ENTREPRENEURIAL MEGABUCKS

ENTREPRENEURIAL MEGABUCKS

The 100 Greatest Entrepreneurs of the Last 25 Years

A. David Silver

JOHN WILEY & SONS

New York   Chichester   Brisbane   Toronto   Singapore

Library of Congress Cataloging in Publication Data:

Silver, A. David (Aaron David), 1941-
  Entrepreneurial megabucks.

  Includes index.
    1. Businessmen—United States—Biography.
2. Entrepreneur—Biography. 3. New business
enterprises—United States—Management. I. Title.
II. Series.

HC102.5.A2S54   1985   338'.04'0922 [B]   85-12089
ISBN 0-471-82184-5

Printed in the United States of America

10 9 8 7 6 5 4 3 2 1

To
Thomas P. Murphy,
Father of the
Venture Capital Club Movement

≡ ACKNOWLEDGMENTS ≡

I wish to give special thanks to my research assistant, Charlene Maes for her relentless pursuit of facts and her unflagging concern for details. I also wish to thank my editor, Michael J. Hamilton, and his assistant, Marilyn Dibbs, and the production staff at John Wiley & Sons. To the venture capitalists and special assistants to chairmen and presidents who supplied biographical data, and responded to requests for more and more data, my deepest thanks. Walter A. Probst of Merrill Lynch Capital Markets, Inc. in New York provided mountains of common stock data as did Linda and Roger Heithaus of Smith, Barney & Co. in Santa Fe, New Mexico. Claude Silver, Caleb Silver, James Charles Cash, and Dayn Schulman combed through my collection of over one thousand new issue prospectuses and updated common stock data and other facts on the companies described within in an attempt to achieve accuracy. Nonetheless, I am fully responsible for all errors.

A. DAVID SILVER

Santa Fe, New Mexico
September 1985

CONTENTS

ENTREPRENEURIAL
MEGABUCKS

INTRODUCTION

Let us now look beyond the praise heaped on America's new hero, the entrepreneur, and examine the process of entrepreneurship. There is no magic or mystery to the entrepreneurial process. As a discipline, it is fairly systematic. It can be learned. The purpose of this book is to explain the process by example.

The examples I have selected are the 100 greatest entrepreneurs of the last 25 years: 92 men and 8 women who have generated aggregate wealth for themselves and their investors of approximately $100 billion—and the amount continues to grow—on initial capital of less than $15 million. These 100 entrepreneurs have created, or saved, over 4 million jobs—and the number, which is larger than the population of Detroit, continues to grow. Moreover, these 100 entrepreneurs have created companies that have solved serious, important, and in certain instances life-threatening problems that affected large numbers of people—and the solution capability of these companies continues to grow. These are America's finest men and women because in every instance these 100 entrepreneurs, their co-founders, and early investors have converted their wealth, gained through problem-solving, to charitable gifts to their communities.

The study of the entrepreneurial process requires an understanding of "greatness." Although we hear the words "great" and "greatness" on a daily basis, they are not properly used. How can the "great taste of a cigarette" be compared with the achievements of a national hero? I felt the need to investigate the lives of national heroes and to examine the perspectives of scholars on the personalities and characteristics of national heroes. Scholarly libraries yielded very little under the heading "heroes"; thus, I selected three bona fide national heroes—Abraham

Lincoln, Winston Churchill, and Chaim Weizmann—and examined the scholarly definitions of heroism applied to these giants of modern history by Carl Sandburg, Isaiah Berlin, and other brilliant minds. With greatness thus defined in Chapter 1, selecting the "greatest" entrepreneurs of the last 25 years was based on the Sandburg and Berlin criteria.

The last 25 years have been a period of intense entrepreneurial activity in the United States and Japan. I reviewed the literature for a similar period in history when poets sang the praises of profitmakers. Much to my surprise and delight, the merchant and the capitalist were the happy subjects of literature in England from roughly 1700 to 1750. Daniel Defoe was the George Gilder of his time, and he gave us *Robinson Crusoe* among others, while Gilder sang the praise of entrepreneurs in 1984 in *The Spirit of Enterprise*.

In Chapter 3, I define the six-step entrepreneurial process, which will not be new to readers of *The Entrepreneurial Life: How to Go for It and Get It*, one of my earlier works on the subject.[1] But the subject is never tiring to someone who wants to solve a large problem affecting many people by developing an elegant solution and building a company to convey the solution to the problem. The principal equation of the entrepreneurial process, $V = P \times S \times E$, is further explicated. The goal of entrepreneurship is to create value (V) by formulating a big problem (P), creating an elegant solution (S) that solves the problem, and forming a capable entrepreneurial team (E) to create a unique system for delivering S to P. The greater the values of S, P, and E, the greater will be V: the value or wealth created by the entrepreneurial process. The 100 entrepreneurial processes described in these pages led to an average V per company of $1 billion. To create large Vs the most important step is to address large problems (Ps). This is known as the *Law of the big P*, that is, a large problem that a bright and qualified entrepreneurial team claims it can solve will frequently achieve a very large valuation (V), long before the solution is delivered. Great entrepreneurs tackle big Ps—and do so with boundless optimism. "Optimism," says James Rouse, one of the entrepreneurs presented within, "is a means of getting things done."

The subject of leverage is described in all of its myriad forms because

[1]A. David Silver, *The Entrepreneurial Life: How to Go for It and Get It* (New York: Wiley, 1983).

America's most successful entrepreneurs have each used it in one form or another. In fact, of the 100 successful businesses described within, only 22 were launched with professional venture capital. The majority of America's finest entrepreneurs used either sweat equity, customer financing, supplier financing, or loans to launch their companies. The process of leveraging is described in detail to provide a better understanding of the individual descriptions of entrepreneurial achievements.

My selection process was one of identifying the 100 greatest entrepreneurs from a list of over 500. I asked a number of experienced colleagues in the venture capital industry to supply names of their candidates, and many of them graciously obliged. My research associate, Charlene Maes, then took three lists of modern entrepreneurs—the Venture 100, the Inc. 100, and the entrepreneurs in the Forbes 400—and wrote or called for biographical data and company histories. Only three entrepreneurs declined to be included in this book, while three others had engaged their own James Boswells, and preferred not to be included.

The seven standards for inclusion derive primarily from the scholarly definitions of greatness applied to our national heroes and adherence to the entrepreneurial process as defined. First, the valuation, or V factor, that the entrepreneur created had to be at least $20 million within five years or $200 million within ten years.

Second, the entrepreneur had to have solved a large problem that was affecting a significant number of people, a problem that would very likely not have been solved without his or her direct involvement. In certain instances, where the problem was relatively small but the solution was extremely elegant and difficult to duplicate, the entrepreneur was included. Social utility was frequently a deciding point in the inclusion process. Real estate developers and extractive industry (oil, mining) entrepreneurs were excluded because the problems they address—shelter and energy—have been around a very long time and there have been no unique delivery systems or elegant solutions to these problems since prehistoric times.

Sustained entrepreneurship was a third criterion. An entrepreneur was excluded from the list if he or she made the cut by all other measures, but ceased solving problems as a way of life. Thus, wealthy entrepreneurs who have turned to corporate raiding or "greenmail," or who have used their wealth to propagandize against segments of society who disagree with them, have been excluded. They have become social problems rather than society's solution finders.

Fourth, entrepreneurs who have tried and failed to start second, third, and fourth companies, notwithstanding their first success, have been excluded. They have shown that their first time at bat was luck and they did not learn the entrepreneurial process for further replication.

The fifth criterion was absence of hubris. A handful of entrepreneurs, having become decimillionaires, act like Plato's philosopher-king, and have attempted to impose their philosophies on the rest of us. For instance, a well-known publisher has laboriously and painfully fed us his philosophy. A fashion industry entrepreneur recently began putting his credo in print alongside his clothing advertisements. A highly successful computer software entrepreneur, with one widely used product, claims that his product and the Union Pacific Railroad have linked the nation together, one in the last entrepreneurial revolution and the other in the present one. These entrepreneurs and others for whom pride has overcome reasoning ability have been excluded.

Sixth, entrepreneurs who did not do the initial *problem formulation* phase of the entrepreneurial process have been excluded from the list. If their fathers started the businesses and they took them over, they are not truly full and complete entrepreneurs. They did not formulate *P* and create *S*, although they may have built *E*, broadened *P* and improved *S*. A large *V*, substantially earned by the inheritor of a business, is not sufficient justification for inclusion in a listing of great entrepreneurs.

A final subjective test was to remind myself to be Emersonian about the task of selecting America's new heroes. I tacked up Emerson's definition of success in front of me while culling the biographies. Ralph Waldo Emerson wrote:

To laugh often and much; to win the respect of intelligent people and the affection of children; to earn the appreciation of honest critics and endure the betrayal of false friends; to appreciate beauty; to find the best in others; to leave the world a bit better, whether by a healthy child, a garden patch, or a redeemed social condition; to know even one life has breathed easier because you lived; this is to have succeeded.

Although most of the men and women on the list do not publish their charitable gifts, a final criterion for inclusion was a positive answer to the question: Have these people left the world a bit better? An outstanding example of the continuous gift-giving character of entrepreneurs is Ewing Marion Kaufmann, founder of Marion Laboratories, Inc., and a member of the list of 100 described herein. Mr. Kaufmann in 1984 began funding and implementing a program in Kansas City, Missouri, to teach sixth and seventh graders how to "manage the temptation" to drink alcohol or experiment with drugs. Approximately 9,000 students began learning to recognize "hidden messages" about the benefits of alcohol usage on television programs. Part of their training included writing letters to the television stations to lobby against programs that include these hidden messages. The mailbags at the Kansas City television stations have never been as full as this year. These stuffed mailbags have made Mr. Kaufmann's gift reciprocal.

I have had the pleasure of working with or for a dozen of the entrepreneurs in this book, I have met many who are included in the list of 100, and I have spent my business life in the company of hundreds more. Although this may or may not qualify me to hand out blue ribbons, it is the overriding purpose of the book to explain by example the process of entrepreneurship so that others may experience its joy.

1

THE NEW AMERICAN HERO

America has a new hero, its first since Franklin Delano Roosevelt, or perhaps Abraham Lincoln. The word *hero* defines someone who is great; someone who has achieved an authentic instance of greatness. A hero is someone who has intentionally taken a large step, one far beyond the capacities of most persons, in solving a problem that affects a large number of people. A hero brings about something that is unlikely to have happened by the mere force of events, by the trends or tendencies of the time. That is, something that is unlikely to occur without his or her intervention. America's new heroes are distinguishable, in the first instance, by the fact that their intervention makes the highly improbable happen.

These great persons do not seek publicity, and as a result are not widely known. They are essentially shy and imprisoned within driven, fanatical personalities. In this involuntary confinement, the heroes have developed a certain independence of outlook. Questions of status, social position, and relative degrees of economic standing—so common in many people—have not affected them. Heroes were raised by frontier mothers, who were strong and self-possessed with energetic and hopeful attitudes toward life. These mothers had a respect for education, for a fully formed personality, for solid achievement in every sphere, together with a clear-eyed, concrete—possibly irreverent—approach to all issues. Above all, they respected effort, honesty, faith, and a critical faculty. "Don't be a sinner," they said. "But worse than a sinner, don't be a sucker."

Their children, our heroes, were raised without safety nets. To supplement for fathers who were frequently or permanently absent, these children developed contingency plans for self-preservation. Later this would be regarded as courage, resisting failure or downside planning. "Shoot at me," our heroes say to their enemies. "I'm going to succeed anyway."

Our new heroes know they are stronger, more imaginative, and more effective fighters than their fellow citizens. They are fearless, understanding, and indifferent to praise or blame.

Our heroes have built groups of followers by convincing them that their view of the future will become reality. Joining the heroes has improved their lives and sheltered them from failure, obscurity, and economic strife. Heroes have become their powerful, self-confident champions who are unafraid of the future. Our hero has immense natural authority, dignity, and strength.

The peculiar quality of greatness and a sense of the sublimity of the occasion stems from a delight in being alive at "the right time" and in control of events at a critical moment in history. The new American heroes thrive on change and the instability of things. The infinite possibilities of the unpredictable future offer endless opportunities for spontaneous moment-to-moment improvisation and for their large, imaginative, bold strokes that cause important events that change the course of history. Although strength comes to our heroes from their clear, brightly colored vision of—and passionate faith in—their views of the future and in their power to mold it, they know where they are going, by what means, and why. This strength enhances their energy and drive as it did Winston Churchill's during the Battle of Britain when he said: "It is impossible to quell the inward excitement which comes from a prolonged balancing of terrible things."[1]

These new American heroes are young, less than 35, casual in their appearance, with an ease of dress. They wear no jewelry and disdain lace-up shoes which require time. They are almost always married or divorced; the latter if the spouses were too frequently left out of things while our heroes fulfilled their dreams. Rarely are they committed to single life. They generally drive European cars which require fewer repairs, live in the city, and vote liberal. Their language, images, and turns of phrase are rooted in strength and individual imagination. They

[1] Isaiah Berlin, *Personal Impressions* (New York: Viking, 1981).

are excellent communicators; these new heroes can convince people to do things for them that they never intended to do before meeting them. They have an extraordinary variety of humor, but never tell a joke that denigrates another race or ethnic group. After all, our heroes have lived on the bottom rung of the economic ladder and have felt the boot of those who would rise in status by stepping on their backs. Our heroes have distinctive physical charcteristics, sometimes carried over from childhood illnesses. The unique aspects of their appearances include physical movements—the manner in which they walk and stand, get up and sit down—their gestures, and the features of their exceedingly expressive faces. Above all is the tone of voice; it is controlled, calm, and self-assured. It does not know bitterness, even when failures seem imminent. Our heroes have an ironical awareness of the shortcomings of all people.

If they have an Achilles' heel, it stems from their capacity for forgiveness of human weaknesses, which causes them to believe, incorrectly, that people whose cooperation they require react as quickly as they do. To compensate for this flaw, our heroes generally attract as partners older persons—proven managers, realists, achievers—who excel in understanding the inner workings of corporations and bureaucracies. Such people are able to organize and prioritize our heroes' dreams and goals; where the heroes are energetic, the corporate achievers are thorough. Heroes have the good judgment to find and hire corporate achievers who untangle plans and implement them by creating functional divisions, reporting mechanisms, systems, and sound management practices.

What large, central human issues have our modern American heroes addressed so successfully? Which major problems that appeared insoluble during the crisis-torn 1960s and affected millions of people have been or are now being solved? For what lasting and important interventions do we now proclaim new American heroes?

First of all, for their achievements in employment, innovation, and productivity. In the 1950s approximately 93,000 new businesses were created each year. In the 1980s the rate is roughly 12,000 per week. From 1970 to 1980 new companies provided approximately 20 million new jobs in America. From 1977 to 1980, Fortune 500 companies lost 3 million jobs, while over the last 10 years, Europe's overall employment declined by 20 million jobs. New companies have created 250 percent more new products than have large enterprises, according to the Small Business Administration. A National Science Foundation study states that new companies produce about four times as many innovations per research and development dollar as do larger firms. Further, new companies take less time to bring innovations to market—an average of 2.2 years compared with 3.1 years for larger companies.

These myriad innovations are not solely technological in nature. In fact, of the 100 greatest entrepreneurial companies of the last 25 years, only one-quarter are high tech. Equally fast growing operations include leasing companies, restaurant chains, free-standing medical clinics, providers of continuing education, physical fitness companies, transportation firms, and the so-called primary activities that catalyze wealth-producing capacity, such as education, training, health care, and information.

Our new American heroes are saving lives with superior medical diagnostic equipment and more responsive therapies for life-threatening diseases; and they are mitigating disease via genetic engineering within the body and in the soil, and in seeds that produce food crops. Virtually every form of life-threatening or unbearably painful disease is being challenged by innovative therapies developed in one of their enterprises. Several of these have begun to receive attention, including interferon, photodynamic therapy, the lithotripter, and magnetic resonant imaging. The lives of thousands have been affected; soon it will be millions. Our heroes have turned around old industries, such as railroads, pipelines, trucking lines, and barge lines that were given up for dead 30 years ago. Public schools have closed due to increasing operating costs and demographic shifts, but our heroes open private ones. Forgotten service institutions that drain the public purses are being addressed with innovative management techniques. These include prisons, garbage collection, hospitals, mental institutions, and nursing homes. They have made entrepreneurship synonymous with personal wellness, by their example of staying fit in order to continually produce the gifts that America requires.

The rejuvenation of the American economy and the extension of our lives as healthier, better-informed, more productive adults are the central issues that our heroes have addressed. We must all assure them that a jealous government bureaucracy will not stunt their growth through central planning and wretched economies. The most precious commodity to our heroes—cash—is the very thing that the government is most likely to take from them through tightened securities laws and higher taxes.

In summary, how can we identify our heroes among those who would pretend to be great but are not? The single most important characteristic of our heroes, one that sets them apart from all others, is *heart*.

Our heroes' hearts focus their knowledge, determine how they use it, and drive them toward whatever goal they choose. They do not childishly strive for wealth or power or to overcome the fear of failure. They have grown out of experiences in their homes, schools, and corporations where these strivings were once important. No longer. Power, wealth, and the fear of failure are not valid reasons for work. They are myths, blown out of proportion by corporate America. Our heroes do not have value systems based on what is *out there*. They did at one time, but have since rejected it. What is important now is what is *in here*, in the heart.

The people who detach the head from the heart work in large corporations where they apply their intellects toward the success of the organization and their movement vertically within the organization. They had hearts once, but the big corporations had them carefully removed. They become frustrated because their work requires them to do the wrong thing occasionally, to keep silent when they should speak up, to knife a coworker in the back. Our new American heroes do not have these frustrations, although they did at one time. They no longer "eat their hearts out."

The people with heart work in the valleys, frequently within a short drive or long walk from their homes. They wear whatever they like to work. They select coworkers who have similar values. They accept *all* of the responsibility for their decisions and never write memorandums to others to protect themselves from failures. They do not fear failure, because the thing they are building is constantly changing and neither failure nor success is quantifiable with so many unknowns. They are free to choose their own destiny; and, although failure would be losing that freedom, they are moving too rapidly to think about failure.

The people with heart create innovation and change in our society. The people without heart look down from the top of the hill and see the people with heart scurrying around in the valley carrying things from cottage to cottage. The people without heart ignore the companies that the people with heart create to market their innovation and change.

"Crumbs from our table," said the heartless people at the telephone company when the people with heart began to sell better and cheaper telephones. "A flyspeck in black pepper," said the airfreight companies when the young man started his small package airline. "We have lost the semiconductor industry to the Japanese," said the venture capitalist to the brothers from Idaho who believed they could make a better, less expensive microchip. Where are they now? The telephone company has been dismantled to allow it to compete. The people who ran the airfreight companies have been fired. The semiconductor industry is once again American-led thanks to the indomitable spirit and courage of the Parkinson brothers.

People with heart always beat people without heart. The reason is quite simple. The people with heart know what drives the people without heart, but the people without heart do not know how the people with heart play the game. So the people with heart build their unique products and pluck from the large corporations the most intelligent people to join their teams. The new recruits, called corporate achievers, get their hearts back along with some ownership in what they are doing, and they work smart, attacking the weak points of the corporations and bureaucracies they know so well. When the chase is over, our new American heroes possess great wealth. It was never their primary goal, but the American system rewards its heroes with wealth. Much of it is returned via charitable contributions to save lives, educate the young, and feed the starving people of the world. Thus, the rewards are spread throughout the world, touching as many lives as possible, although almost always anonymously.

By what name do we refer to the people with heart? Who are these new American heroes, these great persons? They are the entrepreneurs.

Some may say that this song of praise to the entrepreneurs is a romantic illusion. To refute the notion that great people exist only in fiction, one must come face-to-face with an authentic instance of greatness and its works. May I suggest that, to come face-to-face with greatness, all of you who are successful entrepreneurs need only look into the mirror; all of you who are entrepreneurs in mid-chase, maintain your drive, your heart, and your courage; and all others, either invest in or go to work for an entrepreneurial company. Make your life valid. Join the entrepreneurial revolution.

2

THE ENTREPRENEUR CREATES THE ECONOMY

An economy is governed by its entrepreneurs. An economy is the effect for which entrepreneurship is the cause. Without entrepreneurs, there would be no economy. Entrepreneurs set economies in motion; start the game; bring the ball, bat, and gloves.

Economists are usually unable to measure or predict changes in the economy with any degree of accuracy for one simple reason: They do not factor into their elegant, but static tables, the vital role of innovation and the creation of new goods and services—the formation of entirely new industries every 90 days—by entrepreneurs. The U.S. Treasury Department economists, for example, do not maintain records on companies with fewer than 500 employees. An industrial revolution began in 1968, caused by the invention of the microchip and catalyzed by computer software. Statistically it is more important than the Industrial Revolution of 1890 to 1910, but very few significant economists have cited it. Literally thousands of software entrepreneurs have written programs that unleash the power of the computer to perform tasks significantly better, cheaper, and faster than they were performed before. Thus, we begin to incorporate the software, embodied in computers, into our lives universally and tenaciously in much the same way that previous generations got hooked on the telephone, the automobile, and the radio. The most visible effect of software, depending on occupation and living habits, is in sending information: word processors, digital communication, on-line data bases, and telecommunicating. Computer-aided design (CAD) and computer-aided manufacturing (CAM) are software subindustries that significantly lower the manufacturing cost of nearly every product imaginable by simulating all of the design specifications, then testing the simulation, thus obviating the need for costly prototyping. Another branch of CAD is used in medical instruments to spot the onset of cancerous tumors in an early enough stage to save lives. The CAD/CAM industry is almost completely dominated by entrepreneurial companies. Economists have largely ignored it.

While the economists spent the early 1970s warning us that an energy scarcity would cause a structural decline in United States productivity, CAD/CAM and other software entrepreneurs left their jobs, depleted their savings, mortgaged their homes, created thousands of new companies and millions of new jobs, and introduced cost-saving and productivity-improving manufacturing methods that will assure America's competitive edge for dozens of years.

Economic theory that ignores the entrepreneur as a key player is as absurd. Yet a search through economic history indicates that no major economist has ever defined the role of the entrepreneur as the creator of the goods and services that make the markets that create economic prosperity and decline. They have historically failed to place the entrepreneur onto their economic board games. Thus the identity crisis of the entrepreneur. The scorekeepers of our nation's economy do not consider the entrepreneur to be in the game while the entrepreneurs know that they are the leading pitchers and leadoff hitters for both teams.

The word *entrepreneur* appeared originally in the French language in the early sixteenth century to refer to men engaged in leading military expeditions. Two hundred years later, the French began to expand the definition to men engaged in adventures of other sorts, including bridge builders, road contractors, and architects. Finally, a French economist, Richard Cantillon, defined the entrepreneur as a component of the economy when he defined entrepreneurship in 1755 as the process of bearing uncertainty. Other French economists broadened the definition of the entrepreneur by applying the sobriquet to risk takers in construction, farming, and industry. The latter were referred to as risk-taking capitalists; thus, an early linkup of the entrepreneur and the venture capitalist.

The entrepreneur reached the pinnacle as a member of the economy in 1815, in Jean Baptiste Say's *Catechism of Political Economy*. Say's entrepreneur "unites all means of production . . . the re-establishment of the entire capital he employs, and the value of the wages, the interest, and the rent which he pays, as well as the profits belonging to himself."[1] Although Say ignored the creative aspect and responsibility for capital formation—two vital spokes in the entrepreneur's wheel—he is unique among all economists, save Joseph A. Schumpeter, in having defined the role of the entrepreneur in the economy. The definition, although accurate, was ignored by the brilliant economists of the late eighteenth, nineteenth, and twentieth centuries. Adam Smith, Alfred Marshall, John Maynard Keynes, Wassily Leontief, Milton Friedman, Paul Samuelson—prizewinners all—hung no wreaths on the creators of wealth that provided them a field of study, not to mention salaries, royalties, honoraria, and prize money.

In 1934, Joseph A. Schumpeter, an Austrian economist who taught at Harvard University, resurrected the entrepreneur in his *Capitalism, Socialism and Democracy*.[2] Schumpeter gave his students and other economists immense food for thought with his concept of "creative destruction." Schumpeter said that a group of individuals in the economy acted entrepreneurially to seize opportunities, and "shapes the whole course of subsequent events and their 'long-run' outcome." Comparing his hypothesis with productivity statistics and seeing therein a decline, Schumpeter like Karl Marx predicted the eventual decline and obsolescence of capitalism and the rise of some form of equilibrious economy, without innovation, change, and growth.

In 1979 Israel Kirzner, a University of Chicago economist, identified the entrepreneur in the economic system as an "opportunity scout."[3] The entrepreneur, Kirzner says, reacts to disequilibria to create new enterprises. Kirzner does not raise the entrepreneur to the level of initiator. Nor does he see the entrepreneur as an original thinker, or spontaneous reactor to opportunities. Kirzner places the entrepreneur, amidst other barnyard characters, as a pig, ferreting out pieces of corn that the other animals failed to see. Like the universities, governments, and large corporations that keep them clothed, housed, and well fed, econo-

[1]Jean Baptiste Say, *Catechism of Political Economy*, 1815.
[2]Joseph A. Schumpeter, *Capitalism, Socialism and Democracy* (Cambridge: Harvard University Press, 1934).
[3]Israel Kirzner, *Perception, Opportunity and Profit: Studies in the Theory of Entrepreneurship* (Chicago: Univ. of Chicago Press, 1979).

mists have failed to consider the source of wealth and change in the economy that they so myopically study. Not only is the entrepreneur not a bastard child of the economists, the entrepreneur is not even one of their pipe dreams. The entrepreneur is a nonperson to most of the economic thinkers of our civilization.

How have entrepreneurs fared among the artists and intellectuals? Perhaps, because they bear a closer resemblance to them, entrepreneurs are treated better. As I wrote in The Entrepreneurial Life:

> Entrepreneurs and artists have many things in common. Both are problem solvers. The artist tries to solve many of life's problems by expressing solutions on canvas. The entrepreneur focuses intensively on one problem, formulating and reformulating it until he or she is ready to pull out one huge canvas and begin painting. Both species, the artist and the entrepreneur, are individualists, unconventional, sensitive, imaginative, intense, complex, driven, and creative.[4]

Another similarity between artists and entrepreneurs is that they expect very little joy from their efforts. There are so many pitfalls, naysayers, competitive pressures, and obstacles facing both artists and entrepreneurs, that overcoming one or two a day keeps the heart pumping and the smile in place. "Entrepreneurship is a series of random collisions," said David J. Padwa, founder of Agrigenetics Corporation. "Sure you start with a plan and follow it systematically. But even though you start out in the alternative energy business, you are just as likely to end up in real estate development."[5]

Alexander Calder, whose sculptures adorn so many museums, bank plazas, and corporate lobbies, was unable to attract any buyers for his work until he was 54 years of age. Konosuke Matsushita, son of a peasant farmer, picked himself out of the ruins of war-torn Japan at the age of 51, to produce radios. His dreams became Panasonic. Then there is Soichiro Honda, an eighth grade dropout, whose engine factory was

---

[4]A. David Silver, The Entrepreneurial Life: How to Go for It and Get It (New York: Wiley, 1983).

[5]David J. Padwa, speech to members of the Venture Capital Club of New Mexico, November, 1981.

devastated by Allied bombing and an earthquake. He became the world's most brilliant and successful mechanical engineering entrepreneur since Henry Ford.

Soichiro Honda told a graduating class at Michigan Technological University: "Many people dream of success. To me success can be achieved only through repeated failure and introspection. In fact, success represents 1 percent of your work which results only from 99 percent that is called failure." How similar to the autobiographical reflection of Vincent Van Gogh, Wolfgang Amadeus Mozart, and William Faulkner. They were tutored by their failure to capture light, sound, and words in the form and matter that they knew to be possible. How like the artist is the entrepreneur. Picture, if you will, the artist standing in front of a large blank canvas in total rapture that he has an opportunity to fill the canvas. Compare that love of the chase with one of Sony Corporation co-founder Akio Morita's favorite stories:

Two shoe salesmen . . . find themselves in a rustic backward part of Africa. The first salesman wires back to his head office: "There is no prospect of sales. Natives do not wear shoes!" The other salesman wires: "No one wears shoes here. We can dominate the market. Send all possible stock."[6]

Morita's philosophy at Sony Corporation has been to create products for which no apparent demand exists, then create demand. These included a pocket radio, a tummy TV, a digital camera, the Walkman, and the Betamax. Sony Corporation literally burst on the scene in America like Andy Warhol or Roy Lichtenstein.

If there are similarities between artists and entrepreneurs, how have writers treated entrepreneurs over time? Have they raised entrepreneurs to the level of heroes at other times in history, or is the American scene circa mid-1980s the first instance?

Whereas the economists have ignored the entrepreneur, the literati have, in most instances, treated the entrepreneur with hostility. Literature comments on contemporary social life and on society's attitudes toward various components, including merchants and capitalists. The

[6]George Gilder, The Spirit of Enterprise (New York, Simon & Schuster, 1984), p. 193. Copyright © 1984 by George Gilder. Reprinted by permission of Simon & Schuster, Inc.

literary record begins in the sixteenth century, when discoveries abroad opened up people's minds to the new world and explorers brought back to Europe masses of unexpected treasure along with the unlimited promise of more. In England the monastery lands were parcelled out after 1536, releasing large rivers of liquid capital. In 1571 the ban on usury was reversed. These critical events helped to launch capitalism on its inexorable course and with the creation of merchants and capitalists, literature changed as well, from allegorical drama to the classics of Christopher Marlowe and William Shakespeare.

Shakespeare sees all sides of the new mercantilism, in his encyclopedic examination of the human experience: not only the imaginative side of commerce, and the age of merchant adventure, but also the negative, selfish side of aggressive commercialism. Shakespeare, on the whole, is not impressed by narrow capitalist ambition, its materialistic bent, and strident nationalism. In *The Tempest* (1611), Shakespeare captures the spirit of the age of discoveries, suggesting new worlds to conquer, knowledge to acquire, and new ways to feel about discoveries and mercantile ambition. He sees an awakening of the human spirit and the opportunity to gather the commerce of knowledge and spiritually uplifting aspirations as well as the bargain-driving commerce of the merchant class.

Shakespeare's essential treatment of the mercantile process is in *The Merchant of Venice* (1596), written at a pivotal moment at the beginning of capitalism, when the traditional economic order was giving way to a newer, more uncertain one. What seems to catch Shakespeare's attention in *Merchant* is the inadequate moral fiber of those engaged in commerce; at the same time, he is fascinated with the essential money-lending transaction.

It seems that Shakespeare wishes to draw a sharp contrast between spirituality and worldliness, between appealing commerce and despicable commercialism. He goes out of his way to describe both the technical aspects of business and the hard-hearted, nonspiritual aspect of commerce in the Elizabethan age. Shylock leads Bassanio on, creating in him anxious distraction, before saying whether or not he will agree to make Bassanio the loan (*Merchant*, I, iii, 1-7):

"Three thousand ducats; well."
"Ay, sir, for three months."

"For three months; well."
"For which as I told you, Antonio shall
    be bound."
"Antonio shall become bound; well."
"May you stead me? Will you pleasure me?
    Shall I know your answer?"

Antonio then enters the room and Shylock counts his ready cash, complains that he may not have enough, tells a biblical story, negotiates the interest rate, and complains to Antonio how he has been mistreated over the years. Shakespeare sees, in this dragging-out process, motivations of cruelty and sadistic greed. The capitalist is condemned for skillful positioning of the transaction in order to protect his principal and earn the highest rate of interest. An entrepreneur of today sees joy in the expectation of Shylock's eventually making the loan and excitement for dramatic effect in the dragged-out negotiations.

The character of the merchant and his companion, the capitalist, suffered an improved fate from 1650 to 1700. They rose from morally evil to backdrops and comedic characters. John McVeagh points out that George Granville updated *The Merchant of Venice*, as *The Jew of Venice* (1701), to make it more appealing to the modern age.[7] Granville cuts out Shylock's defense of usury, weakens his motivation, and has him eating and drinking with his borrowers.

Restoration drama was indifferent to commerce and the merchant class. Frequently, as in Dryden's *Don Sebastian* (1689), the merchant (in this instance two merchants who come to buy Alvarez, Sebastian's old counselor) is introduced for comic relief. In John Wilson's *The Projectors* (1664), the moneylender is named Suckdry and the exchange broker, Squeeze. Trade is certainly not elevated to a positive force by the eighteenth century, but rather to that of comic relief, which blocks the understanding of anything with humor. At least, by making commerce humorous, the merchants and capitalists were approved.

From 1700 to 1750 Daniel Defoe, himself a trader, discovered commerce and found it absolutely positive. He drew an analogy between business ambition and moral pursuits, as when he condoned Hernando Cortez's policy of liquidating the Indians of Central America who dis-

[7]John McVeagh, *Tradeful Merchants* (London: Routledge Kegan Paul Ltd., 1981).

agreed with him: "I do not see how Cortez could do less than he did; he saw the Surprising Wealth of the Country, he saw himself Environ'd with Mountains of Gold and Silver, and Immense Wealth, Fertility and Production of all kind."[8]

Defoe raises the economically expedient as a principle of just conduct. To Defoe, the actions of the trader are necessary to earn a profit, and therefore correct. To shore up his argument, Defoe describes the various ways in which the trader imperils his life, battling with nature and the elements. In describing the manufacture of a pin, Defoe celebrates the interconnectedness of trading operations, thus of all economic and social issues:

> To bring all this to the same point: With what admirable Skill and Dexterity, do the proper Artists apply to the differing Shapes or Tasks allotted to them, by the Nature of their several Employments, in forming all the beautiful things which are produced from those differing Principles? Thro' how many Hands does every Species pass? What a variety of Figures do they Form? In how many Shapes do they appear? From the Brass Cannon of 50 to 60 hundred weight, to half an inch of brass wire called a *Pin* all equally useful in their Place and Proportions.
>
> On the other Hand, how does even the least Pin contribute its nameless Proportion to the Maintenance, Profit, and Support of every Hand, and every Family concerned in those Operations, from the Copper Mine in *Africa*, to the Retailer's-Shop in the Country Village, however Remote.[9]

There has never been a poet of the entrepreneur such as Daniel Defoe. As McVeagh writes:

> Defoe's pressure on his countrymen to subjugate and use the world, his grief at delay and waste, his brimming excited knowledge of the high rewards and risks involved, his recognition that

[8]Daniel Defoe, VIII (1711) 166-7. (*Review* 1704-13).
[9]Daniel Defoe, *A Brief State of the Inland or Home Trade* (London: 1730), p. 13.

the chance is a short-lived one which will not return if missed: these are the impelling conceptions . . . behind his greatest and best known writings.[10]

Where Defoe saw in commerce a grand harmony of society's energies and needs, within 50 years after his most active period of writing, commerce and those engaged in it were maligned. In the latter half of the eighteenth century, merchants and capitalists were once again condemned in literature. Oliver Goldsmith voiced the fear that commerce, if permitted to continue under its present impetus, would destroy life. He was joined by Tobias Smollett, Henry Fielding, and Edmund Burke. Whereas Defoe saw the wealthy merchant converting his profits to land, housing, and goods from the tradesmen in his village, Goldsmith in the 1760s saw in profits a concentration of power and fortune that signaled odious privilege and the extension of a malign influence over a once independent populace.

In *The Traveller* Goldsmith sees the increasing liberty of the rich few leading to the enslavement of ordinary people. Profit he says leads to selfishness, then to monopoly, then to power concentration, and finally to oppression. Goldsmith's *The Deserted Village* shows how economic development damages lives.

Although in 1776 Adam Smith explained in *The Wealth of Nations* that everyone in England was better off than they had ever been, despite Goldsmith's prophecies of ruin and depopulation, the damage was done. Deeply ingrained distrust of the mercantile class and a hostility to commerce were to last until the Industrial Revolution. The condemnation of the merchant and the capitalist was aided and abetted in 1813 by such as Shelley's *Queen Mary*:

Hence commerce springs, the venal interchange
Of all that human art or nature yield;
Which wealth should purchase not but want demand,
And natural kindness hasten to supply.

[10]John McVeagh, *Tradeful Merchants*, p. 57.

And further in the poem:

> The harmony Land happiness of man
> Yields to the wealth of nations.

The response to industrialism in England was generally to condemn the pursuit of commerce, wealth, and profit. As England passed into the Victorian age, the principal literary spokesperson became Charles Dickens, who positively hated those who lived for personal aggrandizement and profit. This line runs from miser Ralph Nickleby in *Nicholas Nickleby* (1837-1838), through the merchant Dombey in *Dombey and Son* (1846-1848), to manufacturer Bounderby in *Hard Times* (1854), and to financial crook Merdle in *Little Dorrit* (1855-1857). So bitter was Dickens' disdain for merchants and capitalists and so extensive was his influence, that George Bernard Shaw called Dickens an "unconscious revolutionist."

Following the continual denigration of entrepreneurs throughout the nineteenth century, the twentieth dug them up, punched them around, and reburied them without ceremony. Shaw describes capitalist society in dissolution. He saw capitalist economic development as having peaked and on its way to imminent disintegration. Joseph Conrad put another nail in the coffin of commerce. In his *Heart of Darkness* (1899), Conrad condemns the capitalist exploitation of one part of the world by another, advertising itself as beneficial. D.H. Lawrence links commercialism with lovelessness. James Joyce portrays those in commerce as disappointed, futile, and hopeless.

As communism lurched onto the world's economy in the early twentieth century, many writers took hold of it as a crutch that supported their general view of commerce as morally odious. The love affair between writers and the welfare state in the 1930s has been unending. The capitalist and the merchant have been effectively indicted, convicted, hung, and buried without proper ceremony in economics or literature.

The shock of the abnegation of entrepreneurs by the economists and of their murder by the literati did not upset their number until the 1970s. It seems that several informed liberal thinkers, among them Norman Podhoretz, publisher of *Commentary*, and Irving Kristol, author of

Reflections of a Neo-Conservative, changed their spots in public and became conservatives. Kristol became appalled that economists studied economics but not businesses, and journalists studied businesses but not economics.[11]

Not true of Norman Macrae, editor of the *Economist*, who in 1975 wrote "America's Third Century." Some of his points are telling:

> In 1975, when it is fashionable to forecast that world growth is about to stop, technological realism suggests that growth is more probably at an early stage of an extraordinary acceleration. The eightyfold increase in real gwp since 1776 has been based on man's increase in control over matter and energy, at a pace that has risen in each of the last 20 decades after having stood still in the previous 10,000 years. To this matter-cum-energy-revolution there has been added in the past two decades a breakthrough in the processing of information (computers, etc.) and a nascent breakthrough in the distribution of information (telecommunications by satellite, the beginnings of packaged and computerised "learning programmes," maybe even at last a start towards understanding of the learning process itself) . . .
>
> The world's pigs today eat seven times more primary protein than the world's North Americans. The world's horses . . . eat more than the Chinese. The world's cows (a third of them Afro-Asian nonproducers) eat more grain than all the world's people. With apologies to cows, our children will move to rearing foods by conversion of cellulose to enzymes and of petroleum wastes by single-cell high-protein organisms."[12]

Listen to America's J. Leon Potter:

> A pound of bacteria, feeding on crude oil so worthless that it is burned as waste, can grow fast enough to produce 10 pounds of protein in a day. If a yearling calf were able to manufacture pro-

[11]Irving Kristol, *Reflections of a Neo-Conservative* (New York: Basic Books, 1983).
[12]Norman Macrae, "America's Third Century," *The Economist*, December 25, 1976, p. 44.

tein at the same rate, it would end the day roughly the size of a three-car garage and it would have consumed tons of expensive grain in the process. The cost of protein produced from waste effluents is approaching 3 cents/pound, compared with agriculture and animal protein at 10 cents/pound . . .

Other rather obvious points: the world does not actually consume metals at all, but employs them in ways that make them available for re-use after anything between 3 and 25 years . . . most of the industrial materials used today were not even conceptually recognised a short time ago, and most of the materials that will be used in the coming century are not conceptually recognised today; substitutions through plastics, etc., will hugely increase; and microminaturisation with integrated circuits means that it is going to be increasingly economic to put onto a chip the size of a postage stamp properly connected electrical circuits which would previously have required assemblies of machinery that fill a room."[13]

There is something awfully familiar in Macrae's paper. Could it be the similarity between Macrae's love of the marketplace and Defoe's description of the manufacture of a pin?

It is one thing for a distinguished journalist to point out the value of innovation and technological change in the economy. It is quite another for one of our distinguished economists to recognize the entrepreneur as the critical factor in the economy. Peter F. Drucker presented a paper entitled "Our Entrepreneurial Economy" in the Harvard Business Review. It is worth summarizing as well:

It is no longer news that small and new businesses provided most of the 20-odd million new jobs generated from 1970 to 1980 by the American economy. What is not generally known, however, is that this trend has continued, has even accelerated, during the recent recession. Indeed, over the last three years, Fortune 500 companies have lost some three million jobs, but businesses less than ten years old have added at least 750,000 jobs and slightly more than a million new employees.

[13]J. Leon Potter, People of Plenty (Chicago: University of Chicago Press, 1984).

This trend is almost the exact opposite of the typical post-World War II pattern. Between 1950 and 1970, either big businesses or governments created three out of every four new domestic jobs. In any downturn, job losses centered in new and small enterprises. From 1950 to 1970, then, the growth dynamics of the American economy lay in established institutions, but since 1970—and especially since 1979—these dynamics have moved to the entrepreneurial sector.

Contrary to "what everybody knows," high-tech activities—that is, computers, gene splicing, and so on—account for only a small portion of this entrepreneurial sector. True, of the *Inc.* 100 (the 100 fastest growing, privately owned companies that are not less than 5 or more than 15 years old), one-quarter are computer-related. But the *Inc.* sample consists of privately owned new companies and is hardly representative of the whole entrepreneurial group: it has a quite heavy bias in the direction of high tech. Even so, last year there were five restaurant chains in the group.

High-tech companies get more than their share of attention because they are fashionable and fairly easy to finance through public stock offerings. By contrast, such equally fast growing operations as leasing companies, specialized hand tool makers, barbershop chains, and providers of continuing education are far less glamorous and so far less in the public eye. Somewhat more visible are the transportation services like Federal Express . . . whose success has forced our stodgiest bureaucracy, the U.S. Post Office, into inaugurating Express Mail—its first real innovation since it was pushed, kicking and screaming into parcel post all of 70 years ago.

Altogether, a good deal less than one-third of the new entrepreneurship is in high tech. The rest divides fairly evenly into what people usually mean when they say "services" (restaurants, money market funds, and the like) and so-called primary activities that create wealth-producing capacity (education and training, health care, and information). Nor is this flurry of entrepreneurship confined to the Sunbelt. To be sure 20 of the *Inc.* 100 are in California, but the same number are in the supposedly stagnant Mid-Atlantic region: New York, New Jersey, and Pennsylvania. Minnesota has 7, Colorado 5.

Remember, too, that the *Inc.* 100 and similar lists contain only businesses, although the new entrepreneurship is by no means confined to businesses. It is going strong in what we are beginning to call the "Third Sector"—nonprofit but nongovernmental activities. While the government conducts one study after another of the crises in health care, the Third Sector is busily creating new health care institutions—some founded by hospitals, some in competition with them, but each designed to turn the crisis into an entrepreneurial opportunity. There are, for example, independent clinics for diagnosis and primary care, ambulatory surgical centers; centers for psychiatric. diagnosis and treatment; and freestanding maternity "motels."

The entrepreneurial surge is not entirely confined to the United States. Britain now has a booming Unlisted Securities Market (comparable to our over-the-counter market), which allows young and growing companies to raise capital without the great expense of a stock market underwriting. In Japan the fastest growing company during the last ten years has not been a transistor maker or an automobile company but a retail chain that acquired licenses from the United States for 7-Eleven food stores and Denny's restaurants. Italy, too, has a thriving entrepreneurial sector, but it is largely part of the "gray" economy and so does not appear in the figures of tax collectors or government statisticians.

On balance, however, the wave of entrepreneurial activity is primarily an American phenomenon. With respect to the steel, automobile, and consumer electronics industries, America shares equally in the crisis that afflicts all developed countries, Japan included. But in entrepreneurship—in creating the different and the new—the United States is way out in front.

By any reasonable measure, then, the entrepreneurial economy in America is a fact.[14]

[14]Peter F. Drucker, "Our Entrepreneurial Economy," *Harvard Business Review*, Jan.–Feb. 1984, pp. 59–61.

Among the changes that Drucker sees occurring as a result of the creation of an entrepreneurial economy are (1) the emergence of a new industry every 18 months, (2) the most profound changes in the way we teach and learn since the printed book was introduced 500 years ago, and (3) "the emergence of entrepreneurs across a spectrum of activities . . . is a period of great opportunity, of fast-growing employment in certain areas, and of overall growth."

In 1982 the late Herman Kahn saw a revitalization of America as well. His focus was on a reversal of "The erosion of . . . what it means to be a human being." The increasing value of the human being was the effect of three factors:

1. Location independence;
2. Wealth creation opportunities in the social services; and
3. Wealth creation opportunities in the application of high technology.[15]

Kahn did not refer to the role of entrepreneurs, but rather, fastened on the renaissance of the human being. "The man who uses [the computer] feels his own power is intensified . . . . He feels good. The opportunities for both fun and gain, self-fulfillment and self-advancement are great and growing."[16]

In The Spirit of Enterprise, George Gilder, a student of the electronics industry and an economist, writes that the key to economic growth is quite simply creative people with money. Gilder states that entrepreneurial energy is the most critical factor for economic growth. He writes:

the key role of entrepreneurs, like the most crucial role of scientists is . . . to generate entirely new markets or theories. In this they are limited only by the compass of their own imagination and powers of persuasion. They stand before a canvas as empty as any painter's; a page as blank as a poet's. Like creative artists, they

[15]Herman Kahn, The Coming Boom (New York: Simon & Schuster, 1982), p. 82.
[16]Ibid.

bring entirely new things into the world in a process that they themselves control.[17]

Gilder also sees the influence of computer software entrepreneurs on the present entrepreneurial revolution. "More than any other group, the thousands of computer software entrepreneurs epitomize the statistically elusive but explosively creative American economy in the age of information technologies."[18]

John Naisbitt, author of *Megatrends*, described the current transition of America from an industrial society to an information society. "The real increase has been in information occupations," he writes. "In 1950, only about 17 percent of us worked in information jobs. Now more than 60 percent of us work with information as programmers, teachers, clerks, secretaries, accountants, stock brokers, managers, insurance people, bureaucrats, lawyers, bankers, and technicians. . ."[19] The information that so many of us are now reviewing, converting, acting on, and measuring is being created for us by software entrepreneurs.

Naisbitt sees the transition between the industrial and the information economy as a time when entrepreneurs flourish:

The transition times between economies are the times when entrepreneurship blooms. We are now in such a period. The entrepreneurs who are creating new businesses are also creating jobs for the rest of us. During a seven-year period ending in 1976, we added 9 million new workers to the labor force—a lot of people! How many of those were jobs in the *Fortune* 1,000 largest industrial concerns? Zero.[20]

At last the entrepreneur is being recognized as a vital member of the economy by journalists and to a lesser extent by economists. As yet there is no explanation of how the entrepreneurial process fits into the economy. This will come in time when a sufficient number of entrepre-

---

[17]George Gilder, *The Spirit of Enterprise* (New York: Simon & Schuster, 1984), p. 145.
[18]Ibid, p. 52.
[19]John Naisbitt, *Megatrends* (New York: Warner Books, Inc., 1982), p. 16.
[20]Ibid, p.16.

neurs who have accomplished their goals are willing to explain their processes.

But for now, the manner in which 10 million entrepreneurs, employees of entrepreneurial companies, venture capitalists, and other resource people have been spending the years since the mid-1960s is finally being recognized, recorded and, soon perhaps, measured. The shock of recognition is worth noting, but not life-enhancing by any means. After all, the chase is everything. Publicity is a distraction.

3

WHERE DO ENTREPRENEURS COME FROM?

In the early nineteenth century, according to Maccoby and Terzi, "some 80 percent of all Americans were self-employed. By 1950, only 18 percent of all employed persons were self-employed, and this figure shrank to 14 percent in 1960 and 9 percent in 1970."[1]

The Modern Age of Entrepreneurship came about as a result of the launching of *Sputnik* in 1957. Sputnik inflicted pain and embarrassment on American government, industry, and education leaders. Government leaders responded by printing money as fast as they could and awarding contracts to any and all defense contractors who claimed to be able to develop lightweight electronic instruments to make space flight a reality. Within a few years after Sputnik, William Shockley moved from Long Island, New York, to Palo Alto, California, where he developed the transistor as well as the first cottage in Silicon Valley. From Shockley Transistor Corporation came Fairchild Semiconductor Corporation which launched Intel Corporation, Advanced Micro Devices, Signetics, and dozens of other entrepreneurial companies whose solution, in a broad sense, has been to make electronic instruments and machinery smaller, faster, and less expensive.

At the same time as high technology entrepreneurs were beginning

[1]Michael Maccoby and Katherine A. Terzi, "Character and Work in America," in Philip Brenner and others, eds., *Exploring Contradictions: Political Economy in the Corporate State* (New York: McKay, 1974).

to find their hearts, the nation was entering a period of radical social change. Virtually every sacred cow was wrenched loose from its structure, turned upside down, vigorously reexamined for its validity, and restructured. For instance, a safe abortion could not be purchased in America in 1960. By the early 1980s abortions were available in clinics in every American city. The ubiquitous changes in the nation's value system have largely obscured an important reality: entrepreneurial companies are the main driving force for the nation's economic growth.

Virtually every institution in America was reshaped in the 1960s and 1970s, with the exception of the large corporation. The large corporations resisted change forcefully, indeed several of them believed that they were above the law; such was the case of ITT Corporation's involvement in Chilean politics and General Motors Corporation's attempt to discredit Ralph Nader. While almost every social indicator—crime statistics, youth unemployment, number of abortions, and SAT scores, to name a few—were reaching shocking new levels of concern, corporate and national leaders appeared unaware and seemingly uninterested. Large corporations could not be changed from within, and employees interested in changing them from within usually met with frustration and dissatisfaction. They had to leave in order to seize the opportunity that their corporations failed to see. Eastman Kodak Company so frustrated four of its engineers who repeatedly brought forward new product ideas, that they left and formed their own company called ITEK Corporation. ITEK stands for "I'll Topple Eastman Kodak."

Many baby boomers joined the work force in the 1970s with an abhorrence of corporate life. They wanted to do their own thing from the start, and sought the means of solving some of the country's problems in a variety of ways. The opportunities to do things entrepreneurially were enhanced because the federal government had spent itself into moribundity and was beginning to think in terms of doing less, rather than more, to influence change. At the same time the baby boomers realized that being against everything would not put food on the table, and they began to seek positive areas in which to channel their dissatisfaction. They wanted to do several things at once, such was their energy level: solve society's problems, avoid the corporate handcuffs, and achieve personal wellness.

Entrepreneurs, then, are people dissatisfied with their career paths (though not with their chosen fields) who decide to make their marks on the world by developing and selling products or services that will make life easier for a large number of people.

Entrepreneurs are energetic, single-minded, and have missions and clear visions. They intend to create out of their visions a product or service that will serve a central human need and improve the lives of millions. Although entrepreneurs will probably make a lot of money if the solution works and is efficiently conveyed to the problem, entrepreneurs do not care. They are delighted to have their hearts back, to be free of dissatisfaction and frustration, and to be working action-packed 16-hour days for themselves.

Thus, until the time that they developed the insight into large problems searching for solutions, entrepreneurs worked fully within the scope of traditional societal values, perhaps for a corporation, a government, a medical laboratory, or a consulting firm. They had been hired, they believed, for their creative potentials, and were rewarded, they believed, for their creative contributions. The satisfaction was not to last long.

Initially they trusted the organizations that valued them and rewarded them principally for their creative output. The future entrepreneurs had joined these organizations in part because of their prestige; however as they became more energetic and needed increasing latitude and funding for their inventions, the organizations' commitments to their personal creative potentials emerged as less than they wanted, less than they expected. At first surprised, they became increasingly dissatisfied.

At the same time, as trust in the workplace faded, a strong commitment to their own capabilities was unfolding. More and more, they experienced a sense of directedness; their inner voices were asking them questions about personal values, expression of self-worth, and self-sufficiency. These were not the abstract philosophical stock-taking questions that observers and analysts of mid-life change report are raised so frequently; questions like, "What have I accomplished in my life?" "What have I sacrificed?" "What will I do with the rest of my life?" Those questions are as likely to come to entrepreneurs as to anyone else. But at this point in their lives, the "big question" for all entrepreneurs was: "What will I do with my creativity?"

They were intense, deadly serious about homesteading somewhere and being able to exercise confidence in themselves. Before they even knew it had started, the entrepreneurial race was on. For a time, as they continued to do their jobs for their employers, dissatisfaction increased while ideas for the products or services they would develop—that would take the marketplace by storm—were putting down roots in their minds. Although the first growths might be primary shoots that wither, the root systems were secure, come sunny weather or violent storm. And, as I will discuss in more detail, they will be protected by enormous potential to replenish psychic energy, by intense pleasure at their activity, and if they are to be successful, by excellent communication skills and exquisite judgment.

I meet many entrepreneurs at this stage of their growth when they want to discuss their ideas with "an older hand." All of them are complex, intense, determined, imaginative people who have faith in themselves, and whose energy is not sapped by pervasive anger, bitterness, or disappointment. The workplaces have not been satisfying, true, and have not rewarded what they most respect in themselves; the not-yet-active entrepreneurs have put in a lot of time and tried to contribute their best. They have become dissatisfied and to some extent disillusioned. And they are not politically adept, so their pure commitment to human potential irritates rather than inspires management, making it impossible for them to maneuver budgets and forms of influence the way others can to make the organizational dynamics work for, not against them.

Nevertheless, though they resent the system, they proceed in disillusion and go on to create their own reality; thus, true entrepreneurs do not feel victimized. They do not plot and plan retaliation. Rather, they accept that these organizations will not provide places to do what they want to do and believe should be done, and they decide to create such an organization on their own.

Acceptance of reality brings determination, not depression, distraction, or diffuse, flailing attempts to get even, to show them. (They have others to "show," as we will see later on.) Acceptance brings dedication to building on their own strengths rather than to demonstrating the weakness of the organization (and thereby deluding themselves that it would change anything with respect to their positions). They know they cannot reduce corporate power, so they decide to establish their own.

The personal goals and needs that have been emerging as the strongest forces, soon take over to govern their behavior. They direct their psychic and creative energy into building on the emotional self-sufficiency that has been slowly, steadily taking hold. They do this with an ease that astounds people who know or hear about them.

The creative intelligence they brought to their employers' businesses is now directed toward designing products or services and positioning them for the marketplace. They examine opportunities, perhaps for licensing, see nothing available and may work for a short time as independent consultants or for consulting firms. During this time the entrepreneurs continue to see the needs they identified and finally decide to create their own opportunities.

They are getting ready to break ground, carve out niches, and build places in the sun. "Build places in the sun," I said, not "build empires"; empire building is not what they are about. Rather, they are planning for, and are after, self-reliance, a quality-controlled provision for creative output. They talk about building an organization where people will not get lost; where creativity will be rewarded; where salaries and benefits will be just; where participative management (though they do not call it by that name) will be the rule, not the exception. To the amazement of people who are not able to turn anger, energy, disappointment, and dissatisfaction into focused personal directedness, they begin to experience intense pleasure. The undercurrent of basic optimism and trust in their professional power, the certainty that has always existed that their expertise in their fields is unequaled, govern a clear decision to be on their own and succeed. They have no fear of failure, though they make careful, detailed plans to avoid it. Statistics of new business and small business failure offered to them by well-meaning friends and family are dismissed as irrelevant. "Sure, lots of people fail, but since I'm going to succeed, why are you telling me these numbers?" they demand, before going on with their phone calls to bankers, brokers, and friends of friends, and with presentations end to end. Failure is simply not a possibility. They have spotted opportunities and are leaping forward to take advantage of them as rapidly as possible.

With confidence, optimism, courage, focus, and determination newly born entrepreneurs set out to look for money. What happens then depends on whether they possess two other attributes; it seems to correlate as well with several factors in their childhood home lives.

To build successful businesses, would-be entrepreneurs must be able to lead their teams by exercising good judgment—knowing the right thing to do at the right time. But since they may not have a clue about how to do the right things, they will eventually get tangled up in the snare of trying to plan businesses. Without knowing word one about functional areas like strategic planning, sales projections, market research, or even simple accounting practices, they will at this point select managers who do and who can allow the entrepreneur chieftains to maintain leadership.

The higher entrepreneurs reach for managers, the more likely are their businesses to succeed. Entrepreneurs exhibit the keen judgment they are known for when they ask achievers to join them; people who have demonstrated first-class management ability in a growth situation.

, To raise the venture capital that will launch the new businesses, entrepreneurs must be able to make and keep the process simple, and to convince others it is so.

What might make others topple into confusion and frantic despair nourishes their spirit and spirited intellect. Out of the complexity they pull the necessary interim funding from the most unlikely sources—usually on the day the bank loan interest is due; first-rate impressive venture group presentations; corps of dedicated partners or colleagues; determination and confidence enough to refuse equity-hungry venture tempters. Those would-be entrepreneurs who have the products or services and the character prerequisites will become wealthy; those who do not will be wiped out in the marketplace.

You know who some of the well-known personalities are, those who have told of transformations overnight, abrupt decisions to do something on their own. For example, Edwin H. Land, while walking in New York's Times Square one night and staring at car headlights, decided to leave Harvard University in his freshman year. Land believed that he could develop a means to "polarize" light, thus reducing the glare of headlights. Seven years into the development of headlights, the automobile companies turned him down. Land kept his small company, called Polaroid, afloat by producing sunglasses and via the financial expertise of his partner, Julius Silver. Fourteen years after forming Polaroid, Land successfully introduced instant photography.

Kemmons Wilson put his wife and five children in the family station wagon in 1951 for a vacation in Washington, D.C. The motels there charged $2 a head for the Wilsons' children even though they were sleeping in the same room as their parents. Wilson's Scottish blood boiled and he pledged that when he got back to Memphis he would build a chain of motels that would never charge extra for children. One year later, Wilson opened the first Holiday Inn, named for a Bing Crosby movie. To expand Holiday Inns of America, Wilson teamed up with Wallace Johnson, an experienced builder who had the contacts and the financial experience to build an international motel chain.

The lyrics are much longer than merely Land and Wilson, but the melody is the same: young men and women who experience dissatisfaction with their corporate or hierarchical employers, and have not only the insight into problems and their solutions, but also the energy to begin the *chase*—to build companies that will convey the solutions to the problems.

Many people are dissatisfied with their corporate or hierarchical employers and may have important insights. However, lacking the energy to begin the chase, these people indulge in creative hobbies or start side businesses to develop an outlet for their frustration and do something that they can put their hearts into. Writers have many insights into central social problems and frequently feel anguish toward structures that crush creativity. They get their hearts back through their pens, and increasingly, word processors. Entrepreneurs experience the pain, see large problems and unique solutions, and have the energy to build companies to deliver solutions to problems. In so doing, their hearts focus their knowledge and drive them toward their common goal: to solve a serious problem for a large number of people.

4

THE ENTREPRENEURIAL PROCESS

Entrepreneurship expresses a profoundly American art of creation. Entrepreneurs begin with ideas, or insights, and suddenly without notifying anyone of their change, become transformed into fanatical dream chasers. They are frequently fleeing oppression in a foreign land, economic strife, or the pain inflicted on them because they were different from members of their peer group. In their own afflicted lives, they discover that goals will never come easily, that all of human life is a hard predicament, but that failure to achieve the "dream" cannot ever be as brutal as the oppression, deprivation, or affliction that they once suffered.

Jack Tramiel, a short, stout, ravaged-faced survivor of Auschwitz, took Commodore Business Machines to the summit of the home computer market with upwards of 1 million installations in three years, and thereby laid waste the plans and investments of Texas Instruments, Warner Communications, Timex, Coleco, and the Japanese consumer electronics industry. Unable to obtain complete control of Commodore, in 1984 he abruptly left, took a one-month vacation, and resurfaced as the owner of Atari which he purchased from Warner Communications for $140 million in promissory notes.

Kemmons Wilson dropped out of school in the eighth grade because his hard-working mother—so tiny she was known as "Doll"—became too ill to work. Wilson was thrust into entrepreneurship as a teenager. He purchased peanut vending machines by giving the seller a series of postdated checks. To make good on the checks, young Wilson emptied the pennies out of all of his peanut machines each day to run them over to the bank. The hardship of this entrepreneurial existence was inestimably superior to watching his mother's demise and starving in the process. Several years after his major entrepreneurial success, Holiday Inns of America, was an economic success, Wilson's large charitable contributions exhibited the same self-sacrifice as when he left school to support his ill mother.

Jack R. Simplot broke away from a father he feared at the age of fourteen, with guilt and anxiety that he recast as an implacable drive to succeed. His means of survival was to buy bum sheep from farmers. These extra lambs from broods too numerous for the ewe to feed would otherwise have been killed. Jack collected forty of these lambs over a period of several months, raised them to a point where they could be sold back to the farmers, and cleared a $140 profit, a princely sum for an Idaho teenager in 1922. Simplot never stopped entrepreneuring. Ever the contrarian, he was the first to freeze-dry potatoes, and his patented French fried potato is a key element to the success of McDonald's Corporation. As a venture capitalist, Simplot provided most of the $20 million needed to launch Micron Technology Corporation, a Boise, Idaho semiconductor manufacturer with sales that grew to $500 million in 1983, on one-fifth of the capital requirement that semiconductor industry experts such as L.J. Sevin, founder of Mostek Corporation, said was a minimum requirement.

Successful entrepreneurs generally begin with nothing, and they learn the cultural truths of their reason for being during the periods of their greatest suffering, in the face of denigration by established authority. They learn that what is in their hearts and minds cannot be taken from them. They learn that their insight, their dream, is so true and elegant that they will begin building its foundation immediately. Is there a more American expression than "let's get to the bottom of this thing?" By following the dream, building the solution, they will save themselves from failure and solve a problem that affects a large number of people.

The entrepreneurial sacrifice is a religious experience. Entrepreneurs give wholly of themselves, sacrificing everything—their time, their marriages, their assets, and their sleep—for their private, tenacious belief in a redemptive idea. With their funds wasted, families neglected, and friends forgotten, they follow without a moment's self-doubt plans that will launch new companies whose purposes are to convey solutions to large problems. Against all odds, beyond all calculation, and usually in the face of stubborn production obstacles and bankers who bounce the most important of their checks, the entrepreneurs begin to turn the tide, only a little at first, but enough to indicate that they are on the right track. They tunnel up from the bottom each day making some headway, slipping back two yards to avoid a falling boulder, moving forward three yards as soft gravel gives way, even going sideways for a look if the tunnelling appears easier. Day after day, into the evenings, sometimes sleeping next to their prototypes, in basements, rented lofts, abandoned storefronts, the entrepreneurs keep plowing ahead. The smallest of victories during the day brings joy. Holding off a creditor, debugging a tricky software package, convincing a customer to pay in advance or getting the bank to cover Friday's overdraft based on Monday's expected collections: all of these are victories. When they occur, they give entrepreneurs the courage to go another thirty days without salary.

Then one day after digging and clawing for months, a tiny speck of light appears at the far end of the tunnel. It is miles away, but clearly visible. The entrepreneur can see the idea finally validated. The business plan is economically viable. The light provides a shot of adrenalin that speeds the entrepreneur up through the tunnel in the direction of the light.

As entrepreneurs emerge from the "tunnel," or lab, or skunkworks with desks full of unpaid bills and the worried looks of family and friends, they have gained the exquisite knowledge that their ideas are correct, demonstrable, provable. They know that their journeys to the bottom of the world to find their ideas, work with them, shape them and test them were worth the effort; they have found their strength in their ideas. This is the beginning of the process of entrepreneurship and it is as critical as any other stage. Not everyone can run blindly through the night toward some never-before-seen goal, with walls, and cliffs, and low limbs coming out of nowhere to knock them off balance and change their direction. David J. Padwa, who entrepreneured two successful businesses in two unrelated fields, Basic Systems in the 1960s and Agrigenetics in the 1980s, describes the process of entrepreneurship as "A marine landing on a beach, firing at everything that moves. If something he shoots at falls, he runs in that direction."

Some of the anxiety and uncertainty of the entrepreneurial process can be mitigated by an understanding of the entrepreneurial process. It is not true, however, that to understand the process is the same thing as carrying it out in an elegant manner. Everyone cannot be an entrepreneur, but everyone can participate in the entrepreneurial process as a manager, helpful spouse, or active investor.

The fundamental law of the entrepreneurial process is also the cornerstone of venture capital investing. The goal of venture capital investing is the creation of wealth or high valuation (V), through the process of selecting a potentially successful entrepreneur and his or her team (E), who have identified a large problem (P) and created an elegant solution (S) which they intend to convey to the problem via a new company. Stated as a formula:

EXHIBIT 4.1　Silver's First Law of Venture Capital

$$V = P \times S \times E$$

where: V = Valuation
P = the size of the Solution
S = the elegance of the Solution
E = the quality of the Entrepreneurial team

In selecting entrepreneurial companies to invest in, venture capitalists seek large values for P, S, and E. When they are multiplied times each other, the result is a large value for V and wealth is created thereby. Venture capital is lost or wasted when positive values are believed to exist for P, S, and E, but one or more of them, after the investment is made, is discovered to have zero value. Zero, when multiplied by another number, results in zero.

We will return to the first law of venture capital later and apply actual numbers to it to explain why certain entrepreneurial pursuits create innovation, employment, wealth, and solutions to major problems, and why other entrepreneurial endeavors should never have been undertaken. An understanding of the equation $V = P \times S \times E$ will save billions of dollars of capital and perhaps trillions of hours of entrepreneurial time and energy.

The six steps in the entrepreneurial process are:

1. Identifying the problem (P)
2. Creating the solution (S)
3. Planning the business
4. Selecting the entrepreneurial team (E)
5. Producing and test-marketing the product
6. Raising venture capital

IDENTIFYING THE PROBLEM

Problems are markets in search of solutions. All successful entrepreneurs have a unique ability to formulate problems. In economic terms, this means identifying a market or a problem in search of a solution. One of the compliments managers pay to entrepreneurs whom they join usually goes something like this: "She has the ability to see the whole market, from those customers who are ready to buy to those who need years of education."

Gloria Steinem, the co-founder of Ms. magazine, is a successful entrepreneur. She problem-formulated brilliantly in the wispy, smoky, uncertain arena known as women's liberation. This problem area runs the gamut from women not receiving equal pay for equal work, to sexual harassment on the job, to abortion, to the political arena. A more complicated, multiarena problem area probably does not exist. Steinem absorbed it all, and realized that the cacophony of women's liberation problems needed to be indexed. What better way to sell an index to a market eager to learn more about women's liberation problems than through a magazine? Broadly read magazines attract advertisers, and so the index should pay for itself. The first entrepreneur to attack a new problem usually becomes its indexer. Pat McGovern did the same thing in software with the publication of Computerworld.

Steinem perceived that corporations would pay her to help them solve large problems dealing with women as customers. For example, truck drivers were increasingly becoming husband-and-wife teams in the 1970s, and the truck manufacturers wanted to learn more about designing a cab suitable for women. What better place to go for help than to the women's liberationists? A $250,000 consulting contract from a major truck manufacturer has more profit than the sale of $250,000 worth of advertisements in the magazine.

Let us assume that the women's liberation market was not problem formulated in detail, but, rather, that an entrepreneur began selling services to truck manufacturers to help them redesign cabs for a newly created female driver market. The entrepreneur in this instance creates the solution before properly identifying the market. The truck manufacturers would rebuff the entrepreneur in one of the following ways:

I was not aware that we had the problem that you are describing.

We would like some assistance in solving that problem, but how do we know you have developed the solution?

We have the problem, you have the solution, but what endorsements do you have in this field?

These three questions deal with three lacks: lack of information, lack of trust, and lack of credibility. Marketing professionals frequently know how to overcome them, but entrepreneurs usually do not.

Many new business failures are the result of inadequate problem formulation. Entrepreneurs make the mistake less frequently than small businesspersons and large corporations. It is the plight of small businesspersons such as merchants to open stores whose products interest them and to locate them in convenient or available locations. Unfortunately, the market is not interested. Large corporations rush solutions to the market, and then try to use brute force to place them onto the shelves and millions of dollars of advertising to move them off the shelves only to pull the product after a few years of red ink. Feminine deodorant spray is a case in point. "Real" cigarettes produced a $45 million loss for R.J. Reynolds Industries, Texas Instruments' home computer was too expensive. Topps Chewing Gum brought us chocolate bubble gum in 1980. Watching McDonald's Corporation grope for new customers in an attenuating market with such obvious gestures toward the black market as McRib Sandwiches makes one realize how quickly a meteorically successful company can lose its entrepreneurial zest. Even the mighty Xerox Corporation blew it in the personal computer market by selling dumb hardware instead of solutions-oriented software. According to the International Franchise Association, one reason that 95 percent of all franchised stores succeed for at least three years is that their franchisor problem-formulates for them and writes out the solution delivery method in long, detailed training and operations manuals.

Entrepreneurs and artists have many things in common, principally their desire to overcome a deprivation by saving some portion of humanity with a joyful creation. In this respect, both are problem solvers. The artist tries to solve some of life's problems by expressing solutions on canvas. The entrepreneur focuses intensively on one problem, formulating and reformulating it until he or she is ready to pull out one huge canvas and begin painting. Both species, the artist and the entrepreneur, are individualists, unconventional, sensitive, imaginative, intense, complex, driven, and creative. Although one could argue the differences, the similarities are greater in number. Therefore, the study of creativity among artists by Jacob Getzels and Mihaly Csikszentmihalyi has a bearing on our investigation of the entrepreneurial process.[1]

The participants in the study were young male art students. Each participant first completed a still life for the researchers based on an arrangement he made from a collection of objects provided. Afterward, the artists answered several questions.

One question was: "Could any of the elements in your drawing be eliminated or altered without destroying its character?" The objective of the investigators was to determine whether a student considered his work fixed or flexible.

The answers to this question enabled Getzels and Csikszentmihalyi to draw a correlation between ability and recognition of the possibility of change. A panel of judges rated each artist's drawing. Those who received the highest ratings overall were the ones who said their work might be changed. A follow-up study seven years later by the same investigators indicated that more success had come to the artists who earlier had seen the possibility for change.

Certainly the committed artist is a perfectionist. Why then would there be a correlation between willingness to change a finished piece and artistic success? Quite simply, perfection is too costly to achieve.

[1]Jacob Getzels and Mihaly Csikszentmihalyi, *The Creative Vision: A Longitudinal Study of Problem Finding in Art* (New York: Wiley, 1976).

Rather than spend the time and effort to be perfect, a successful artist will spend less time and be satisfied. Satisfaction is the goal in problem finding, not perfection. The potential entrepreneur should free his or her mind of any notions of finding the perfect problem and supplying that demand curve with a perfect solution. In the entrepreneurial process, random collisions are the norm.

Getzels and Csikszentmihalyi learned something about the work methods of the artists and their professional success. The most effective artists displayed these work traits: In arranging the objects that they were preparing to paint, they manipulated them more, moved them about and then rearranged them more, moved the mechanical parts more, and chose more unusual objects. They tended not to have a predetermined theme in mind prior to beginning to paint, but discovered arrangements through handling the objects.

As they began drawing, they more often rearranged or substituted objects, changed paper, switched media, and transformed the scene and subject of the drawing. The final structure of the drawing tended to emerge later rather than earlier. These artists reported that they tried to develop the drawing beyond the physical objects. In addition, after completing the drawing, they admitted that it could be altered without destroying its character.

The researchers regarded the artists' problem finding as a measure of creativity. The more creative artists, who indeed became more successful seven years later, devoted more time to problem formulation. The actual drawing, or problem-solving activity, remained open to further changes in matters such as the arrangement of the objects which seemed to have been settled during the problem-finding stage. That is, the more creative artists often found new problem formulations even while working from the original one.

The late George Quist, a venture capitalist who began in the early 1970s providing seed capital to some of the most successful entrepreneurs in the country, said essentially the same thing: "The road to success isn't always going to be straight. The smart guy will realize there will be a lot of turns—changes in the market, for instance. The honest entrepreneur can face up to that."[2]

One example is Ward Parkinson, the founder of Micron Technology

[2]"Do You Have What it Takes?" Forbes, August 3, 1981.

Corporation. This Boise, Idaho, semiconductor manufacturer beat all of the established American and Japanese semiconductor companies in the development of 64K DRAM chips, ignored the elegant visions of chip design engineers, and focused on providing as much space on the chip for memory as possible. In the personal computer, memory size is one of the biggest problems. His trial and error methods eventually led to the technological breakthrough that his former boss, L.J. Sevin, founder of Mostek Corporation, turned down.

Another example is William Benton, who sold his interest in Benton & Bowles in 1935 and, in his words, "began making money by mistakes." Soon thereafter, Robert M. Hutchins hired Benton to do public relations for the University of Chicago. Benton knew that Sears, Roebuck & Company wanted to sell *Encyclopaedia Britannica*, because it needed to be updated. He convinced Sears to donate it to the university, but he was unable to convince the university's trustees to pay to have the encyclopedia revised. Benton agreed to invest $100,000, to have it updated, for which he received two-thirds of the stock. The encyclopedia has become a cash cow. Benton expanded the company by enfolding the Merriam-Webster Company in the mid-1950s.

The message seems loud and clear—find an interesting problem and carefully observe every aspect, because once it becomes the *raison d'être* of your business, the various components of the problem will collide with one another and with other variables and force you to rearrange the business plan. Finding problems is a relatively simple procedure. A mere look at five or ten processes currently being managed by a large corporation or bureaucratic organization will indicate that 80 percent of them are being managed inefficiently or suboptimally. If the entrepreneur's preference is to buy rather than start a business, virtually every conglomerate or multinational company has dozens of subsidiaries for sale.

The newspaper is the best source of lift-off opportunities in the country. Large city newspapers index the world's problems and serve potential entrepreneurs a banquet of opportunities. Comedians provide a menu of ideas for the problem-finder as well. Humor and pathos address problems differently, but without problems there would be neither.

Problem formulation requires continual failure and frustration. If it comes too easily, some important component was overlooked. Laser interactive video discs have left CBS and RCA Corporation bloodied and bowed, each emptying over $100 million in the field. They built the devices without software to make them interesting. Rarely is the entrepreneur successful who launches a company with all the capital that is required. Rolm Corporation, which developed the most efficient automated telephone exchange, PABX systems, was launched with $200,000 and struggled for a destiny from 1964 to 1974. Ten years later, International Business Machines Corporation acquired Rolm for $1.8 billion.

Entrepreneurs also find problems in services undertaken by the government but systematically done poorly. Post offices are a case in point. You can set up a private post office nearby to a U.S. Post Office and charge a premium for stamps and box rental. Your unique services would be speed and courtesy. You need only promise that the line of customers would never exceed two. If more than two people are waiting in line, another service person would come to the counter.

Scott Adler, a 35-year-old electrical engineer, opened several storefront post offices in the Los Angeles area in 1982. He accepts packages for shipment by United Parcel Service, Federal Express, Trans-box, and U.S. Postal Service. All the services receive their normal fees. Several times a day Adler's post offices turn their mail over to the appropriate carriers. His handling fee is $1 to $5 per item, frequently greater than the postage cost. Adler's solution—offer speed, convenience, and courtesy—is simple. His problem formulation was complex and unique.

Adler's post offices are in malls and near banks, places that people visit once a day. The closest U.S. Post Office is located out of the way in a cluster of government buildings noted for traffic snarls and inadequate parking. United Parcel Service and Federal Express require that the sender or receiver be home when they arrive; thus, people frequently prefer to take those kinds of packages to the courier. Adler's post office centralizes that function. His fee represents a savings in gasoline, driving time, and parking hassles. His post office idea can be replicated and should be franchised for speed of multimarket penetration. When it is, the U.S. Postal Service will be whittled down to an efficient, manageable size.

Another entrepreneurial success story that underscores the value of problem formulation is a mail order business known as the Horchow Collection. Roger Horchow publishes a catalog chock-full of beautiful personal items, very expensive and very chic. Others also publish handsome catalogs, but Horchow does better. The problem that he identified goes by many names, but has to do with simple vanity. People love themselves and every once in a while like to strut their stuff. So Roger Horchow has prepared a catalog for gift-givers in which he encourages the customer to put the initials of the recipient on the gift. He knows that people are too vain to return gifts with their initials on them.

How does one problem-formulate? Like the successful artists, it is necessary to adopt a problem, index its many features and parts, and begin arranging and rearranging the parts until you identify areas that appear to be receptive to solutions.

When I first learned that I could solve problems for entrepreneurs, only one aspect of the problem appeared to me: raising venture capital for them. I subsequently learned that the universe of entrepreneurs was quite broad, and some segments of it needed entirely different kinds of solutions than other segments. For example, I estimated that approximately one million people in the United States annually consider the possibility of becoming entrepreneurs. I based this on readership of entrepreneur-oriented magazines and attendance figures for franchise, small business, and new technology conferences. These people were probably at the dissatisfaction and energy peaks of their personal development curves, but lacked insight as to what to do about it. A possible solution was to steal a page from Gloria Steinem: Index the problems of becoming an entrepreneur and the many resources available to entrepreneurs, how to access them, and when. The perfect product was a book, which I called *Upfront Financing*.[3]

A smaller group of would-be entrepreneurs, perhaps one hundred thousand per annum, has a different set of problems. They want to share their problem with others, discuss specific areas such as attracting a manager, packaging a product, and dealing with suppliers. This group of entrepreneurs would prefer to come together in a conference room environment. The multiple solutions for this group are Venture Capital Clubs, conferences, and discussion groups. I started the Venture Capital Club of New Mexico at about the same time.

A yet smaller group of entrepreneurs has completed its journey

[3]A. David Silver, *Upfront Financing* (New York: Wiley, 1982).

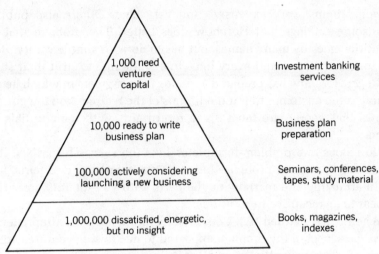

FIGURE 4.1.   The Market of New Entrepreneurs

through the tunnel, put it all together, and is ready to write a business plan and to raise venture capital. I estimated approximately ten thousand entrepreneurs go through this rite of passage each year.

And finally, approximately 1,000 entrepreneurs will seek the assistance of an investment banker each year to help them find a merger partner or raise venture capital or other forms of cash.

Thus, when I problem-formulated the market for my services, I saw four tiers, each interested in a separate and distinct product having its own price, payment terms, and means of conveyance. Figure 4.1 tells the story better.

By addressing only one segment of the market, for example, investment banking, I would have been ignoring much larger aspects of the market which not only feed into one another but also can easily be serviced profitably by the overall entity. The pyramid method of problem-formulating seems to be applicable in a number of service industries.

Service companies are unique in two respects: many entrepreneurs are attracted to the idea of starting service companies; and, it is very difficult to raise serious amounts of capital for them. Venture capitalists have protested that the problem with service companies is that the "assets" go home every night and may not return. Thus service company entrepreneurs, lacking the enormous sums of start-up capital lavished on their fellow entrepreneurs who have tires to kick, have in desperation come up with unique financing methods. Coincidentally, the sources of capital come from the people with the problem; that is customer financing. Approximately 20 percent of the greatest entrepreneurs of the last 25 years relied on customer financing for their venture capital. A substantial number of successful service companies have been customer financed because it occurred to the entrepreneurs that their customers could be persuaded to risk capital upfront. The insurance industry was launched with customer financing. Many customer-financed companies are well-known and include Arthur Murray Dance Studios, Weight Watchers International, Century 21 Real Estate, EST, Esprit, Evelyn Wood Reading Dynamics, ComputerLand Corporation, CMP Communications, Renovators Supply, Mary Kay Cosmetics, Avon Products, Shaklee, Time, Maxicare, and others. The primary forms of customer financing are the following:

Franchising

Facilities management

Newsletters, seminars

Direct mail marketing

Licensing

Consulting

Party plan selling

The advantages to customer financing are that it preserves equity, the V factor, for the entrepreneurial team; it involves the customer directly in developing the solution to the problem; and it is a faster means of raising capital than making presentations to investors and their attorneys. The disadvantage to customer financing is that there must be no delay in delivering the service or product that the customer has paid for in advance. Thus, the entrepreneur must prepare the product or service in advance in order to be ready to deliver it within 60 days of receiving payment. Society benefits because the customer is involved with the development of an appropriate cost-effective solution to the problem, which saves time, and venture capital is conserved for more capital-intensive projects. An exhaustive problem formulation process can be less painful and anguished if the entrepreneur analyzes various forms of customer financing to see if the problem is sufficiently large and propinquous to ask for and receive payment in advance to finance the preparation and development of the solution.

Franchising

The franchisor raises money by selling exclusive rights in a region to a franchisee who pays an initial fee—the franchise fee—plus royalties based on monthly revenues. The latter might be tied to volume, and can range between 1 and 10 percent of revenues. Frequently, but not always, the franchisor agrees to purchase national advertising with a portion of the monthly fee. Some franchises begin with zero capital investment by the franchisor. This results from very creative new business ideas. For example, the entrepreneur who founded the Wiks 'n Stiks candle shop chain ran an ad offering to sell candle shop franchises. When someone sent him a check, he was in business, and busily created the logo and other appurtenances that would create value for the franchisees. The company was very successful from the beginning, partially because the admission ticket was a comfortably low $2,500.

Setting the franchise fee is not scientific. The price is equal to what the market will bear. For example, McDonald's currently charges in excess of $100,000 for a franchise, but it is able to document a large number of franchisees who achieve revenues in excess of $1 million per annum. A wide range of franchises is offered every Thursday in the classified section of the *Wall Street Journal*. Most of them are relatively new, hence their fees are less than $20,000.

Prior to the famous legal battle of the early 1970s known as the Chicken Delight case, a franchisor was able to force franchisees to buy certain necessary products through or from it. This was not only profitable to the franchisors, but as was claimed by Chicken Delight's attorneys, necessary to control the quality of the product and provide a means of counting how much chicken was sold, hence giving a revenue count to the franchisor. Monthly royalties were then matched against the internal count. The court found in favor of the franchisees, stating they should be able to buy at the lowest price, so long as the standards were maintained. As a result, franchisors must be extremely careful not to step on their franchisees' toes.

Throughout the 1970s, the laws restricting the sell-now-deliver-later axiom of the franchising business grew tighter and tighter. One needs skilled legal counsel to interpret the laws because they vary from state to state. Most franchisors adapt to the most restrictive state law and follow it, in order to be covered in all of the other states as well.

Notwithstanding legal fees and perhaps some logo design fees, the cost of launching a franchise-oriented business lies in creating the system. For example, let us say you start a brain scan equipment leasing business based on the leasing of medical equipment by all large hospitals, which are currently seeing a revenue erosion due to growth of urgent care 24-hour medical centers. We will name the company Scanning Equipment Leasing Corporation or SELCO. The justification to the hospitals is that they can provide a financing service to the doctors who are taking hospital business into their entrepreneurial clinics. Thus hospitals can regain some of their lost loyalty and provide capital for necessary equipment. The franchisors then obtain a credit arrangement to enable them to assign the leases to a third party and carry the paper once their net worth fattens up. It is not uncommon for a leasing company to have a debt-to-worth ratio of 10:1, with 6 or 7:1 closer to the norm. SELCO must also offer other features to make the franchise worthwhile, such as low-cost insurance and national advertising. An insurance company, looking at the potential of thousands of policies that will come over its transom without having to beat the bushes, is likely to propose a low flat rate. The final step is a national advertising campaign, which can be sketched out in draft form until enough franchises are sold to create the need for a national customer-generating campaign. The SELCO entrepreneurs also need to develop some on-site items, such as window signs, brochures, forms, and perhaps a file cabinet.

How do you price this franchise? One method might be the discounted cash flow of the income the dealer might make over 10 years. A simpler method is to sell a franchise to the most highly regarded and best-known dealer, perhaps one of the premier teaching hospitals, such as Baylor or University of Tennessee, and put a representative on the SELCO board, thus justifying a ground floor price of, say, $15,000. With the large hospital's endorsement, the price could be moved up swiftly to $25,000 for the next five, $35,000 for the next five, and finally to a tummy-warming $60,000.

Assuming that a happy medium is reached, SELCO can project sales of perhaps 10 franchises per month in the first few months, increasing exponentially as word spreads to penetration of as many as 20 percent of the large U.S. hospitals with 200 beds or more, or about 1,600 sales at an average of $58,000 per sale. As soon as the system is installed at a dealership, SELCO can record the sales as income; but in the meantime it has already generated $9 million in cash to operate with (1,600 × $58,000). Using conventional borrowing ratios, the company could borrow approximately $54 million to buy CAT scanners and magnetic resonant imaging instruments, each of which costs from $500,000 to $1 million per unit. As net worth builds, SELCO can increase its borrowing and begin to offer additional services to its franchisees. An early public offering could raise enough capital for SELCO to repurchase its best franchisees.

Nothing is easy in business, even though these business examples may strike you as "Why didn't I think of that" simplistic no-brainers. Problem formulation and customer-financing methods require a considerable amount of analysis, discussion, and trial and error. They are not taught in any MBA program, but require some business experience and some serious failures until they are well understood.

A note of caution on franchising. It is an elegant means of raising money but a difficult form of business organization to hold together. The better franchisees should be acquired by the franchisor in order to prevent them from going out on their own, litigating for a better slice of the pie, or asking embarrassing questions about relative wealth. When the better franchisees are acquired for stock in the franchisor and made wealthy, the less efficient franchisees have a goal to strive for.

Facilities Management

The essence of this business is to find a fair number of large organizations that share a similar problem and offer to deliver a solution at the price they currently pay for the problem. Automatic Data Processing did this magnificently with corporate payroll processing and Bradford

Computer Systems did equally well with mutual fund data processing. Electronic Data Systems Corporation (EDS) took over entire data processing departments and was rewarded with a meteoric rise in value, to a $2.5 billion acquisition price in 1984 by General Motors Corporation. The start-up capital provided in 1964 by the entrepreneur, H. Ross Perot, and his mother was $24,000. The customers did the rest.

One of the most popular areas to sell facilities' management contracts is in municipal services. The Scottsdale, Arizona, fire department was taken over by a private contractor in the late 1960s. Several other cities followed. Municipal garbage collection has gone that route in certain instances as well. By raising capital from insurance companies and pension funds, venture capital funds are selling facilities management contracts of a sort: taking over the venture capital investment operation from these large organizations. For example, if a two-partner venture capital fund raises $50 million from 10 investors, it is saving the administrative and analysis time of 10 people, and conceivably doing a better job of investing the funds.

Entrepreneurs are becoming aware of the profit of the opportunities available in offering facilities management contracts to state and local governments. Prison management, school management, and other new facilities management companies are being formed at a rapid pace.

In *Capitalism and Freedom*, Milton Friedman suggests numerous government-operated enterprises that could be better run by profit-oriented companies.[4] Included in the list are the U.S. Postal Service (initially a private company in Pony Express days, Friedman points out), school systems, sanitation, street cleaning and maintenance, and the fire department. *Capitalism and Freedom* was published nearly 20 years before the founding of Federal Express Corporation, which appears to be well on its way to becoming our nation's leading private mail delivery service.

To launch a facilities management company, one must prove to the first customer an unquestioned ability to provide the solution at the price the customer is currently paying; that is, the cost of operating the department. Institutional food service companies, such as Saga, have been successful in operating corporate dining rooms by tackling this as-

---

[4]Milton Friedman, *Capitalism and Freedom* (Chicago: University of Chicago Press, 1961).

signment. Often entrepreneurs in facilities management companies worked previously for the first customer, or a close competitor. Once again, some assurance that the job will be done as promised, plus the endorsement of the people in the facilities management company, is essential to getting contracts. An example would be a division of Fox-Meyer Corporation, launched by then 28-year-old William Y. Tauscher. This company stocks, staffs, organizes, installs fixtures, and does advertising for thousands of pharmacies, which in turn order their supplies from FoxMeyer. Frequently contracts are let on a trial basis whereby the entrepreneurs are given one or two aspects of the problem to solve before the entire contract is given to them. Of course, after two or three contracts are in process, some equipment can be merged or eliminated, and there will be some people savings as well. Assume that a new facilities management company wins three $2 million contracts in its first year and makes a 30 percent savings in equipment and people; its operating income, before overhead, would be $1.8 million. That is a comfortable base from which to launch a business. That was approximately the size of Perot's first full fiscal year's income, and, of course, EDS's capital injection. Revenues grew to $36 million by the fifth year and at its initial public offering in 1969 the market put a valuation (the V factor) on the company of approximately $1 billion.

Perot's problem-formulation process was the epitome of elegance. EDS would take the corporations' payroll and equipment costs in its budget (i.e., absorb the cost of the problem) and deliver data processing solutions. In so doing, if EDS was efficient, it could keep the difference as its profit. Perot located in the problem EDS was to address the eight

---

EXHIBIT 4.2.   The Eight DEJ Factors

---

1. Existence of qualified buyers
2. Existence of competent sellers
3. Homogeneity of buyers
4. Large number of buyers
5. Lack of institutional barriers to selling
6. "Hey, it really works!" phenomenon
7. Optimum price-cost relationship
8. Invisibility of the new company

---

most important predictors of a new company's economic success, which I refer to as the "DEJ factors," or factors of "Demonstrable Economic Justification." These are shown in Exhibit 4.2.

All entrepreneurs should hold the mirror of the eight DEJ factors up against their proposed new companies to measure the economic validity of their ideas. The more of the eight factors that their new companies possess, the greater the V or wealth they will create. Let's examine the DEJ Factors that EDS had going for it.

Existence of Qualified Buyers. Corporate data processing inefficiency was a very real problem in the mid-1960s. Buyers did not have to be educated—that is, told they had a problem. Buyers knew they had a problem and knew they had to pay for a solution. A minimal amount of buyer education was required.

Existence of Competent Sellers. Perot hired managers who were skilled in providing solutions to the problems of the EDS customers. Perot, a former IBM salesperson was an able marketer and he hired personnel in his image. He was competitive and competent and so were the managers he hired. Numerous service company entrepreneurs have profited by offering customer service in markets where the principal suppliers offer products, but fail to emphasize customer service.

Homogeneity of Buyers. The problem that EDS solved was essentially the same for all buyers, with minor differences in degree of severity. The solution did not have to be tailor-made or customized for each buyer. Selling off the racks is cheaper and provides more rapid cash flow than selling custom made.

Large Number of Buyers. The number of potential buyers sharing essentially the same problem was in excess of 3,000 corporations and institutions. Assuming each one had an annual data processing budget of $1 million, the market size for EDS's solution was $3 billion and no other competitor was within two years of sharing a piece of the pie. More than any other single factor, this explains why EDS's initial public offering was at a common stock price in excess of the then unheard of 115.0 times earnings. Facilities management, five years after EDS began operations, was to become the fastest growing segment of the data processing industry. It is destined for even greater wealth creation in government and hospital markets, two of our largest problem gardens.

Lack of Institutional Barriers to Selling.   The buyers were not organized. They belonged to no association. There was no regulatory body to which they were responsible for their activities, such as the American Medical Association or the Federal Aviation Administration. The buyers were new to computers and new to their problem. Their purpose in seeking a solution was to generate data cost-efficiently, a purpose that did not require them to seek permission or clarification from an outside institution.

"Hey, It Really Works!" Phenomenon.   EDS's solution was passed along from buyer to buyer by word-of-mouth advertising. Not only is word-of-mouth the cheapest form of advertising, it is also the most effective. Advertising is one of the most inefficient consumers of capital and the excessive use of it serves to reduce the entrepreneur's wealth.

Optimum Price-Cost Relationship.   The price of the solution was equal to the cost of the problem, that is, the buyer's data processing budget. EDS's price could not be questioned as being excessively high or unwarranted, because the buyer was paying the same price for the problem that had to be paid to have it solved. If the same $100 that brought problems would now bring solutions, the buyer was $100 ahead. As they say in *The Godfather*, EDS made them an offer they couldn't refuse.

Invisibility of the New Company.   EDS operated quietly and without fanfare. It did not advertise or promote heavily. It did not gain attention so that it could be copied by competitors. In 1973, 10 years after the formation of EDS, General Electric Company was the first company larger than EDS to enter the facilities management business. By that time, Perot had banked nearly $1 billion in capital gains.

Just as Perot taught us facilities management, one of the more brilliant means of launching a new business on the customer's capital, he also underscored the difficulties of achieving a second entrepreneurial success. Perot's attempts to operate an efficient Wall Street investment banking firm cost him millions and a reduction in the height of his pedestal.

Newsletters, Seminars

No business is simpler to launch than the newsletter business on customers' advance payments. The first entrepreneur to make money in a new industry is usually the newsletter publisher. The service the publisher provides is to identify the problem that the new entrepreneurs of that industry are intent on solving. Frequently the newsletters grow into magazines, or branch into seminars, cassettes from the seminars, and conventions, all of which are managed by the entrepreneur. Sheldon Adelson's COMDEX, the leading trade show of the personal computer industry, grosses more than $175 million per annum.

Many new social issues are in need of careful and frequent indexing of their problem segments on a fairly regular basis. *Ms.* magazine looked at the women's liberation market when it was relatively new and identified the problems created by male chauvinism. Each month this very fine, upbeat publication indexes the problems, problem solvers, and solutions in the complex area of the changing role of women. *Ms.* is a newsletter that serves a sufficiently wide market to attract advertisers. Because it elected to have a wide rather than a narrow appeal, *Ms.* allowed *Working Woman* and *Savvy* to capture the narrower segments.

Electronic funds transfer systems (EFTS) is another market in search of more precise definition. Commercial bankers believe that if they do not begin to offer off-premises banking in stores, then the stores themselves or, heaven forbid, the less closely regulated savings and loan industry might do it. Sears, Roebuck & Company purchased Dean Witter Reynolds for $600 million in order to begin offering brokerage and banking services to its 21 million Sears credit cardholders. The checkless society is coming, but no one is quite sure how, why, when, or where. A perfect scenario for a newsletter.

An eastern EFTS company, Payment Systems, acquired in 1975 by American Express Company on attractive terms for its founders, noticed quite early in its short business life that the banking industry had four levels of sophistication regarding EFTS or the "checkless society":

1. The largest group had heard or read about it and wanted to learn
   more.

2. The next largest group felt they should begin to see how they
   might implement different phases of EFTS, such as automatic
   tellers or debit cards.

3. The third largest group was ready to hire consultants to begin
   implementing one or two phases.

4. The fourth largest group was very well informed about EFTS,
   had studied its costs and benefits, and wanted someone to install
   a computer-based system.

Since the market was pyramid shaped, with the biggest dollars in
group 4, among one or two banks, Payment System's job was to move
potential customers up the pyramid. Group 1 bought a newsletter,
group 2 attended seminars, group 3 hired the company for consulting,
and group 4 engaged the company for facilities management of their
EFTS facility.

The newsletter, however, provided the cash flow to support the
other activities until the company matured. Thousands of banking institutions and computer peripheral component manufacturers sub-
scribed to the newsletter. Their dollars subsidized the more sophisticated but poorer cash flow segments of the business.

Other markets that come to mind as likely candidates for newsletters
as a base for launching new products or services are: the nutrition market, with follow-on nutritional products; the alternative energy markets; the genetic engineering market; the home computer market; the
home video market; the step-parenting market; the post-operative cancer patient market; and the frequent flyer prize-optimization market.

Aside from the newsletter's ability to generate cash up front on a
subscription basis or monthly on a newsstand basis, a newsletter in and
of itself is very inexpensive to initiate. The entrepreneur needs a mailing list and a printer willing to prepare a lot of postcards. An optimistic, persuasive publisher is able to convince the owner of the mailing
list and the mail order printer to be paid out of initial subscriptions.
The founders of *Psychology Today* launched their magazine on the
strength of their initial mailings and with virtually no money in the
bank. They convinced the printer to prepare the direct mail postcard

"on spec," and they, the entrepreneurs, only had to pay for the postage. The problem was sufficiently large and the direct mail piece was right on target.

A large number of service company ideas can be launched by offering a newsletter indexing the various facets of the problem to those who have the problem. In the wellness and health care fields, these include child abuse, anorexia and bulimia, lasers in medicine, stress and distress, teenage suicides, alcoholism, and the implications of genetic engineering in family health care. How does an entrepreneur capitalize on these opportunities? T. George Harris launched *American Health*, a monthly wellness magazine that rapidly grew to 600,000 subscribers. As a wide-ranging magazine, it cannot provide sufficiently thorough service in the specific segments such as stress, child abuse, or anorexia. Thus, the market is wide open for newsletters in this field, followed by seminars, followed by consulting services.

The newsletter-seminar launch should be given careful consideration by entrepreneurs who have not as yet developed a solution to a problem, but have a great deal of information about the problem. Perhaps they are employed by a large corporation that does not wish to address the problem. Yet the entrepreneurs very much want to.

Following the typical entrepreneurial pattern, their internal drivers will not let them remain employed where they are. Their ideas overcome them and they leave their jobs, incorporate, describe their services in writing, send out letters to potential customers offering the service, and await the invitations. They do not come. Then they get on the telephone to see if the people they sent the letters to would prefer a meeting. They would not. The entrepreneurs have lunch with people well placed to help them, but these people do not feel right making introductions because they do not understand the services being offered.

The entrepreneurs rewrite the descriptions of their services, rearrange them on paper, and ship them back out to the likely purchasers, the people with the problem that only they can solve. They receive a few calls, and two or three meetings are held. The services are fairly well understood, but the potential customers need to understand their problems a little better before they go out and buy the new solution. After all, they may find solutions in-house. For each entrepreneur, one small study contract comes out of a $5,000 investment in stationery, word processing, postage, and telephone calls. The entrepreneurs know their services are valid, but the people with the problems are not ready to buy them. The entrepreneurs may be too far ahead and they will go broke waiting for the market to catch up with them.

The solution: Put on a seminar. Whenever a problem is not well understood by the people who have the problem, it is not only difficult, it is impractical to try to sell a solution to it. People who are not concerned with the immediacy of their problem will not pay for its solution. They will, however, pay for more information about the problem.

Over the last several years, the customary means of enlightening people about their problems is holding a seminar. People seem to enjoy paying $150 to $750 to join others in the same situation in a conference room at a hotel, motel, or resort and hear speakers describe some new developments that they should all begin to worry about. If the seminar attendees are sufficiently pleased with the seminar and if they feel comfortable with the level of awareness of the problem to which they were elevated, they might begin to seek a solution. The seminar company would be pleased to offer the solution, but at a higher price.

In the back of each seminar room is the ubiquitous table full of tapes and books, including an order form for a tape of the present seminar and a subscription form for the entrepreneur's newsletter. The attendees can buy the tape and play it when they return to their homes or offices to amplify things that they missed at the live performance.

Personal computer seminars are very popular at the moment. People are paying $100 to $150 to attend seminars to learn how the personal computer may be used in their businesses or professions. Self-actualization seminars have been popular for years, under a variety of titles, Est, transactional analysis, Psi, Scientology, and many more. The prices can be as high as $500 for a session.

Looking at areas where the entrepreneur would be wise to sell seminars about a service rather than the service itself, one that rushes to the front is software for cable television. We know that more and more channels will soon be available to us on cable television, affording opportunities to independent producers to generate programs. John Coleman, the "Good Morning, America" weatherforecaster, recently completed a venture capital financing to produce a weather program to be sold to cable television. How did he do it? Whom did he see? What is important to the cable television broadcasters? How much is a program worth in that market? A seminar entitled "How to Sell Programs to Cable TV" would do well at $300 per head. If the seminar were held 12 times per annum in New York, Chicago, or Los Angeles for an average audience of 30 per seminar, the seminar entrepreneur would achieve gross revenues of $108,000. Assuming conference rental and food and beverage costs of $300 per session, or $36,000, the entrepreneur would earn slightly over $70,000. The seminars would very likely lead to other revenue sources, principally consulting contracts.

Other seminar ideas include stress relocation for corporate human resource officers, corporate alcoholism and corporate physical fitness addressed to the same market, and ideas for businesses to launch, addressed to potential entrepreneurs.

Candidates for seminars are most easily located by direct mail, but it is possible to reach them, although not as effectively, with newspaper advertisements. For a cost of one insert in the local newspaper, perhaps as low as $300, one can see if the seminar business might be a way to bail out of a cash flow problem. The mechanisms for reaching the market are not difficult to learn. The point to remember, however, is if you cannot sell the solution, sell information about the problem.

Direct Mail Marketing

No other business is quite as easy to enter as direct mail marketing, as witnessed by all of the shop-by-mail catalogs you are offered. The business is going electronic as well, so that owners of personal computers can log onto hundreds of catalogs, then order their products via mail, courier, or United Parcel Service.

Direct mail or mail order is the fastest growing segment of retailing. It is a $150 billion per annum business, and it represents about 15 percent of total annual retail sales.

Roger Horchow made the first significant change in direct mail marketing since Aaron Montgomery Ward produced the first mail-order catalog in 1872. Horchow was the first entrepreneur to publish a catalog independent of a store, which he did exactly 100 years after Ward. His catalogs are full of attractive items that appeal to the vanity of upscale women aged 35–60 whose names and addresses he and other mail-order entrepreneurs locate by renting lists of American Express cardholders. These names are then merged and purged against other lists, to make certain that the recipients of the catalogs have expensive taste and a direct mail purchasing habit. With nothing more than an idea and the experience of having been in charge of Neiman-Marcus Company's mail-order department, but no investment in inventory, Horchow built a business whose sales now exceed $50 million per annum.

Horchow lit the lamp so that hundreds of others could follow. Whereas he cataloged new products, other direct mail entrepreneurs have discovered opportunities in niches, such as baseball cards, antique eye wash cups, rare coins, commemorative plaques and, lest we forget, trivia.

When Claude and Donna Jeanloz were kicked out of Africa by a new dictator who turned against the Peace Corps, they returned to their renovated home in Millers Falls, Massachusetts, and began tossing around ideas for a business that they could do together. The idea suddenly came to Donna to launch a mail-order catalog full of renovators' supplies for couples such as themselves who were renovating old houses. In 1979 they launched *The Renovator's Supply* with $50,000 that they earned from the sale of another home. Within five years the Jeanlozes had built a $10 million (sales) mail order business with enough cash flow to launch a chain of retail stores.

For the direct mail entrepreneur who has the idea, but lacks the $25,000 to $50,000 to rent mailing lists and purchase postage, there is the stuffer. American Express Company, other credit card companies, oil companies, and department stores will include a stuffer describing a product to their customers receiving monthly billings. This is a widely used means for selling small appliances, giftware, housewares, decorative accessories, and art prints. One of the typical pricing methods is for the credit card issuer to incur all of the marketing costs in exchange for 50 percent of the retail selling price. For art prints that are marked up about 800 percent, the value of a Sears, Roebuck & Company mailing to 21 million Sears credit card customers is extraordinary. Assume that an artist charged an entrepreneur $10,000 for a drawing and that prints could be reproduced for $5 apiece and sold for $40. Assume further that a department store stuffed this direct mail offer into 2 million envelopes and that 1 percent of the recipients (20,000) ordered a print. Revenues would be $800,000, of which the department store would keep $400,000. Costs would be $100,000, for a net profit before taxes of $290,000. Even with a one-half of 1 percent response you would come out handsomely.

The direct mail method of financing a new company assumes that the entrepreneur is able to produce and deliver the product within about six weeks to 60 days.

After six to eight weeks, the customers will be getting anxious about the product. Failing to deliver a product for which an entrepreneur received cash in the mail is mail fraud, a serious felony. The entrepreneur must return the money or face serious consequences. Very few entrepreneurs are larcenous; but those who have defrauded the public by failing to deliver a product have cast an aura of foul play over direct mail in general, mitigated in large part by the fine firms that are increasingly entering the business.

Smell and Sense of Taste.   It was discovered in the late 1970s that the odor of vanilla in enclosed malls was practically irresistible. People who had gone years between eating cookies would be drawn into cookie stores by the odor of fresh cookies. Workers in Thom Mc An shoe stores adjacent to Mrs. Fields' Cookies stores report the onset of an addiction. Thus the rise and success of cookie stores, initially a direct mail success made famous by Famous Amos, but carried to new revenue heights by Debbi Fields. Mrs. Fields began her cookie chain in 1977 by handing out fresh baked cookies in the streets of Palo Alto to attract customers. In seven years, her chain has grown to 180 stores in 15 states with revenues estimated by a competitor at $80 million.

When you wish to learn a new skill, such as public-speaking, or a foreign language, or become better informed in general, the spoken-word audio cassette firm of Jeffrey Norton Publishers, Guilford, Connecticut will sell you the cassettes via direct mail. Many people who spend several hours a day in their cars use "learning cassettes."

One of the world's leading sportswear companies is Esprit de Corp, founded in the late 1970s by Douglas and Susie Tompkins. It was founded on a direct mail catalog idea that encourages young women to pile on layers of beautifully designed, colorful clothing. Seasonality and sizes are largely ignored. The clothes are cheerful and trendy and if cold weather sets in, a few more layers are added. The 2.5 million catalog recipients drove sales to $613 million in 1984. The Tompkinses intend to convert the profits into a chain of Esprit boutiques.

Many messages can be drawn from happy-go-lucky direct mail entrepreneurs. First, customer financing is an excellent means of testing
whether or not the P, or problem factor, is strong. If it is not a serious
problem, the direct mail marketing brochure or catalog will generate
very few coins. If it is a serious, contemporary problem, the customers
will mail in the capital to launch the company.

The reason that direct mail entrepreneurs seem to be smiling all of
the time is they have used "leverage" and that is a happy event when
done well. Chapter 5 describes leverage.

Licensing

An ideal licensing opportunity exists when the entrepreneur can sell to
a third party the rights to manufacture and market a product in that
market. Films are frequently financed by selling the distribution rights
in advance to various distributors in all of the principal markets. Cable
television was a boon to film producers because it provided a new
source of cash from licensing. A greater boon is home video, largely ignored by everyone except Andre Blay, a Southfield, Michigan, entrepreneur. His company, Magnetic Video Corporation, quietly acquired
the home video rights to over half of the existing movies made prior to
1976. Because the industry did not have the same feel for the potential
of VCRs, Blay paid next to nothing to build his library. In 1985 home
video has become one-fifth the size of the overall U.S. movie industry.

Walter O. Heinze, a 76-year-old entrepreneur when he founded International Water Saving Systems Inc. (IWSS) in 1979, needed capital
to develop, manufacture, and market his unique water-saving toilet.
The IWSS toilet required several cups of water to properly dispose of
human waste, whereas conventional toilets in the United States use
two gallons per flush. Heinze read that the Saudi Arabians were attempting to float a large iceberg from Antarctica to the Persian Gulf to
provide some of their water requirements. He immediately began to research the size of their problem and the effectiveness of his solution.

Because it needs more water than it can produce, Saudi Arabia has
been seeking innovative means to generate or save water. It uses 36 billion gallons of water per year flushing toilets, and it does not have 36
billion gallons of water in a year. It is water short, and some people

must discharge waste without toilets, which leads to typhus and cholera epidemics. Countries such as Saudi Arabia were approached by IWSS not just for the granting of manufacturing licenses, but also for the exclusive rights to sell the toilets in their markets. The price for this privilege was approximately a $1 million down payment and minimum royalties for each of the next 10 years in the range of $1 million per year. At a royalty to IWSS of $50 per toilet, that could represent minimum sales of 20,000 toilets per year in the Middle East, and enough to finance the U.S. operation.

An ideal licensing situation is one in which you can sell off an exclusive product or territorial right, like the IWSS example, and use the proceeds therefrom as capital to finance the development of the major activities of the company. This type of opportunity exists principally with multimarket proprietary products, but perhaps surprisingly, with commonplace products as well. Looking back at the direct mail example with framed art print offers sent as credit card stuffers, those same framed art prints could be licensed to a catalog, premium, or direct mail firm, or to a publisher for inclusion in a book, and so forth.

Licensing has myriad ramifications. While in the problem formulation stage, the important licensing related questions are:

1. Is there a submarket for my product willing to pay a premium for it because of a serious problem that my product solves?

2. Is there an entity in that submarket that can manufacture and market my product?

3. Is it large enough to pay me a substantial down payment and to guarantee the payment of future minimum royalties?

4. What is the potential size of that submarket in number of units (dollars) per annum?

5. What is the highest level contact that I can establish with that entity? (An introduction through an investment or commercial banker is preferred.)

In the process of problem formulation, many an entrepreneur has hit upon the idea—usually when desperate for cash—of selling to a third party the right to the solution (S) that the entrepreneur has developed for that market. Frequently the market is a foreign one, but occasionally the licensee represents a different channel in the U.S. marketplace. For example, an entrepreneur might develop a unique, high-performance tomato picker to build a company around. To raise capital, the manufacturing and marketing rights in the United States, Canada, France, and West Germany are licensed to Deere & Company for $1 million plus a 10 percent royalty on sales. This leaves the entrepreneur with the manufacturing and marketing rights for Central America, parts of Europe, the Middle East, and the Far East. The company may not end up to be what the entrepreneur had in mind, but the cash advance and the future royalty stream will free him or her up for more product development.

It is important to include "out" clauses in licenses, because frequently the licensee fails to perform and the entrepreneur gets back the rights due to nonperformance, without having to forfeit any advances. This happened to Dr. Lyman Smith, inventor of Chymodiactin and cofounder of Smith Laboratories, Inc., whose entrepreneurial process has led to a unique solution to the pain of slipped and herniated discs.

A struggling, young Xerox Corporation sold the European rights to manufacture and market the Xerox copying machine to Rank S.A. Gene Amdahl was raising venture capital for his IBM-compatible Amdahl Computer Corporation in the illiquid mid-1970s and sought the financial muscle of Fujitsu, which cost Amdahl the Japanese rights. When Francis Coppola was arranging the financing for *Apocalypse Now*, he sold the French distribution rights in advance for $100,000. The French distributor made his best deal ever, because *Apocalypse Now* was the number one movie in France for the better part of a year.

The emerging personal computer industry contains numerous opportunities for licensing because European companies have—for the most part—arrived late to this particular party. Thus, struggling IBM-compatible personal computer manufacturers should look to European partners for the financial muscle to do battle with IBM, Apple, and the Japanese manufacturers, while licensing the manufacturing and marketing rights to Europe. Since software is the blade and computers the razor, the licensor can look to a bright future of selling software into an installed base of computers in Europe.

Another side to licensing does not raise capital for the entrepreneur, but gains certain rights and advantages. This side is the entrepreneur as licensee. For the entrepreneur who wanted to build a chain of dance studios in the 1940s, what better name to license than Arthur Murray? It has become one of the most profitable franchises ever. The name set the company apart from other dance studios and imputed a national image and a quality reputation to an infant company.

Products are frequently licensed from well-known institutions to attract customers who seek quality brands and a "name you can trust." Thus, the best known word processing package for home computer users is produced and marketed by Broderbund Software, but bears the name Bank Street Writer, under a license from the renowned Bank Street private school in New York. Charles Schulz has licensed his Charlie Brown and Snoopy characters to numerous manufacturers of toys and children's products, as has George Lucas his *Star Wars* characters. These licenses are frequently worth the royalty that the entrepreneur is asked to pay because the characters or names licensed have millions of advertising dollars and many years of good will behind them. Thus, for the entrepreneur developing a chain of wellness clinics, the name of a popular physical fitness personality such as Jane Fonda or Bruce Jenner could be very useful. For a line of running clothes, the name Carl Lewis could help to spur sales. Larry Hagman's name and face could possibly lift a cowboy hat's sales above the pack.

Frequently a trade association will endorse a product in a related field in exchange for a royalty. In education software, most publishers have obtained the endorsement of one or the other of the many associations of teachers, schools, or parents. The use of staid, conservative associations in testimonials often gives entrepreneurial companies the early endorsement that they need. As a new industry begins to mature, usually an entrepreneur forms a laboratory-type company that reviews and critiques all of the products of that industry for the purpose of selling evaluative information and seals of approval. Clever is the entrepreneur who can set himself up as the "Good Housekeeping Seal of Approval" for a burgeoning industry, chock-full of confusing new products. By making the company the toll booth in a new industry, the entrepreneur forces companies to pay to get onto the highway. You could call these mandatory licenses.

The number of toll booth opportunities for entrepreneurs is staggering because of all the new industry formations. In the health care industry, for instance, a new reimbursement system has been formulated by Medicare, and quickly followed by systems from other insurance companies. The reimbursement system is known as "diagnostic related groups" (DRG), and it means that hospitals are to be reimbursed on a rate schedule determined by Medicare, and not based on what the market will bear. DRG is a potent attempt to cut health care costs at the source.

Lucky is the entrepreneur who sets up the first DRG electronic data bank code to enable doctors to immediately down-load evaluative information on alternative and health care services and their DRG costs. This toll booth could result in one of the largest service companies in the health care industry.

Stevan Cloudtree, the 35-year-old founder of One Point in Walnut Creek, California, had a similar thing in mind for the business software market. He and his staff have loaded evaluative information on approximately 6,000 software products into a computer's electronic data base. Prospective purchasers of business software can dial up One Point's catalog and down-load information about the products they have an interest in, such as spread sheets, word processors, or accounting packages. One Point provides a description of the products, published reviews, prices, warranty information, operating system information, and comparative data. The retail chains, in particular, are very pleased with this information because it helps them satisfy their customers. Corporate software users demonstrate their satisfaction with One Point by ordering software from the company.

Gatekeeper businesses are the best kind. The gross profit margins can be in excess of 80 percent. Controlling access to a marketing channel can be very profitable. Entrepreneurs should read *The Godfather* from a business viewpoint to see the benefits of being a gatekeeper.

Consulting

Frequently entrepreneurs are consultants for several years before becoming entrepreneurs. This situation occurs because the person who recognizes the existence of a large problem, develops an affinity and an attachment perhaps, as well as a thorough understanding of the problem, but is unable to develop a solution to the problem. Without a solution, and with a desire to become completely occupied with the problem, the person leaves the corporate employer and becomes a consultant.

The combination of forces that pull a person out of a corporate position and into the fanatical world of entrepreneurship is dissatisfaction, insight, and energy. The usual pattern is that the person has identified a problem that affects a large number of people and recommends to superior officers that the corporation attempt to solve it, adding that the problem is sufficiently large and propinquous to develop quickly into a market. The person fancies himself or herself as the project head, with a six-figure budget and several research assistants. At some point in the near future, when this person and the staff have identified the magnitude and dimensions of the problem and the matrices of the possible solutions, the person imagines becoming a division manager, perhaps vice-president, maybe more. Identified as one of the bright young executives, this person is capable of leading the corporation to unheard of heights and undreamed of levels of earnings in the near future.

Alas, the aspiring corporate leader is told by superiors that his or her insight is considerably off the mark, that the problem identified is not very large; in fact, it is quite small. The aspiring leader is also told the corporation would have no interest in pursuing it as a potential market and to get back to business and stop dreaming. The person's dreams and plans for corporate excellence via this new market are trashed, leaving the young dreamer shattered.

Suddenly the former aspiring leader leaves the corporation because the P has taken hold of him or her and time is required to develop the insight to create S. The violence of this sudden transformation frequently rocks the future entrepreneur's marriage. The spouse has not been sufficiently informed that his or her mate is going through a period of intense dissatisfaction, and that an entrepreneur is about to emerge from the body of Clark Kent.

A consultant is frequently an entrepreneur in the making. A young man or woman who has identified a large P, but needs the space and time to create S and to pull together the components of E. To make a living during the transitional period, consultants sell the P. That is, they call on groups of people, large corporations, and institutions that are willing to pay to learn more about this particular P. The consultant explains P, indexes P, classifies P, provides the history of P and analyzes the possible ramifications of P. This is done in memorandum form, with statistical data bases, overhead projection, and oral communication. The consultant dances P, sings P, paints P, and plays it on the piano. By becoming a consultant prior to becoming an entrepreneur, the consultant is paid to problem-formulate. By generating cash in front to study the problem, the consultant maintains a positive cash flow in the preentrepreneurial stage. Some consultants do well enough financially to be their own sources of venture capital.

When the second factor—insight for S—strikes the consultant, a prototype is developed, frequently with the help of others, particularly for a technically complex solution, and it is tested. A prototype test on the entrepreneur's premises is known as an alpha test, and a test on a customer's premises is known as a beta test. A satisfied beta test customer is permitted to purchase the product or service at a discount. An unsuccessful beta test, of course, sends the entrepreneur back to the drawing board.

The third factor required to launch the consultant into entrepreneurship is energy. A person who is sufficiently dissatisfied to leave an employer and who has the insight to formulate P and to create an elegant S that can be packaged and sold to the people with P, must have the necessary high level of energy required to build a company that will convey S to P. A person with dissatisfaction and insight, but lacking energy, generally becomes a journalist or remains a consultant.

Consulting is a stage between working for someone and entrepreneurship. The consultant needs to spend time with the problem. In addition to becoming comfortable with the problem, the consultant must see if it is central to a group of people whom he or she likes, and would like to help in a meaningful way. There are lots of problems, many opportunities, and the wise consultant wants to pick the one that suits him or her best. Each of us knows only limited ways to make money, and it is important for our happiness that we find the right method.

Happiness is finding and retrieving one's heart in the marketplace and then pursuing a goal directed by the heart. Consulting is a process of recapturing one's heart. A longtime corporate or government employee loses his or her heart. The corporate employer requires qualities that exclude and deny the directions of the heart, including competence, coolness under stress, and self-confidence. The qualities of the heart, of extreme importance to the entrepreneur, include compassion, cooperativeness, generosity, sense of humor, openness, spontaneity, independence, and loyalty to fellow workers. Michael Maccoby, a serious student of the corporate worker, believes that corporate employees who are the most loving, caring, sensitive, and compassionate move up the corporate ladder more slowly than do the cool, dispassionate, and insensitive. Might entrepreneurs be superior lovers? That is the subject of someone else's book.

Party Plan Selling

This marketing channel—variations of in-home selling—is not included merely because it is a cornerstone or even an important leg of the stool of entrepreneurship. Rather, this creative form of marketing is all too infrequently considered by entrepreneurs. Mary Kay Cosmetics, Shaklee Corporation, Amway Corporation, Tupperware, Discovery Toys and Transart Industries have all achieved rapid sales growth via the party plan method, and moreover, with very modest start-up capital. After all, party plan selling is the ultimate form of customer financing.

In party plan selling's classical structure, the universe—say North America—is divided into 10 geographic regions, and a regional marketing director is found for each. This person is trained in the sale, installation, and servicing of the company's product, and of equal importance, in the recruitment and training of a sales staff. The regional directors are then *sold* their initial inventories by the company, and a mutually agreed upon quota is set for their purchase of more inventory. The faster they can recruit, hire, and train sales teams for their regions, the quicker they can turn over their inventory and make their commissions.

The commission structure is carefully arranged so that the regional sales manager earns an override on all sales in his or her region; so that the divisional sales managers hired and trained by the regional sales manager earn overrides on all sales in their divisions; so that the district sales managers hired and trained by a divisional sales manager earn overrides on all sales in their districts; and so that the sales representatives—the people who are doing substantially all of the in-home selling—earn healthy commissions for their sales. Indeed, there is even one more layer of commissions: "finder's fees" are paid to the person who calls her friends over to the party. If the friends purchase products, the finder is paid a commission on their purchases.

All of these commissions may add up to from 40 to 50 percent of the retail selling price, which may strike the casual observer as a large percentage, but it is frequently less than the discounts charged by monopsonistic mass merchandisers. The latter pay 120 days after they sell the products, whereas in the party plan method, the customer pays for inventory in advance. A typical commission structure for an in-home selling company might appear as follows:

Regional sales manager	5.0%
Divisional sales manager	7.5
District sales manager	10.0
Sales representative	17.5
Finder's fee	10.0
Total commissions	50.0%

In addition to these commissions, the company must incur the costs of preparing selling materials, national advertising costs, public relations, convention costs, prizes and awards, premiums, and sales support. This could add up to another 15 percent of the total retail selling price.

Transart Industries, the leading merchandiser of framed art work, calculates that its average sale is approximately $65 and that its cost of goods sold is in the neighborhood of $6.50. If total selling expenses are approximately 65 percent of the retail price, or $42.25, the company will earn· approximately $16.25, or 25 percent per unit before general and administrative expenses. Transart grew to more than 20,000 employees in 40 states in less than five years from the sale of framed art via party plan selling. Its employees were largely housewives who wanted to earn second incomes. Many of these women quickly began earning more money than their husbands.

How new a creation is party plan or in-home selling? Do you think it originated in the postwar era with Tupperware or Mary Kay, when Rosie the Riveter of World War II fame grew up to become a button-down lady sales executive, aided and reassured by her subscription to *Ms.* magazine? Although this sounds plausible, it is far from the truth.

In-home and party plan selling began in the late nineteenth century. The first company to use it was Investors Diversified Services, Inc. (IDS) whose product is a service, mutual fund investing. Sales representatives have subsequently been licensed to sell insurance, another service sold on an in-home basis since the nineteenth century. As perhaps the most truly American of marketing concepts, in-home selling needs to be considered seriously by today's entrepreneur.

The marketing of home computers and home computer software could become more efficient if party plan selling techniques were adopted. Other consumer electronics products, possibly home video products, wellness services and products, and a venture capital investing service—how unusual does that sound relative to mutual funds in 1896—could benefit by in-home or party plan selling.

Problem formulating, if done wisely and enthusiastically by the entrepreneur, is the most creative aspect of entrepreneurship. It is boundless and far-reaching. No other stage in the entrepreneurial process is as *free* as problem formulating. It is a happy time, one of almost total creativity, exploration, and idea generating. There are places one can go in the United States to meet with other potential entrepreneurs who are also at the problem-formulation stage. Thirty different cities now have Venture Capital Clubs, an idea launched by Thomas P. Murphy, the *Forbes* columnist and successful venture capital investor, in 1974. For a concentrated four-day total submersion in problem formulation, The Center for Entrepreneurship in Tarrytown, New York, is in a class by itself. Founded by Robert Schwartz in the late 1970s, the center requires potential entrepreneurs, who stay in former Nigerian embassy buildings overlooking the Hudson River, to bounce entrepreneurial ideas off one another for two weekends. The experience is, in a word, cathartic.

In his *Memoirs*, Jean Monnet, the architect of the European Economic Community, tells how he said to a friend:

George, you should stop diffusing your energies. You should select a single, great objective and concentrate on it until it is accomplished. You may have to make short-term tactical detours, but you must never lose sight of your central goal, even when the road ahead seems hopelessly blocked.[5]

CREATING THE SOLUTION

Entrepreneurship is not creating a solution to a problem already defined. Rather, it is the formulation and reformulation of the problem until a solution emerges through the process of raising all of the questions, examining the problem from all angles, and restating and reframing the problem until it has been examined as thoroughly as possible. The entrepreneur who formulates the problem in a thorough, exhaustive manner will develop a larger P and more elegant S than will the entrepreneur who invents a superior S without examining all of the nooks and crannies of P. The latter is usually done by inventors; they are a far different breed than entrepreneurs.

If the process of entrepreneurial creativity is to be understood fully, the study of what the entrepreneur does cannot be restricted to the visible solution, the finished product. It must include the earlier, crucial step: formulation of the problem to which the solution is a response. In addition, the formulation of the problem is not a constant, but rather, a cumulative process of discovery which begins when the potential entrepreneur enters the period of dissatisfaction, extends through the development of insight into the problem, and often does not end even after the entrepreneur appears at the corner of Wall and Broad streets for the listing ceremony on the New York Stock Exchange of his or her company's common stock.

Thinking, we know, is equated with rational, methodical, unadventurous problem solving; the unfolding of symbolic links from given premises to known conclusions. Creative thinking does not follow the known path. Rather than accepting the premises of a structured problem, creativity fashions a new problematic configuration. Instead of striving to reach a known solution, the cognitive efforts of a creative person are frequently targeted at goals that previously had been considered inconceivable or not achievable. If behavioral scientists skilled in

[5]Jean Monnet, *Memoirs* (New York: Doubleday, 1978), p. ii.

structuring measurement systems would observe entrepreneurs at work, query them continually, and qualify and correlate the results against standards, we would learn more about the creative process that entrepreneurship involves than we would from my or any other lay observations.

One method of measurement would be to put 20 significant problems on pieces of paper, have the entrepreneurs select the one that they would like to build a business to solve, and then formulate the business plan. The launch itself would require capital aplenty, not a long commodity at universities these days; thus, measuring the competence of an entrepreneur by the success of the business against his or her creative process will probably have to be postponed until there is funding for the full study. Still, behavioral science is sufficiently developed to measure the creativity in the entrepreneurial process.

The study of creativity by Getzels and Csikszentmihalyi mentioned earlier in this chapter also investigates the social, emotional, and experiential "baggage" of artists and their social typologies, not dissimilar from our discussion as it applies to entrepreneurs and managers. The social typologies of artists and entrepreneurs have more similarities than we might at first imagine. The media play a nasty game with entrepreneurs, reminding us that their scorecard is wealth and not the chase, whereas artists are supposed to love the chase and abhor the comforts of life. Artists and entrepreneurs, on the contrary, have quite a bit in common, not the least of which is the desire to do some one thing extremely well.

The art students who scored highest in seeking power as a social value became applied artists and entered advertising and marketing. Their skills, the tests showed, were more in the area of problem solving than that of problem finding. In advertising, one is paid to motivate people to want certain things—from products to political candidates—and to guide people toward certain ends. In the measurements of personality characteristics, advertising students are most similar to the general population, reflecting interest in power and persuasion rather than the inner drives that we have found in entrepreneurs. This raises more questions about the kinds of people who become entrepreneurs. Is an advertising-trained individual who creates a successful shampoo an entrepreneur in our definition, or a promoter? Where does one place John DeLorean, who created a new car in a marketplace

where supply clearly exceeded demand? That would make DeLorean a
problem-producer rather than a problem-solver, a promoter rather than
an entrepreneur. Or would it? His dissatisfaction at General Motors
Corporation, his divorce and remarriage, and other personality characteristics that we were bombarded with in *Pathfinders*[6] and *Playboy*,
among others, would characterize him as an entrepreneur. What seems
to be lacking, however, is the problem-finding characteristic, the formulation, reformulation, and continual examination of the market that
one intends to address with a new product. What problem did De-
Lorean find that he could deliver a solution to? Clearly there was none.
Perhaps if we knew more about the entrepreneurial process, we could
prevent the waste of capital on products such as DeLorean cars.

Getzels and Csikszentmihalyi observed 31 male fine art students and
then followed their careers over seven years. Of these, 16 were engaged
in artistic work and 15 left the field. Eight of the 16 artists had achieved
success, as measured by gallery owners and art critics. The backgrounds of the successful artists are shown in Exhibit 4.3.

EXHIBIT 4.3. Backgrounds of Successful Artists

Father's occupation:	50% executives, merchants or professional; 50% white collar jobs, skilled and unskilled workers
Mother's occupation:	62% mothers employed outside the home
Family broken due to death or divorce:	13% disrupted
Sibling position:	81% first born
Religious background:	19% Protestant

(Source: Getzels and Csikszentmihalyi, p. 164.)

The successful artists came from more well-to-do families. "The
mother's education and occupation are more related to the son's success than the father's education and occupation. Finally, despite common belief to the contrary, family disruption through divorce, separa-
tion, or death of parents was three times more prevalant in the
unsuccessful than in the successful group."[7]

[6]Gail Sheehy, *Pathfinders* (New York: Morrow, 1981).
[7]Getzels and Csikszentmihalyi, *The Creative Vision*, p. 165.

There are similarities between successful entrepreneurs and successful artists. As we have seen, the relationship with the mother is a critical variable. In my interviews with hundreds of successful entrepreneurs, approximately 80 percent said their dominant personality characteristics were derived from their mothers. Erik H. Erikson warns us to be wary of second sons, particularly where the maternal grandfather was a dynamic individual. Thus, sibling position is an important criterion. It forces the issue to find more parallels. Indeed, entrepreneurs carry more pain and other emotional baggage than do artists. They have a hurt that drives them to build a far more complex thing than a work of art. Although artists occasionally surface at their openings and sometimes teach, they have the privilege of working alone and marching to their inner drumbeats; entrepreneurs, however, must get involved with hundreds of moving variables. Entrepreneurs are more complex and idiosyncratic than artists. But the creative processes in art and those in entrepreneurship are not dissimilar.

The creative process in entrepreneurship has not been investigated thoroughly, and is only now being studied in artists and scientists. However, the studies by D. N. Perkins, Getzels and Csikszentmihalyi, and Anna Roe provide a large body of ideas from which we can draw to learn more about the creative process as it applies to entrepreneurs.[8] D.N. Perkins provides us with good principles of creativity:

Try to be original. If you want to be creative you should try to build into any outcomes the property of originality. This sounds almost too silly to mention, but I don't think so and have given some reasons for that. Many supposedly intrinsically creative pursuits like painting can be pursued in very humdrum ways. Major figures in the arts and the sciences often were certainly trying to be original. Creativity is less an ability and more a way of organizing your abilities toward ends that demand invention.

[8]Anna Roe, in a 1963 paper, concluded that creative physician-scientists were (1) very open to experience, (2) highly observant and prone to see things in unusual ways, (3) extremely curious, (4) accepting of unconventional thoughts, (5) ready to recognize and reconcile apparent opposites, (6) tolerant of ambiguities but liking to resolve disorder into order, (7) appreciative of complexity, (8) highly independent in judgment, thought, and action, (9) self-reliant, and (10) not responsive to group standards and control.

Find the problem. This recalls the Getzels–Csikszentmihalyi concept of problem finding. Early in an endeavor, explore alternatives freely, only gradually converging on a defined course of action and keeping even that flexibility revisable. The evidence is that creative people do this. The principle makes all the more sense because later on in the process is often too late—too late to build in originality or intensity or other qualities you might want.

Strive for objectivity. Problems of accurately and objectively monitoring progress pervade creative activity. The judgment of the moment would prove different tomorrow, the revisions of today wrong in a week. Makers have adopted many strategies to cope with the caprice of their own impressions, such as setting a product aside for a while. Also, learning to fashion products that have a potent meaning for others as well as for yourself is a complex process. Beginning with the child's first experiences of language and picturing, the problem of reaching others reappears throughout human growth in more subtle guises and plagues even the expert maker. Sometimes, it may be best to ignore such hazards and freewheel for a while. But if you always freewheel, you never really take advantage of your own best judgment.

Search as necessary and prudent. That is, explore alternatives when you have to, because the present option has failed, or when you had better, because taking the obvious course commits substantial resources that might be better spent. Of course, the conventional advice of many works on creativity is to explore many alternatives routinely.

Try, but don't expect, to be right the first time. The research found that people trade quality for quantity. Aiming at fluency, they lower the standards governing their production of ideas, select imperfectly, and achieve no net gain. This is advice against doing just that. Instead, ask your mind to deliver up the best possible results in the first place. Notice that this does not mean fussing over initial drafts, trying to make them perfect by editing in process. Neither does this say that the results will be right the first time. They likely will need revision, maybe extensive revision and maybe the wastebasket and a new start. This is why you have to adopt a paradoxical attitude: trying, while being perfectly comfortable about falling short. The point is to bias the quick unconscious mechanisms that assemble the words we say, the gestures we make, toward doing as much of the work as possible and leaving as little as possible for deliberate revision. To put it another way: ask yourself for what you really want—you may get it, or at least some of it.

Make use of noticing. The ability to notice patterns relevant to a problem is one of the most powerful gifts we have. This can be put to work deliberately by contemplating things connected to the quest. Suppose, for example, you are designing an innovative house and need ideas. Walk around a conventional house and see what transformations suggest themselves. Or examine a conventional house in the mind's eye with the same objective. The latter can be particularly powerful, and the mind's eye takes a willing traveler to places inconvenient for the body or billfold. Often books on creativity recommend exposure to seemingly unrelated things to stimulate ideas. This certainly sometimes works, as Darwin, Archimedes, and other have taught us. But, in my experience and judgment, sensitive scrutiny of things related to the task at hand usually yields a richer harvest of ideas.

When stuck, change the problem. Early on in the space race, NASA spent much time and effort seeking a metal robot strong enough to withstand the heat of reentry and protect the astronauts. The endeavor failed. At some point, a clever person changed the problem. The real problem was to protect the astronauts, and perhaps this could be done without a material that could withstand reentry. The solution, the ablative heat shield, had characteristics just opposite to those originally sought. Rather than withstanding the heat, it slowly burnt away and carried the heat away from the vehicle. Let me generalize this and similar examples into a heartening principle. Any problem can be solved—if you change the problem into a related one that solves the same real problem. So ask yourself what the real problem is, what constraints have to be met and which ones can be changed or sacrificed. (There may be more than one way of formulating the real problem.)

When confused, employ concrete representations. Darwin's note-books, Beethoven's sketchbooks, a poet's drafts, an architect's plans all are ways of externalizing thought in process. They pin down ideas to the reality of paper and prevent them from shifting or fading in memory. All of us do this at one time or another. However, despite such habits, we may not realize that making thought concrete can help to cure confusion on nearly any occasion. When paths lead this way and that, circle back, and refuse to show the way, make notes, make drawings, make models. Think aloud or form vivid mental images, for such internal concreteness helps some, too.

Practice in a context. Most advice on how to be creative urges the learner to apply it everywhere. However, sometimes "everywhere" is so indefinite and daunting a notion that it turns into nowhere. When people want to improve their creativity, my suggestion is for them to choose some likely activity they often undertake and try hard to be more creative in that. Focus breeds progress. No need to hold back in other activities, but be sure of one.

Invent your behavior. That is, people should think about, criticize, revise, and devise the ways they do things important to them. Too often, inventive thinking is limited to the customary objects of invention—poems, theories, essays, advertising campaigns, and what not. But part of the art of invention is to select unusual objects of invention—objects like your own behavior. This isn't just nice; it's needed. Performances do not necessarily improve, even when you do them frequently. Indeed, it's common lore that people often end up practicing and entrenching their mistakes.

There, then are some possible plans up front, another contribution to that young and hopeful technology of thought. These principles and others like them try to define and impart the limited but very real "edge" which is about the best you can hope for from very general principles. Perhaps the plans mentioned are hard to take, at least as advice. Their prescription is too broad, too much in the direction of telling the daydreamer to pay attention or the grind to daydream more. Just what they mean in particular cases and how one persuades oneself to behave accordingly are serious questions. But take them as general principles and take seriously the problem of translating them into practice, and then they make more sense. There's no reason why the right principles (whether these are they or not) have to be as easy as a recipe for boiling water.[9]

The elegant solutions come to the deeply committed entrepreneur, not as the result of invention but frequently after working with all of the elements of the problem, much as Monet painted the church facade at different times during the day in order to capture sunlight on canvas. Clearly he did not, but he produced some beautiful impressions of sunlight. Edwin H. Land did not invent instant photography as a solution to the problem of delayed film development time. He worked for 14 years on the problem of headlight glare and the possible solutions from polarizing light. His daughter asked him one day while he was snapping her photograph with a Kodak, why it took so long to get her picture back. Land was struck by the question and sought the answer within the field of polarizing light. Chester Carlson, a patent attorney, came up with the idea for xerography as a solution to his particular need to make neater copies of patent applications than were available with a mimeograph. Fred Smith named his overnight small package courier Federal Express because he believed that the Federal Reserve Banks would be his most important customers due to their perceived need to move money around rapidly. They did not become a very significant customer. In many cases, the solution fits into the problem randomly, but effectively, because the entrepreneur recognizes the accidental fit and causes it to happen.

THE BUSINESS PLAN

The preparation of a business plan is the creation of a schematic design that the company will follow as it is launched. It begins with an ex-

[9]D. N. Perkins, *The Mind's Best Work* (Cambridge, Massachusetts: Harvard University Press, 1981).

haustive problem-formulation exercise, where answers to questions are
plotted against time in what is known as a PERT (program evaluation
and research tool) chart. Questions are asked regarding location sensi-
tivity, equipment requirements, laboratory instrument requirements,
technician requirements, time necessary for testing, staffing, marketing
personnel needs, marketing and sales support, and timing until production models are ready for customer tests. Who are the potential
users? What are the various means of locating them? What is the estimated cash flow deficit until break-even? A typical PERT chart that
plots these key factors appears in Figure 4.2.

In each PERT chart block there is a cost. It may be only travel, lodging, or lunch, but there is a cost. The entrepreneur, or the achiever partner, must count the beans from the start or the project will be weakened
throughout by its initial shoddy bookkeeping. Further, there will be a
risk of raising too little capital, a frequent cause of business failures.

Once the costs for the six-month period are counted, the PERT chart
should be reformulated to a six-month delay of a key variable, such as
obtaining the performance contract from an important first customer.
Note that the salaries and overhead will have to be paid for an additional six months without any revenues. Then, assume that suitable
software and hardware products cannot be located by Month 5 as
shown in the original PERT chart, but take until Month 7. Again, costly
delays and more airplane tickets to visit with advisors, producers, and
manufacturers. It is frequently not in the nature of the entrepreneur to
do this much planning and to exercise this much caution, but that role
can be handled effectively by the achiever or manager, the second
member of the entrepreneurial team.

In addition to the PERT chart, the entrepreneur must write a complete and thorough business plan, one that contains all of the data relevant to a sophisticated investor. The purposes of the business plan are
to provide a map for the entrepreneur to follow and to attract financing
at the appropriate time.

The entrepreneur's version of the business plan should be complete
and exhaustive with every detail accounted for. It can be stored on a
word processing disc and updated monthly as factors change. For purposes of raising venture capital, portions of the business plan can be
pulled off the disc and printed out. The executive summary is an over-
view, a one- or two-page summary that defines why the game will be

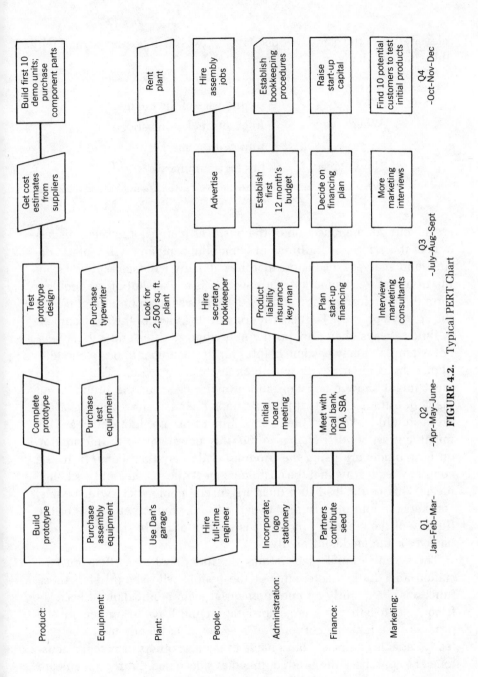

FIGURE 4.2. Typical PERT Chart

played, where the game will be played, how it will be played, and why the game will be won.

Why played	Boundaries of the business
Where played	International, domestic, limits of the market
How played	Strategy summary
Why won	Competitive advantages

The environment section of the business plan is a thorough discussion of the external conditions in which the company will grow. It defines and analyzes the factors that the company will face as it looks out the front door at its market. This section is a snapshot of the problem formulation/reformulation activity that plays such an important part in the creative process. To the entrepreneur, the view of the environment is fluid, always changing, posing new opportunities and submarkets. For example, it may become helpful for the customer to be able to telephone the company with questions about the product. The environment might show a constant and growing need for the product, but many questions as to its utility. Perhaps the customer's name and address should be kept on file to send him or her product updates. This might suggest another change: a monthly newsletter with information on how others are using the product. Calls may then come in to the company requesting that the customers meet one another and exchange ideas. This could lead to a quarterly users' conference, with panels, speakers, and an opportunity to sell add-on products. Because of the fluidity of the creative process, this section of the business plan may have to be updated continually.

The organizational plan defines the functional areas that must be staffed and the characteristics of the people who should staff those functions. Frequently an entrepreneurial team is unbalanced because friends get together at a large corporation and leave to implement the product idea that the corporation rejected. The friends might be perfectly capable engineers, but unable to manage others or persuade customers to purchase the product they have designed. Entrepreneurs are frequently reluctant to delegate responsibility to others, either because no one else can do the job or because they think that is the case. The company crawls when it should trot for lack of a barn-burner marketing person or a thorough production person or a financial officer.

By using an organization plan outline, entrepreneurs can alert themselves to the functional skills that must be hired and when. This section ties in neatly to the PERT chart.

The product plan forces the entrepreneur to think about the solution that the company will be offering to the market. What should it look like and feel like? The name is important, as is the packaging. What should the price be? Should it be sold with a service contract, maintenance contract, in-house instruction, or installation service? Should these have prices? Should there be a lease option? This section of the business plan should define the decisions made about the product, how they were arrived at, alternative plans, and opportunities for ancillary, add-on, and peripheral products.

The manufacturing plan details the technical requirements to manufacture the product that exist in-house and the support necessary for this operation. It describes the physical equipment requirement, the plant requirement, and the people resources. The manufacturing plan is written in stages, beginning with initial requirements, then tracking the production rate as the company enters an operating mode.

The sales and merchandising plan enables the entrepreneur to think of the optimal means of getting the product to the customers. The marketing plans utilized by competitors and similar companies can be observed. For example, microcomputer entrepreneurs might model their marketing plans after their minicomputer predecessors. Or, they might discard traditional methods and set out on a new course, such as party plan or direct mail marketing.

The merchandising plan describes how the product will be presented and positioned. Notice IBM's use of Charlie Chaplin in its advertisements for the personal computer. Chaplin is considered friendly, easy to get along with. IBM wants people to come in and test its personal computer, not to consider it awesome and only for programmers. A product's advertising, promotion, and positioning are as important as its technical qualities. Entrepreneurs know relatively little about advertising and promotion as shown by the juvenile advertisements and common themes in most trade publications in the newer industries. Most printed circuit boards, for example, are floating in space. Most word processing systems are on top of a desk with a pretty girl in front of them. The equivalent advertisement in *Vogue* would be to show the lipstick and list its contents rather than the gorgeous face of Lauren Hutton. I am a proponent of turning the advertising responsibility over to professionals early in the game.

The financial plan, which is a 36-to-60-month forecast that quantifies the actual and forecast results of the business plan, should carefully track the PERT chart. Entrepreneurs should do the financial plan manually, not with a software package, in order to obtain a more thorough knowledge of their business.

It bears pointing out that as a strategic plan to be carefully followed, the business plan is as important to the entrepreneurial team as a road map for a cross-country trip. However, it is doubly important as a means of attracting venture capital. The business plan, in most instances, points out a cash flow deficit in the early months—it is known as the well of the "S-curve." This well is filled with water from the venture capital bucket, customer financing, loans, or other sources. A carefully prepared business plan is essential to raising capital. Thoroughness counts big at this stage of development.

THE ENTREPRENEURIAL TEAM

The third critical factor in the equation $V = P \times S \times E$, is E, the entrepreneurial team. In its primary stage, E is made up of an entrepreneur and a corporate achiever partner. Subsequently, other team members are added. The entrepreneur and the corporate achiever have different backgrounds and value systems, different energy levels and different work habits. In fact, they are strange bedfellows all the way around.

It is exceptionally difficult to form effective entrepreneurial teams. My research indicates that, in the most successful entrepreneurial teams, managers are an average of 16 years older than entrepreneurs. The development stages of the entrepreneur and the achiever partner are markedly different. The personality characteristics and social values overlap in relatively few areas. The social values of the entrepreneur are usually more liberal. This could be a function of age and life experiences, but a 27-year-old entrepreneur and the 43-year-old former corporate manager that he or she selects are bound to have different views of life. The manager is outer-directed, and the entrepreneur is inner-directed. An entrepreneur is more likely to have few assets, live in the city, and drive a European car. The manager has a house in the suburbs and other assets, and drives an American car. They vote differently and have different opinions on marijuana, politics, premarital sex, taste in music, and use of their leisure time.

The unifying factor is that both members of the team want to build a successful company. The manager's goals are perhaps more capital gains oriented, while the entrepreneur's goal is to do some one thing extremely well. But the partners need each other for several very important reasons, not the least of which are: (1) entrepreneurs need managers around to direct their talents, focus their energies, and orchestrate the increasing number of people and departments; (2) managers need energetic, innovative, imaginative entrepreneurs to provide them with growing companies to which they can apply their managerial talents.

The entrepreneurial team works somewhat as follows: Two people decide to go on a photographic safari to Africa. The first person boards the plane in casual attire, unburdened by carryon luggage. The second carries six cameras, filters, guidebooks, camping equipment, a tent, and other paraphernalia. The plane lands in Kenya and the two set off on foot into the jungle. The first traveler goes out in front and the second decides to stop and put up the tent. The first is about a mile away from where the tent is being set up when a tiger jumps out from behind a tree, growls, and charges. The first traveler spins around and runs back to the tent as fast as can be, with the tiger in hot pursuit. The tent is partway up, and the tiger's would-be prey runs into the tent, swings around the pole, and heads out in the same direction, shouting back at the busy partner: "This tiger is for you. I'm going to go back for mine."

Entrepreneurs can generate weeks of work in the first three hours of the day, drop it off on the managers' desks to be organized and implemented, and then change their minds by the afternoon. Managers are delighted for the opportunity to clean up after the entrepreneurs. They are used to making management decisions; now, for the first time, they own a meaningful portion of the company that they manage.

The method by which entrepreneurs select their partners is, alas, all too frequently random, uncertain, and subject to chance. As venture capitalists become more knowledgeable about the lift-off stage, they are able to step in and advise the entrepreneur that management talent is needed, that it is a criterion for financing, and that they intend to assist in the interview process. Executive search consultants are very valuable people. Entrepreneurs and venture capitalists are turning to these hiring professionals, often called "head hunters," with increasing regularity to assist them in building the entrepreneurial team. When the Santa Fe Private Equity Fund formed Mesa Diagnostics, Inc., we needed to locate both an entrepreneur and a manager. Using the criteria described herein, we selected a marketing manager out of Abbott Laboratories, John Lonergan, 35, to be the entrepreneur, and a project manager, also from Abbott, Ross U. Robinson, 50. This team has the balance of high energy and high thoroughness that we were striving for.

Some pairings of entrepreneurs and managers do not work out. I suspect the premise on which they get together is incorrect. The worst premise is capital: the manager has some capital and wants a business to run. In all likelihood he or she knows little or nothing about the entrepreneurial process; almost certainly the manager knows very little about the technology or innovation that is at the heart of the business. But the entrepreneur is desperately out of capital and has been living hand-to-mouth for months. The manager, with $100,000 to invest, time to help run the business, and experience in management looks like the white knight. Without thinking about all of the things that could go wrong, the entrepreneur accepts the capital and trades equity at far too low a price.

The $100,000 runs through the business like General William T. Sherman through Georgia; in a month's time, the company is once again out of funds, and the manager cannot bring order to the chaos. He or she tries to impose rigidity on an amoebalike organism but cannot generate sales because of a failure to learn the product. Several key engineers tell the entrepreneur that if the new manager does not leave, they will.

But the manager has a no-cut contract; that is, if fired, he or she gets to keep the stock. The entrepreneur senses that it may be better to try to work things out than sever the relationship quickly. The two of them visit the manager's bank and jointly guarantee a $100,000 loan. The entrepreneur elects the guarantee over issuing more stock to the manager.

But the bank sees that the entrepreneur has no assets. It is looking to the manager for protection. Thus, the manager asks the entrepreneur to pledge some of his or her stock in the company to secure the loan partially. If the company fails to begin growing and needs another injection of capital, the manager will continue accumulating equity. This becomes an untenable position for the entrepreneur, who must use the equity to attract and keep people and for major injections of capital. To keep adding to the manager's stack of chips does not serve any purpose other than enriching the manager.

When the blowout comes, as it inevitably does, there is a legal battle, and someone ends up with the company and the other person ends up with cash. Both parties will have incurred substantial legal bills and bitter memories. They will have wasted their time.

The error frequently made is to look for a manager and capital from the same source. Rarely does a manager have enough capital to really matter. A truly qualified manager has been extremely busy climbing the corporate ladder. Although this is not always the case, the median age of managers in start-up companies is 43, and that is relatively young to have begun accumulating liquid wealth. Even if a manager is capable of making a meaningful investment, managerial skill is being sought by the company, not his or her capital. The 5 to 10 percent equity position that a manager is entitled to in a rapidly growing innovative or high-technology company could make him or her very wealthy; a lot depends on the management skills. Witness Frank Lautenberg's unique contribution to Automatic Data Processing (ADP). A computer-based payroll processing company doing several million dollars' worth of business a year when Lautenberg joined entrepreneur Henry Taub in 1956, ADP is currently one of the most successful computer service companies in the world, with annual revenues in excess of $800 million. Lautenberg diversified the company through dozens of acquisitions, hired and trained a middle management team to manage the acquired companies, and led the company from batch processing to data networks and other markets.

A primary aspect of the venture capitalist's occupation is to locate, interview, and hire corporate achievers to join entrepreneurial companies. Over time, like the artisans in Plato's cave, one develops some definite opinions about the shadow casters on the walls we stare at all day. The shadows are the characteristics of the corporate achievers. The objective is to choose well, so that the choice need not be made again.

I have found that the most important criterion for managers of entrepreneurial companies is a strong desire to get their hearts back. The most successful transplants of corporate jungle fighters onto entrepreneurial teams are tigers who, like the Tin Man in *The Wizard of Oz*, desperately want to work with their hearts. Their corporate background has instructed them well in systems, production methods, marketing organizations, introducing new products, lines of command, and the difference between strategy and tactics. They want to stop eating their hearts out and begin regaining their sensitivities and feelings. They want to become valid. They want to help make lasting contributions. They want to be stimulated by their work. They want their hearts back.

PROTOTYPE TESTING

The entrepreneurial process holds its breath at this critical stage of development. The product or service could fail its test and the marketplace rejection could kill the dream or send the entrepreneurial team back into the skunkworks for further development. Many entrepreneurs have experienced harsh turndowns at this stage, only to alter their plan and emerge with a more exciting, more marketable alternative. A number of bugs have appeared for the first time during software beta tests. Fuses have blown in electronic instruments. A medical diagnostic product proclaimed to be able to diagnose viruses and bacteria within minutes was unable to distinguish between strains of bacteria, strep throat, and St. Louis flu during its first beta test.

The value of mistakes such as these is that they teach the entrepreneurial team to be more careful before releasing the product. Although it is a drain on cash and an agony to be pushed back from the goal line at fourth down and one yard to go, it is a humbling and enlightening experience as well. Jesse L. Acker, co-founder of two successful medical instruments manufacturers, Akro-Medic Engineering and Personal Diagnostics, tells of sleeping on the floor of his basement alongside his prototype blood analyzer for fear that something might go wrong during the instrument's first 24-hour burn-in test.

In the direct mail business, the most important test is mailing a relatively small number of brochures, say 1 percent of the eventual mailing or 70,000 names, if the principal mailing is to seven million names. The critical issues that are tested include the product description price, the appearance of the brochure, and the mailing list. For a catalog of up-scale personal products such as those carried in the Horchow catalog or The Sharper Image, it is important to describe the products in a manner that the average retail store clerk is incapable of doing, not because of incompetency, but rather the difficulty of mastering the specific details of so many products. Thus, these catalogs always describe size, weight, options, colors, price, and price of options. The availability of detail makes direct mail shopping valid.

But valid is useless without target marketing. The mailing lists to be tested must be appropriate for the products to be sold. In major cities mailing lists may be rented from list brokers who generally provide advice and assistance along with the lists. The most expensive lists are of those people who recently purchased an expensive product via direct mail, the kind of product that is relatively nonessential. These names are proven direct mail purchasers, and the list broker must rent them for a higher fee, because the owner of the list will ask more for the names. A less expensive list of names, for instance, might include subscribers to a magazine which advertises relatively expensive, nonessential personal use items—BMWs, Chivas Regal, deBeers, or Pierre Cardin. The rental price might be seven cents per name for the first list and four cents per name for the second. For a test mailing of 350,000 names, the difference is $10,000. A $24,500 test versus a $14,000 test may seem insignificant at first glance, but what if the cheaper list, if tested, would generate a 1 percent response and the more expensive list a 3 percent response? Investing in seven million names from the cheaper list to launch the company could be a waste of money, if the more expensive list pulled six times as well for less than two times the cost. This is shown in Exhibit 4.4.

Responses from the less expensive list are fewer and more interested in the less expensive items. The more expensive list generates greater responses and more expensive products. There would be no means of predicting the quality of the lists in advance of the mailing without a

EXHIBIT 4.4. Comparison of Mailing Lists

	More Expensive List	Cheaper List
Names	7,000,000	7,000,000
Cost per name	$.07	$.04
Total rental cost	$490,000	$280,000
Response rate	3%	1%
Average price of item ordered	$200.00	$150.00
Revenues from mailing	$42,000,000	$7,000,000

direct mail test. The direct mail business has killed many entrepreneurs who did not test their products and lists before renting millions of names.

Another variable to determine from a direct mail test is the optimum time to use direct mail. Although the casual observer might think that the Christmas season is the best, there is an argument against producing a catalog for the Christmas season because most of the department stores and the established mail order companies do their heaviest mailing during this time. An entrepreneurial direct mail company might achieve superior results at another time of year. People are in buying moods at other seasonal changes, such as Labor Day and Easter.

Another form of consumer product testing involves "focus groups." Potential users are invited to come to a conference room where they view, handle, and manipulate the product. Then they are asked questions about the product, and their responses are recorded in an unobtrusive manner. The questions are very specific, such as "Does this product fill your need?" "Where might it be improved?" "What price would you pay for it?" "What additional features would you like to see?" Although focus groups are not a foolproof means of testing consumer reaction, they are better than shooting at the target blindfolded.

There is a reluctance on the part of many entrepreneurs to spend the necessary amount of time at the prototype testing stage. After all, the war cry of entrepreneurs is "READY. FIRE! AIM." So confident are they of the absolute fit between their solutions and the problems that they have identified, that many entrepreneurs skip over or dodge around the testing stage, only to lose a good portion of their capital and frequently their companies. The corporate achiever schooled in the principles of market research, focus groups, prototype testing, beta sites, and direct mail tests, generally accords this stage the importance it deserves. The better mousetrap hypothesis is among the most inaccurate in all of economic history. The old mousetrap will keep selling because it solves its problem very cost effectively. The most successful entrepreneurs have an awareness of their vulnerability and are sensitive to the requirement of testing.

RAISING VENTURE CAPITAL

Upon reading the biographical sketches of America's new heroes, you may be surprised by how few of them raised conventional venture capital. There are several explanations for this: First, venture capitalists are a relatively ethnocentric group of people who tend to avoid risks. For the most part they are 30- to 35-year-old males who have earned Bachelor degrees in Electrical Engineering and Master degrees in Business Administration from Ivy League schools, plus Stanford and the University of Chicago.[10] Second, although there are definite exceptions, the organized venture capital community prefers to invest in productivity improving or cost-saving industrial products. Electronic test and measurement instruments fit this label very nicely. So do special purpose computers such as those produced by Tandem Computers, Apollo Computer, Altos Computer Systems, and Computervision Corporation—whose founders are among the list of heroes—and computer peripheral equipment: printers, monitors, input-output devices, and controllers. Third, of the 100 heroes included herein, only 22 of the entrepreneurs received conventional venture capital. Although one hears a great deal about venture capital's role in the entrepreneurial revolution, there are several reasons why organized venture capital has backed very few of the outstanding companies. However, the principal reason is that the entrepreneurs cited herein launched companies that in many respects did not require start-up capital. This situation resulted from an unusually big P, so that the company could be financed initially by the stock market, or the availability of customer financing

---

[10]A. David Silver, *Who's Who in Venture Capital* (New York: Wiley, 1984).

or vendor financing. In some instances, the product or service had such large profit margins that the company was self-financed.

The law of the big P says that if the problem that the entrepreneur (E) will be able to solve (S) is very big, the stock market will accord it a start-up valuation (V) of a very great number, frequently equal to the size of the problem (P).[11] The law of the big P, then, is $P = V$.

A typical example of a big P company is Genentech Corporation, which had an initial public offering in 1981 and a first trading day valuation of more than \$800 million—more than Chase Manhattan Bank's valuation on the same day. Genentech at the time was a promising genetic engineering company engaged in research, primarily with interferon, to develop genetic implants to successfully treat diabetes as well as other diseases. The basis for the law of the big P is that the stock buying public is made up of members of the movie-going public. In the United States, the most popular movie today is the "chase scene" movie. Members of this genre include the *Star Wars* series, *Close Encounters of the Third Kind*, the *Rocky* series, *Chariots of Fire*, and *E.T.* In chase scene movies, the young blond-haired star, with a powerful but unique force is attacked by a dark, fierce, evil problem, an exciting chase results, followed by a duel, and the good guy wins. In *Star Wars* it was Luke Skywalker with the Force versus Darth Vader. In Genentech, it was Bobby Swanson with interferon chasing diabetes. The stock market, or movie market, sent both *Star Wars* and Genentech to record-setting valuations. Other companies that went directly to the public stock market because their Ps were so large include Cetus Corporation, Biogen, Molecular Genetics, and Enzo Biochem.

Fourth, another group of companies in our list of entrepreneurial success stories attempted to raise conventional capital but were turned down. They did not fit the mold preferred by most venture capital investors. Their companies were in the service industries, sold products to consumers, or were in the distribution industries—three areas typically ignored by most venture capital investors during the last 25 years. As these industries become better understood, and as high technology companies become too plentiful and lose their lustre, conventional venture capital will gravitate to distribution and service businesses. Thus entrepreneurs who are currently in *medeas res* should give seri-

[11]Silver, *Venture Capital*.

ous consideration to preparing a business plan and visiting members of the venture capital community. In order to make this task more cost-efficient, my staff has created a data bank of the more than 700 United States venture capitalists, their areas of interest, their occupational backgrounds, their list of investments, and their addresses and telephone numbers.[12]

In most instances, the final step of the first stage of the entrepreneurial process is to raise venture capital. Approximately 12 sources of capital, in addition to conventional venture capital funds, are capable of providing start-up and first stage capital to entrepreneurial companies. These sources are listed in Exhibit 4.5 and then summarized.

EXHIBIT 4.5. Alternative Sources of Start-up Financing

Accounts Receivable Financing	Leveraged Buy-Outs
Government Guaranteed Loans	Business Development Corporations
New Issues Market	Joint Ventures and Licensing
Grants	Minority Enterprise SBICs
R & D Limited Partnerships	Small Business Investment
Public Shells	Companies

Accounts Receivable Financing

This form of borrowing is generally provided by commercial finance companies, whose business is to make asset-based loans. Because they understand the assets they lend against, and more important, know where to sell the assets if they have to and at what price, commercial finance companies will frequently make loans to companies that lack positive cash flow or secondary collateral.

Certain rules of the road govern dealing with commercial finance companies. Their preference runs to the most liquid assets on the balance sheet—accounts receivable, finished goods inventory—and not to equipment, unless that is a specialty of theirs as it is with certain finance companies, nor to real property or other nonliquifiable assets.

[12]The data bank can be found in A. David Silver, *Who's Who in Venture Capital* (New York: Wiley, 1984).

Two other important rules exist: high interest rates and prepayment penalties.

Commercial finance companies do not have relatively inexpensive depositors' dollars to relend. Rather, they borrow from commercial banks and in the commercial paper market at interest rates that average a shade less than prime rate. The range of their charges for money is between prime + 4 percent and prime + 10 percent.

Commercial finance companies like to hold their borrower for at least a year. They understand that the borrower will leave them at the first opportunity to go with a less expensive lender. Therefore, commercial finance companies build prepayment penalties into their loan agreements. The penalty can be as stiff as one year's interest payments if the loan is prepaid prior to 12 months; or as lenient as two months' interest payments if the loan is prepaid prior to six months. In easy money economies, which have not existed since the prime rate reached 20 percent for the first time in 1979, the prepayment penalty is either watered down or eliminated.

Government Guaranteed Loans

One person among the 100 greatest entrepreneurs of the last 25 years launched her business with a bank loan guaranteed by the Small Business Administration (SBA). An SBA guaranteed loan is available to a small business in amounts up to $500,000 for seven years, repayable usually in 84 equal monthly installments at an interest rate governed by the U.S. Congress, but usually a few points over prime. The higher the interest rate, the more aggressive the lenders. The SBA guarantees 90 percent of the face amount of the loan, thus the entrepreneur must persuade a commercial bank or an SBA approved lender, such as a Business Development Corporation, to provide 10 percent of the loan. In fact, the lender puts the full amount of the loan in the borrower's bank account and either earns interest on the full amount of the loan or sells the guaranteed portion to a buyer of government guaranteed loans at a premium. The bank can earn a monitoring fee for processing the loan for the secondary buyer and a spread between the rate the borrower pays it and the rate it charges in the secondary market. The processing charge is usually around 1 percent per annum on the total loan, the spread is about half that amount. Couple these charges with its rate on the unguaranteed portion, and banks that are active in the SBA guaranteed loan business can earn over 30 percent per annum on that portion of their loan portfolio.

Grants

A wide variety of grant money sources is available to entrepreneurs, but none of the grants is particularly easy to obtain. The smallest research and development grants are those offered by the National Science Foundation (NSF). NSF awards $25,000 to an individual for the purpose of conducting original research in an area that NSF believes is socially useful. In recent years, NSF has favored energy-saving projects and alternative energy sources. The State of Connecticut offers grants of up to $350,000 for the development of a product that could lead to increased employment of scientists in the state. These kinds of grants are relatively narrow and small. The application for the $25,000 NSF grant is rather lengthy and can only be submitted during a brief period once a year.

The large and more interesting grants are those at the private foundation level: Ford, Rockefeller, Kellogg, Carnegie, and many of the other family foundations. Like Andrew Carnegie, these founders believed that their wealth should be held in trust for the benefit of the country. The literally thousands of foundations in the country are listed in directories giving their assets, location, and key decision makers. Determining if their assets are managed internally or delegated to a third party can be done with a telephone call.

R&D Limited Partnerships

Section 174 of the Internal Revenue Act provides that: "A taxpayer may treat research or experimental expenditures which are paid or incurred by him during the taxable year in connection with his trade or business as expenses which are not chargeable to capital account. The expenditures so treated shall be allowed as a deduction." The phrase "in connection with his trade or business" was clarified in 1974 when the U.S. Supreme Court held that a new limited partnership organized for the purpose of developing a new process or product is entitled to deduct research and experimentation expenditures. In other words, the investor need not be the manufacturer or even in business to get the tax deduction on research carried out in his behalf.

Therefore, an R&D tax shelter is usually organized as a partnership, and the research is usually conducted by a company under contract with the partnership. The same company is typically granted the option to license the technology developed and to manufacture products utilizing the technology. The partnership's remuneration is then tied to product sales that result from the research; but there can be no guarantee of remuneration or, for that matter, repurchase of the technology from the partnership, for if that were the case, the partnership would not be at risk on the research.

Other expenditures in an R&D tax shelter may be treated differently. The costs of obtaining a patent, including legal fees, are deductible. Expenditures for the acquisition or improvement of land or property to be used in connection with research and experimentation are not deductible if the partnership acquires rights of ownership in the property. However, if the partnership acquires no ownership rights in the property, the entire cost of such property is deductible. The only property that the partnership should acquire an ownership right to is technology; for example, patents, designs, drawings, data, research, prototypes, formulas, trade secrets, processes, and know-how. The cost of acquiring patents owned by someone else is not deductible. Therefore, the research agreement should specifically exclude transfer to the partnership of patents, prototypes, production, or processes already in existence.

If the research is intended to improve on already existing technology, the owner of that technology can grant a nonexclusive license to the partnership for the term of the research agreement. The costs allocable to the acquisition of such a nonexclusive license are also deductible. The costs of market testing, management studies, consumer surveys, inspection of materials, quality control, advertising, or promotions are not deductible.

Leveraged Buy-Outs

A leveraged buy-out is the purchase of a company, using its assets to secure loans that are used to pay the seller. If the assets are inadequate to attract the full sales price, the seller must be persuaded to take promissory notes or the buyer must attract equity capital. The more equity capital required, the smaller the percentage of ownership the entrepreneur is able to keep. If the company's asking price is too high or the cost of debt financing too dear, then more equity capital is required to the point of diluting the entrepreneur's interest. At some point the entrepreneur will have to walk from the deal.

The best candidates for leveraged buy-outs are divisional spin-offs from large industrial corporations. These giants periodically go through a housecleaning exercise in which they discard small divisions or subsidiaries appended to larger companies acquired many years ago when the corporation's goals and objectives were perceived differently. These small divisions are frequently not attractive to other corporations because of their size, thus making them candidates for entrepreneurial purchase. Private or family-owned companies are less attractive leveraged buy-out candidates because the record keeping is usually sloppier, and there is no assurance that the family is truly a willing seller. Sometimes they will put their company on the market merely to establish a value for estate planning purposes. In a divisional spin-off, the board has authorized the president not only to sell, but also to get the best price with the most cash. Further, the division is usually audited every year, and the key general ledger items are normally maintained on computer.

Business Development Corporations

Perhaps the most flexible lenders in the country are the Business Development Corporations (BDC), which are chartered by 27 states to make loans to small businesses where the end result is *job creation*. BDCs are a well-kept secret. Very few entrepreneurs know of their existence, hence they are substantially underutilized. Curiously, slightly less than half the states do not have BDCs, and many of the non-BDC states are capital importers with few venture capital funds. The states that have BDCs are Arkansas, California, Florida, Georgia, Iowa, Kansas, Kentucky, Maine, Maryland, Massachusetts, Mississippi, Missouri, Montana, Nebraska, New Hampshire, New Mexico, New York, North Carolina, North Dakota, Oklahoma, Pennsylvania (2), Rhode Island, South Carolina, Virginia, Washington (2), West Virginia and Wyoming.

Some BDCs are owned by a group of private investors who take the trouble to obtain a license from the state; others are owned by financial institutions and large corporations in the state. Funding is generally provided by individual financial institutions and corporations in the state whose interests are served by the increased availability of jobs.

Joint Ventures and Licensing

Joint venturing is a frequently overlooked source of seed capital and a method for launching a new company. A joint venture is a partnership of two or more entities formed to undertake a certain project. A joint venture opportunity exists when each partner brings to the project a property that the other partner or partners do not have, but regard as integral to the success of the project.

An entrepreneur in search of seed capital must honestly confront the fact that more than money is necessary to launch a new company. Although the project may call for manufacturing or distribution of a certain product, merely obtaining capital does not make the entrepreneur the most efficient manufacturer or the most successful distributor of the product.

Licensing has myriad ramifications. In terms of raising venture capital, however, one should ask:

1. Is there a submarket for my product willing to pay a premium for it because of a serious problem that my product solves?

2. Is there an entity in that submarket than can manufacture and market my product?

3. Is it large enough to pay me a substantial down payment and to guarantee the payment of future minimum royalties?

4. What is the potential size of that submarket measured by the number of units (dollars) per annum?

5. What is the highest level contact that I can establish with that entity? (An introduction through an investment or commercial banker is preferred.)

The optimal licensing arrangement involves a substantial down payment by the licensee and relatively high annual minimum sales goals.

Minority Enterprise Small Business Investment Companies

The Department of Commerce created a new division of the SBA in 1964, to assist minorities in entering the entrepreneurial process. This division was the Office of Minority Business Enterprises (OMBE). Having participated in some of the early planning sessions in 1966–1967, I am aware of its purpose and goals. OMBE was created to assist blacks in owning businesses in inner cities. As white flight led to black blight in burned-out downtowns like Detroit and Chicago, OMBE looked for mechanisms by which blacks could own automobile dealerships, retail stores, and fast-food franchises to enhance commerce in fast eroding downtown business districts. OMBE came up with a stepchild of the Small Business Investment Company (SBIC) program then in full flower: the Minority Enterprise Small Business Investment Company (MESBIC). A MESBIC would loan venture capital to minorities. If you wanted to form a MESBIC you showed a net worth of $150,000 to the SBA, and it would grant a MESBIC license, then invest $600,000 (a ratio of 4:1) in your preferred stock, with a 3 percent dividend rate after five years and a 20-year redemption period. Many large corporations formed MESBICS—Ford Motor Company, General Foods Corporation, Equitable Life Assurance Society of the United States—and, indeed, for the first time blacks and other ethnic groups had a special way of obtaining capital. Approximately 200 MESBIC licenses were granted, and the program was launched at top speed. Alas, the 1974 recession eliminated many minority entrepreneurs whose retail establishments were thinly capitalized and about half of the MESBICs, like many SBICs, collapsed and died.

To breathe new life into the MESBICs, the SBA broadened the definition of a minority in 1976, thus enabling MESBICs to target loans to a variety of businesses, not merely inner city retailers and small manufacturers. The 1976 redefinition included men and women deprived of economic advantages for any number of reasons. Thus Caucasian males over 50 years of age, persons deprived of economic opportunity due to ill health, American Indians, women of all races and ages, persons of Hispanic origin, and Vietnam-era veterans could obtain venture capital from a MESBIC. The formation of MESBICs took on a new head of steam, as clever investors saw the 4:1 leverage as a new government trough at which to feed. Indeed, several movie production companies formed MESBICs, right after the movie tax shelter loophole was closed in 1976. The Hollywood MESBICs would loan money to produce black and martial arts films employing hundreds of minorities, and then the parent company, having risked but one-fourth of the capital, would distribute them. Several larger MESBICs have operated almost like SBICs funding emerging businesses with the caveat that they are majority owned by "disadvantaged" people. Disadvantaged borrowers should bear in mind that these MESBICs are interested in first-stage and mezzanine-stage companies that manufacture a fairly basic product. When a MESBIC seeks to stretch the definition of "disadvantaged," permission must be obtained from the SBA, but that has not been difficult. For some reason not clear to the SBA or other observers, very few women and physically disadvantaged people have stepped up to the MESBIC window. However, Hasidic Jews, classified as disadvantaged because they represent an ethnic minority, have been obtaining MESBIC loans in relatively large numbers.

New Issues Market

The three centers of underwriting activities in the new issues market are Denver, Jersey City, and New York City. The Denver underwriters appear to favor start-up companies and common stocks priced at 25 cents or less. These are commonly referred to as "penny stocks." One of the problems associated with penny stocks is getting them up to more than $1 where national investors become interested. In fact, Californians are restricted from buying common stocks having initial underwriting prices of less than $3. Investors in penny stocks have the mentality of slot-machine players in Las Vegas. When the stock they purchased goes from 10 to 50 cents, the tendency is to dump it. With this kind of resistance, it is difficult over the near term to get the price of the stock up to the range of decency even when earnings improve. For the entrepreneur, a penny stock issue certainly raises capital, but it may be years until any stock can be used to acquire other companies, attract key management, be pledged as collateral, or sold. Favorite issues of the Denver underwriters appear to be oil and gas related and high technology. A spate of penny stock offerings between 1979 and 1981 by Denver underwriters backed geologists in their search for oil. Few endeavors are as risky as oil exploration, but risk is apparently what the investors like.

Jersey City, New Jersey, is a step up in quality of new issue underwritings. Although Jersey City happens to have a fair number of small underwriters, the name applies to a number of regional underwriters in Albany, New York, Philadelphia, Pennsylvania, and other towns near New York City. The basic Jersey City new issue offering is a common stock priced at $1–$2 per share. Whereas the Denver style is to authorize 20 million shares, issue 8 million to management, 4 million to treasury, and 8 million to the public at 10 cents per share ($800,000 in gross proceeds), the typical Jersey City deal is to authorize 2 million shares, issue 800,000 to management and sell 800,000 to the public for two dollars per share ($1.6 million in gross proceeds). The Jersey City underwriters prefer more quality, such as an operating history, or an initial investment by the founding entrepreneurs of $20,000 or so. The qualifications of many of the companies who flog their paper on an unsophisticated public are extremely weak by many of the standards described herein. Yet LTV Corporation, a New York Stock Exchange Company, began with Jimmy Ling doing a self-underwritten new issue from a booth at the Texas State Fair in the early 1960s. Control Data Corporation, whose founding entrepreneur, William C. Norris, is among the 100 greatest, also began operations with a self-underwritten initial public offering that raised $1.6 million. A handful of other successful companies raised their initial capital with a dollar issue through small, regional underwriters.

Across the Hudson River in lower Manhattan is Wall Street where, it has been said, "gentlemen come to raise money." Most of the New York City underwriters who are inclined to manage new issues will not underwrite start-ups; but that rule is broken frequently. The venerable Allen & Company, early backers of Syntex Corporation, developer of the birth-control pill, raised $5 million for Codenol in 1981, a start-up laser development company. Goldman, Sachs & Company—investment banker to Ford Motor Company, the *New York Times*, and others—underwrote a new issue in 1981 for Hybritech Corporation, a monoclonal antibody research and development company which had nominal revenues.

The Wall Street-sponsored underwriting has a higher price per share —somewhere between $5 and $20—and the number of shares is correspondingly fewer, with the average offering producing approximately $10 million for the company. Certain new issues can raise more capital if the problem that the company purports to be addressing is large, if the management team is extremely well experienced, or if there are promising aspects, such as important contracts, numerous patents, or the blessings of important customers or suppliers. This was the case with Genentech Corporation, one of the premier biotechnology companies that manufactures interferon, a possible cure for several diseases.

Why go public as a start-up or first-stage company? There are several good reasons, the most important of which to some entrepreneurs is to create paper wealth. Although shares of common stock of a public company cannot be sold for approximately two years after the offering according to the Rule 144 requirement (except in a private transfer where the buyer is willing to hold onto the stocks for the required length of time, while buying them at a steep discount from market), some entrepreneurs enjoy or need to be "paper millionaires." It's a macho thing.

A second reason is that the public will generally pay a higher price for the stock of new companies than will private investors. This translates into more working capital. For the 18-month period ended September 30, 1980, half of the 111 new issues were start-ups. The initial public offerings for these start-ups raised on average $2 million for one-half of the companies' equity. The average size of private placements of early-stage companies during that same period was $1 million for approximately one-third of the companies' equity. Frequently half of the company's ownership is sold to the public, but many entrepreneurs regard that as a fair trade-off for a larger amount of capital to test the business plan.

A third reason is to obtain currency. A common stock with a market value (although restricted in its transferability) is a form of currency, one step removed from complete illiquidity. It can be used to make acquisitions, attract key people, award bonuses, and it can be pledged as secondary or side collateral. For an entrepreneur with a boat manufacturing business who would like to acquire a catamaran manufacturing business, the stock can be offered to the seller in lieu of cash or notes.

In summary, the entrepreneurial process is a five-to-seven-year intense, energetic, exciting period. It begins when the entrepreneur sees the P and feels compelled to solve it. The entrepreneur formulates and reformulates it, looks at it in several different lights and from all angles until he or she understands it as would a person with the problem. The entrepreneur then creates an S and builds a prototype to test it. Then S is brought to P in a test situation to see if P is satisfied with S. If there is a positive response, the entrepreneur begins building a team (E), first by attracting a corporate achiever to manage the company. They write a business plan and begin raising capital. With all of the components in place—indeed, while the components are being fitted into place—the company is launched. The entrepreneurial process ends when a high value for V is created. Generally this takes around five years, plus or minus two; the time frame is subject to economic and stock market conditions.

5

LEVERAGE

At the age of 26, with a thoroughly written and documented business plan in hand, Frederick W. Smith raised approximately $96 million in debt and equity in less than 18 months to launch Federal Express Corporation, a service company that many of us cannot live without. At the age of 60, with a rabbit's foot, a piece of stainless steel, two sheets of paper, one with typing on it, and some grey powder, Chester A. Carlson raised practically no capital in five years for Xerox Corporation, a company whose product many of us cannot live without. Other things being equal, Smith and Carlson should have created roughly the same size V, or wealth for themselves and their investors, because the P factors were both very high and the solutions were, and remain, very elegant. Smith created a considerably larger personal V than did Carlson because Smith knew more about leverage: getting people to do things for you that they never had any intention of doing before you began talking to them. Xerox Corporation sprang from an idea in the mind of a charming, slightly disheveled New York City patent lawyer in 1937 to its peak market valuation, or maximum V of $16.4 billion in 1972. Federal Express Corporation began in the term paper of a Yale junior in 1964 and grew to its maximum V of $1.7 billion in 1984; and it is still growing. The fate of Xerox Corporation, whose market value at the end of 1984 was $3 billion is to be studied in business schools as a company that makes one major diversification mistake after another. Many entrepreneurs leverage their way into a new market that Xerox Corporation has stumbled into and fumbled out of. Nobody has managed to live off of a Federal Express Corporation mistake.

Typical of Xerox Corporation's confusion was entry into the retail computer store business. Xerox Corporation manufactures computers, typewriters, and copying machines, as well as related peripheral equipment; it also has a local area network that links disparate computers together. Xerox Corporation has an excellent reputation for service and an intelligent, handsome, well-spoken army of sales engineers calling on offices throughout the world. Selling and servicing computers and office equipment from retail stores would seem to be a natural. Xerox Corporation management agreed and it quickly opened more than 30 stores in 1980–1981.

Alas, software sells computers, not the other way around; the most popular software did not operate on the Xerox computer. In fact, Xerox Corporation stocked very little useful software. In the meantime, the Radio Shack chain of 6,000 consumer electronics stores was busily introducing its TRS-80 computer with the popular Peachtree Software line of accounting packages and popular games such as Temple of Apshai.

Along came David Norman of Businessland in 1982, laden with $26 million in venture capital; he offered Xerox Corporation $30 million for its chain of 40 stores. Xerox Corporation turned Norman down. It would have worked out well for both companies, as we will see, because Norman went to the public trough in mid-1983 and raised $50 million at $11 per share, which when added to the $26 million of venture capital, enabled him to open the 40 stores that he tried to buy for $30 million. Businessland has been unable to make a profit and its stock price has traded in the $3 to $7 per share range ever since it went public.

One year after rejecting Norman's offer, Xerox Corporation accepted another offer for approximately $14 million in cash and notes, from The Genra Group, an entrepreneurial consortium, that came up with the $4.5 million in cash from a group of investors including the founder of Steak 'n Ale. The Genra Group entrepreneurs added a few more stores, but without sufficient capital they were unable to rapidly expand the chain and had to locate a merger partner. One of Genra's suppliers, Moore Business Forms, a $2 billion forms vendor, stepped up to the altar and acquired The Genra Group along with its obligations to Xerox Corp.

At the time that Businessland's common stock was offered to the public, the small, struggling computer retail chain industry had a handful of publicly held companies: Computer Factory, Computer-Craft, CompuShop, and Prodigy Systems. Although not very profitable, these four companies had managed to go public and raise desperately needed capital by selling 30 to 50 percent of their shares to the public for an aggregate of approximately $15 million. The stock market, never agog over retailing, was valuing the computer retail industry at their annual revenues. That is, revenues of $10 million accorded that chain a market value of approximately the same amount.

Along came Businessland, with its 26 esteemed venture capitalists and led by the doyen of new-issue underwriters, Hambrecht & Quist, for a new issue that raised $50 million at a valuation to revenues ratio of 40 to 1. Clearly the market had to wonder about the pricing of this issue. The small investors who had purchased shares in scrappy little Computer Factory and ComputerCraft through their small regional underwriters turned their backs on Businessland. The investors that Norman and Hambrecht & Quist assembled were, for the most part, pension funds and insurance companies. Norman used his venture capitalists and his underwriter to leverage the large financial institutions.

If Businessland can become profitable and get its stock moving once again, leveraging the big guys will have been a positive strategy. However, if Businessland runs out of time or money before it can generate operating earnings, it will have no substantial financial sources to turn to. An expression on Wall Street has a bearing on this story: Bulls win, bears win, and pigs go to the slaughterhouse.

Most entrepreneurs do not have Norman's background and access to enormous sums of venture capital or blue chip underwriters and computer manufacturers. In fact, because of Norman's contacts at International Business Machines Corporation (IBM), Businessland was awarded a much sought after IBM personal computer dealership *before* it had opened its first store. Indeed Norman had been the founder and chief executive officer of Dataquest, a market research firm which he built from scratch and sold twice, profiting very nicely on both occasions. Businessland is very highly leveraged. Entrepreneurs who can pull off the big V more than once are very few and far between.

The typical entrepreneurial company deals with less zeroes in its early years than did Carlson, Smith, or Norman. The leverage is smaller as well but of singular importance to the survival of the company.

Leverage is borrowing. It is acquiring an asset, generally by persuasion, barter, or notes, for which payment is deferred until a later date. Professionals and skilled craftspeople do not employ leverage. They earn a fee for a job performed in time, and they can do nothing else while on that job. Employees of large corporations and institutions cannot leverage their time either. Professional service people and employees of large corporations and institutions frequently do not understand leverage nor do they understand when they are being leveraged. Thus, the opportunity for entrepreneurs to leverage them. For instance, corporations are the largest consumers of consulting services. Consultants, Carl Ally once said, are a clever bunch of people who borrow your watch to tell you the time, then charge you for it. Successful consultants sell their services to the corporate market on a monthly retainer basis. They agree, for instance, to provide information to 10 similar pharmaceutical companies on new diagnostic instruments being developed at national laboratories. Their research is the same for all of the clients, and the report is as well although the cover page changes. Thus, they have leveraged their time and personnel ten-fold.

But that's not all. If they maintain title to their intellectual property—that is, their research—they can peddle the report, ostensibly in a modified version, to various retail markets. Where the 10 corporate clients paid the consultant $10,000 per month for three months, an aggregate of $300,000, the retail market is likely to purchase the report (1) in book form; (2) as a monthly newsletter; (3) in cassette form; (4) as a TV special for PBS; (5) as an article in *Scientific American*; and (6) it's good for three or four speeches to audiences who are keenly interested in technology transfer, enough to pay an honorarium. Another $300,000 could roll in to the entrepreneurial consultant who understands leverage.

The story is not over. When the reports have been submitted to the pharmaceutical companies and the retainer payments are in the bank, the consultant provides the 10 clients with the next logical stage of their inquiry. Rather than solving all of their problems for $30,000 the consultant explains to them that a more fertile field of inquiry is "How can the pharmaceutical company obtain rights to these instruments?" The price for that service, somewhat more complex perhaps, is $10,000 per month for five months.

The entrepreneurial consultant can find yet one more item to lever-

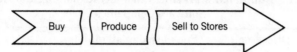

FIGURE 5.1.   Software Companies Operating Plan

age in this scenario: the names of prestigious clients. The consultant prepares a handsome brochure listing those clients served and begins contacting those potential customers who would be most impressed with dropped names of corporations manufacturing medicines. These customers are most likely to be hospitals, medical clinics, and group practices.

With large corporate cash flow sustaining the consulting practice in the medical field, the entrepreneurial consultant can pursue hiring less expensive personnel to serve clients. The consultant can leverage employees by paying them what they are worth, say $40 per hour, but charging the clients the full rate, say $100 to $150 per hour. Accounting firms have done this with skill, grace, and charm for many years.

Software publishers have missed numerous leverage opportunities that are the norm in most information industries. But then, the computer software industry is composed of many small companies, most of them still run by their entrepreneurial founders, who are programmers. Programmers look out at the world from the inside of computers through monitors. Their vision, for the most part, is quite narrow. The typical software company operates in the simple three-step manner shown in Figure 5.1.

Software is bought by screening hundreds of submissions and selecting those that have potential "hit" quality. Once selected, the programs are produced for the major personal computer operating systems, tested in focus groups, reworked, packaged for the market, then pushed through the retail distribution channel: buy from programmers, produce to run on the most popular computers, and sell to the computer dealers and mass merchandisers.

When the computer dealers and mass merchandisers have an excess of inventory due to slack sales, as occurred from March 1984 through mid-1985, the system breaks down. Software companies respond to slower sales in the only way they know how: increased advertising to create consumer demand and laying off personnel in the headquarters

EXHIBIT 5.1. Additional Marketing Channels Remaining Undiscovered by
Software Companies

Direct mail	Franchised retail outlets
Mail order	Foreign licensing
Party-plan	Licensing computer manufacturers

cost centers. If sales fail to turn up, software companies look to the venture capital community for help; failing that, to a merger; and failing
that, go into bankruptcy.

Software companies that hit the wall in 1984 in just this manner include Peachtree Software, whose sales dropped from $20 million in
1983 to $16 million in 1984, while its losses grew from under $500,000
in 1983 to over $11 million in 1984. Others were Human Engineered
Software, VisiCorp, whose VisiCalc was the largest selling software
package ever, Imagic, Synapse, Sirius Software, Business Soft, Ovation,
Knoware, Rocky Mountain Software, Jane, and dozens more. This
waste of capital and time could have been avoided by using leverage
techniques discovered, developed, and perfected in other markets.

The first place to institute leverage is the mass merchandisers and
other distributors. Alternative marketing channels could be developed
to mitigate the perils of relying on distributors Softsel, MicroD, First
Software, and the other members of the monopsony. Alternative marketing channels include those described in Exhibit 5.1.

Facilities management has worked beautifully for mainframe software companies, but it has been largely ignored in the personal software market. It could work somewhat as follows: A publisher of education and entertainment software could contact an industrial company
that sells products in the home but has largely missed the software revolution. Candidates might include most of the food processors, health
and beauty aids manufacturers, and many consumer electronics companies. The list is large, and runs the gamut from General Foods Corporation to RCA Corporation. The software compay could propose a
contractual arrangement with say Nabisco Brands to develop a line of
Nabisco software, from soup to nuts, for Nabisco Brands to push
through its channels. The software company could earn a front-end fee
plus a publisher's profit, perhaps $10 per box of software. Nabisco
would provide its name and marketing clout in order to get shelf space
in supermarkets for which it would earn a royalty.

Franchised software stores in enclosed malls could be another relatively inexpensive way of opening up another distribution channel. Franchising is a classic form of customer financing, and a relatively rapid means of opening up a market. The stores would necessarily have to be small, and perhaps carry products other than just software to achieve the volumes necessary to break even. Complimentary products may include books, home video tapes, modems and other peripherals, inexpensive home computers, magazines, and perhaps high-tech furnishings. Automobile parts have been distributed through captive retailers. Movie theaters were at one time owned by producers until their monopoly profits offended the government.

Party plan selling is uniquely well-suited for education and entertainment home software. Software packages cost around $4 to produce and sell at retail from $20 to $50 per unit. Party plan selling if done on a pyramid basis generally requires an 80 to 90 percent gross profit margin to permit large commissions to local and regional sales personnel. In-home selling of software requires the salespersons to be knowledgeable about computing and the educational material in question. What better sales staff than teachers who have a genuine interest in making additional money in the evenings and who know how to explain the merits of remedial reading or memory-expanding software. To get into party plan selling, the software companies need only to lure away from Mary Kay Cosmetics or Tupperware an experienced manager anxious to take a crack at "intrapreneurship" (entrepreneurship within another company).

A fourth channel is direct mail or catalog selling. This marketing method has been used successfully since 1872 and is currently popular in the trade book and audiocassette fields, cousins to the software industry. The Book-of-the-Month Club could be copied with relative ease by the software industry, but as yet it has not been.

As desperation caused by lack of capital begins to permeate the computer market, leverage will begin to appear, and along with it some new and exciting marketing channels will be developed. How about a software dispensing machine located next to Coke machines and restocked every week by local service organizations. Can you picture software coupon books? Or "Software by Wire?" Or software marketed via direct response television advertising, such as, "Remember those great software hits of 1982? Gridrunner I, Lodestar, Choplifter, Zork and Temple of Apshai? Well, they're yours now for only $9.95 each or 5 for $39.95, plus $5 postage and handling, by calling 1-800-555-5555." It's only a matter of time. Desperation is the mother of leverage.

The software industry could take notes from the movie industry. Here producers (a fancy name for movie entrepreneurs) put together multimillion-dollar products out of thin air. Let's examine the exquisite leverage of producing a movie.

Let's say the producer is male. Here he sits in New York, reading a script just presented by a writer. The producer likes it and signs an option to pay the writer $75,000 plus 5 percent of the distributor's gross income (the box office receipts less 50 percent which is the theater's cut). The producer must deliver $25,000 within 90 days and $50,000 by the first day of shooting.

The producer thinks that a semi-unknown actor who costarred in a recent successful film would be a good male lead, because he is considered affordable, bondable, and bankable. These are important characteristics. Some stars, such as Marlon Brando, are simply not affordable by most independent producers. They want several million dollars plus a large percentage of the distributor's gross income, sometimes as much as $5 million plus 10 percent. Bondable means that the collection of actors, actresses, and directors have the reputation for hard, focused work in order to bring the film in on budget. Some stars have been known to come to the set too drunk to work, thus blowing a day of shooting at great cost to the producer. Performance bonds are not obtainable on these people. And without bond, the producer cannot convince lenders that the budget is realistic. If overruns are not financed, the film cannot be released; thus no revenue stream.

Bankable means that the revenue projections are believable. If an actor's last few movies had box office results of $10 million, $8 million, and $6 million, in that order, then projecting that his next film will do $15 million will convince absolutely nobody. If his last film achieved box office results of $10 million, projecting $8 million for the current project is more sensible.

The producer calls the semi-unknown actor's agent to ask that he read the script. That is accomplished rapidly (sometimes the producer sits in the adjoining room and pushes telephoning to new heights of excitement in order to demonstrate the "moving train effect") and the actor agrees to take the role. The producer and the agent negotiate a flat $250,000 price for the actor's services, payable $25,000 on signing,

$112,500 on the first day of shooting, and $112,500 on the last day of shooting. This is a rather modest contract and fee. Certain stars have the right to change the script, approve the director, receive a percentage of the gate, and select where their name will appear in the advertisements. Whenever you see a strange grouping of stars of relatively equal ranking, such as Michael Caine, Sean Connery, and George C. Scott, you can be sure that each wanted to appear to the left of the other two and not on a line below. The compromise is sometimes a pyramid or a pyramid of their faces and the names on a straight line. The negotiations are so tedious and difficult that movie producers sometimes survive on antacid liquids and tension relievers.

The independent producer now has a script and a star. He needs a director. In most cases, the good directors and stars are booked well into the future, so it is up to the producer to find out who is available, what his or her track record is, and what he or she will cost. For this, the producer flies to Los Angeles and begins brainpicking, telephoning, and searching for the optimum candidate. This process is excruciatingly difficult because the director is as critical to a movie as a chief operating officer is to a business. The director is the conductor. He or she will determine the budget, the scenery, the locations, and most of the crew as well as the other actors and actresses. He or she may want a script rewrite. Budget overruns are largely a matter that rests with the director's abilities and emotions.

The difficult search for an available, bankable, bondable, and affordable director continues until the producer and the director's agent sign a contract. Let us assume that in this situation the director agrees to $400,000 for 16 weeks of shooting and 16 weeks of editing, plus 5 percent of the distributors' gross. The director receives $80,000 on signing, $120,000 on the first day of shooting, and $200,000 on the final day of shooting, protected by a letter of credit. For the $80,000 advance, the director agrees to deliver a budget and an edited shooting script to the producer within 60 days of the date of signing the contract.

To summarize what has happened at this point, an independent producer has obtained the rights to a script and the services of an actor and a director for a certain period of time. The producer's balance sheet at this time is shown in Exhibit 5.2.

The producer must deliver $520,000 by the first day of shooting, some 60 days in the future. In addition, he must raise the amount of

EXHIBIT 5.2. Independent Producer's Balance Sheet

Assets		Liabilities and Net Worth	
Cash[a]	—	Payable to:	
		Writer	$ 50,000
		Actor	225,000
		Director	320,000
			$595,000
Script	$ 75,000	Net worth	(520,000)
		Total liabilities and net worth	
Total assets	$ 75,000		$ 75,000

[a]The independent producer has spent the following sums:

Travel, telephone, legal	$ 20,000
Writer advance	25,000
Actor advance	25,000
Director advance	80,000
Total out-of-pocket expenses	$150,000

capital that the director says it will cost to shoot the film. Let's assume those costs are $4 million, which includes a 20 percent cushion for overruns. Therefore, the overall costs of this film come to $4,670,000 —say $5 million after additional travel and legal costs. At this point, the revenue stream has been diluted by 10 percent to the director and writer and another 10 percent to friends of the producer who put up a $175,000 war chest. The producer has 60 days to raise $5 million, and he is working with 40 percent of box office receipts.

The independent producer has several off-balance-sheet assets to sell:

United States Theatrical Distribution. The producer can sell the right to distribute the film to U.S. theaters for a fee equal to from 25 percent to 60 percent of the distributor's gross income. A U.S. distributor such as Twentieth Century Fox Film Corporation or MGM might advance all or a portion of the budget. The more they advance, the greater their percentage. Independent producers would rather negotiate with more tender lambs for the money than enter the jaws of the U.S. distributors, but dealing with them is practically inevitable. Technological change will someday permit movie distribution from studio to theater via satellite and obviate the distributor; but that is two or three years away.

Foreign Theatrical Distributors. The right to distribute the film in 30 to 50 foreign countries is quite easily sold at the film industry's annual trade show: the Cannes Film Festival held every May on the French Riviera. A French distributor advanced Francis Coppola $100,000 for the French rights to *Apocalypse Now* and when the film was number one at the box office for most of 1980, the French distributor made over 20 times his investment. Winners like this one keep the market very active and responsive.

United States Network Television. The three major U.S. television networks are forever in the market for products. They buy movies "by the pound"; that is, four hours' worth costs twice as much as two hours' worth. One hour's worth of outtakes were put back into the two-hour film *King Kong* for the television sale. This brought the price up from $5 million to $7.5 million. The film *Annie* was sold to a network for $20 million to finance the shooting.

United States Independent Television. After a couple of runs on one of the networks, the independent stations would like to fill some of their hours of programming time with Hollywood's finest. Because the air time will be further out in the future, the advance from the independents is less than from the networks; but the product is nonetheless salable to them.

United States Cable Television. An increasingly important market for Hollywood's product is cable television. It has the audience, hence the capital to pay a fair penny for its chance to show the film. Twenty million homes are wired for cable television. The only major city in the United States today without cable television is Chicago. Cable and pay television frequently advance as much as 20 percent of the amount advanced by network television.

Home Video. With the explosive sales of video cassette recording (VCR) devices, the market for watching movies at home is currently estimated at one-fifth of theater attendance. If a film grosses $10 million at U.S. box offices, it should generate $2 million in home videocassette rentals over the subsequent three to five years. Thus, the film can be discounted at something under $2 million; perhaps $1.2 million in advance of shooting.

Military and In-Flight.   These are two small but interesting markets in which to sell the rights. For in-flight, the film must be rated G or PG and be less than 90 minutes long.

Book Rights.   Is there a paperback book possibility in this script? There may very well be that and more. Some people have sold paperback books on the making of their movie. The photographs are there, after all, and so are a few thousand words.

Product Rights.   In the film *Rocky III*, when Rocky smiles at his little boy and says, "Wheaties! What are Wheaties?" and the child giggles uncontrollably and says to Rocky, "The breakfast of champions," I could see the check from General Mills to the *Rocky III* producers. My estimate: $300,000. When Apollo Creed, the former heavyweight champion of the world, appeared in training with his Nike workout suit on, I said to myself, "$150,000." I never quite saw the name on Rocky's motorcycle, but it had a three-minute spot in front of an audience of 30 million viewers, so my estimate was "Honda: $250,000." I missed a few of the obvious advertisements that appeared during *Rocky III*, but I mentally raised $600,000 to pitch into the budget.

Other Rights.   If you are Gary Kurtz or George Lucas, capable of conceiving the Federation and producing the movies that depict the wars between the stars, then you might end up with toys, games, calendars, clothing, beach blankets, bed linen, and robots. Lucasfilms could be one of *Fortune* 500's largest industrial companies on its product sales alone. The $40 Darth Vader mask has sold close to 25,000 copies. The producers of *Star Wars* own a bank. Lucasfilms has sold some of the ancillary, and done so very carefully. I would estimate that the remaining rights to the *Star Wars* series are worth more than most American steel companies.

At any rate, we return to the fearless independent producer who must raise $5 million in 60 days on the strength of a script, a director, and a semi-unknown actor. There are some bicycle scenes and some running scenes in the movie, so the producer bases the U.S. box office projections on the figures generated by the recent hits, *Breaking Away* and *Chariots of Fire*. Their revenues are generally known, and he cuts them down by 75 percent. He projects $10 million in box office receipts for his "bicycle film." Were this the case, the distributors' gross would be $5 million, less perhaps $2.5 million or 50 percent of net box office receipts to the U.S. theatrical distributor, less perhaps $500,000 for advertising and prints, less $500,000 to the writer and director, and $500,000 for the producer's friends. The producer would keep the remaining dollars, or $1 million, for his efforts. This, of course, is subject to his being able to sell the other rights and to raise the $5 million.

The $5 million might be raised as follows:

Foreign theatrical (20 countries sold preshooting at an average $25,000 each)	$ 500,000
United States network television (assume $1 million per hour and a two-hour film)	2,000,000
United States independent television (not to run for three years, thus a steep discount)	400,000
United States cable television (20 million homes have cable, or 40% of the United States population, thus networks value × 40%)	800,000
Military, government, and in-flight	150,000
Products (assume bicycles, soft drinks, running clothes, one flight on United Airlines, and other advertisements)	
Book advance	750,000
Total	50,000
	$5,050,000

The independent producer scampers around from source to source picking up contracts and checks and arrives on location to give everybody his or her advance. He banks the contracts with a film lender which provides working capital for the film, gets eight hours' sleep the night before the shooting, and stays on the set for 16 weeks to assist the director.

No entrepreneur works harder or more intensely than the independent film producer. This entrepreneur is the most masterful user of leverage in the American economy. Other entrepreneurs have much to learn from producers. The difficulty of continual bootstrapping leads to a high rate of burn-out in Hollywood. A producer's profits are very hard to come by. The nature of the business demands that the independent film producer know how to sell off assets without giving up the basic business.

Another group of entrepreneurs who are becoming as much a part of the entrepreneurial landscape as movie producers are the leveraged buy-out entrepreneurs. These fearless young men and women have been buying dull manufacturing companies for hundreds of thousands and occasionally millions of dollars for the last 10 years, without two nickels to rub together. The leveraged buy-out is classic entrepreneurship. The leveraged buy-out begins with a search.

Since the entrepreneur has no cash, a fully leverageable seller is the target. The search begins. Merger and acquisition brokers and investment bankers are contacted, lists of sellers are scoured, and advertisements are placed in the *Wall Street Journal*. After weeks of reviewing acquisition candidates, the entrepreneur finds a fully leverageable tent manufacturer. Its financial statements appear in Exhibit 5.3.

Assume that the seller's price is $335,000 cash for the entire business. Small, nonproprietary manufacturing companies are quite difficult to sell. Frequently, other competitive manufacturing companies are not interested, would prefer to see a competitor leave the market, or are prevented by antitrust laws from making a horizontal acquisition.

Also, acquisitions are sometimes frightening to people, because they are stressful and upsetting. Thus, attractive little companies such as the $1.4 million (sales) tent manufacturer cannot demand a premium price. They are sold off at or below book value and usually for a package of cash and notes, rarely for all cash. Thus, the seller might accept $300,000. Let's see if that amount can be raised from the balance sheet.

Conventional loan ratios used by asset lenders such as commercial finance companies are 85 percent against the value of accounts receivable less than 90 days outstanding, 50 percent against the value of fin-

EXHIBIT 5.3.   Tent Manufacturer Leveraged Buy-Out Candidate

Balance Sheet, Fiscal Year Ending 12/31/82

Assets		Liabilities and Net Worth	
Current assets:		Current liabilities:	
Cash	$ 35,000	Accounts payable	$ 90,000
Accounts receivable	245,000	Accrued expenses	25,000
Inventories	180,000	Notes payable	120,000
Total current assets:	460,000	Total current liabilities	235,000
Plant, equipment (net)	85,000	Stockholders' equity	335,000
Other assets	15,000		
Total assets	$ 560,000	Total liabilities and net worth	$ 560,000

Operating Statement, 12 Months Ending 12/31/82

		Percent
Sales	$1,350,00	100.0
Cost of goods sold	904,500	67.0
Gross profit	445,500	33.0
Selling expense	135,000	10.0
General and administrative expense	222,500	16.5
Net operating income	88,000	6.5
Interest expense	20,000	1.5
Net profit before taxes	$ 68,000	5.0

ished goods and raw material inventories, and 75 percent against the liquidation (auction or quick-sale) value of property, plant, machinery, and equipment. If we assume that all of the accounts receivable of the tent manufacturer are less than 90 days old, that two-thirds of the inventories are either raw material or finished goods, and that net book value of plant and equipment is equal to liquidation value, then the entrepreneur can raise the cash from the tent manufacturer's balance sheet as shown in Exhibit 5.4.

From the $342,000 cash advance, we must deduct the $120,000 note payable, which will have to be repaid. This leaves $222,000 to pay the seller. To squeeze more cash from the balance sheet, we ask the seller to guarantee the collectibility of 100 percent of the accounts receivable. Normally sellers will agree to this request. The negotiation is quick and

EXHIBIT 5.4. Cash Raised from Balance Sheet

	Book Value	×	Loan Ratio	=	Cash Advance
Cash	$ 35,000		–		$ 10,000[a]
Accounts receivable	245,000		0.85		208,250
Inventories	120,000		0.50		60,000
Net plant, equipment	85,000		0.75		63,750
Total	$485,000				$342,000

[a]Excess over amount needed to operate the business.

simple. If the seller will not guarantee their collectibility, then the buyer surely does not want them. The seller can keep the accounts receivable as part of the purchase price in order to borrow 100 percent of the value of that particular asset. In any event, an additional $36,750 in cash can be squeezed out of this balance sheet, bringing total cash on hand at the closing date to approximately $260,000. Some of that is needed for closing costs. Assume then that the entrepreneur offers the seller $230,000 in cash and a $50,000 note secured by the inventory in second position to the commercial finance company, bearing interest at 9 percent per annum and due in five years. With the lure of a condominium nestled behind the fourteenth green of a Tarpon Springs, Florida, golf course beckoning the seller, he or she is not likely to refuse.

Not so fast, you say. How can the entrepreneur afford the debt service on a $260,000 loan at 20 percent interest, of which the equipment portion amortizes in 84 equal monthly installments immediately, plus 9 percent on $50,000? The first year's debt service is:

$$\$260{,}000 \times 0.20 = \$52{,}000$$
$$50{,}000 \times 0.09 = 4{,}500$$
$$63{,}750 \div 7 = 9{,}107$$

$$\text{Total annual debt service} = \$65{,}607$$

The company's net operating income is $88,000 per annum, so it can fairly comfortably support $65,000 in debt service. However, if sales slip by 10 percent, the company will be operating at the break-even point. Fortunately, in leveraged buy-out situations, general and administrative expenses are frequently overstated. The wife's car is occasionally a company expense, as are country club dues, lots of travel and entertainment card charges, and the ubiquitous indigent brother-in-law in the shipping department. Rather than $88,000, adjusted net operating income is more like $108,000. Further, the entrepreneur can work for a smaller salary than the seller, thus adding to cash flow. The result is an extra cash flow of approximately $40,000 after debt service ($108,000 minus $65,000) plus $40,000 in salary savings. This results in close to $7,000 per month additional cash for the combined operations.

Furthermore, the entrepreneur received from the lenders a check for $260,000 at the closing, paid his professional fees of $10,000, and handed over $230,000 to the seller. The additional $20,000 can be used as a reserve. The additional cash flow of $80,000 can be used to launch a new business.

Even if the seller had refused the package and held out for more cash, the entrepreneur could have found ways to squeeze more cash out of the balance sheet. A favorite method is to sell the equipment to a leasing company or partnership of individuals and lease it back.

Another is to let the seller keep the inventory and sell it to the buyer for cost as orders are taken. Still a third is to find a subordinated lender to add $50,000 to the inventory loan. The Small Business Administration will frequently do this. However, in instances where speed and timing are critical, it is best to sit and hammer out a deal with the seller who wants to tee up at Innisbrook as badly as the entrepreneur needs to have his own company.

The newest form of high-stakes leverage is that of the "target entrepreneur" or "greenmailer." This person has a larger stack of chips to play with than does the movie producer or the leveraged buy-out entrepreneur. The target entrepreneur identifies an asset-rich company with uncreative management and begins buying its stock. After accumulating approximately 7 percent ownership, the entrepreneur announces to the Securities and Exchange Commission the intention of taking control of the target company and replacing senior management with a new slate. The target company's management team does what every frightened group of aging men would do when their company is the subject of a raid: they protect themselves with "golden parachutes," huge severance payment arrangements. The raids on Gulf Oil, Phillips Petroleum, TWA, Avco Corporation, Walt Disney Enterprises, and other giant corporations have filled the pages of the financial press in 1985.

Saul Steinberg's raid on Walt Disney Corporation resulted in a payoff to Steinberg of more than $30 million for his time and trouble, plus a profit of about $75 million in Walt Disney Corporation stock.

Other target entrepreneurs include Irwin "The Liquidator" Jacobs, Joe Steinberg, Ian Cummings, T. Boone Pickens, Asher Edelman, Carl Icahn, and Ivan Boesky. They have enriched themselves by seeing the underlying values of the assets of very large companies, too large one might say, for their complacent, well-paid managements to have noticed. Target entrepreneurs are a healthy segment of the economy. By acting in the manner of sharks in the ocean, they keep all of the other fish awake and alert.

All successful entrepreneurs understand and use leverage with the offhandedness and regularity that the rest of humanity uses a toothbrush in the morning. It is second nature, and a part of the entrepreneur's anatomy. But customers, suppliers, and asset-rich companies are not all that entrepreneurs leverage. They make better use of time than any other group of individuals in society. In Exhibit 5.5 are listed some important entrepreneurial timesavers.

Entrepreneurs place an inordinately high value on time. They flock to locations where time is in their favor, such as the more western time zones, industrial parks near major airports, and areas that employees are able to reach conveniently. Entrepreneurs drive quickly, take early flights, avoid maintenance breakdowns or other time-eaters, speak rapidly, and walk at a quick pace. Entrepreneurs are rarely significantly overweight, because they do not overeat. Entrepreneurs practically never get sick.

These tactics may involve merely a few minutes of each day, but they add up to hours. If an 80-hour workweek is a typical entrepreneur's schedule, adding 10 more hours here and there is a 12.5 percent increase in assets. This optimal use of time is a fundamentally Marxian principle for it was Karl Marx who was the first to define labor properly as a form of capital. For the cash-poor entrepreneur, the substitute for capital is labor or as some call it, sweat equity.

Where others strive for prestige, wealth, and power, the entrepreneur seeks time to build a problem-solving machine. Appreciating the complexity of the work involved, the entrepreneur realizes that if he or she has the time, there will be less need for capital and employees and

EXHIBIT 5.5. Entrepreneurial TimeSavers

During the day:
    Sleep little
    Eat little
    Never get sick
    Speak quickly
    Wear short hair
    To avoid shaving, grow a beard
    To avoid haircuts, wear long hair (but never comb it)
    Wear the minimum number of articles of clothing (12 or less)
    Wear no jewelry
    Don't initiate idle conversation

Automobile rules:
    Drive fast
    Own two radar detectors; one may get stolen
    Own cars that rarely need overhauling
    Own cars that maneuver well in traffic
    Own a car (or cellular) telephone

Airport, airplane rules:
    Do not check baggage
    Do not carry or wear a metal object that will be picked up by metal detectors
    Avoid being behind people with thick-soled, comfortable-looking shoes prior to entering the metal detectors because they enjoy setting off the buzzer
    On the airplane, sit in any aisle seat in the nonsmoking section for rapid exit
    Avoid eye contact with your neighbors; it could lead to their initiating conversations
    Take the earliest flight to and the latest flight from the appointment in order to avoid ground and air traffic delays
    Bring lots of work to do
    Walk quickly to the car rental counter in order to beat people who care to understand what all the rates, circles, checks, numbers, and letters mean
    Do not talk to the rental car bus driver; he or she may slow down in order to extend the conversation

other resources. Time is the single most important asset for the entrepreneur. Many of the success stories in the biographical sketches in the next chapter are the result of entrepreneurs leveraging time.

6

THE 100 GREATEST ENTREPRENEURS OF THE LAST 25 YEARS

In the biographical sketches that follow, the personality of the entrepreneur is juxtaposed against the company that he or she founded, launched, and helped to build. The objective is not to parade 100 beauties out onto the stage and give their measurements, but to describe the *process* by which they built successful, problem-solving companies. The manner of presentation, however, includes a scorecard. The size of the problem (P) is quantified wherever possible, and described if it is not actually measurable. The solution (S) is described and distinguished as to its proprietariness or elegance and, if not proprietary, the uniqueness of its delivery system. The members of the entrepreneurial team (E) are described as well. For ardent box score readers, the company's V is described. It is less important for us to know how much wealth the entrepreneur made personally—100 percent of the entrepreneurs that we chose are believed to be worth more than $20 million—but the companies' Vs are an important indicator. A high V with many beneficiaries—entrepreneur, managers, employees, and investors—means profits for reinvestment. Finally, the scorecard includes a description of the entrepreneur's and his or her company's social utility. How many new jobs did this dream create? How many entrepreneurs, and which ones, spun out of this company and with the experience gained there went on to launch their own entrepreneurial companies? Where the entrepreneur has provided us with some examples of social utility, such as charities, endowments, and personal projects for the betterment of humanity, these have been listed as well.

This entrepreneurial scorecard is not believed to be wholly accurate and complete, although that is certainly one of its important goals. Any errors or omissions are accidental, unintentional, and regrettable.

SHELDON ADELSON

Name of Company:	The Interface Group, Inc.
Date Founded:	1971
Location:	Needham, Massachusetts
Description of Business:	The company produces computer industry trade shows, most notably Computer Dealer's Exposition (COMDEX), the largest computer show in the world. In addition, the company operates the fifth largest tour business in the United States, initially started to manage the travel needs associated with COMDEX
Description of *P*:	An industry trade show is needed to bring together buyers and sellers several times a year for information-sharing purposes. The revenues of all computer trade shows probably exceed $500 million in a year, of which The Interface Group's share is an estimated $175 million.
Description of *S*:	COMDEX is designed for vendors to display their wares to dealers and distributors—the middlemen of the personal computer industry—rather than the end user. The dealers are asked to pay $25 to attend COMDEX and the vendors an average of $15,000 each for their booths. The elegance of this marketing method encouraged 100,000 dealers and other visitors to attend the five-day November 1984 COMDEX in Las Vegas.
Members of *E*:	Richard Katzeff, vice-president, Irwin Chafetz, president of Five Star Airlines Division, Ted Bernard-Cutler, president of GWV Travel.
Size of *V*:	The Interface Group is privately held, thus no figures are reported. However, assuming earnings before taxes of $25 million, applying a corporate tax rate of 45 percent and multiplying by a

price/earnings ratio of 15x, The Interface Group is possibly worth $180 million.

Social Utility:

The Interface Group employs 600 people full time and 500 are hired for each conference. Dealers are treated royally and for a nominal charge attend outstanding seminars with speakers such as Esther Dyson and Portia Isaacson, which are top-drawer, and a dealer can learn more about the business at COMDEX than back at the office.

Principal Source of Venture Capital:

Family and friends; Adelson owns 51 percent.

SHELDON ADELSON has been an entrepreneur since he was 16 years old, a stretch of 35 years, when he purchased Vend-A-Bar, a candy bar vending company, for $10,000, a price financed by his paper route savings, the seller's note, and a $3,000 loan. Adelson repaired the broken machines, installed them in factories and repaid his loans with the nickels that the machines generated. When cash flow turned positive he bought a truck with ice chests and sold ice cream at the factories in the summer. Adelson was already fully conversant with the fundamentals of leverage: while making a trip to collect payment, sell another product. He may have learned business from his mother, who owned a knitting store in Boston. Adelson, his immigrant parents, and three siblings lived behind the store in a one-bedroom apartment.

His vending business was interrupted by the Korean War. However, Adelson learned court reporting at night school in order to try to avoid battlefield duty. Indeed, it worked. Adelson's tour of duty was in New York City. When the war ended, he became private secretary to Celia D. Wyckoff, owner of the financial magazine, *Magazine of Wall Street*. Adelson began selling ads for the publication and graduated to advertising manager, in which capacity he became acquainted with most of the investment and commercial banks in New York's financial district.

He left Ms. Wyckoff in 1963 and with a partner founded Dashel Associates, which acted as a "finder," a company that locates capital for companies. Adelson became relatively successful, at least enough to induce him to begin investing his own capital in small companies, prior to locating investment banks to take them public. When the stock market plummeted in 1970, Adelson suffered a serious reversal and he abandoned the role of investment intermediary and venture capitalist. "One day I woke up in 1970 and found myself a million-and-a-half in the hole," Adelson told the authors of The Computer Entrepreneurs.[1]

His interests turned to condominium conversions, but to keep his fingers in publishing, Adelson purchased Communications User magazine in 1972. He attended a condominium conversion trade show in 1972 and learned that the show's sponsor also published a magazine. Like the 16-year-old vending machine owner who began selling ice cream bars when he went to collect his nickels, Adelson immediately visualized trade shows as "living magazines," or "magazines in the flesh." In 1973 after changing the name of his magazine to Data Communications User, Adelson sponsored his first trade show, the Data Communications Interface show, where manufacturers of data processing equipment exhibited their products for end users. He learned the trade show business thoroughly over the next six years. In 1979 as the personal computer was emerging, Adelson saw the need for a trade show aimed at dealers and distributors. Eight months after the idea for the first COMDEX Adelson's dealer-oriented trade show rolled out and it has not stopped rolling since. In fact, computer industry trade shows that appeal to hobbyists, and those that appeal to corporate data processing users, have been left in COMDEX's dust.

The Interface Group has entered into facilities management contracts to operate more than 30 trade shows. It has founded other profitable spin-off businesses, such as tour operations, publishing the COMDEX Show Daily and other trade shows' newspapers, and exhibiting books and other materials that utilize Adelson's skills.

---

[1]Robert Levering, Michael Katz, Milton Moskowitz, The Computer Entrepreneurs (New York: New American Library, 1984), p. 366.

MARTIN A. ALLEN

Name of Company:	Computervision Corporation
Date Founded:	1969
Location:	Bedford, Massachusetts
Description of Business:	The company designs, develops, and manufactures computer-aided design, engineering, and manufacturing (CAD/CAM) systems for automating various development and industrial processes.
Description of *P*:	The need to automate various design, development, and manufacturing functions in many industries, including aerospace, electronics, construction, and plant design has generated a $556 million (1984 revenues) CAD/CAM industry of which Computervision has sales of $400 million.
Description of *S*:	The company has several lines of fully integrated workstations that incorporate computers, specialized processors, graphics capability, plotters, storage, and software.
Members of *E*:	James R. Berrett, president (formerly with Honeywell); Philip L. Read, senior vice-president; Robert P. Gothie, vice-president; Robert L. Callaway, vice-president.
Size of *V*:	$1.2 billion as of December 1984, approximately 7,000 stockholders own 28.5 million shares of common stock which traded at an average price of $45 per share in 1984.
Social Utility:	The company employs approximately 5,300 persons and earns a 17.5–20 percent return on equity.
Principal Source of Venture Capital:	First Capital Corporation, a subsidiary of the First National Bank of Boston

MARTIN A. ALLEN, 54, was inspired to launch a new company that would solve the costly industrial problem of product design via computer-aided design while at the Smithsonian Museum in 1964. He became mesmerized by a display of George Washington in his surveying days. It struck Allen that the rudimentary equipment used by Washington had not changed very much in 200 years. In fact, the drafting tools used by Allen himself had not evolved much beyond "the triangle, straight edge, slide rule, and a couple pieces of string."

Experiencing that brief flash of inspiration from which entire industries have sometimes sprung, Allen wondered: "Why not link the computer to the costly and excruciatingly long process of product design?" The solution to that problem, he calculated, could be worth as much as 40 percent of the research and development budget.

For Allen the big breakthrough came in 1969, when he left Singer Company and struck out on his own with Computervision Corporation, a fledgling company that at the time, he recalls, had "no distinction whatsoever." Since then, however, Computervision Corporation has become the largest producer of CAD/CAM systems. Revenues in 1984 exceeded $400 million.

In 15 years, Computervision Corporation has built up a clientele of nearly 3,000 companies, including such big CAD/CAM converts as General Motors Corporation, Westinghouse Electric Corporation, Ford Motor Company and Boeing Company, whose orders run anywhere from $100,000 to millions for CAD/CAM components and systems, all of which can be interconnected with each other. One of Computervision's biggest contracts was awarded by the U.S. Navy, which placed a $62.9 million order for a complete range of CAD/CAM and GNA (graphics network architecture) systems. When in place over the next several years, the Navy's systems will constitute the largest interconnected turnkey CAD/CAM operation in the world.

Yet the company is a long way from having saturated the CAD/CAM marketplace. "The demand is so great, the need so immense," Allen told a Dun's interviewer, "that we still have some ways to go."[2] Indeed, considering Computervision's top-of-the-art technology, its solid finances, and a growth rate of some 30 percent a year, securities analysts

[2]R. Levy and others, "Visionary at Computervision," *Dun's Business Monthly*, Vol. 119, p. 53.

rate Computervision Corporation as one of the most professionally managed of the high tech companies.

Born into bleak poverty in Des Moines, the son of a struggling laborer, Allen took his early schooling in California, where a high school chum introduced him to the wonders of building crystal sets and electric motors. At 14, he bought a '34 Chevy and a tool set, which he used to take the car apart. "I was perpetually fascinated by mechanics," Allen recalls.[3]

Putting himself through the University of California at Los Angeles, engineer Allen worked at Northrup Corporation, Servomechanisms, Ramo Woolridge and the Martin Company, before joining Singer Company in 1962. There he formed a close friendship with Philip Villers, a colleague who shared Allen's excitement over his visit to the Smithsonian. After endless weekend discussions of "what might be done to computerize the design process," the two budding entrepreneurs recruited a group of Massachusetts Institute of Technology professors and mapped the formation of a company to produce turnkey CAD/CAM systems. Venture capitalists listened, liked what they saw, and plunked down $1.1 million to launch Computervision Corporation.

Although Villers left the company to head his own concern, he still holds about 9 percent of Computervision Corporation's stock. So does Allen, whose shares have made him extremely wealthy. But as Allen puts it, "When one grows up in poverty, one has a desire to make a dramatic, monumental change in one's estate. (Now) I want to do something for mankind."[4]

[3]"High Priests of High Tech," March 1982 (Press Release).
[4]Ibid.

MARTIN ALPERT

Name of Company:	Tecmar, Inc.
Date Founded:	1974
Location:	Cleveland, Ohio
Description of Business:	The company designs, develops, and manufactures computer peripheral products that expand the capabilities of the IBM PC and Apple personal computers and those compatible with them.
Description of P:	Computers are dumb machines without the peripheral equipment and software to make them useful. Sales of peripheral equipment for personal computers reached $300 million in 1984 of which Tecmar represented approximately $100 million or 30 percent.
Description of S:	The company grabbed the lead in IBM PC peripheral equipment at the 1981 COMDEX and has never let down its energy and drive. Tecmar produces on average one new product per week from memory extenders and speech synthesizers to insertable boards that permit two PC operators to share one printer.
Members of E:	Carolyn Alpert, wife of Martin Alpert, has been the company's principal business manager from the beginning. Kenneth Stern, vice-president—Engineering, has been critical in the design and development of new products.
Size of V:	Estimated 1984 revenues were $100 million. A conventional return on sales for similar publicly held companies is 10 percent, and at a p/e ratio of 15x, Tecmar valuation is an estimated $150 million.
Social Utility:	The company employs 425 people and its employees are visibly proud of having built a Silicon Valley success story in Cleveland, Ohio.

Principal Source   Self-financed as a start-up; subsequently from
of Venture   cash flow.
Capital:

MARTIN ALPERT is the over-achieving, only child of refugees who
survived several Nazi concentration camps. Alpert's Yiddish-speaking
parents found work in a storm door factory and a bakery; their savings
financed his tuition at Cleveland's highly regarded Case Western Reserve University. This combination of factors made the typical child
prodigy feel sufficiently guilty to study medicine as his parents
wished. Indeed, Alpert, whose first love was electronics, earned a medical degree from Case and practiced medicine part-time until 1983
when Tecmar became all-consuming.

He met his wife, Carolyn, in 1971 when both were undergraduates.
As motivated as he, Carolyn held down two jobs while her husband attended medical school.

After becoming a physician and opening a practice, Alpert began developing microprocessor-based medical instruments in the couple's
living room. Approximately $50,000 was diverted by Alpert from his
medical practice to the increasingly cluttered business taking shape on
the living room floor. Seeing his direction before Alpert did, Carolyn
enrolled in an MBA program. When annual sales reached $1 million
and the living room was occupied by 15 engineers making 20 products,
Tecmar moved into a 10,000 square foot office nearby in April 1981.

In August 1981 International Business Machines Corporation (IBM)
announced that it would begin marketing a personal computer in the
fall and Alpert announced to his staff that they would make enhance-
ments for it. When the IBM PC was released on October 7, 1981, Alpert
dispatched Tecmar's vice-president—Marketing, David Westman, to
buy the first two models and bring them back to Cleveland. Working
around the clock with food sent in, the Tecmar engineers
systematically tore apart the PCs to find out how other products could
be attached. Then they doubled their efforts to build a line of these
products.

Six weeks later, at the fall COMDEX, the Tecmar booth was second
in popularity only to IBM. For in the Tecmar booth were 20 fully operational peripherals for the IBM PC. Tecmar has never looked back since,

and no competitor is anywhere near approaching the company. Many of the company's engineers have been given stock and the personnel are rewarded with other perquisites including a fleet of company-owned Porsches, a wine cellar, and a music room. At 35 Alpert has apparently achieved a level of respectability of which his parents can be extremely proud.

J. REID ANDERSON

Name of Company:	Verbatim Corporation
Date Founded:	1969
Location:	Sunnyvale, California

Description of Business: The company designs, develops, manufactures, and markets removable magnetic data storage media, including floppy discs and data cassettes, which are used to record and store digital information for use in word processors, personal computers, minicomputers, and other data collection equipment.

Description of P: The problem that Anderson identified in 1969 was a need for a small, low cost medium to store digital information to replace paper tape. Anderson bet on data cassettes and floppy discs. Aggregate sales of these media in 1984 were approximately $850 million, of which the company represented 20 percent.

Description of S: The elegance of the solution is based on timing and fit. The floppy disc fits into a drive mechanism which contains recording and playback heads, together with a motor-driven mechanical device for moving the media in relation to the heads. In 1973, IBM introduced the floppy disc and Anderson obtained a license to manufacture it. In 1977 Shugart Associates introduced a smaller version and Anderson secured an additional license. Verbatim's timing was perfect, because Anderson had formulated the needs of the market and was in the right place at the right time.

Members of E: Malcolm B. Northrup, president (formerly with Rockwell International) and Polly Anderson, wife of the founder.

Size of V:	The approximately 23 million shares of Verbatim common stock outstanding have traded between $10 and $29 per share in 1984, for an average market value of $460 million. In March 1985, Verbatim became the object of a tender offer by Eastman Kodak.
Social Utility:	Verbatim employs 2,800 people at five locations, earns about 30 percent on stockholders' equity and has created sufficient freedom for Anderson to devote his time and capital to assisting entrepreneurs in launching high technology companies.
Principal Source of Venture Capital:	Personal resources from a previous venture plus family and friends and a small amount of outside capital

J. REID ANDERSON, 67, was born in Wheeling, West Virginia, the son of a stockbroker who lost everything during the Great Depression. He loved the clarinet and engineering, and upon graduating with degrees in physics and engineering, Anderson joined Bell Laboratories in Murray Hill, New Jersey, where he was happily employed for 17 years. The competition for advancement was keen at Bell, so Anderson jumped to NCR Corporation in Dayton, Ohio, in 1956 as director of physical research.

Many entrepreneurs go through a consulting stage in order to pull together the tangled ideas of a potential new business. In 1958, Anderson left NCR to join the esteemed consulting firm, Stanford Research Institute, Palo Alto, California. Here he was involved completely in innovation; every assignment involved a new business idea. Anderson left SRI five years later to launch his own company.

Anderson's first venture into the waters of entrepreneurship was to produce a metronome, the Tempo Tuner, which he sold to music stores. He enlisted the services of his son and wife, and Palo Alto had another of its soon to be well-known garage start-ups. Unfortunately, the Tempo Tuner saturated its marketplace within three years. Anderson was in the market for ideas when he met another consultant, Ray

Jacobson, whose background was marketing and finance. In 1967, while visiting SRI, they were exposed to an acoustic data coupler, a device for transferring data over telephone lines. Anderson felt that he could produce them quite inexpensively, and Anderson Jacobson Corporation obtained a license from SRI. However, friction between the partners developed within the year, and Anderson left.

His plan was to produce magnetic tape data-storage devices, as a replacement for paper tape storage, but after his new company, Verbatim, had been in business for four years, it became apparent that a newer medium, floppy discs, would obsolete magnetic tape. Verbatim, which was by then well capitalized with Anderson's capital gains from Anderson Jacobson, obtained licenses from International Business Machines and Shugart to produce and market floppy discs that fit their disk drive mechanisms. Sales grew from $7 million in 1975 to $120 million in 1983. Earnings grew as well, from $500,000 in 1975 to $14.3 million in 1983, but the growth trend suffered in 1980–1981 (earnings fell from $4.5 million in 1979 to $1.8 million in 1980 and $1.1 million in 1981) when Verbatim shipped some faulty products that had to be recalled. Anderson had not built a strong management team, possibly as a result of some scar tissue from the earlier Jacobson disagreement. In 1981, Malcolm B. Northrup was hired from Rockwell International Corporation to manage the company. He is credited with having introduced a new disc, the DataLife, which was sold with a five-year warranty, an industry first. Anderson has been permitted the opportunity to retire from the day-to-day activities of Verbatim and to invest in and provide advice to entrepreneurial companies.

Among the wisdom that Anderson will be able to impart to these entrepreneurs in the process of launching companies, is the role of corporate achievers to guide rapidly growing companies and the central theme of survivability. Anderson is also in an excellent position to remind entrepreneurs that they need not be the pioneer in an industry; producing a product that adds value to the pioneers' products certainly can prove rewarding as well.

MARY KAY ASH

Name of Company:	Mary Kay Cosmetics, Inc.
Date Founded:	1963
Location:	Dallas, Texas

Description of Business: The company produces and sells cosmetics through an international network of marketing consultants using the party-plan method.

Description of P: Many women prefer to purchase facial cosmetics in the privacy of their homes where they can experiment more freely than in a store. Avon has proven this with annual sales of more than $3.1 billion. Mary Kay Ash added another feature: create high incomes for her lady marketing consultants, liberate them from the chores of the housewife, and gain their loyalty for life.

Description of S: There is nothing proprietary about the Mary Kay line of cosmetics. However, the delivery system is not easily duplicable: over 200,000 "independent beauty consultants" operating in five countries with an evangelical leader who continually admonishes them with the courage to believe in themselves. At a recent convention she told her women: "If you are here today, you are too smart to go home and scrub the floors."[5] They have rewarded her with sales of $324 million in 1983.

Size of V: With approximately 30 million shares outstanding and a common stock price that averaged $15 per share in 1984, Mary Kay's valuation is $450 million.

Members of E: The company's chief executive officer since the beginning has been Mary Kay's son, Richard Rogers.

[5]Kathy Latour, "What Motivates Mary Kay," *American Way*, October 1984, p. 154–158.

Social Utility: The company has generated employment and a
                             high sense of self-worth for over 250,000 women.
                             In addition, 1,500 people are employed at Dallas
                             headquarters. More women earn over $50,000 per
                             annum for Mary Kay Cosmetics than for any other
                             company in the country.

Principal Source   The founder's life savings of $5,000
  of Venture
  Capital:

MARY KAY ASH founded her own company in 1963, about three
months after retiring from another direct sales company where she had
worked for 25 years. She entered the direct sales business as a divorced
mother of three children. She wanted to create a company in which being a woman would not hinder upward mobility and financial rewards
and where motivation was based on what goals and objectives are important to women and not to men. Her entrepreneurial insight was in
creating a unique motivational system that would attract, hold onto, motivate, and reward an all-women marketing organization. The
unique product or elegant solution to a large problem was not part of
Ash's initial formulation, although clearly the product would have to
possess economic validity for her company to be successful.

    She chose a cosmetic that she had been using for years, a skin-care
line based on formulas developed by a hide tanner, which until Ash's
endorsement of them, had been sold only by the man's granddaughter.
She rented a store front in a Dallas office building and began selling the
products to generate revenues. She pulled her son, Richard, then aged
20, out of college to assist her. Ash immediately began recruiting and
training beauty consultants to begin home demonstrations. Although
practically every male friend, advisor, and counselor tried to dissuade
her, Ash claims to have been given the courage to succeed by her previous successes in direct sales and her mother's admonition and encour-
agement.

    Revenues grew slowly in the 1960's as the foundation was being
laid, but reached $31 million in 1974 and since have grown ten-fold.
The company has consistently earned more than 20 percent before

taxes and its stockholders' equity exceeds $140 million, of which cash ($26 million) is approximately 20 percent. The company has virtually no long-term debt. Ash has built a cash-generating machine that, moreover, has turned over a quarter of a million women into self-employed businesswomen with lots of ability and "handsome bank accounts." As in many party plan companies, the wives begin outearning the husbands.

How did Ash accomplish this? She created a feeling of family in her company, a hierarchical organization chart which had a system of rewards and penalties, like any family. Through frequent seminars attended by the independent beauty consultants, Ash "preaches" to her women like a tent-meeting evangelist. Typical of her gospel are the following precepts:

"If you are here today, you are too smart to go home and scrub floors. You are spending one dollar time on a one penny chore."[6] This admonition not only gives the women pride, but encourages them to hire housekeepers so that they can spend more time recruiting additional beauty consultants and selling more cosmetics. "I created this company for you," she tells them. This and similar preachments enhance the spirit of family and the excitement of a crusade.

Mary Kay Cosmetics depends for its success on the continual attraction of new independent beauty consultants. After training, they purchase their initial inventory and begin calling on friends to have parties. The company does not advertise for women; rather, it relies on word-of-mouth. Thirty percent of its 250,000 direct sales personnel are college graduates. When the economy is weak and inflation is strong, women flock to Mary Kay in greater numbers than when the economy is buoyant. To counter this situation, the company has introduced the Mr. K line of male cosmetics. Can this vibrant lady and her skillful son enter the second line as successfully as they did the first? Only time will tell. But, win or lose on Mr. K, Ash is one of the most valuable entrepreneurs in the country.

Perceiving greater value for her company than does the stock market, Ash announced her plans to take the company private via a leveraged buy-out in June 1985. She and Rogers will become the principal owners should the buy-out be accepted by the Mary Kay shareholders.

[6]Ibid, p. 158.

HENRY WOLLMAN BLOCH
RICHARD A. BLOCH

Name of Company:	H & R Block, Inc.
Date Founded:	1955
Location:	Kansas City, Missouri

Description of Business: This company is the largest preparer of federal income tax returns for individuals. The company prepared over 10 million returns in 1984.

Description of *P*: Henry Bloch recognized the growing complexity of income tax forms in the mid-1950s and believed that a trustworthy, careful tax preparation service with a national reputation could be successful.

Description of *S*: In the case of a nonproprietary service such as tax preparation, it is critical to open a large number of offices on a national basis as quickly as possible in order to make life difficult and expensive for the competition. The best means to achieve this is via franchising.

Members of *E*: William T. Ross, vice-president, secretary; Donald W. Ayers, vice-president, treasurer.

Size of *V*: There are approximately 12 million shares of common stock outstanding, which traded in a range of $37 to $50 per share in 1984 for an average valuation of $522 million.

Social Utility: The company has created 12,000 jobs and second incomes for numerous families who purchased franchises.

Principal Source of Venture Capital: Customer financing

HENRY W. BLOCH, 62, and RICHARD A. BLOCH, 60, have created one of the most successful cookie-cutter businesses in the country: a national tax preparation service. There are approximately 9,700 tax preparation offices nationwide, of which 4,200 are company-owned, 3,300 are satellites of company-owned stores, 760 are located in Sears, Roebuck & Co. stores and approximately 1,570 are franchisees. Roughly 89,000 students enrolled in Block's tax preparation schools in 1983–1984. The schools provide the majority of the company's tax preparers.

Nearly 10 million people had their taxes prepared by H & R Block in 1983–1984. The average fee for its service in 1983–1984 was $40.35, up from the prior year's fee of $38.32. With tax preparation revenues of approximately $400 million, H & R Block dominates its business.

Nonetheless, tax preparation has two major problems: first, it is intensely seasonal—all revenues occur between January and April; and second, the business is reliant on the government's making income tax payments increasingly complex. The former is the risk that H & R Block can do the most to offset, and it has made two interesting acquisitions outside of its primary industry. The first is Compuserve, Inc., a rapidly growing network for the transmission of data via computer. There are over 90 data banks that download information to personal computer users via Compuserve. Stock market data, airplane flight information, and gift catalogs are three of the most frequently used of these data banks. Revenues have grown from approximately $15 million to $50 million over the last year.

A second acquisition, Personnel Pool of America, provides supplemental medical, industrial, food service, and clerical personnel through 57 owned and 259 franchised offices. Revenues of this subsidiary have grown to $60 million in 1983–1984 compared with $24 million the previous year.

A third acquisition is Hyatt Legal Services, Inc., a chain of storefront legal offices started five years ago by Joel Hyatt in Columbus, Ohio. Hyatt's revenues were $12 million in 1983–1984. Although Hyatt and Compuserve have not broken even, Block's management permits their entrepreneurs a great deal of autonomy and provides them with ample capital to grow. H & R Block has adroitly used its extraordinary cash flow from tax preparation to play venture capitalist to three new businesses, all of which are in exciting, rapidly growing markets.

Henry W. Bloch's leadership and determination in building a totally new business in America undoubtedly was inspired by the achievement of prominent pioneers on both sides of his family. Bloch's maternal great-grandmother was Betty Wollman, one of the first pioneer women to enter Kansas and whose picture now hangs in the Kansas State Office Building in Topeka. Bloch's paternal grandfather came to the Midwest as a guide with Kit Carson, settling near the Kansas-Nebraska border to start a general store.

On his mother's side, the Wollman family was well known in New York financial circles, founding the brokerage firm of W. J. Wollman & Company. Henry Bloch's great-aunt built the Wollman Skating Rink in Central Park and presented it as a gift to the people of New York City.

Henry, along with his brothers, received his early education in Kansas City and graduated from Southwest High School. He attended the University of Kansas City and the University of Michigan, where he majored in mathematics until he was called into the U.S. Army Air Corps.

Special schooling in the Air Corps in England allowed him to complete his college degree in mathematics and he was graduated from University of Michigan in absentia. As part of his Air Corps training, Bloch also attended the Graduate Business School at Harvard University completing courses in statistical control.

A first lieutenant and navigator aboard a B-17 Flying Fortress, Bloch flew 31 combat missions over Germany, including three bombing runs on Berlin during the height of the Allied campaign. He was awarded the Air Medal with three Oak Leaf Clusters.

Returning from the service, Bloch worked one year for a Kansas City brokerage firm. He then borrowed $5,000 from his aunt to go into business with his older brother, but the loan was repaid within 30 days because it "wasn't needed" as operating capital.

When the older brother returned to school to obtain a law degree, Henry joined forces with his younger brother, Richard, in the formation of the United Business Company, offering small businesspeople bookkeeping, management assistance, collection, and income tax preparation services.

Henry visited clients to pick up their records, while brother Dick ran the office. At first, the preparation of income tax returns was an added free service to their bookkeeping clients. But their customers began to tell their friends about the Blochs and soon they were being asked to prepare income tax returns by the score . . . for a fee.

By 1954, income tax returns and United Business Company's regular services had the Bloch brothers working seven days a week and nearly every night.

Then came the idea. Why not a business limited to doing income tax returns exclusively? In 1955, United Business Company was dissolved and a new company specializing in income tax preparation was born—H & R Block, Inc.—with Henry Bloch as President.

Bloch's numerous activities include directorships in Southwestern Bell Telephone, Commerce Bank of Kansas City, Employers Reinsurance Corporation, and National Fidelity Life Insurance Company. His other affiliations include vice-chairman and member of the executive committee of the Kansas City Art Institute; vice-president, Menorah Medical Center; co-chairman of The Kansas City Area Economic Development Council; trustee of the University of Missouri at Kansas City; executive committee member of Midwest Research Insitiute; and president of the H & R Block Foundation.

WINTON MALCOM BLOUNT

Name of Company:	Blount, Inc.
Founded:	1946
Location:	Montgomery, Alabama

Description of Business: The company is a leader in constructing "one-of-a-kind, first-of-a-kind projects" around the world, such as waste-to-energy plants, missile silos for the U.S. Air Force, launch complexes for NASA, and the New Orleans Superdome.

Description of P: Blount saw the need at a very young age to undertake large, complex projects, often hazardous, because they were more profitable and had fewer competitors. Blount's sales in 1984 were $819 million.

Description of S: To hedge its bet against bidding too low or not being able to complete a certain job, Blount maintains a relatively liquid position. It also acquired several unrelated manufacturing and agri-business companies.

Members of E: Paul Hess, an early member of management, Oscar J. Reak, president, and Jack P. Glynn, executive vice-president.

Size of V: There are approximately 11 million shares of common stock outstanding which traded in a range of $15 ⅞ to $10 ¾ in 1984 for an average valuation of $138 million.

Social Utility: The company employs approximately 10,000 people and Blount has given his fortune to numerous charities including the arts.

Principal Source of Venture Capital: Personal savings and sweat equity

WINTON M. BLOUNT, 62, and his brother Houston, dropped out of the University of Alabama in 1942 to enlist in the armed forces. Their father died while the young men were in the service and by the time they returned home to Union Springs, Alabama, his sand and gravel business had deteriorated. Winton went to Atlanta to buy some surplus Army sand and gravel equipment. But the cheap price on some tractors and scrapers was irresistible to Winton. When he brought them back home, Houston asked him, "What are we going to do with that stuff?" Winton replied, "We're going into the contracting business." That was the beginning.

The first jobs were small, but the company gained experience in building roads, bridges, office buildings, and other structures. In 1952, the company completed a very technical job—a wind tunnel for the Air Force's Arnold Engineering Development Center near Tullahoma, Tennessee. "Its successful completion," says Blount, "proved to those of us at Blount Brothers that we had the talent, ability, and courage to tackle high-risk jobs."

Houston left Blount Brothers in the mid-1950s after helping to pull together various companies into Vulcan Materials Corp., of which he is president and chief executive officer. At that point, Blount began bidding on national jobs. His timing could not have been better. He answered the Air Force's and NASA's needs for heavy-duty, complex construction "employing hospital-type cleanliness." The space projects kept coming—Cape Canaveral, Huntsville, Tullahoma and Sandusky, Ohio. The company became known for its first-of-a-kind, one-of-a-kind jobs. These included building an indoor ocean for the Navy at Carderock, Maryland; nuclear reactors for Oak Ridge National Laboratories; a cyclotron for Oak Ridge; and the Atlanta airline terminal. The growth of the company was dramatic.

To offset the risks and cycles of its construction business, the company began diversifying. It acquired manufacturing companies in fields that it knew something about, such as pipe manufacturers, agricultural equipment and tools.

In 1968, Blount took a leave of absence to serve as Postmaster General in President Nixon's Cabinet. He could do this because of the management structure that he had in place.

In the mid-1950s, while the company was still quite small, Blount wrote his company's mission statement. It reads as follows:

The Blount Philosophy

We want to create within the Blount organization a place where people can and will want to come and devote their lives. To do so, we seek to create a climate where individuals can develop to their maximum potential. It is our belief that if people are set free to express themselves to the fullest, their accomplishments will be far beyond their dreams, and they will not only contribute to the growth of the company, but will also be more useful citizens and contribute to the larger society.

We hold a deep and abiding faith in the American Enterprise System. We understand and have tolerance for a wide range of individual interpretations of this system, but we brook no adherence to any other way of life. We believe in a person's responsibility and duty as a citizen to look beyond the office, and we encourage participation in civic, cultural, religious, and political affairs of our country. WE DO NOT SEEK CONFORMITY; WE DO SEEK PARTICIPATION.

We believe we have no greater responsibility to the American Enterprise System than to insure our business operates at a reasonable profit. There is no way to provide opportunity for growth or job security other than to make profits. To accomplish this on a continuing basis, we believe it is necessary to grow. We believe growth is necessary to provide opportunities on an ever increasing scale for our people to make their mark. Therefore, we are dedicated to growth—growth as a company—growth as an organization—and growth as individuals.

This is what we stand for. This is what we are about.[7]

---

[7]Winton M. Blount, The Blount Story, "American Enterprise at its Best," October, 1979, p. 20 (pamphlet).

ROSE BLUMKIN

Name of Company:	Nebraska Furniture Mart, Inc.
Date Founded:	1937
Location:	Omaha, Nebraska
Description of Business:	The company owns and operates a large retail furniture store.
Description of P:	The problem that furniture solves is similar from one merchant's goods to the next. Thus, Nebraska Furniture Mart must have been doing some unique things to generate sales of $120 million per annum out of one location.
Description of S:	Blumkin's secret of success, she told the *Wall Street Journal*, is to "sell cheap, tell the truth, don't cheat nobody and don't take kickbacks."[8]
Members of E:	Louis Blumkin, president
Size of V:	Berkshire Hathaway Inc. acquired the company in 1983 for $60 million.
Social Utility:	The company has created 500 jobs and Blumkin is a living testimonial to the finest qualities that entrepreneurship stands for.
Principal Source of Venture Capital:	$500 personal loan

ROSE BLUMKIN came to the Midwest from Russia in 1917 without a penny to her name. She has built an empire by hard work and by selling quality furniture at prices lower than the competition. The 91-year-old, 4-foot-10-inch czarina of Nebraska Furniture Mart moves through her 250,000 square feet of selling space on a motorized three-wheeled cart. She speaks with vendors, salespersons, and customers, making

[8]Frank E. James, "Furniture Czarina, Still a Live Wire at 90, A Retail Phenomenon Oversees Her Empire," *Wall Street Journal*, May 23, 1984, p. 1.

buy-sell-hold decisions as she buzzes around her store. In 1983 New York University (NYU) awarded Blumkin an honorary doctorate in commercial science, the first woman to be so honored.

When asked by *Wall Street Journal* reporter Frank E. James how the illiterate daughter of a poor rabbi should be thus awarded, Blumkin replied in broken English: "I'm born, thank God, with brains. In Russia you don't have no adding machine or nothing, so you have to use your head. So I always used it." Laurence Tisch, a member of NYU's board of trustees said: "She's more of a business leader than anyone we've ever honored before."[9] Other recipients of NYU's award include chief executive officers of Citicorp, Exxon Corporation, and General Motors Corporation.

Blumkin began in the basement of a pawnshop at the age of 43 with a borrowed $500. She had helped her husband run the pawnshop until 1950, renting shotguns and selling the miscellany that comes into pawnshops. When her husband died, Blumkin had to make her own way in the world. Where that might have crushed other single mothers, this single mother had faced far greater obstacles in her life. In 1917, she bribed her way past a Russian border guard, then came to America via China and Japan on a peanut boat. Her drive to succeed was an offshoot of her drive to be free. It seems that in the case of immigrants-turned-American-entrepreneurs, there is no such thing as being "too far" from the border guard.

Running hard and being smart is not sufficient to assure entrepreneurial success. Blumkin understands leverage. During the Korean War, she borrowed $50,000 for 90 days from a banker when she could not pay her suppliers. Blumkin was fearful that she would not be able to repay the banker. So she rented a hall and had a three-day sale which generated $250,000 in cash, enabling her to pay off the loan. Since then, Blumkin has dealt in cash, and achieved its leverage by shrewd and careful buying, giving attention to detail, and selling quality products at 20 to 30 percent below the prices of other retailers. Having all of the furniture under one roof has helped keep overhead down as well.

Her reason for selling to Warren Buffett's Berkshire Hathaway Inc. in 1983 for $60 million was to resolve her estate. Buffett trusts Blumkin so much that he bought the store without an audit. Buffett, whose entre-

[9]Ibid, p. 1.

preneurial achievements appear next, told the *Wall Street Journal*: "Put her up against the top graduates of the top business schools or chief executives of the Fortune 500 and, assuming an even start with the same resources, she'd run rings around them."[10] Someday when universities recognize entrepreneurship as more than a temporary aberration in economic history, Blumkin will be called back to the podium for more awards.

[10]Ibid, p. 1.

WARREN E. BUFFETT

Name of Company: Berkshire Hathaway Inc., See's Candy Shops, Inc. Blue Chip Stamps, Capital Cities Communications Inc. plus several banks, insurance companies, and newspapers

Date Acquired: 1965

Location: Buffett resides in Omaha, Nebraska; Berkshire Hathaway is located in New Bedford, Massachusetts.

Description of Business: Buffett acquired control of Berkshire Hathaway, a textile manufacturer with a long record of unprofitable operations in 1965, and installed new management. He has used Berkshire Hathaway as a source of cash to buy control of or make investments in other companies.

Description of P: Buffett believes that most businesses are poorly run and moreover require three rare commodities: capital, research, and management that works for the benefit of the stockholders. Venture capital propositions are even worse investments because most of them soon fail. Buffett seeks investments in "gross profits royalty" companies. These kinds of companies benefit from the large capital investments of the companies they serve, while requiring little capital of their own. Examples include TV stations, advertising agencies, and newspapers.

Description of S: The characteristics of America's most wonderful businesses according to Buffett are:
1. They have a high return on capital
2. They are understandable
3. Their profits are generated in cash
4. They have strong franchises and the freedom to raise prices

5. Their earnings are predictable
6. They are not natural targets of regulation
7. They have low inventories and high asset turnover ratios
8. They do not take a genius to run
9. The management is owner-oriented
10. The best business is a royalty on the growth of others, requiring little capital itself

Size of V: Employing these investment principles plus a keen sense of timing, Buffett has generated over $1 billion in valuation, most of which is owned by him, from a base of practically nothing within the last 20 years.

Members of E: Buffett works with a small staff

Social Utility: Assuming Berkshire Hathaway would have eventually folded, Buffett can be credited with having saved over 7,000 jobs.

Principal Source of Venture Capital: Personal savings

WARREN E. BUFFETT, 55, demonstrated a knack for making money as a teenager. He tells the following story, reported by John Train in *The Money Masters*:

When I was a kid at Woodrow Wilson High School in Washington, another kid and I started the Wilson Coin-Operated Machine Company. I was 15 years old. We put reconditioned pinball machines in barbershops. In Washington you were supposed to buy a tax stamp to be in the pinball machine business. I got the impression we were the only people who ever bought one. The first day we bought an old machine for $25 and put it out in a shop. When we came back that night it had $4 in it. I figured I had discovered the wheel. Eventually we were making $50 a week. I hadn't dreamed life could be so good. Before I got out of high school I bought myself an unimproved 40-acre farm in northeast Nebraska for $1,200.[11]

Buffett's father, Howard H., was a four-term conservative Republican congressman from Omaha who later became a stockbroker. He was a man of unusually high integrity, having once returned to the U.S. Treasury a $2,500 raise in pay. He was amused by young Warren's money-making activities, and hoped his son would become a member of the clergy. The young man was fascinated by the stock market and became hooked after reading *The Intelligent Investor* by Benjamin Graham. The following year he enrolled at Columbia University because Graham was teaching there. Buffett believed in working for the smartest person available, and he offered his services to Graham for nothing. After being rebuffed, Buffett returned to Omaha and kept in touch with Graham. In 1954 at the age of 24, Buffett was invited by Graham to come to New York, where he remained for two years analyzing hundreds of companies.

Benjamin Graham's investment philosophy involved finding and investing in companies that were selling for two-thirds of their working capital, and selling them again when they rose in value to 100 percent of their working capital. Although this philosophy was immensely successful for Graham, it was too mechanical for Buffett.

He returned to Omaha and started a family partnership with $100,000 capital. As manager, he received 25 percent of the profits above a 6 percent annual return on capital. He terminated the partnership in 1969 when it had grown to about $100 million in value because he wanted to be independent. Also, he had become fond of one of the partnership's principal investments, Berkshire Hathaway; and as its chairman, he wished to devote his time to building it.

And build it he did. Berkshire Hathaway's earnings have grown more than 20 percent per annum over the last 15 years. A lot of growth has come from capital gains on investments made by Buffett. He has selected primarily companies that have royalties on the sales of large corporations such as advertising agencies, Ogilvy & Mather International, Interpublic Group of Companies, TV station conglomerate Capital Cit-

[11]John Train, *The Money Masters* (New York: Harper & Row, 1980). p. 4.

ies Communications and a variety of big city newspaper publishers. Buffett told John Train that his favorite company is the *Wall Street Journal*. Train writes:

> Buffett considers the *Wall Street Journal* one of the most perfect business franchises, one you probably could not duplicate for a billion dollars. (Two others are *TV Guide* and the *Racing Form*, both apparently price-insensitive.) The most profitable publication in the country, the *Journal* offers a product for which many users would gladly pay double the price . . . . When a media executive asked a friend on the *Journal* why it did not tie its ad salesmen's compensation more closely to their productivity, the friend replied, "Why, the salesmen would just go across the street." The executive answered, "There ain't no *across the street* from the *Wall Street Journal*."[12]

At the risk of immodesty, how like the demonstrable economic justification (DEJ) factors is Buffett's dictum to invest in "gross profits royalties" companies. (The DEJ factors are described in Chapter 4.)

[12]Ibid., p. 26.

DONALD C. BURR

Name of Company:	People Express Airline, Inc.
Date Founded:	1980
Location:	Newark, New Jersey

Description of Business

The company is a low-fare airline operating primarily in the eastern United States; it offers passengers substantial fare discounts resulting from low labor costs and productive equipment scheduling.

Description of *P*:

Burr has created the fastest-growing airline in the history of aviation. By bringing fares down to the price of car or bus transportation, he has attracted new airline passengers. The company's 1984 revenues were over $450 million.

Description of *S*:

Cost reduction and waste rejection is a state of mind at this company. It puts more seats in a Boeing 737 than other airlines; by innovative scheduling it keeps planes in the air longer—10.4 hours per plane per day versus an industry average of 7.12 hours per day—and it cross-utilizes its employees; that is, no employee does the same job all of the time.

Members of *E*:

Robert J. McAdoo, chief financial officer; Hap J. Pareti, secretary; and William P. Hambrecht, director.

Size of *V*:

The approximately 24 million shares of common stock outstanding on a fully diluted basis traded in a range of $25⅞ to $9⅛ in 1984 for an average market value of $408 million.

Social Utility:

The company has created aproximately 4,000 new jobs.

Principal Sources of Venture Capital:

The entrepreneurial team plus the investment banking firm of Hambrecht & Quist and its clients

DONALD C. BURR, 43, has "designed a product which is so popular we can't satisfy the demand for it."[13] The product is a seat on an airplane that flies between Newark and some other major city, primarily in the eastern United States, but also Los Angeles, Minneapolis, Houston, and London, England. This may seem a bit unusual since major airlines like Eastern, Braniff, Frontier, and Western are sinking in red ink, Delta recently lost money for the first time in history, and Laker folded trying to carry passengers between New York and London. Burr's airline, People Express Airlines (PEA), has grown to sales of more than $450 million and earnings of over $12 million in 4 years. PEA has an average passenger load factor of 84 percent versus 60 percent for the airline industry. Because its operating costs are lower than any other carrier, PEA charges its passengers roughly 50 percent less than its competitors and is more profitable than many of them. Furthermore, at its current rate of growth, the company may be the first ever to achieve $1 billion in annual revenues within five years.

Born and raised in South Windsor, Connecticut, Burr developed an early love for airplanes. Every Sunday he cajoled his parents into driving him to the Hartford airport where he would remain mesmerized for hours. He was also fascinated by business. While other boys would fantasize about baseball, Burr would wonder how the local merchants ran their stores.

Upon graduating from Harvard Business School in 1965, Burr became a securities analyst for National Aviation Corporation, a closed-end investment company that specializes in aerospace industry securities. Six years later at age 31 he became president of the company and completely knowledgeable about the financial aspects of managing an airline.

Texas International, a regional carrier in serious financial straits, approached Burr to bail it out. He did so with a low-fare idea called "peanut fares," which increased traffic and brought the company back into the black. In June 1979 Texas International made Burr its president. Six months later he resigned.

Congress had passed the Airline Deregulation Act of 1978 which freed existing airlines to compete aggressively in route selection and pricing, and encouraged new entrants. Burr sensed the end of 40 years

[13]Lucien Rhodes, "That Daring Young Man and His Flying Machines," *Inc.*, January, 1984, p. 42.

of regulation as the moment for him to accept a new challenge. He was dissatisfied with the way corporations dehumanized employees and wanted to elevate workers, train them to do meaningful functions, and reward them with equity in their own company. Burr's challenge was to launch a new airline and incorporate his ideas for creating a loyal, intelligent, wealthy group of employees. Texas International's senior vice-president of planning, Gerald L. Gitner, and Burr's executive assistant, Melrose Dawsey, resigned one day after Burr, and they moved into an office in Houston to conceive the idea for what would become PEA. One year later, after the three co-founders drained their savings to come up with $545,000, PEA became the first company to apply to the Civil Aeronautics Board (CAB) for permission to form a new airline. The application cited a plan to raise $5 million and to lease three planes that would operate out of Newark International Airport. The general manager of Newark had heard the same story many times since deregulation, but did not believe any of them. Bill Hambrecht believed Burr, and the esteemed judge of entrepreneurial horseflesh handed Burr $24 million in venture capital, raised from the public market, in October 1980. Neither has regretted the transaction, nor have the stockholders who are flying about as high as PEA airplanes.

RONALD E. CAPE

Name of Company: Cetus Corporation

Date Founded: 1971

Location: Emeryville, California

Description of Business: The company develops commercial products through genetic engineering. Areas of interest include human health care, immunology, and agriculture.

Description of *P*: This is a "big-*P*" company; that is, it has convinced the investment community and its corporate investors that through its research activities in genetic engineering, it will develop solutions to fatal diseases and world hunger. The company achieved something of a record in 1981: the biggest initial public stock offering, some $115 million.

Description of *S*: Cetus's revenues of $18.5 million are largely from research contracts. The corporations that have purchased Cetus stock along the way, and the rights to the fruits of specific research projects, include Chevron Corporation, Amoco Corporation, National Distillers and Chemical Corporation, Weyerhauser Company, W. R. Grace & Company, and Nabisco Brands, Inc. The company has very artfully "sold the problem."

Members of *E*: Co-founder Peter Farley, M.D., who resigned in 1983; and Donald Glaser, a biologist and Nobel laureate.

Size of *V*: The just over 22 million shares of common stock outstanding traded in a range of $19 to $10½ in 1984 for an average valuation of $330 million.

Social Utility: The utility of Cetus and similar genetic engineering companies is in the future. If they can effectively treat disease genetically and identify crops that can be grown in the Sudanese desert, their names will be blessed by millions.

Principal Sources of Venture Capital: Chevron Corporation invested $14 million for 20 percent ($70 million valuation) in 1978, followed by three other corporations; then the public invested $115 million in 1981; in 1983, $75 million was raised via a research and development limited partnership.

RONALD E. CAPE, 51, has raised more capital from corporate venturers, the public stock market, and tax shelter-oriented investors by selling the "problem" than any other entrepreneur in recent memory. The problems are cancer and hunger. The solutions, to hear Cape and other genetic engineering entrepreneurs talk, lie with recombinant DNA; with the ability to transfer DNA from one form of life to another, making it possible to produce in great quantities substances whose natural availability is very limited.

Human insulin produced through genetic engineering is already on the market; the Food and Drug Administration is expected to approve a genetically engineered growth hormone within the next two years. In the works are vaccines against hepatitis and herpes. What the market is looking for, hoping for, are effective substances for treating cancer and heart disease, and for genetically engineered seeds that will permit food to grow in desert lands.

To solve these multibillion-dollar problems requires millions of dollars of capital to pay for scientific research. Those dollars are attracted by painting a picture of a disease-free world, as Cape recently described to a visitor:

This is our interferon pilot unit. In this one vessel we can make ten thousand patient-doses of interferon overnight. We take a human gene, stick it into a bacterium and say: "Do it!" And the project is real human interferon, not a close animal relative to it. Interferon is a hot prospect for the treatment of cancer, and possibly for other "autoimmune" diseases—diseases in which your body's

EXHIBIT 6.1.   Capital Raised by Ronald Cape

Year	Approximate Amount Raised	Investor	Post Financing Valuation
1973	$2,000,000	Venture capitalists	$10,000,000
1974	3,000,000	Venture capitalists	37,500,000
1977	5,000,000	Amoco	17,800,000
1978	14,000,000	Chevron	70,000,000
1979	14,000,000	National Distillers	70,000,000
1981	115,000,000	Public Market	500,000,000
1983	75,000,000	R & D Ltd. Partnership	
	$228,000,000		

own chemicals are destroying you: muscular dystrophy, maybe multiple sclerosis, probably rheumatoid arthritis . . . Tay-Sachs disease and sickle-cell anemia . . . . Almost everything that kills people except heart attacks and car accidents potentially can be attacked by these methods.[14]

That is hard selling, but quite effective. The speaker, Ron Cape, was born in Canada and earned an A.B. degree *summa cum laude* in chemistry from Princeton University in 1953, and an MBA degree from Harvard University with distinction in 1955. After working for Merck & Company (1955–1956), Professional Pharmaceutical Corporation, and his family's Montreal cosmetics business, Cape saw a research study about DNA and enrolled in McGill University, which awarded him a Ph.D. in biochemistry in 1967. Cape then moved to the University of California at Berkeley to further his studies in molecular biology, whereupon he met Dr. Peter Farley and they launched Cetus Corporation. Its purpose then as now is "the innovative use of microorganisms in the profitable production of materials to fill human needs."

Although Cetus has thus far not delivered solutions, Cape has been a terrific raiser of capital. Look at the statistics in Exhibit 6.1.

[14]Gerard K. O'Neill, *The Technology Edge: Opportunities for America in World Competition* (New York: Simon & Schuster, 1983).

To have raised $228 million on the strength of pulling together a team of brilliant scientists to address a variety of genetic engineering solutions is a monumental achievement. As the best-financed biotechnology company, the market expects a great deal from Cetus Corporation.

CURTIS L. CARLSON

Name of Company:	Carlson Companies, Inc.
Date Founded:	1938
Location:	Plymouth, Minnesota

Description of
Business:

The company owns and operates restaurants and hotels as well as a trading stamp business and other operations.

Description of *P*:

Curt Carlson is a one-man conglomerate with primary interests in Gold Bond trading stamps, food wholesaling, sports equipment, construction and interior design, catalog showroom selling, jewelry manufacturing, and home building. His initial entrepreneurial success was with Gold Bond trading stamps, known as the incentive business. It began when Carlson sold a book of stamps to a grocer for $14.50, which his customer later redeemed from Carlson for $10 worth of merchandise. Carlson's profit was the spread, plus the float on the $14.50. When the stamp boom began to fade in the 1960's Carlson diversified into hotels (The Radisson), restaurants (Country Kitchen, TGI Fridays), and other interests. Annual sales exceed $2 billion.

Description of *S*:

It is rare for an individual to launch a company and manage it successfully into the ranks of the 100 largest corporations in America. It is rarer still to accomplish this sublime goal without accessing the public markets. Carlson attributes his success largely to respect for people. He motivates his managers and employees with goals and blue ribbons. As for his customers, Carlson says: "Only as long as a company can produce a desired, worthwhile, and needed product or service, and can command public respect, will it receive the public dollar and succeed."[15] Homilies maybe, but the track record says it's fact, not fiction. There are 75 different businesses within the Carlson Companies, all commanding "public respect."

Members of E: Co-founder Truman Johnson was bought out in 1958; likely successor to Carlson is son-in-law Edwin C. Gage.

Size of V: As a privately held company, valuation data is unavailable. Reasonable estimate: $500 million.

Social Utility: Carlson Companies employ 30,000 people. Carlson is a personal inspiration to thousands of entrepreneurs.

Principal Sources of Venture Capital: Carlson delayed his rent for one month and invested the $50 in Gold Bond stamps.

CURTIS LEROY CARLSON was born in Minneapolis in 1914, the third of five children of Letha and Charles Carlson. The elder Carlson emigrated from Sweden and worked for grocery wholesalers for several years until he opened his own small self-serve grocery store.

From early on, Carlson remembers, "I was always very independent, and I was always thinking of ways I could earn money." He ran as many as three paper routes at one time, caddied at the local golf course and worked as a bellhop. "When you don't have any money," he says, "and then can put $15 a month in your pocket, you realize it's a whole new world. All my life I knew that there was all the money you could want out there. All you have to do is go after it."[16]

Carlson entered the University of Minnesota in 1933, earning his tuition through his paper routes and by selling advertising on the college bulletin boards to local retailers. In 1937, he received a degree in economics.

For the first time since the start of the Depression, job recruiters began appearing on campus, and Carlson signed on as a salesperson with

[15]Curtis L. Carlson, "Personal Business Philosophy" (Press Release).
[16]Mary Granius, "$1 Billion is Not Enough," *Success Unlimited*, 1979, p. 4.

Procter & Gamble Company (P&G) at $110 a month. His territory included the small grocers in the Minneapolis area.

The job was anything but glamorous. Merchandising tactics of the day were aggressive: his sales manager told him that if he were not thrown out of at least one store a week, he was not doing his job. Carlson became the top salesperson in his district during the first six months, and he eventually rose to become one of the top two producers nationally. His sales manager assured him that his future with the company was bright.

Quite by accident, Carlson spotted his opportunity and bolted from P&G in 1938 to begin an entrepreneurial period. While selling P&G's soap to grocery stores, Carlson noticed that any incentive—two for one or a cents-off deal—increased sales. At that time only department stores gave trading stamps. Carlson saw that they did not fit. If a customer wanted *that* suit or *this* pair of shoes, stamps would not influence the purchase. But why not try them in grocery stores? As Carlson says, "They sell identical items, all known brands. So if everything else is equal, the one giving stamps will have an advantage."[17]

He was absolutely correct, but his Gold Bond Stamp Company, launched that year, needed perseverance and Carlson's persuasive powers to succeed, because it did not have any capital. The customers were being asked to provide that.

He chose the name "Gold Bond" for an interesting reason. "If you have funds to advertise," Carlson told *Success* magazine, "you should pick an unusual name or coin a name—such as Lux for soap—so, through your advertising, people will always identify the name with your product. But if you have no funds to advertise, as in my case, you should pick a name that will itself inspire the buyer to think what you want him to think about your product."[18] Because he had no money, Carlson drew up his own incorporation papers and tried to persuade mom-and-pop grocers that they could combat the giant chains with trading stamps. Carlson's wife, Arleen, donned a drum majorette's costume and worked the floor of the local groceries. Still the grocers refused to see him or chased him out.

Carlson would not allow himself to become discouraged. "You've

[17]Maurice Barnfather, "Capital Formation," *Forbes*, March 29, 1982, p. 95.
[18]Granius, *Success Unlimited*, p. 5.

got to be success-minded. You've got to feel that things are coming your way when you're out selling; otherwise, you won't be able to sell anything."[19]

Carlson also has some important thoughts on avoiding discouragement. "A salesman must also have flexible goals. You may say, 'I want to sell 10 accounts this week,' and you sell five. You're ready to die. But you tell yourself, 'Five isn't too bad. You know, next week maybe I'll sell 10.'"[20]

Within three years after launching Gold Bond, Carlson had 200 accounts. Then World War II shortages set the company back for nearly 10 years. Carlson took a part-time job to feed his family. By 1952 Gold Bond landed its first national chain, Super Valu Stores, and Carlson did $2.4 million in sales. By 1960 all but 1 of the 20 largest supermarket chains gave stamps, and Gold Bond was the third largest in the business. Shrewdly, Carlson realized that the business had peaked and he began diversifying into hotels, restaurants, and other services.

For Curt Carlson, the preeminent goal-setter and motivator, goals are not exactly what one might think. He says: "I consider a goal as a journey rather than a destination. And each year I set a new goal."[21]

[19]Ibid.
[20]Ibid.
[21]Curtis L. Carlson, "Personal Business Philosophy" (Press Release).

FRANK L. CARNEY

Name of Company:	Pizza Hut, Inc.
Date Founded:	1958
Location:	Wichita, Kansas
Description of Business:	The company operates the world's largest chain of pizza restaurants.
Description of P:	Carney rode the crest of a long wave of World War II baby boomers who wanted a quick meal, nice atmosphere, and moderate prices. In the 1960s and 1970s he gave them pizza. In the 1980s with his second venture, Chi-Chi's, Carney is giving them a family-style restaurant serving Mexican food and alcoholic beverages.
Description of S:	Carney has the ability to observe demographic shifts in the eating habits of the largest segment of the American public and to cater to that need. He is currently thinking of a chain of quality cafeterias serving bland food to serve the baby boomers as they grow older.
Members of E:	Daniel Carney, co-founder and chief operating officer, who is Frank Carney's older brother.
Size of V:	Pizza Hut was acquired by PepsiCo in 1977 for $300 million. Chi-Chi's has approximately 26 million shares outstanding and its common stock traded between $29 and $14 per share in 1984 for an average valuation of $550 million.
Social Utility:	Pizza Hut has created 70,000 jobs and Chi-Chi's, 14,000. Approximately 150 Pizza Hut franchisees sold their restaurants back to the parent and became significant stockholders; the same thing is occurring with Chi-Chi's.
Principal Source of Venture Capital:	Family and friends invested the seed capital, but the principal investors were the franchisees.

FRANK L. CARNEY opened his first Pizza Hut restaurant in 1958 as a University of Wichita freshman because he needed money for tuition. He and his brother, Dan, opened the business in a tiny brick building across the street from the family's grocery store where Frank was making $16 per week. Nineteen years later, Pizza Hut had become the largest pizza chain in the world with 3,100 outlets. PepsiCo acquired it for $300 million and Carney joined PepsiCo's board. He headed up their food services division until 1980, spearheading the acquisition of Taco Bell, the nation's largest Mexican fast-food chain. Carney left PepsiCo that year and bought the mid-Atlantic franchise for Chi-Chi's. Within two years, Carney had opened eight Chi-Chi's and had three under construction; sales were $26 million. Chi-Chi's bought out Carney and his partners for 396,000 shares of stock worth $7.8 million. Carney joined Chi-Chi's board.

Classical franchising in its most elegant form is Carney's principal achievement. He, perhaps more than any other entrepreneur, executed the most classically perfect use of the financial leverage that franchising can generate. Many franchise entrepreneurs fail because they use franchising as an operating method. Carney understood franchising as an excellent and efficient means of raising cash from customers.

Carney generated cash by selling franchises and collecting the franchise fees. When earnings were attractive in 1969, Pizza Hut went public and the proceeds were used to purchase about 40 percent of the franchisees, increasing company-owned units from 12 to 129 at the time. A broad-based management structure was created along with a system for financial controls that could monitor the revenues and expenses of each store on a weekly basis. Then the company entered a period of managed growth to the 3,100 store level. It responded to competition from regional pizza chains by experimenting with menu changes, finally settling on thick, Chicago-style pan pizza, which now accounts for 55 percent of Pizza Hut's sales.

When Carney left PepsiCo to become a Chi-Chi's franchisee, he left the security of a large company for the uncertainty of entrepreneurship. Having made various venture capital investments (a 14 percent interest in Scandia Down Corporation, a 45 percent stake in Carbo Company, and a 14 percent stake in Classic Corporation, among others) and having guaranteed $10 million of loans to open his Chi-Chi's restaurants, Carney bet quite a few of his chips to see the dealer's next card. Naturally, since Carney knows fast-food as well as anyone, he won.

In his leisure time, 46-year-old Carney is a professional sports car racer on the national circuit. He enters his 2.5 liter Datsun 280ZX in about 15 rallies a year. In between races, Carney is launching a new ethnic food chain in Kansas City, Pastificio, which means pasta factory in Italian.

ALEXANDER V. d'ARBELOFF
NICHOLAS DeWOLF

Name of Company: Teradyne, Inc.

Date Founded: 1960

Location: Boston, Massachusetts

Description of   The company is a leading manufacturer of auto-
Business: matic test equipment for the semiconductor,
                    printed circuit board, and telecommunications
                    industries.

Description of *P*: d'Arbeloff, and his co-founder, Nick DeWolf, un-
                    derstood well the needs of engineers in the fledg-
                    ling semiconductor industry. Their biggest need
                    was to test the reliability of the systems they were
                    building.

Description of *S*: "What the customer demands is last year's model,
                    cheaper," DeWolf told *Electronic News*. "To find
                    out what the customer needs you have to under-
                    stand what the customer is doing as well as *he* un-
                    derstands it. Then you build what he needs and
                    you educate him to the fact that he needs it."[22]

Members of *E*:   Nick DeWolf, co-founder, plus members of man-
                    agement, Windsor H. Hunter, Lennart B. Johnson,
                    Joseph B. Lassiter III, Dennis P. O'Donnell, and
                    James A. Prestridge

Size of *V*:   The approximately 22 million shares of Teradyne
                    common stock outstanding traded in a range of
                    $21¼ to $39⅜ in 1984 for an average valuation of
                    $666 million.

Social Utility: Teradyne has created 2,450 jobs in the Boston
                    area.

---

[22]*Electronic News*, August 1974.

Principal Sources
of Venture
Capital: d'Arbeloff and DeWolf each contributed $25,000 and one of Boston's oldest venture capital funds, Greylock & Company, invested $250,000.

ALEXANDER V. d'ARBELOFF and NICHOLAS DeWOLF started Teradyne in a loft over a hotdog stand in downtown Boston because they wanted to be able to walk to work. It was 1960 and both men were 32 years old. DeWolf walked away from a top engineering job at Transitron to find a partner who could help him build a company.

Eleven years later, after he and d'Arbeloff had "fought" Teradyne into existence, pushing it to the top in an industry that barely existed before they began, Nick DeWolf walked away again. He plunged into the jungles of Asia with his camera, spending six months taking 35,000 pictures before returning to the states to pursue still newer ventures. Teradyne had become too big to afford a president like Nick DeWolf, who preferred working alone in the lab to lunching with Wall Streeters.

Teradyne has probably sold more computer-controlled systems for testing electronic components than all of its competitors combined. Last year, the firm increased its net income nearly 500 percent, from $4.3 million to $21.4 million, on sales that nearly doubled, from $176 million to $251 million. In short, the company has come a long way from its days over the hotdog stand.

Nick DeWolf had almost become a legend in the young semiconductor industry as engineering director at Transitron in Wakefield. He was famous for his applications work with germanium diodes and other components, and he and Transitron prospered. But with that prosperity came a sense of security that bored DeWolf.

He decided to start his own company, and quit Transitron before he knew what he wanted his company to do. He began looking for a partner. DeWolf and d'Arbeloff first met when they lined up alphabetically in an ROTC class at Massachusetts Institute of Technology, in the late 1940s. After graduation, the two men went their separate ways and met again some 10 years later.

d'Arbeloff had held three jobs in the four years before he and DeWolf began discussing a possible business partnership. d'Arbeloff had become disenchanted with the climbing of corporate ladders and had an itch to start *his* own company.

The two men sat down in DeWolf's living room in the fall of 1960 to draw plans for their new venture. First they chose the company name. "It had to have a 'D' in it," DeWolf says. "'Tera' is the prefix for 10 to the 12th power and 'dyne' is a unit of force. To us, the name meant rolling a 15,000-ton boulder uphill."[23]

With a total of about $250,000, including $25,000 each of their own money, DeWolf and d'Arbeloff opened Teradyne's doors officially early in 1961, on the floor above Joe & Nemo's hotdog stand at the corner of Kingston and Summer streets. DeWolf recalls,

We blew our bankroll on our first product, a "go/no-go" diode tester, and we took it around to five or six guys who could buy it and put on a song and dance act to show off our wonderful toy.

Three of these guys, who were really good friends in this club of diode makers I had belonged to at Transitron, took me aside after their companies had formally refused to buy a tester and told me we had failed and that they felt sorry for me. That's a pretty low point. When your *friends* not only say "no," they say "no" and "we feel *sorry* for you."[24]

By the end of the first year, Teradyne had nine employees who had accounted for the sale of one $5,000 diode tester, finally, to Raytheon Semiconductor. Things looked brighter by the end of 1962. The company employed 20 people and shipped 19 testers. By 1963 Teradyne had 35 people, who shipped 59 testers worth more than $431,000.

"Two years after we started peddling that first diode tester we couldn't make enough of the very same machine for those very same people who had told us we had failed," gloats DeWolf.[25]

In the early 1960s, few sophisticated testing machines were operating on factory floors. Production testers were typically slow to operate and limited in the tests they could perform. "The sophisticated test instruments were in the hands of the mad scientist in the laboratory," DeWolf says. "Our machine was designed to be used at the heart of the

[23]John Day, "Teradyne: The House That Nick and Alex Built," *The New Englander*, Nov. 1974.
[24]Ibid.
[25]Ibid.

production process. When we started, the electronics industry had factories with hand-operated test equipment and labs with glamorous equipment. We were putting glamorous equipment in the factories."[26]

While DeWolf was designing, d'Arbeloff says he was "laying out printed circuit boards, chasing after parts, and getting products out the door." Both men were learning how to run their own business from the ground up. "When you start a company," d'Arbeloff says, "there's no mail. There are no telephone calls. You don't even know how to get the trash out. You want to ship some parts back, and they just sit on the desk until you find a box and some brown paper and string."

d'Arbeloff says starting a company is like getting a square wheel rolling. "Nothing happens unless you push it, and when you've pushed it, nothing happens unless you push it again and you keep on pushing until the corners begin to chip off."[27]

DeWolf and d'Arbeloff and their small group of employees kept pushing, and Teradyne doubled its sales volume for six of its first 10 years. The company acquired more and more room over Joe & Nemo's.

The semiconductor industry recession pummelled Teradyne as it did other companies. d'Arbeloff and DeWolf laid off 100 employees and survived by going back to the drawing board to come up with special niche products. When Teradyne pulled out of its slump, DeWolf resigned. "I'm a sleeves-rolled-up-guy," he told *Electronic News*. "And I had become pretty much a figurehead."

d'Arbeloff has built a management structure that has carried the company to six times the size it was when DeWolf left. The 56-year-old co-founders remain friends and both have prospered by the company's growth.

[26]Ibid.
[27]Ibid.

CECIL B. DAY
RICHARD C. KESSLER

Name of Company:	Days Inns of America, Inc.
Date Founded:	1970
Location:	Atlanta, Georgia
Description of Business:	The company owns and operates a chain of 320 budget motels located primarily in the southeastern United States.
Description of *P*:	Day saw an opportunity to capture a sizable portion of the lodging market by offering rooms that looked like Holiday Inns, at a 30 percent lower price. His target customers included retired people, business and government travelers with small expense accounts, and families.
Description of *S*:	Kessler executed the plan. Days Inns have very little wasted space—there are no meeting rooms, lobbies, or bars. The buildings are standardized and personnel do several jobs. Kessler's attention to detail is legendary. Revenues for 1984 were approximately $270 million.
Members of *E*:	Kenneth Niemann, chief financial officer
Size of *V*:	The company is privately held; it has an estimated current valuation of approximately $180 million using standard valuation techniques.
Social Utility:	The company has created 6,032 jobs.
Principal Sources of Venture Capital:	Day sold an apartment building in Atlanta for $350,000 to finance the first Days Inn.

RICHARD KESSLER was 23 years old when he became CECIL B. DAY's personal assistant for $9,000 per year just as Days Inns of America, Inc. began. Cecil Day's father was a Baptist minister in a little town near Savannah, Georgia, where Kessler grew up. The two families had known each other for years. At Day's suggestion, Kessler studied industrial engineering at Georgia Institute of Technology. During summer vacations he trained for a future in real estate development by building duplexes and gas stations with financing provided in the beginning by his father, a plumbing contractor. When he graduated, Kessler joined Day "so he could teach me the business." Day did just that until he died of cancer in 1978.

After the first Days Inn was built in Savannah, Kessler looked for a second location in Florida. Kessler says, "In 1972 I took a trip to Orlando and I felt the potential of what Disney World was going to do. I came back to Cecil and said, 'Somebody needs to go to Florida and set up an office and just build Days Inns, because it's coming.'"[28] Kessler's enthusiasm has frequently been likened to that of a revival preacher.

Day sent Kessler to Orlando at age 25, agreeing to give him 30 percent of the equity in each motel he built. As Kessler hired more people for these ventures, Day gave up still more equity. The system worked so well that Kessler was soon traveling up and down the east coast setting up similar teams whose real estate companies would build motels and lease them back to Days Inns, the operating company.

In 1974 Day was in Texas most of the time opening motels, Kessler was on the eastern seaboard opening motels, and the nation was plunged into a deep recession. Days Inns of America had $20 million in assets, $19 million in debt, and only $100,000 in cash. Kenneth Neimann, who joined the company at that time as its first professional controller, described the picture back at headquarters: "We didn't know how much money we had in the banks. We didn't even know which banks it was in. There were no controls. Even the reservations system—it was on a blackboard, with the people who had good eyesight sitting in the back of the room and the people with bad eyesight in the front." Day called Kessler back to Atlanta promising to make him chairman and president if he cleaned the mess up. "Things were real loose," relates Kessler.[29]

Nonetheless, Kessler saw an opportunity to buy properties cheaply

[28]Jane Carmichael, "I can see it coming," Forbes, May 10, 1982, p. 84.
[29]Ibid, p. 84.

in the pit of the recession. He and Day put up all their motels as collateral and personally guaranteed bank loans to buy $18 million worth of almost-new motels, including two Holiday Inns and a Sheraton in Florida. The gamble doubled Days Inns of America's asset size. The chain became one of the most profitable in the country. Its pretax margin per property is 50 percent greater than for Holiday Inns or Sheraton Corporation, according to Laventhol & Horwath, an accounting firm that specializes in the lodging industry.

The Days Inns of America business plan calls for Holiday Inn-like rooms at 30 percent below Holiday Inns' prices coupled with a fanatical attention to costs. All buildings are standardized so materials can be purchased in bulk. The architect's fee for a Days Inn motel is equal to that for two rooms at a Sheraton. The Day Break restaurants next to the motels are freestanding in order to attract local customers. All tables can be served from behind the counter. The breakfast waitress at the Day Break is the same one who cleans rooms at the motel four hours later.

There is something of People Express Airlines at Days Inns: Offer high quality and convenience at a budget price and the revenues and profits scoreboards will light up time after time.

C. NORMAN DION

Name of Company: Dysan Corporation

Date Founded: 1973

Location: Santa Clara, California

Description of Business: The company develops, produces, and markets rigid and floppy discs used as memory storage in computer systems. It also makes venture capital investments.

Description of *P*: Dion is a double problem-solver. First he identified a need for rigid and floppy magnetic data storage media, which products have become ubiquitous commodity products. To hold onto valuable employees and to create customers and vendors for Dysan's rigid and floppy discs, Dion launched a second venture: providing seed capital in the form of Dysan's cash flow to launch new businesses.

Description of *S*: The company is among the industry leaders in the manufacture of rigid discs storing up to 300 megabytes and 3¼-inch and 5¼-inch floppy discs used in personal computers. Its revenues in 1984 were in excess of $214 million.

Members of *E*: William L. Harry, president; George L. Farinsky, chief financial officer

Size of *V*: The approximately 17 million shares of common stock outstanding ranged from $25 to $5¼ in 1984, for an average market value of $250 million. The company merged with Xidex in early 1985, a move which will strengthen its market position against invasion by giants such as Eastman Kodak.

Social Utility: The company has created approximately 3,500 jobs, and the affiliates launched by the company have created an additional 2,000 jobs.

| Principal Sources of Venture Capital: | Initially personal savings; subsequently Rhone-Poulenc, a French manufacturer of chemicals provided $2.5 million for 20 percent of the company. |

C. NORMAN DION, 53, removed himself from the day-to-day management of Dysan Corporation several years ago in order to play the role of seed capitalist to new entrepreneurs, many of whom were Dysan employees. "You can have a lot of fun making people rich," Dion says.[30] And in so doing, Dysan has made as much as $75 million in capital gains on one investment alone—Seagate Technology Corporation, a Winchester disc drive manufacturer that Dion seeded in 1979 with $500,000 for 48 percent ownership.

Whereas a venture capitalist will typically take two out of the five risks of a start-up company, the seed capitalist will take four of the risks. In exchange for more risk, the seed capitalist buys more cheaply. The comparison is shown in Exhibit 6.2.

Within months after Dion's investment in Seagate, valued at $1 million, Oak Investment Partners, a venture capital fund, witnessed a demonstration of the product, and anted up $2 million for 20 percent, raising the valuation of Seagate's stock to $10 million. Nine months later, Seagate went public selling 20 percent of its common stock for $40 million, and the public market quickly bid those shares to $160 million, making Dysan's $500,000 investment worth more than $100 million, after selling half its holdings for $55 million. In early 1985, Dysan sold an 8 percent interest in Brown Disc, Colorado Springs, Colorado, and 45 percent of DyPy S.A., a French disc manufacturer for $23.4 million. Further, Dysan has been expensing its investments on its operating statement as research and development, a clever use of leverage.

Dion has enjoyed the various roles he has played throughout his interesting life. Born and raised on a chicken farm in Fall River, Massachusetts, Dion abandoned farming when he discovered engineering during the Korean War. He then earned a degree in engineering from Southeastern Massachusetts University in 1959 and joined International Business Machines Development Laboratory in Poughkeepsie, New York. IBM transferred Dion to San Jose in 1963 to solve problems

[30]Roger Neal, "Millionaire Maker," Forbes, September 12, 1983, p. 172.

EXHIBIT 6.2.   The Five Risks of Investing in Start-ups

	Usually Taken By
1. Can the product or service be developed?	Seed capitalist
2. If developed can it be produced?	Seed capitalist
3. If produced can it be marketed?	Seed, venture capitalist
4. If marketed can the company be managed profitably?	Seed, venture capitalist
5. If managed profitably can the company be grown?	Public investor

with its information mass storage device. "It was an incredible training ground," Dion says. "I was so happy at IBM I guess I stayed longer than I had expected."[31]

Dion left in 1967 for Memorex Corporation where he developed the equipment that gave Memorex its entry into disc pack manufacturing. After making Memorex into the industry leader in memory storage, Dion left in 1973 to launch Dysan.

Whereas much of Dion's business career has been based on fundamentals, planning and manufacturing skills, in his new role as a seed capitalist, Dion is gambling on risks that, although he knows a great deal about, he may not be able to control. But seed capital is scarce and Dion's 18 individual investments are related to businesses that he knows or involve entrepreneurs who have worked for him. That is an intelligent way to play the riskiest of all investment games.

[31]C. Norman Dion, "Biography," p. 23 (Press Release).

RICHARD DOTTS

Name of Company:	Pedus International, Inc.
Date Founded:	1979
Location:	Los Angeles, California
Description of Business:	The company provides cleaning, maintenance, and security personnel for office buildings in the West and Southwest.
Description of *P*:	The cleaning and security business had concentrated in several large diversified corporations. The customer was not well served and middle managers were increasingly frustrated because their pleas about delivering high-quality service for a reasonable price were unheeded. Dick Dotts felt trapped. But he had an idea for "collecting entrepreneurs" in the cleaning and security field, eliminating the bureaucracy and memo writing, and delivering quality services to the customer. In five years, Pedus has grown to sales of $70 million.
Description of *S*:	Dotts's plan was to acquire small cleaning, janitorial, and security businesses, and divisions of conglomerates located in the West and Southwest, particularly those with strong management. He created incentive compensation systems for the management and gave them lots of autonomy. He bought the first company in 1979 for $85,000, a guard service company. This was followed by a cleaning company. He introduced the first company to the second company's customers and vice-versa. He repeated this formula, expanding revenues and profits thereby.
Members of *E*:	Peter Dussman, co-founder and principal investor; Tim Gilmore; and Harold Shapiro

Size of V:	Pedus is a privately held company. Applying conventional financial ratios, the company's current market value is probably around $35 million.
Social Utility:	The company employs 10,000 people. Introducing entrepreneurial flexibility to a straitjacketed industry has been instructive to other potential service industry entrepreneurs.
Principal Sources of Venture Capital:	Peter Dussman, a Munich entrepreneur, who parlayed a janitor's job into a large European janitorial company, invested $200,000.

RICHARD DOTTS was convinced he should have been promoted to the presidency of the $36 million (revenues) security and cleaning subsidiary of The Bekins Company in 1979. After all, he had served them well for 10 years. But he was passed over, which brought to mind earlier disappointments while he put in five years learning the business at Pacific Telephone Company. So, he left Bekins Company in 1979 and wrote a business plan which outlined a strategy for building a West Coast labor services company. Dotts showed his plan to Peter Dussman, a Munich entrepreneur seeking a U.S. investment in the janitorial and guard services field, who struck a deal with Dotts within an hour. Reportedly Dussman said to Dotts as he handed him $200,000, "I'll plant the first tree, you grow the forest."[32]

Dotts acquired a 63-person security company for $85,000, asked his wife to join him as bookkeeper, and set up an office on Wilshire Boulevard. He spent a lot of time with his customers discussing their needs and determining which additional services he could sell to them. Dotts bought four more smaller companies, cross-fertilizing customer needs with his newly acquired solutions.

In 1980 Pedus International acquired the $12 million (sales) Los Angeles operation of New York-based National Cleaning Contractors and two years later, Pedus International purchased Dotts's former employer, Bekins. Like so many entrepreneurs, the only way Dotts was ever going to be the president was to start a business.

[32]Curtis Hartman, "The Cleanup Crew," *Inc.*, December 1984, p. 62.

Dotts problem formulated brilliantly. He determined correctly that managers of security and janitorial businesses were in over their heads with responsibilities. As Dotts told an *Inc.* reporter: "With most of them, their size has outstripped both their management skills and their resources. By my assuming some of those burdens, they're back in the hunt. They can concentrate on doing what they enjoy doing—building a business."[33]

With every acquisition, Dotts was buying managers and giving them back their entrepreneurial spirit. He designed incentive programs which they love, removed management and financial worries, and they gave Dotts their hearts and drives. The people he acquired shared Dotts's feeling for customer service and his pride in delivering quality work. Dotts eliminated committees, insisted on everyone being on a first name basis, and gave his managers autonomy.

At this stage in its growth, Pedus International is *Inc.*'s fastest growing privately held company in the United States. At 41, Dotts is stopping to catch his breath before enlarging his forest beyond $100 million in sales by 1986.

[33]Ibid, p.62.

WILLIAM FRANCIS FARLEY

Name of Company:	Farley Industries, Inc.
Date Founded:	1976
Location:	Chicago, Illinois

Description of Business: In April 1985 Farley and Ben W. Heinneman, reached an agreement wherein Heinneman would sell Northwest Industries to Farley for $1.5 billion via a leveraged buyout. This conglomerate of essentially manufacturing companies is one of the largest privately held companies in the country.

Description of P: The leveraged buy-out is one of the most effective ways to bring new energetic management into tired old manufacturing companies. An entrepreneur identifies a company with fully depreciated assets, excessive employees, and other expenses, and borrows on the reappraised assets to buy the company. Frequently, management of the purchased company is cut in on the equity and they redouble their energies and enthusiasm.

Description of S: Farley learned the tools and mechanics of leveraged buy-outs while at an investment banking firm on Wall Street. He bought his first company with no personal cash investment, while employed by another. Dozens of people do this every month now, but in 1976, Farley's coup was unique and elegant.

Members of E: William Hall, chief operating officer, Kevin Moore, vice-president acquisitions and mergers, William Vrba, vice-president finance.

Size of V: *Forbes* places the valuation of Farley Industries at more than $150 million.[34]

---

[34]"The Richest People in America, the Forbes Four Hundred," *Forbes*, Fall 1983.

Social Utility: Farley has revitalized seven tired companies and
                         increased employment by 8,000.

Principal Sources   Farley's personal guarantee on bank financing
of Venture
Capital:

WILLIAM F. FARLEY was part of the syndicate that bought the Chicago White Sox in 1980. Entrepreneurs love baseball because of its open-endedness and optimism. Farley has had an open-ended entrepreneurial career, and at 42 is one of the most successful leveraged buyout people in the country. He has not engaged in "greenmail" tactics either. When he buys them, he grows them.

Take his first purchase, Anaheim Citrus Products, which he bought for $1.7 million in 1974 while working at Lehman Brothers. The purchase was 100 percent financed in 1974 when interest rates were in excess of 18 percent for this kind of financing. Farley's personal guarantee stood behind the assets, but he chose to use it at the best time: when there was not much to lose. At the time of purchase, Anaheim Citrus Products' sales were $4.5 million per annum. In 1983 they reached $21 million.

In 1976 he purchased Baumfolder Corporation, a manufacturer of graphic arts equipment and folded it in with Anaheim Citrus into Farley Industries. He left Lehman Brothers when life in the fast lane became more exciting. How does one train to become a leveraged buy-out entrepreneur? Work for one.

Born in Pautucket, Rhode Island, Farley attended Bowdoin College, and upon graduating joined Collier Encyclopedias. Not fulfilled, he returned to school, this time to Boston College for a J.D. which he earned in 1969. Farley then joined the mergers and acquisitions department of NL Industries in New York. He was quickly named director of long-range planning and acquisitions for NL's largest division. He set the acquisition strategy, then went out and bought the companies. To improve his skills, Farley took courses at New York University's Graduate School of Business.

In 1972 NL Industries transferred Farley to Chicago to become regional manager for midwest operations of its $50 million metals division. There is not much fun in managing a $50 million metals division, when you've been doing mergers and acquisitions on Wall Street. Thus, Farley left to join Lehman Brothers' Chicago office which put him back into the deal flow. The midwest is a more efficient location for buying companies on a leveraged basis, because there are more smokestack-type companies within one hour of Chicago than any other metropolitan area.

After buying Anaheim Citrus Products and Baumfolder Corporation, Farley improved their cash flow, restructured his debt, and went after bigger game. Farley Industries bought NL Industries metal products division for $118 million, of which $3 million was his equity and the rest leverage. In 1984 he won a proxy fight for Condec Corporation; this prize cost $140 million, substantially all leveraged.

At some point, we expect to see Farley offer the public an opportunity to share the growth of Farley Industries, or parts of it. At a higher price than he paid, of course. After all, that is what baseball is all about—to see if the next batter can get on base or drive in a run.

TOM J. FATJO, JR.

Name of Company:	Browning-Ferris Industries, Inc.
Date Founded:	1970
Location:	Houston, Texas
Description of Business:	The company is one of the largest providers of solid and liquid waste collection, processing, recovery, and disposal services for commercial, industrial, governmental, and residential customers.
Description of P:	Fatjo's Houston subdivision was experiencing unsatisfactory garbage collection. In a community meeting, Fatjo suggested that the neighbors buy a truck and provide services for themselves. A neighbor said to him, "Tom, this is a civic club, not a damn garbage company! Why don't you buy a garbage truck and be our garbage man?" Although Fatjo was a partner in a small accounting firm at the time, this "crazy idea" as he calls it got hold of him, and he did just that. Moreover, he learned how to do it efficiently and that communities in many other cities required efficient garbage collection as well. Browning-Ferris Industries (BFI) grew to sales of approximately $1 billion in 1984.
Description of S:	Five days after the community meeting, Rice University graduate Fatjo was up to his chest in garbage. He signed up his subdivision as the first customer. In order to succeed, Fatjo developed some positive innovations all learned while driving the truck for over a year, from 4 to 8 A.M., prior to going to his accounting business.
Members of E:	Lou Walters, first chairman of BFI; and Harry J. Phillips, first president of BFI

Size of V:	The approximately 34 million shares of common stock outstanding traded in a range of $26½ to $44½ in 1984 for an average valuation of $1.2 billion.
Social Utility:	BFI has created 16,800 jobs, given local garbage collection businesspeople a means of obtaining liquidity for their estates and improved the operations of a difficult, labor-intensive business.
Principal Sources of Venture Capital:	Fatjo borrowed $7,000 to buy his first truck and took $500 from personal savings for working capital.

TOM J. FATJO, JR., 44, has written his entrepreneurial autobiography along with a description of the entrepreneurial process.[35] He has the script for converting entrepreneurial drive into profitable businesses. The book is one of a kind and must reading for entrepreneurs.

After building BFI into the leader in waste removal and installing Harry Phillips to manage it, Fatjo has put his entrepreneurial ability to other important uses. With other investors he bought a small bank in 1970, helped to grow its deposits nearly 10-fold in 14 years, and then merged it into a Texas banking conglomerate. He founded a mortgage banking firm in 1974 which was servicing $400 million in mortgages when he sold it in 1978. With other investors he purchased Criterion Group in 1976; today this private investment management company manages $9 billion in investments.

Fatjo's interests for the last five years have centered around the Houstonian, a wellness center on a 20-acre wooded tract in Houston. The goals of the Houstonian are (1) to help executives and professional people and their families discover and develop the highest quality of personal life and health possible and (2) to provide a place where entrepreneurs, innovators, managers, and others who are concerned about the renewal of a free society could meet and begin to dream together. Lofty goals, you say? A neoutopian, out of his depth? Don't discount the ability of this one-in-a-million entrepreneur.

[35]Thomas J. Fatjo, Jr., With No Fear of Failure (Waco, Texas: Word Books, 1982).

Fatjo's interest in wellness grew out of the damage that he did to his body and first marriage while building BFI. Here are some descriptions of some of the agonies that he, like many other entrepreneurs lacking adequate business experience, went through while launching a company.

The first incident occurred in the earliest days of Fatjo's entrepreneurial experience.

I continued driving a truck for over a year. I wanted to learn the waste business thoroughly, to know how much time it actually took to work a block or make a round trip to the dump. Such information would be invaluable to us if we expanded further.

Some days I'd get up very early, work on a route from four to eight, then take a shower, change into my president-of-the-company-and-accounting-partner clothes and get on with the day. I was working almost all the time, and although I had an incredible amount of energy, I was just barely able to keep my nose above water in each area of my life.

I have to smile now when I think of my own intensity to get the job done in those days. Within a few weeks after we started we began to experience truck breakdowns. One day the compactor didn't work on the large truck I was driving, and we had about seventy more homes to service before completing the route. When the compactor went out, I was determined to finish the route. I called out to my helpers, "Hey, one of you guys jump in the truck and we'll throw the cans up, and you can stomp the garbage down." Both of them said they weren't about to get into the truck with all that garbage, so I climbed up into the truck. That was when I found myself up to my armpits in garbage.

As I was getting out of the truck that day, I thought to myself, "Life really isn't bad at all." The company was going well, and we were getting new business. A sense of well-being flooded my thoughts.[36]

[36]Ibid, p.30.

The second incident occurred in the first year of operations as Fatjo was wrestling with the dilemma of throwing off the security blanket of the accounting profession and accepting the risk of entrepreneurship.

Within a week I was almost frantic. My food wouldn't seem to digest, and I had a big knot in my chest. When I was doing one thing, I thought of two others which had to be done that same day.

The pressure just kept building. Even though it was cold, my body was damp from continuous perspiration. Since so much of what I was doing in the accounting firm had to be done by the end of the tax year and involved important decisions with key clients, I needed to spend time thinking through problems and consulting with them as they made decisions. I was caught in a triangle of pressing demands, and I felt my throat constricting as if there were wire around my neck . . . .

That night I was exhausted, but I couldn't sleep. As I stared at the ceiling, I fantasized all our trucks breaking down at the same time. I was trying to push each of them myself in order to get them going. My heart began beating faster in the darkness and my body was chilled. The horrible thought that we might fail almost paralyzed me.

I wanted to quit and run away. I was scared to death, very lonely, sick of the whole deal. As hard as I tried to think about my life and what was important to me, my mind was just a confused mass of muddled images . . . . I remembered committing myself to make it in the garbage business "whatever it takes!" I lay back on my pillow and felt a deep sigh within myself—"Good Lord, so this is what it takes," I thought, then rolled over and got some restless sleep.[37]

Within a year, Fatjo's business grew to $300,000 per annum and he had $80,000 in the bank. He began learning methods to beat the competition and to improve customer service. He attended seminars around the country to learn all he could about the solid waste business. Fatjo

---

[37]Ibid, p.32.

made the decision to expand out of Houston. He figured perhaps one or
two other Texas cities, but an investigation of other cities put a much
larger idea into his head and led him on a breakneck acquisition plan
that included 150 separate acquisitions in a six-year period.

Fatjo continues:

When I drove to the Houston International Airport to begin that
trip, I was an excited twenty-eight-year-old who was enjoying
the building of a growing local business. As I began to talk to the
best garbage company operators in the world, I was impressed
with their dedication to the business of keeping their communities clean. I listened to what they had to say, and was surprised
that several of these men began to discuss their problems with
me. It seemed that few people realized the effect the enormous
increase in solid waste was beginning to have in the cities.

Almost all the companies needed additional capital to expand
their services—just to take care of their present clients, not to
mention the hundreds of thousands of new residential and commercial customers moving into the cities every week. Not only
was the increase in waste material a practical difficulty in itself,
but the ecologists also had seen that the burning of garbage was
posing serious health problems. Recent governmental regulations
had eliminated this major way to dispose of the mammoth mountains of garbage. So existing companies were having to learn the
landfill business to survive, and this involved even greater needs
for capital.

I moved on across the country. In one city, an older operator
talked about the fact that if he died his estate would be crippled
because of the high estate taxes his heirs would have to pay. And
since a garbage company's assets are very illiquid, the heirs could
be wiped out with no source of cash to pay the taxes. By the time
my tour was over, I saw that this was a general problem in the
industry.

One night at the end of the second week I sat down alone in my
hotel room and began to jot down some of the things I was discov-
ering. I was beginning to see a need and an opportunity which

was so large, so preposterous, that my mind wouldn't consider it at first . . . . For some reason—perhaps because no one had ever come to listen, perhaps because the pressures had built inside with no one to tell them to—these men had also told me about their personal needs and frustrations relating to the industry as a whole.

As I sat there in my room . . . and realized that, at that moment in history, I might be one of the few people anywhere to see the nature of the crisis America was facing . . . . It dawned on me then that I was beginning to see an emerging need for a large *national* solid-waste company . . . . It was as if . . . God was telling me, "The time to build this national company is right now, Tom, and you're the man who's supposed to do it!"[38]

Entrepreneurs do not as a rule convey their feelings and emotions too well. Tom Fatjo is different. He has poured out his heart onto paper, and entrepreneurs forever more owe him a debt of gratitude.

[38]Ibid.

WILLIAM ARTHUR FICKLING, JR.

Name of Company: Charter Medical Corporation

Date Founded: 1969

Location: Macon, Georgia

Description of Business: This rapidly expanding hospital management chain operates 50 psychiatric, acute care, and addictive-disease hospitals throughout the United States and England.

Description of *P*: A National Institute of Mental Health study in 1984 stated that 3,285 people out of every 10,000 in the United States will suffer substance-abuse or psychiatric disorders during their lifetime. The treatment facilities must be in place to handle this large number of cases.

Description of *S*: Fickling saw the need to provide treatment facilities for substance and psychiatric disorders. He acquired hospitals, converted them and ran them efficiently as psychiatric hospitals located in numerous metropolitan areas.

Members of *E*: Ray Stevenson, president; and James T. McAfee, Jr., executive vice-president.

Size of *V*: The Approximately 20 million shares of Charter Medical outstanding traded in a range of $18½ to $32 in 1984 for an average valuation of $500 million.

Social Utility: The company provides humane treatment of emotional problems with high-visibility psychiatric hospitals.

Principal Sources of Venture Capital: Personal savings

WILLIAM ARTHUR FICKLING, JR., 52, lettered in three sports in high school while graduating near the top of his class. He earned a basketball scholarship to Auburn University where he became the Southeastern Conference hurdles champion twice and was named to the school's basketball "Team of the Decade" in the late 1950s. He graduated with honors and married Neva Jane Langley, a few months after her tour as Miss America 1953.

Fickling joined the U.S. Air Force for two years, then returned to Macon, Georgia, to join his father's mortgage banking firm. He helped to transform the firm into a residential builder and diversified development and construction company.

In 1969, he left to specialize in building, acquiring, and operating hospitals. The public stock market was suffering as Charter Medical began, and it was denied access to large chunks of capital. Growth was primarily via leverage. Charter's bank debt has always been very high and today it carries a debt to worth ratio of 2-to-1. "As long as cash flow is covering our interest and debt reduction schedules, we feel comfortable," Fickling told Jay Gissen of *Forbes* magazine. "Coverage is more important to us than the ratio. If somebody's expecting us to pay off our debts, they ought to buy some other stock."[39]

Fickling can joke about Charter's leverage today, with revenues in 1984 topping $425 million and net income $34 million. But 10 years ago, Charter was a hodgepodge of shopping centers, real estate holdings, and hospitals. It was then that Fickling conducted a "strategy audit" and found a solution to Charter Medical's identity crisis: the psychiatric hospital. Charter Medical already had three showing better returns on assets and profit margins than its general hospitals. And the cost of building a psychiatric hospital—as little as $6 million—is about 40% of the cost of a general one. Finally, Fickling saw growing acceptance of psychiatric care.

The result of this was Charter Medical chopped away almost all of its holdings save its hospitals and a couple of medical office buildings and emphasized psychiatric care. "We became a lean company with a central directive to do one thing and do it well," says Fickling.[40]

---

[39]Jay Gissen, "Do One Thing and Do It Well," *Forbes*, Dec. 5, 1983, p. 153.
[40]Ibid.

Fickling believes in the active participation by business executives in a "strategy audit" for the United States and in helping to manage it. In 1980–1983, he served as Chairman of the Federal Reserve Bank of Atlanta. In addition, he writes and speaks extensively about citizens' responsibility to the state. He says:

> If the free market is allowed to function as in other parts of our economy, it will assure that the highest quality care is delivered in the most cost-effective manner. We would not have to worry whether it is more appropriate to spend 9.8 percent of GNP on health care than, for example, to spend 2.7 percent on alcohol and tobacco. The marketplace—the most effective determinant of these kinds of questions—would tell us.[41]

Fickling also believes the greatest contribution he can make in the next five years is to reduce the cost of superior health-care service. There are valid reasons for the cost escalation in health care, he thinks; it's an unusual business in that the customer doesn't make the buying decision—the doctor does. And a third party pays the bill—Medicare, Medicaid, or an insurance company. Fewer than 10 percent of patients pay their own hospital bills. About half the patients' bills are paid for on a cost-plus basis by the government, downplaying the incentive to worry about costs. Fickling says he'd like to change that. The Federal government's diagnostic related group law, effected in 1984, and the growth of health maintenance organizations, will help him do that more quickly.

[41]Ibid.

DEBBI FIELDS

Name of Company:	Mrs. Fields Cookies, Inc.
Date Founded:	1977
Location:	Park City, Utah

Description of
Business:

The company owns and operates a chain of more than 200 cookie stores throughout the country and in the Far East.

Description of *P*:

John Naisbitt's "high tech/high touch" principle is at work in the rise of chocolate chip cookie chains.[42] The more people are isolated from each other by the introduction of technology into their lives, the greater their need for human contact in shopping malls, movies, and restaurants, as well as their need for simple things that remind them of less technological times. The chocolate chip cookie says it all. Americans spent over $200 million on freshly baked chocolate chip cookies in 1984.

Description of *S*:

Mrs. Fields Cookies reach the public through owner-operated retail stores in shopping malls and free-standing locations. Store managers and other employees are selected for their ability to "ham it up" with customers, to have fun with their customers, and to be caring. All cookies over two hours old are given to the Red Cross, so that the customer receives only *warm* cookies.

Members of *E*:

Randy Fields, Mrs. Fields' husband; Taylor Devine, chief operating officer, formerly with Arthur D. Little, Inc.; and Stanley Slap, vice-president—operations

Size of *V*:

The company is privately held, thus an accurate valuation is not available. Retail food chains are

[42]John Naisbitt, *Megatrends* (New York: Warner Books, 1982), pp. 35-40.

frequently acquired by major food processors for the value of their sales. At that rate, Mrs. Fields Cookies is worth about $50 million.

Social Utility:

The company has created more than 1,000 jobs and Debbi Fields, a 28-year-old mother of three, has and will continue to be an inspiration to thousands of young mothers seeking to become valid in other areas in addition to the home.

Principal Sources
of Venture
Capital:

The company was launched with $50,000 of personal savings.

DEBBI FIELDS borrowed $50,000 from her husband eight years ago to open a cookie store in a Palo Alto, California shopping mall. Fields had developed an ultra-chocolatey cookie and she "wanted to take a shot at it." At first, no one came in the store, so Fields went outside and handed out cookies to passersby. Within a week, the store was profitable and Fields never looked back. Her success formula: "I use nothing but the best ingredients. My cookies are always freshly baked. I price cookies so that you cannot make them at home for any less. And I still give cookies away."[43]

According to the Small Business Administration, about 1,600 bakeries in the United States are owned by women as are another 800 food-related businesses, but Fields is the only woman bakery entrepreneur; the others are small businesswomen.

She has made cookie buying and eating a "Mrs. Fields Experience," a "feel-good feeling," according to Chief Operating Officer Taylor Devine, a dignified, mature New Englander, formerly a strategic planner with Arthur D. Little. Although customers think they came into the store to buy cookies, Fields thinks they came in for "caring." She continues, "You make the cookie and you're standing there and you sell the cookie. You put it over the counter and this person says, 'This is great, this is better than homemade, this is . . . ' whatever. And that

[43]Micki Siegel, "Cookies Are Their Fortune," Good Housekeeping, Sept. 1983.

fuels the individual to do a great job, because he doesn't want to let that customer down."[44]

Fields is smart. She knows the ease of entry into her market, so she makes the business seem complex, in the sense of requiring "heart," to keep out Nabisco Brands, Inc., Pillsbury Company, Hershey Foods Corporation and the other food processors whom she, Famous Amos, and David's Cookies have scooped. Keys to her company's success include corporate achievers such as Taylor Devine, Randy Fields, and Stanley Slap who run day-to-day operations. For example, two vice-presidents at the corporate level oversee eight regional operations managers, each of whom is responsible for about thirty stores. Store managers, some of whom may manage two or three stores, get help from team leaders selected from the hourly employees.

At some point, the number of cookie stores will approach market saturation and Mrs. Fields Cookies will either be acquired or go public and diversify into other markets. How high is up for this smartly run company? Can a high-touch business become as large as one that is high tech? Easily.

[44]Tom Richman, "The Cookie Wars," *Inc.*, July 1984.

ARYEH FINEGOLD

Name of Company:	Daisy Systems Corporation
Date Founded:	1980
Location:	Mountain View, California
Description of Business:	The company is a leading manufacturer of computer systems that design electronic circuits, known as computer-assisted engineering or CAE systems.
Description of P:	The cost of designing electronic circuits which are subsequently reduced in size to fit onto silicon wafers increases geometrically as the circuitry becomes more complex. Months are now needed to handle very large scale integration (VLSI) and the design costs have become staggering.
Description of S:	Finegold led a team of engineers to develop computer programs that let design engineers simulate the performance of thousands of circuit elements as they are drawn on the screen. This eliminates months from the time it takes to design and test computer chips.
Members of E:	Fred Adler, principal investor.
Size of V:	Approximately 17.2 million shares of Daisy Systems' common stock outstanding traded in a range of $18 to $36 per share in 1984, for an average valuation of $413 million.
Social Utility:	The principal social value of Daisy Systems is that without computer-aided engineering of semiconductors, further technological breakthroughs in the design of chips would be very few and slow in coming. The miniaturization of medical implants, for example, might not be possible.
Principal Sources of Venture Capital:	Fred Adler provided start-up capital.

ARYEH FINEGOLD, 38, the president of Daisy Systems Corporation, came to the United States from Israel on a student visa in 1977 with his wife and baby and $800. To support his family until the fall term at Stanford Business School, Finegold took a temporary job at Intel Corporation. When Intel offered him a permanent job, he accepted and never looked back at the plans he cast aside. Now he speaks with pride of his training in the Intel "business school."

At Intel, Finegold was a manager responsible for input/output architecture within the product-line architecture department. He also served as engineering manager, where he headed up the design of an enhanced member of Intel's mid-range microcomputer family. Finegold directed logic design and prototyping of the 8089 input/output processor and developed an application system for it.

Finegold co-founded Daisy Systems in August 1980 to design a computer that would automate the most time-consuming portion of the VLSI design cycle, the two-thirds of the design process that translates the concept for a new device into logic diagrams and schematics. The first Daisy Systems' product to provide this capability was the LOGICIAN, delivered to the market on schedule in November 1981. Since then the Company has introduced the GATEMASTER and CHIPMASTER for integrated circuit layout, the MegaLOGICIAN and MegaLOGICIAN PMX for system integration and verification, and the Personal LOGICIAN for low-cost design entry.

With sales of $69 million in fiscal 1984, Daisy is a dominant force in the computer-aided engineering marketplace.

The idea for Daisy came to Finegold at Intel when a conversation with a fellow manager revealed that they had much the same set of problems in speeding up design. Finegold found an ideal backer in Fred Adler, the hard-nosed venture capitalist known as much for one of his favorite catch-phrases—"Happiness is positive cash flow"—as for having helped start Data General Corporation, at one time a significant player in the computer industry. Finegold announced his first product, the LOGICIAN work station, in November 1981, one year after he left Intel. Daisy Systems turned profitable in the first quarter of 1982 and has stayed that way since.

Though it was first to market, Daisy Systems might not be today's sales leader without Finegold's unique management style. He takes his cues at Daisy Systems from the only other sizable outfit he has man-

aged—a company of paratroopers that he led through Israel's wars of
1967 and 1973 without losing a man. The secret, he says, was that "I'm
a born paranoid, a hysterical woman. I fear every shadow in the hills—
and I defend against each one."[45] As an aggressor he's fearless.
Finegold encourages paramilitary sales tactics and once fired a salesperson who was 50 percent over quota on the suspicion that he should
have sold even more.

Of course, Daisy Systems owes its success to more than Finegold's
paranoia. The company has focused its marketing on chipmakers and
on users of semicustom chips, a $450-million market that is doubling
every year. Buyers of semicustom chips do the final design work themselves, choosing from suppliers' catalogs of chip elements.

[45]Bro Uttal, "Free-for-All in Computer-Aided Engineering," *Fortune*, July 11, 1984.

DR. THOMAS F. FRIST, SR.
DR. THOMAS F. FRIST, JR.

Name of Company: Hospital Corporation of America

Date Founded: 1968

Location: Nashville, Tennessee

Description of
  Business: The world's largest owner/operator of hospitals.

Description of *P*:   Dr Frist, Sr. was unhappy with the quality of care his patients were getting at the local hospitals. He felt that he could do better. Over the last 17 years, Hospital Corporation of America (HCA) has grown rapidly via acquisitions to revenues of more than $4 billion in 1984 and earnings of approximately $240 million. In April 1985, HCA announced that it intended to acquire American Hospital Supply Corporation, Evanston, Illinois, which would double its size. His presumption of 24 years ago was correct: a well-managed chain of hospitals would satisfy patients, doctors, and investors alike.

Description of *S*:   The advantages of professionally managed hospitals over not-for-profit are in economies of scale (buying Band-Aids by the boxcar, for instance, is less expensive per Band-Aid), which are passed along to the patients and to the bottom line. Hospital managers who receive bonuses based on earnings carefully watch *all* of their costs. HCA's return on equity over the last 10 years has averaged 17 percent.

Members of *E*:   Donald S. McNaughton, chairman; Joe B. Wyatt; John Hill, Jack Massey, and numerous active investor-directors.

Size of *V*:   The roughly 86 million shares of common stock outstanding traded in a range of $35¾ to $44⅞ in 1984 for an average valuation of $3.4 billion.

Social Utility: HCA has created 110,000 jobs and delivered lower
                             cost health care in 409 hospitals throughout the
                             country.

Principal Sources   Dr. Frist, Sr. and 10 individual investors provided
  of Venture   the initial capital.
Capital:

DR. THOMAS F. FRIST, SR., 75, gathered together a handful of investors in 1960 to build the first investor-owned hospital. The group then went looking for the best doctors, technicians, and administrators they could find. "Quality attracts quality," Frist told a *Forbes* reporter. "Good people generally have good people as their friends, and I hired them too."[46] The initial hospital was built, operated, and debugged. In 1968, Thomas F. Frist, Jr. left the U.S. Air Force to join HCA and one of this country's most successful expansion plans began.

As of March 31, 1984, HCA owned 170 general hospitals in the United States with 28,225 beds; 25 psychiatric hospitals with 3,182 beds; and managed for others 177 units with 23,297 beds. Overseas, the company owned 24 facilities with 2,109 beds and managed two units with 500 beds. HCA's U.S. patient care days were 6,842,914 in 1983, down from 7,143,902 in 1982. Occupancy rates in the United States were 63.4 percent in 1983, down from 65.8 percent in 1982. Hospital admissions are declining as a result of the growing trend toward ambulatory care centers and the cost-cutting pressures of diagnostic related groups (DRGs), but HCA has managed to maintain its growth of revenues by a steady program of acquisitions. Earnings have not suffered, primarily because of belt tightening.

HCA's formula is traditional conservative management. It has strict inventory controls, computerized billing, and low-cost purchasing. If certain procedures increase during the period of a month, they are flagged to see if so many were essential.

The publicly owned hospitals have accused the investor-owned hospitals of "skimming"; that is, accepting patients covered by insurance carriers who pay more than Medicare or Medicaid. Frist, Jr. has rebutted those charges by showing that HCA owns hospitals where pa-

[46]Paul B. Brown, "Band-Aids by the Boxcar," *Forbes*, August 31, 1981, p.88.

tients stay much longer than they do in not-for-profit hospitals. Humana, a large, investor-owned competitor of HCA, hired Dr. William DeVries, an expert in artificial heart implants, in order to develop an important specialty and leadership role in this critical area. Humana has gained much publicity through Bill Schroeder and other heart implant patients. HCA recently built a 109-bed cancer treatment center in Nashville, Tennessee. HCA and Humana are aggressively entering the HMO business, a means of holding down health care costs.

Frist, Jr. says, "You and I were brought up thinking hospitals shouldn't make a profit. They were there to provide quality health care, period. Well, that was in the days when if you needed a $1 million addition, you could raise half through donations. Today, that addition might cost $20 million, and you probably still couldn't raise more than $500,000 in donations. We have been the stimulus for a cottage industry to reorganize itself."[47]

If Frist is correct, and HCA's record is testimony to steady, unerring growth of revenues and profits, then there are other institutions that should be managed by entrepreneurial companies in order to deliver quality service. Could investor-owned universities be next?

[47]Ibid, p. 89.

JOHN BROOKS FUQUA

Name of Company:	Fuqua Industries, Inc.
Date Founded:	1964
Location:	Atlanta, Georgia
Description of Business:	This diversifed company is engaged in the manufacture and distribution of lawn and garden equipment, recreation products, and seating; it also provides photofinishing services.
Description of *P*:	Tired, old companies with second generation family management represent problems for the economy, because they are not growing, innovating, and creating new jobs and profits for their investors. Leveraged buy-out entrepreneurs, like fish that keep the pond clean, snap up these weaker companies, change their managements, and turn them into rapidly growing, innovative, and productive companies.
Description of *S*:	The key to leverage buy-outs is understanding financial leverage, re-examining assets that have been written off, and using them as collateral to support buy-out debt.
Members of *E*:	L. P. Klamon, president
Size of V:	The approximately 9 million shares of common stock outstanding traded in a range of $20 to $30¼ per share in 1984 for an average valuation of $225 million.
Social Utility:	The company employs 9,000 people. Fuqua has devoted 10 years to government service and he has been charitable to Duke University and to other schools and organizations.
Principal Sources of Venture Capital:	Financial leverage

JOHN BROOKS FUQUA was born in Prince Edward County, Virginia. Shortly after his birth, his mother died. As his father lacked the resources to properly raise a son, Fuqua was adopted and raised by his maternal grandparents.

Fuqua realized early that he wanted more from life than farming. While attending county public schools he learned it was possible to borrow books by mail from the library at Duke University. Throughout high school, he read books on finance and management. During this period he was prompted by a radio advertisement to send in 25 cents for a booklet on ham radio operation. Receiving the booklet, he studied it and built a ham radio station at the age of fourteen. Fuqua's hobby became the first stepping stone of his career.

Graduating from Prospect High in 1935 and realizing that there was no money for college, 17-year-old Fuqua passed the test for a commercial radio operator's license and joined the U.S. Merchant Marine as a radio officer. Two years later at 19 he was the youngest chief engineer of a broadcasting station in the country. Two years later he found three investors who would help him become manager and part owner of a radio station, WGAC.

Fuqua established a bank credit line and began buying land, building on it, and then selling the whole property for a profit. He did this repeatedly. Meanwhile he made a lucrative investment in the Royal Crown Bottling Company. Before age 30, Fuqua had amassed a six-figure estate.

Fuqua bought and sold radio stations using bank financing. In 1950 he applied for and received a television license to operate in Augusta, Georgia. This required a $250,000 investment in television equipment. Later the station sold for nearly $30 million.

Interested in politics, Fuqua ran for and was elected to the Georgia Legislature in 1957, where he served for eight years. He served three terms in the House and one term in the Senate. While in the legislature, Fuqua was the chairman of the Senate Banking and Finance Committee and the House Banking Committee. He was elected chairperson of the state Democratic party from 1962 to 1966. "I spent some of my best years in politics," says Fuqua.[48]

---

[48]Commentary from Horatio Alger Association of Distinguished Americans, April, 1984 (Press Release).

After a decade in public life, Fuqua returned to business, bought Natco—a $12 million brick and tile manufacturing firm—and changed its name to Fuqua Industries. He used it as the starting point for a conglomerate which includes farm, home, and industrial products; recreational products and services; and seating. Among the companies are Snapper Power Equipment; Islander Yachts; Klemp Corporation (metal bar grating); Ajay Enterprises Corporation (golf, exercise, and other sports equipment); Colorcraft Corporation (photofinishing); Shoreline Products (boat and motorcycle trailers); and American Seating Company.

Fuqua commented:

Unless you have some goals, I don't think there's any way to get above the pack. My vision was always well beyond what I had any reason to expect.

Accessibility is a major factor in success, because if you try, you can learn something from everybody you meet. When I was in high school, I was very much impressed by something one of the early philosophers said: "I am a part of all whom I have met." I have always remembered that, and, therefore, I try to meet as many people as possible. I do as much listening as possible and as little talking as possible.[49]

[49]Ibid.

WILLIAM GATES
PAUL ALLEN

Name of Company: Microsoft Corporation

Date Founded: 1975

Location: Bellevue, Washington

Description of
Business: The company has developed the most popular and widely used operating system for personal computers, licensed to International Business Machines Corporation (IBM) and others. It also develops other software packages for Apple Computer, IBM, Tandy Corporation, and Japanese personal computer manufacturers.

Description of *P*: A computer is a dumb machine without software. Gates was one of the first entrepreneurs to see the need for personal computer software that would make the machine easy and efficient to use.

Description of *S*: Applications packages that operate on personal computers must be managed by an operating system. Gates wrote the most popular program, called MS-DOS. Sales in 1984 were approximately $150 million and the company is estimated to be highly profitable.

Members of *E*:   Jon Shirley, chief operating officer

Size of *V*:   The company is privately held. On a comparable scale it is probably worth $300 million.

Social Utility: The company employs in excess of 600 people.

Principal Sources
of Venture
Capital: Gates self-financed the company with personal savings. A venture capital firm subsequently invested to help the company grow professionally.

WILLIAM GATES was born and raised in an upper middle class home in Seattle. In the seventh grade, he learned how to program a computer. By his senior year in high school, TRW had pulled him to Vancouver, Washington, to write programs for one of its divisions. Gates entered Harvard University at 17, but he dropped out and moved to Albuquerque, New Mexico, with Microsoft Corporation co-founder PAUL ALLEN. There a small company called MITS had put Intel's 8080 microchip on a board and soldered wires to the board leading to the keyboard and a monitor. Many of the early microcomputer entrepreneurs had read about the MITS computer in *Popular Science* magazine and had descended on Albuquerque.

Gates and Allen rented a cheap motel room in Albuquerque and adapted the first popular BASIC language to create an operating system for the first microcomputer. There were other operating systems of equal or greater popularity in the late 1970s—CP/M being the most widely used—but MS-DOS was selected by IBM when it built its IBM PC in 1981, and as the sportscasters say, the rest was history.

Thirty-year-old Gates is generally acknowledged in the personal computer industry as a man of brilliance and perspicacity beyond his years. David Bunnell, publisher of *PC World*, was also a resident of Albuquerque during the birth of the personal computer; he says of Gates: "When the history of the microcomputer industry is written, Bill Gates will be remembered as the guy who wrote the first successful program for the mass market."[50]

A single product company less than 10 years old would not ordinarily qualify for a list of the 100 greatest entrepreneurial companies of the last 25 years. As a measure of Gates' maturity, he has been diversifying Microsoft Corporation rapidly and vertically. The company has a highly successful spreadsheet package called *Multiplan* and released a windowing package in 1985. As for horizontal diversification, Gates recently wrote an operating system for the Japanese personal computer manufacturers called MSX, which is expected to become the principal operating system in Europe.

[50]*Esquire*, December, 1984, p.29.

FRED GIBBONS

Name of Company:	Software Publishing Corporation
Date Founded:	1981
Location:	Mountain View, California
Description of Business:	The company designs, develops, produces, and markets a broad range of productivity-improving personal computer software packages.
Description of P:	The principal utility of the personal computer is that it makes its user more productive in a number of ways: he or she can process words or data more rapidly, reach more people, and maintain records in a more meaningful manner. The size of this market, according to *Future Computing*, reached $400 million in 1984, of which Software Publishing Corporation (SPC) had a 6 percent market share.
Description of S:	The product line developed by SPC is of the highest quality; it contains seven applications packages that are easy to use. The company went public in 1984 in order to be in position to make attractive acquisitions during the software industry shakeout.
Members of E:	John Page, vice-president—research and development; Janelle Bedke, vice-president—productivity software.
Size of V:	The approximately 6 million shares of common stock outstanding traded in a range of $7 to $10⅝ in 1984 for an average valuation of $67 million.
Social Utility:	SPC has created 169 jobs and demonstrated a three-year average return on capital of approximately 50 percent, laying waste to the premise that investors cannot do well in the software industry.

Principal Sources of Venture Capital:	Gibbons invested $50,000 in seed capital, then $1 million was provided by Jack Melchor, a venture capitalist, plus entrepreneurs Les Hogan (Fairchild), Robert Noyce (Intel), Robert Maxfield and Kenneth Oshman (Rolm), and attorney John Friedrich.

FRED GIBBONS, 36, has maturity and practicality that are uncommon in the personal computer software industry. While his competitors keep their success private (Microsoft Corporation) or place their emphasis on a single product (Lotus Development Corporation, MicroPro International, Digital Research) or raise so much money from megafunded venture capitalists (Knoware, Ovation) that they lack the pressure to perform, Gibbons set his cap on a simplified business plan: to produce a high-quality, easy-to-use, broad line of productivity-improving software. Entrepreneurs have played the role of jockey to the personal computer horse for the purpose of improving productivity for industry for over 30 years. Gibbons did not reinvent the wheel.

Born in Boston, the son of a sea captain, Gibbons' first foray into entrepreneurship was at 17 when he designed a canvas ski bag. The profits paid for two degrees at the University of Michigan, the latter in computer science. He joined a small computer company in Boston to gain small-business experience, and enrolled in Harvard Business School to learn the fundamentals. If this sounds programmed, it is. Gibbons believed that some experience at a large company would round out his business education. He joined Hewlett–Packard Company, where he stayed for six years and became one of their youngest marketing managers.

The idea for a productivity-improving software company occurred to Gibbons in 1979 while he was at Hewlett–Packard Company. He proposed it to his boss, who rejected the idea. Two coworkers, John Page and Janelle Bedke, liked the idea and the threesome agreed that Bedke would leave to begin writing the first package, *pfs: file*, a data base management package, while Gibbons and Page would support her with evening and weekend labor plus half their paychecks and Gibbons' $50,000 of savings. Following in the footprints of the founders of Hewlett–Packard Company, their headquarters was Bedke's garage.

In September 1980 Bedke had completed *pfs: file* and sent announcements to computer dealers throughout the country. The orders rolled in enabling Gibbons and Page to leave Hewlett–Packard. They presented their story to venture capitalist Jack Melchor, who pulled together the necessary funds to broaden the line and begin marketing.

As Gibbons told the authors of *The Computer Entrepreneurs:* "There's no status in the company. I don't have a secretary. Everybody has vocational work that has to be done, even me."[51] The Hewlett-Packard experience shows clearly throughout the company in its egalitarian, teamwork-oriented, spartan working conditions. Further, the products are excellent. *Pfs: file* has sold close to 200,000 copies, and the company has introduced a bestseller every year since 1980.

[51]Robert Levering, Michael Katz, Milton Moskowitz, *The Computer Entrepreneurs* (New York: New American Library, 1984), p. 168.

ROBERT L. GREEN

Name of Company:	Community Psychiatric Centers
Date Founded:	1962
Location:	San Francisco, California
Description of Business:	The company is the largest publicly owned operator of acute psychiatric hospitals; it also operates a chain of kidney dialysis centers and a home health care business.
Description of *P*:	In the late 1950s, psychiatric care in the United States was emerging from the insane asylum stage. Mentally and emotionally disturbed people were "put away" as demonstrated in *David and Lisa*. Hospitals did not have psychiatric units. Community Psychiatric Centers (CPC) led the revolution in treating mental illness as a disease with drugs and therapies in attractive suburban hospitals.
Description of *S*:	CPC treats patients in a comprehensive manner, beginning with an evaluation of their symptoms, needs, and resources and then developing a personalized treatment plan using drugs and psychotherapy. The company operates over 20 psychiatric hospitals and 44 dialysis centers. In 1983 CPC entered the home health care business. Revenues were about $160 million in 1984, on which the company earned 19.75 percent or $36 million.
Members of *E*:	James W. Conte, president
Size of *V*:	The approximately 19 million shares of common stock outstanding traded in a range of $25⅜ to $35½ in 1984 for an average of $570 million.
Social Utility:	The company has created 3,761 jobs; but its leadership role in treating psychiatric illness on a for-profit basis is perhaps its greatest social achievement.

Principal Sources of Venture Capital:	Green and friends formed a small business investment company and launched the company with the government's three to one leverage.

ROBERT L. GREEN, 53, was raised without a safety net, his father having died when he was 12 years old. So, perhaps his cap was set early, as it is with many fatherless entrepreneurs, to make it on his own. Green earned a B.A. and an LL.B. from Stanford University (1952 and 1957) and then became a certified public accountant (1959). He began working in 1959 as an attorney with a San Francisco firm.

At that time the small business investment company (SBIC) had recently become a popular means of starting new companies. Anyone whose hands could reach up to a counter to put down $100,000 could get a license from the Small Business Administration (SBA) to make investments. The SBA would put up three dollars for the SBIC's one dollar. Green formed Sutter Capital as an SBIC in 1962 and it immediately acquired Belmont Hills Neuropsychiatric Center located on 18 acres near the San Francisco Airport. Green's plan was to build apartment houses there, but once he began to look closely at Belmont's numbers, his goals changed. Belmont was affiliated with the Stanford University School of Medicine for training resident physicians in psychiatry. In 1968 CPC acquired Alhambra Neuropsychiatric Hospital. In 1969 with a balance sheet that showed $2.5 million of debt and $174,000 of equity, and a deficit working capital of $385,000 (give Green credit for leveraging his initial leveraged purchase), the company had an initial public offering by selling 300,000 shares at $12.50 per share, plus 100,000 founders' shares. Earnings for the previous year were $.06 per share. The public seems to flock to companies that attempt to solve large medical problems. CPC currently sports a p/e ratio of 20x, but now has substantial earnings and a historical average return on equity of more than 25 percent.

Just as the leverage of 1968 may have been unusually high, the balance sheet of 1984 is quite liquid. There is about $50 million in cash on the balance sheet and only $23 million of funded debt. Perhaps Green and CPC's president, James W. Conte, are planning to catch another trend in health care delivery at the bottom rung.

ANDREW GROVE
GORDON MOORE
ROBERT NOYCE

Name of Company:	Intel Corporation
Date Founded:	1968
Location:	Santa Clara, California

Description of
Business:

The company designs, develops, manufactures, and markets microprocessors, or "computers on chips." Intel Corporation has continually led this revolutionary yet highly competitive industry.

Description of P:

The cost and size of core memory used in mainframe computers could be sharply reduced by developing semiconductor memories and placing them on tiny silicon chips. The founders of Intel Corporation did not realize then that this development would make possible the personal computer and spawn the birth of many new industries, based on the microprocessor, every 180 days since the late 1970s.

Description of S:

Four movements came together at the same time to cause Intel Corporation's technological breakthrough: (1) awareness of the properties of silicon; (2) development of the metal oxide semiconductor technology at Fairchild Semiconductor Corporation; (3) the push for large-scale integration (LSI); and (4) the laws of binary computer theory. Intel Corporation pioneered the commercial recognition that bits of information could be stored very cheaply on a microchip of silicon as the presence or absence of electrons at microscopic sites on the chip. A shock went through the electronics world in 1970 when Intel Corporation announced that it had stored 1,000 bits of information on a thumbnail-sized piece of silicon.

Members of *E*:	Ted Hoff, leader of the design team; Arthur Rock, principal backer
Size of *V*:	International Business Machines Corporation purchased 12 percent of Intel Corporation for $250 million in 1981, which established the company's value at more than $2 billion.
Social Utility:	Intel Corporation has created 25,400 jobs and it has set the standard of quality and achievement among technological companies.
Principal Sources of Venture Capital:	Arthur Rock and his partners invested $2 million without seeing a business plan.

ANDREW GROVE, 48, GORDON MOORE, 56, and ROBERT NOYCE, 58, left Fairchild Semiconductor Corporation in 1968. Without a business plan, they convinced Arthur Rock to invest $2 million to launch a company that would develop a microprocessor. Along with Texas Instruments, Fairchild developed and commercialized the integrated circuit. By 1963 its Palo Alto, California, plant had become one of the most exciting places on earth for young scientists to work. More than two dozen physicists and engineers in their thirties, 2,000 miles away from their parent company, were learning how to sell products and build a business into hundreds of millions of dollars. Noyce told Dirk Hanson, author of *The New Alchemists*: "Fairchild was the first time that the scientists and technologists really got themselves in the position of controlling the operation, with high financial rewards for successful experimentation. We had a policy of spreading those rewards through the ranks and pretty soon Fairchild became the premier semiconductor laboratory in the world. It trained a hell of a lot of people in this new technology."[52]

Soon the spin-outs began. Rheem left first, and his company became Raytheon Semiconductor Corporation. Next, Jean Hoerni left to found Amelco, which became Teledyne Semiconductor. Then Richard Lee and William Hugle left to form Siliconix; Jerry Sanders left to start Ad-

[52]Dirk Hanson, *The New Alchemists* (Boston: Little, Brown, 1982), pp. 100–101.

vanced Micro Devices; Charles Sporck left in 1967 to start National Semiconductor Corporation. Three new chip makers were launched in 1966; three more in 1967; 13 in 1968; and eight in 1969. Engineers running companies became acceptable, and Fairchild was gutted to give birth to Silicon Valley.

Intel Corporation rose to preeminence among all of these chip makers because its three-man team had gained management experience at Fairchild. They understand management, as evidenced by Grove's outstanding book, *High Output Management*;[53] Noyce can market his products with as much charm as anyone, and Moore and Hoff are preeminent scientists who attract the top engineers that keep Intel Corporation at the top technologically. When venture capitalists are asked to cite the most outstanding start-up entrepreneurial team, it is always Noyce–Grove–Moore.

Moore, a deputy sheriff's son and California Institute of Technology educated engineer, is the company's technical visionary and chief engineer. Grove, a Budapest dairyman's son who fled Hungary in 1957, landed in New York unable to read a newspaper headline, but three years later graduated as valedictorian of his class at City College of New York. He sped through his Ph.D. in three years at the University of California and then joined Fairchild. He is Intel Corporation's president and chief operating officer. Noyce is the son of an Iowa minister who studied electronics at Massachusetts Institute of Technology. He is an urbane Renaissance man who once conducted his own madrigal ensemble; he is also a venture capitalist and a pilot.

When one thinks of Intel Corporation, one thinks of the microprocessor. It was developed from the start as a commodity item with broad user appeal. Intel Corporation lets others design specific applications for it. Intel Corporation will sell them all they want. Moore and Hoff built a standardized small computer that simulated any kind of logic. Early customers used it to design calculators and in the mid-1970s the microprocessor gave birth to the personal computer. Moreover, it is reducing the cost of medical appliances; making possible the development of home medical diagnostic products; and permitting cost savings in telecommunications, driving, banking, and hundreds of things that

[53]Andrew Grove, *High Output Management* (New York: Random House, 1983).

we take for granted every day. Intel Corporation is the Ford Motor Company of the modern economy.

Listen carefully when Moore, Grove, or Noyce speaks about the industry or its role in the economy. They are frequently accurate. In 1960, for instance, Moore predicted that chip complexity, or the number of individual circuits on a chip would double every year. This has happened. In 1974 when the installed base of computers was 200,000, Moore predicted 20 million computers would be in operation by 1984. He was right once again. Moore and his engineers, of course, reproduced the entire mainframe computer on four silicon chips, and by 1971 were selling $9 million worth of these chips per annum to calculator manufacturers.

Noyce has recently sent out a warning of another kind. "The character of *this* industry, this industrial revolution—innovation intensive, rapidly growing, intensely competitive—really played into America's hands. Because America is an enterprise where the pioneer is still admissible. We won that game. Other societies not organized to promote innovation and entrepreneurial activity got left behind. But as the business becomes more mature, in the sense that it's becoming more capital intensive, the elements of success are changing, too. And several of the elements are playing into the hands of the Japanese winning the next round."[54]

As for Grove, any manager of an entrepreneurial company who ignores his book, *High Output Management*, is losing ground to those who have read it.

[54]Hanson, *New Alchemists*, p. 174.

WILLIAM HAMBRECHT

Name of Company:	Hambrecht & Quist, Inc.
Date Founded:	1968
Location:	San Francisco, California
Description of Business:	The company is an investment banking firm that specializes in underwriting the common stock issues of entrepreneurial success stories and in managing several venture capital funds.
Description of *P*:	Personal and institutional investors in the 1970s were in search of an investment banking firm that understood high technology. The major firms were poorly represented in the entrepreneurial caldrons of California and Massachusetts. Further, the investors were burned in the stock market collapse of 1969–1971, yet they knew that fortunes could be made by choosing the right technology companies in Silicon Valley.
Description of *S*:	Hambrecht & Quist was the first investment banking firm to separate the wheat from the chaff in the high technology garden for the public to invest in.
Members of *E*:	George Quist, partner of Bill Hambrecht for over 15 years
Size of *V*:	Hambrecht & Quist (H&Q) is a privately held company, thus valuation is unknown. A similar investment banking firm with an exceptional money management subsidiary, Donaldson, Lufkin & Jenrette, was acquired by Equitable Life Assurance Society of the United States in 1984 for $460 million.
Social Utility:	The company has created approximately 400 positions and provided a professional image to venture capital investing and investment banking.

Principal Sources   Five wealthy individuals invested $1 million.
of Venture
Capital:

WILLIAM HAMBRECHT, 50, and his deceased partner, George Quist, filled an important need that the major Wall Street investment bankers left unattended in the mid-1970s: merchant banking for rapidly growing, high technology companies. In classical merchant banking, a profession that dates back to 19th century England, the bankers buy a small company, fatten it up, then sell it at a higher price. Hambrecht & Quist (H&Q) formed several venture capital funds to buy or invest in small high technology companies. The partners of the venture capital funds found managers for the portfolio companies who fattened them up. Then H&Q took the companies public at prices greater than they paid in their venture capital funds. The script became quickly learned and several H&Q officials left to knock off the master, but H&Q's preeminence has never been seriously questioned.

Not too many entrepreneurs were raised on Long Island as the son of an executive of Mobil Oil, and educated at Princeton University. But unlike other Ivy Leaguers, Hambrecht drove a Pepsi truck during summer vacations.

Following a brief stint on Wall Street, Hambrecht joined a small investment firm in Orlando, Florida, which was acquired three years later by A.C. Allyn & Co., a Chicago investment bank. Hambrecht moved to Chicago, but A.C. Allyn was acquired by Francis I. duPont & Co., a major Wall Street firm, whose managers sent Hambrecht to San Francisco in 1965 to manage their office. In San Francisco, Hambrecht met George Quist, who was running Bank of America's venture capital arm.

Hambrecht became dissatisfied with F.I. duPont and Company; he had an insight about a high technology merchant bank and he had the energy to make it happen. Shortly after opening its doors in San Francisco with a satellite office in New York, a severe bear market forced H&Q to close its New York office. When some of their investors wanted out, the partners mortgaged their homes and bought them out.

H&Q managed $2.2 billion of underwritings in 1983 and its dominant position as the most knowledgeable high technology merchant banker was solidified.

JOHN K. HANSON

Name of Company:	Winnebago Industries, Inc.
Date Founded:	1958
Location:	Forest City, Iowa
Description of Business:	The company designs, develops, manufactures, and markets recreational vehicles.
Description of *P*:	The completion of the interstate system opened up the United States to automobile and truck traffic, and Americans hit the road. Motel chains and campgrounds did not satisfy all tastes; some people wanted to travel in the comfort of their own homes. This demand was satisfied by the advent of the recreational vehicle, a market that grew to $411 million in annual sales by 1984. Of this amount, Winnebago owned a 60 percent market share, with sales of approximately $250 million.
Description of *S*:	Winnebago Industries introduced recreational vehicles (RVs) in the mid-1960s. RVs are mobile homes that rest on a medium-duty truck chassis including the engine and drive components. The company has consistently been the industry leader to the extent that the name "Winnebago" is practically synonymous with RVs.
Members of *E*:	Ronald E. Haugen, President
Size of *V*:	The approximately 25 million shares of common stock outstanding traded in a range of $8¾ to $14¼ in 1984 for a valuation of approximately $250 million.
Social Utility:	The company created 2,893 jobs in a small town in Iowa, made dozens of Iowans very wealthy, and created a camaraderie, spirit, and loyalty that are unique to "home town heroes."

Principal Sources of Venture Capital:	Personal savings plus family, friends, and members of the community.

JOHN K. HANSON, 71, has done quite a bit for the reputation of local entrepreneurs making it big in a small town and creating wealth for his neighbors. Frequently, entrepreneurs leave their origins for reasons of mutual dissatisfaction, search for themselves in the cold, grey labs of an uncaring corporation, and emerge with the truth in a faraway, sunny clime, where preppy venture capitalists provide fuel for their launch, and an unknown pride of pension funds receives capital gains five years later. The nice thing about the Hanson story is that he created jobs and wealth for a large number of people in a small town in Iowa. Winnebago Industries is the entrepreneurial process at its finest.

He was 13 years old in Thor, Iowa, when his father set him up in business. As the only son among seven children, Hanson was his father's protege. Knut Hanson helped his son set up a food stand for a Fourth of July parade. "He banked me," Hanson said, adding that he hired his own classmates. "I made $39 that Fourth of July—more than most people made all summer."[55]

"You see, you get the basic ingredients and you put in other things—education, scouting . . . ," Hanson said, leaning forward in his cushioned chair and enumerating the points with his fingers. "I was an instinctive leader by the confidence my parents gave me," he said, proudly noting he attained the Eagle Scout rank. "You do what you set out to do."[56]

To ensure that his son got broad business experience, Knut Hanson made him change jobs every year. "That frustrated me," Hanson conceded. "I could have made more money had I stayed in one job." But his employers served as important role models, Hanson said, recalling a boss who was an "up-front man," always with a ready smile and handshake, anxious to please the customer. "A system of quality service was pounded into your head," he said. "You had to do all the services or they would boot you."[57]

[55]Jan Lovell, "The Amazing John K," *Globe*, Feb. 3, 1985.
[56]Ibid.
[57]Ibid.

Hanson also spent his teen years working in his father's furniture, appliance, implement, and mortuary businesses. He graduated from Forest City High School, Waldorf College, and became the youngest licensed embalmer in the state of Iowa after studying mortuary science at the University of Minnesota.

He returned to work at the family businesses, later buying out his father. "I was nervous," Hanson said of those early business years. "And there were periods of worry and frustration. But there always would be a goal. My goals were so terribly simple," he added, noting that he wanted to make $50 in sales each day. If he hadn't sold that much by 5 P.M., he would put some furniture in the truck, head down the road, and peddle his wares house to house until the goal was met. "If you're not in the hole one day, you won't be in a week."[58]

Hanson's appliance, furniture, and mortuary businesses flourished during his early years, thanks in part to novel promotion. He received national publicity from *Time* magazine in the 1940s by translating the prices of his furniture and appliances into hog pounds or bushels of corn. For example, a four-poster bedroom set was offered for 65 bushels of corn, a 623-pound hog, or $149.50.

For Hanson, that business success eventually meant "there was no challenge left." So he spent his free time fishing and camping with his family.

Looking for new challenges, Hanson decided to spearhead the effort by a Forest City, Iowa, development group to persuade the California firm of Modernistic Industries to build a travel trailer manufacturing plant in Forest City in the late 1950s. When the plant began to flounder, Hanson responded to the challenge by agreeing to take a year off his other businesses to get the company back on track again. Hanson took it over full-time in 1959.

The idea of the RV is rather simplistic, and poor people had been doing it for years: building enclosures on the back of flatbed trucks for their families to sleep in while traveling. Hanson added all the features of motor homes: kitchens, toilets, showers, comfortable beds and seating areas, heating and air conditioning.

The product was an instant success and when Hanson took Winne-

[58]Ibid.

bago public in 1971, the stock rose 462 percent making two dozen local folks millionaires. Hanson became the toast of the town.

When gasoline prices rose in 1974–1975, RV stocks fell, Winnebago's along with them. Hanson sent his design teams into overtime to develop more fuel-efficient vehicles. A line of more fuel-efficient RVs was introduced in 1976, and Hanson put himself on the shelf in 1979 at the age of 65. His son took the reins but high interest rates and gasoline prices decked the company. In 1980, sales fell from $215 million the previous year to $92 million.

Hanson returned in style. "I came in like Wyatt Earp," he said. "I just lined 'em up and shot 'em down."[59] He plunged the company into a crash program to replace its old behemoths, and in May 1981 unveiled an $18,800 model that gets an improved 15 mpg. An even more economical diesel version followed close behind. Even though he hoisted Ronald E. Haugen up to the role of President, and himself to Chairman, Hanson has a way of not really being retired. When your friends and neighbors are stockholders, that's the right and proper thing to do.

[59]"Winnebago Industries: Gambling on two hybrids to win back lost territory," *Business Week*, Corporate Strategies, Nov. 15, 1982, p.147.

NEIL S. HIRSCH

Name of Company:	Telerate, Inc.
Date Founded:	1969
Location:	New York, New York
Description of Business:	The company operates the Telerate Financial Information Network, a computerized financial market information system. Subscribing securities firms and banks receive prices, other market information, and financial news services.
Description of P:	Hirsch saw an opportunity to gather all prices on securities, currencies, and commodities that trade on major exchanges and to provide them on an on-line, real time (that is, instantaneous and accurate) basis 24 hours a day, 7 days a week.
Description of S:	Hirsch sold information. If you put a Telerate screen on your desk in New York, you could see the price of the dollar change against the pound or Deutschmark continually. You could trade for profit, while others without the Telerate screen had to await delivery of their *Wall Street Journal* the next morning. Sales increased from $17.2 million in 1978 to $114 million in 1984; and earnings from $3.6 million to $28.7 million.
Members of E:	Esther Zimet
Size of V:	The approximately 44 million shares of common stock outstanding traded in a range of $13½ to $23¼ in 1984 for an average valuation of $792 million.
Social Utility:	Telerate has created 320 new jobs.
Principal Sources of Venture Capital:	$30,000 loan from his father.

NEIL S. HIRSCH, 37, has created a very successful company by re-packaging information that he gathers for free in a marketplace of giant information providers who overlooked this opportunity to repackage and sell information. Hirsch started Telerate in 1969 when he noticed that nobody had created stock quote machines for money market in-struments—commercial paper, Treasury notes, and other securities. He learned that money market instruments were not traded in a central place, like stocks, bonds, and commodities were. To get price informa-tion, a trader had to call a half-dozen banks. Hirsch set himself up as the first clearinghouse for this information. Shrewdly, he told custom-ers that if they bought a monitor from him they could have access to his data. This made Telerate a network, and he operated the network (think of many interconnected highways) down which other information could be shipped for a fee.

Telerate opened in a ten-by-ten-foot cubicle in a room at Two Penn Plaza that Hirsch shared alongside 50 other fledgling businesses who had also rented small cubicles. He hired a family friend, Esther Zimet, to be vice-president. Eager to convince potential customers that Tele-rate was a large company, Zimet would pretend to switch them from re-ception to sales to administration departments by changing her voice. Hirsch and Zimet fielded phone calls from issuers of money-market in-struments and punched current prices up for their handful of compu-ter-screen viewers. Whenever Hirsch went to install or service the com-puter screens, Zimet would get phone calls from executives who were concerned that the long-haired guy in blue jeans and tennis shoes was Telerate's president. Zimet assured them that he was not.

Telerate changed the way institutions bought and sold money mar-ket instruments. Telerate's sales spread to banks throughout the United States. Even the U.S. Government's Treasury Department could more effectively price the sales of its $1.5 trillion debt. To make Telerate seem more proprietary—notwithstanding public-domain information is as free as the air we breathe—Hirsch hired programmers to make the data more interesting, putting it into chart form or bar graphs with color. When the company went public in April 1983, albeit a frothy time, it had a valuation (V) of $1 billion. The number of subscribers leasing Telerate terminals has more than quadrupled in the past five years to more than 14,000 and includes investment firms and finance companies worldwide. The system now has 300,000 miles of phone lines, 2 satellites, and a network of computers to transmit 500,000 quotations every day in foreign exchange rates, financial futures, Euromarkets, options, and precious metals.

"At first I never thought we would get this big," Hirsch told *Esquire*. "Now I know we're going to get much bigger."[60] Someday soon Hirsch says every major company will have a Telerate terminal or two, and so will every securities and investment banking firm, every commercial and mortgage bank with deposits of more than $25 million. He can predict this because Telerate has no major competitors in its field. For another company to compete directly with Telerate, it would need a broad base of subscribers who want the information and the contributors willing to supply it; at this point no company could enter the market for $30,000 as Telerate did.

But Hirsch didn't know that Dow Jones & Company, McGraw-Hill, Inc., and the major wire services owned the information market. He was a Bridgeport University dropout who stopped at a Merrill Lynch & Company office one day in 1969 and asked if the prices of money market instruments were available on the quote machine. They were not and Telerate is. In July 1985, Dow Jones & Co. and the Oklahoma Publishing Co. announced their intent to purchase a 52 per cent interest in Telerate for $564 million.

[60]Terri Minsky, "The Wiring of Wall Street," Dec. 1984, pp. 348–349.

SOICHIRO HONDA

Name of Company: Honda Motor Company, Ltd.

Date Founded: 1948

Location: Tokyo, Japan

Description of Business: The company is one of the world's leading manufacturers of motorcycles and an increasingly important producer of automobiles.

Description of P: Honda broadened the marketplace for motorcycles by convincing "nice people" to buy them. Honda's sales exceeded $11 billion in 1984.

Description of S: Whereas motorbikes seem to be the kind of product that people want less of the richer they become, Honda produced a step-through bike that combined the power and excitement of big machines with the convenience and efficiency of scooters, and priced them well below the competition. Its brilliant ad, "You meet the nicest people on a Honda," gave its motorbike mass market appeal. The motorbike dealers became a distribution channel for the Honda automobile brought forth in the wake of the motorbike.

Members of E: Takeo Fujisawa, chief operating officer, Kiyoshi Kawashima, engineer

Size of V: The approximately 88 million shares of common stock outstanding traded at an average price of $50 per share in 1984 for a market value of $4.4 billion.

Social Utility: The company has created over 100,000 jobs in the United States and Japan and provided low-cost transportation for millions of people.

Principal Sources of Venture Capital: Income from the founder's machine shop.

SOICHIRO HONDA, the single most brilliant mechanical engineer-ing entrepreneur since Henry Ford, was pierced by one unique, fixating idea that was to drive him through periods of hunger, pain, and falling bombs. It drove him through the kind of terror and despair that only those with the need to survive in order to accomplish an idea survive. In 1938 Honda was in a desperate, round-the-clock pursuit of a per-fectly cast piston ring. He slept at his machine shop, covered in grease, without savings or friends, and having pawned his wife's jewelry. The first batch of piston rings was rejected by Toyota Corporation, so it was back to the drawing board. At his industrial engineering classes, Hon-da's designs brought laughter from his professor.

Two years later, Toyota Corporation found the piston rings satisfac-tory and placed an order, but the Japanese government was tooling for war and denied Honda the cement to build a plant. Unfalteringly, Honda and his men learned how to make their own cement. When the war came, Toyota Corporation advanced badly needed working capital of $260,000 while Honda began training women to replace the men who went to war. His factories were bombed out twice, but after each attack, Honda rushed out to pick up the extra gasoline tanks U.S. fight-ers threw away as they flew by. Honda called these cans "Truman's gifts," because they provided raw materials for his manufacturing pro-cess. When an earthquake finally leveled his factory, Honda sold his piston ring operation to Toyota Corporation for $125,000.

After Japan's surrender, Honda created a fast rotary weaving ma-chine, but he ran out of funds in 1947 before the manufacturing stage. Because of the gasoline shortage, he was unable to use his car to get food for his family. In desperation, Honda attached a small motor to his bicycle. A neighbor asked for one and then another neighbor, and another, until his supply of motors ran out. Then he decided to build motors.

As there was no gasoline in war-ravaged Japan, Honda made a motor that ran on pine resin. "We squeezed the resin from the pine root," Honda says, "then mixed it with gasoline bought on the black market. The mixture gave off such a stench of turpentine that I could insist we were violating no gasoline controls by operating the motorbike."[61]

With the income from motorbikes, Honda set out to fulfill his

---

[61]George Gilder, *The Spirit of Enterprise* (New York: Simon & Schuster, 1984), p. 179.

"dream of speed," and build real motorcycles. He brought in as a full partner Takeo Fujisawa and gave him complete authority in finance and strategic marketing. By 1951 Honda's machine was ready for the market, notwithstanding a lack of working capital. Fujisawa relied on customer financing. He wrote letters to Japan's 18,000 bicycle shop owners and told them about Honda's dream, the history of the bicycle and its evolution to the motor-driven bicycle, and finally, he sold the dream of a new Japan and their role in it. Five thousand dealers signed up, but only the hard-core motorcycle riders wanted Honda's "dream." He needed to downsize the motorcycle to a small, inexpensive, quiet, step-through, motor-driven bicycle in order to expand the market from "class" to "mass." The small motorbike, called the "Cub," became an overnight winner, and Honda was awarded the emperor's medal.

It was Honda's good judgment to bring Fujisawa in to handle finance and marketing. Because Fujisawa had been raised in the home of a frequently failing small businessperson, he knew how to design stretch-outs for bankers and creditors, and how to stretch the stretch-outs. As the company prepared to expand into Europe and the United States in 1953, it overextended itself with the purchase of $1 million of machine tools, and if the loan from the Mitsubishi bank has been called, Honda Motor Company would have been gobbled up by the atavistic Mitsubishi Heavy Industries. Fujisawa persuaded the bank to extend the loan and the company remained independent. By 1955 the Honda motorbike was on its way to capturing the hearts and minds of the postwar baby boomers in Europe and America. Honda and Fujisawa built a dealership network in the United States from bicycle dealers who were looking for a new, high profit margin product. When Honda Motor Company introduced its automobiles to the United States in the 1970s, its dealership organization was in place. Through continual change and innovation in its product line, Honda's reputation for quality grows stronger.

ROGER HORCHOW

Name of Company:	Horchow Collection
Date Founded:	1973
Location:	Dallas, Texas
Description of Business:	The company is a direct mail merchandiser of luxury items and collectibles for affluent people.

Description of *P*:

A combination of demographic changes created the need for the Horchow Collection. First, expensive gift items require explaining to the customer, but retail store clerks have become increasingly less capable of learning about their merchandise and communicating this knowledge to others. Second, a catalog can fully describe a product, its sizes, colors, optional features, and other data. Third, catalog shopping via 800 numbers and credit cards is more convenient than driving around to several different stores.

Description of *S*:

Roger Horchow is a passionate collector of beautiful, functional gift items; his taste is similar to that of the market he serves. He caters to *vanity* in several unique ways. For instance, people rarely return items given to them if their initials are on them. Thus, the returns to the Horchow Collection are minimized by pushing the initialing feature.

Members of *E*:

Clay Johnson, president, James A. Mabry, vice-president—controller

Size of *V*:

The Horchow Collection is privately held, but its revenues are believed to be approximately $50 million. Companies that create distribution channels have numerous capabilities for spin-off businesses. Thus, they are valuable to larger companies, perhaps worth more than their revenues.

Social Utility:	The company has created approximately 600 new jobs and Horchow serves as a prime example of successful customer financing.
Principal Sources of Venture Capital:	Family and friends

ROGER HORCHOW, 56, has been collecting brightly colored, unique objects since he was in kindergarten. His grandfather ran a general store near Zanesville, Ohio. This store supplied Horchow's earliest collections of matchbook covers, promotional pamphlets, clippings, photographs, letters, and mementos.

After graduation from Yale, Horchow spent three years in the United States Army, eight years as a buyer at Federated Department Stores (owners of Bloomingdale's), and another eight years at Neiman-Marcus Company, where he was put in charge of the mail-order catalog division from 1969 to 1971. Here the idea occurred to him to launch a catalog independent of a famous department store.

In 1971 he joined Kenton Corporation, a retailer of luxury items in New York, to start a catalog for them. When Kenton's fortunes waned, Horchow bought the catalog from Kenton owner Meshulam Riklis for $1 million, most of it raised from friends, and renamed it. Since then he has built the Horchow Collection into a $50 million business.

The computer has dramatically altered the direct mail business from that day back in 1872 when Aaron Montgomery Ward mailed his first catalog to customers. The computer can process thousands of names and addresses of affluent people; merge various lists together (for example, readers of Town and Country, RCA VCR warranty card signers, American Express Gold Cardholders, and Bloomingdale's credit cardholders in zip code 10021); purge the names that have no mail-order purchasing experience; and then drop out the duplicates. This is known in mailing list management parlance as "merge-purge-dupdrop." The list can be refined to obtain other purchasing propinquities. For example, you can ask the computer to mail the catalog to this "clean list" purified to include only those people who have charged an item of $500 or more or ordered their Town and Country subscription within the last 30 days. Thus, it is possible to reach virtually any group of potential customers with a catalog of goodies.

The goodies have to be very well picked, and Horchow has one of the best reputations in the country for selecting gift items that affluent people love to buy for themselves, as well as their families and friends. He has always trusted his abilities. When he started the Horchow Collection, his exboss, Stanley Marcus, told him that a catalog detached from a well-known retailer would never work. Marcus said that the customers wanted to identify with a famous merchandiser. To counter this argument, Horchow put his picture in the catalogue and the pictures of his family. Whom else could Horchow provide but himself? The courage of the entrepreneur is truly boundless.

K. PHILIP HWANG

Name of Company:	TeleVideo Systems, Inc.
Date Founded:	1975
Location:	Sunnyvale, California

Description of Business: The company designs, develops, and manufactures video display terminals, personal computers, and intelligent workstations which it markets primarily through computer dealers as well as to computer manufacturers for resale.

Description of P: Hwang identified the early need for a "smart" video display terminal, one that could display uppercase and lowercase letters, permit text editing, and recall data in blocks rather than line-by-line. The manufacturers of dumb terminals ignored TeleVideo Systems' (TVS) encroachment into the video display terminal market, even though TVS's smart terminal was less expensive than their dumb terminals.

Description of S: TVS's initial terminal was built simply to facilitate its servicing. It has four basic subassemblies: video module, power supply, keyboard, and logic board. The terminal is handsomely packaged in a tight, tough plastic molded case, all manufactured in Korea under tight quality control standards and shipped to Sunnyvale for assembly. The terminals are less expensive than the competition and TVS can ship hundreds of terminals within hours of receiving the order. Its sales in 1984 were in excess of $163 million on which it earned $4.5 million.

Members of E: Richard A. DuBridge, executive vice-president; and Gemma Hwang, whose income paid the bills during the start-up years.

Size of V: The approximately 42 million shares of common stock outstanding traded in a range of between

	$19⅛ and $2½ in 1984 for an average market value of $460 million.
Social Utility:	TVS has created 1,233 new jobs and Hwang has provided entrepreneurs everywhere with an example of a classical letter of credit start-up.
Principal Source of Venture Capital:	Personal savings, wife's income, and sweat equity

K. PHILIP HWANG, 48, pulled off a "sting" on three established terminal manufacturers—ADDS (a division of NCR Corporation), Lear-Siegler, and Hazeltine—by introducing bargain-priced video display terminals that outperformed their terminals. Between 1979 when TVS began shipping and 1981, NCR Corporation and Hazeltine did nothing more than criticize TVS's cutthroat pricing. "They thought, oh those guys are just trying to buy the market," says Hwang. "They thought we would last three months, maybe six months. Our competitors thought we were losing money from the beginning. That was good for us. They didn't challenge us because they thought we would be out of business before long."[62] TVS shipped 7,500 terminals in its first year at prices 30 to 40 percent below its competitors for twice the performance; 27,500 in its second year; and 120,000 in its fifth year, 1983. It has become the dominant independent supplier of smart terminals in the country and it achieved this position without an injection of equity capital.

Philip Hwang was born in Hungnam, North Korea, and developed a survival instinct when he escaped to Pusan, South Korea, at age 14. When the war ended, Hwang quit his $5-a-month job as an errand boy for the U.S. Tenth Army to attend school in Seoul. He sold pencils and pads and kept up his studies during rigorous 18- to 20-hour days and repeatedly took examinations to qualify for overseas study. Eleven years later, in 1964, he enrolled in Utah State University with a scholarship and $50 to his name. He would have starved in his first year except for a Christmas basket of damaged cans of pumpkin pie filling given him by a kindly Presbyterian minister.

[62]Gene Bylinsky, "The All-American Success Story of K.P. Hwang," Fortune, May 18, 1981, p. 86.

He married a friend from Seoul in 1966, Gemma, and they worked in Lake Tahoe restaurants in the summers. After graduation, Hwang worked for several big companies—Ford Motor Company, Burroughs Corporation, NCR Corporation—but his entrepreneurial urge made him restless. He jumped to a small Silicon Valley electronics company and in that fertile nursery of innovation, it did not take long for Hwang to begin thinking of his own business.

To generate some business experience, he and Gemma acquired a 7-Eleven franchise, at which she and he worked day and evening shifts. The Hwangs pulled $9,000 out of the sale of the 7-Eleven and Hwang and two partners set up shop in a garage to manufacture video game monitors. When they could not raise venture capital, the two partners left.

Hwang had the idea of going to his homeland, where he made the rounds asking seven Korean television companies to make monitors for him. Six turned him down; the seventh was conditionally interested if Hwang could order several thousand monitors per month.

He returned to California and approached Atari and other game manufacturers. They were interested because of Hwang's low price. He went back to Korea and struck a deal for 5,000 monitors per month, raising the capital with letters of credit backed by orders. When Hwang needed more capital, he pledged his house, furniture, and car to a bank for $25,000 and then went back to Atari. In exchange for cutting the price by 5 percent, Atari provided Hwang with additional credit and he was off to Korea with a firm order for 6,000 monitors. Although Hwang's operation was profitable in its first few years, the video game business was becoming very crowded and he decided to switch to video display terminals for computers.

By designing the components of his terminal carefully for ease of service, and emphasizing a tough case and superior quality control, the upstart TVS turned the lights off on Lear-Siegler, ADDS, and Hazeltine. In 1981, two years prior to its initial public offering, TVS began diversifying into personal computers, a significantly more difficult market than smart terminals. The entry into personal computers has created sharp losses for the company in 1985. Can Philip Hwang pull off another sting? Do not bet against a cat who has nine lives and has only used up half of them.

MASARU IBUKA
AKIO MORITA

Name of Company:	Sony Corporation
Date Founded:	1946
Location:	Tokyo, Japan
Description of Business:	Designs, develops, manufactures, and markets consumer electronics products, including color television sets and videocassette recorders.
Description of P:	Ibuka and Morita have had a unique ability to identify consumer needs ahead of others, and to satisfy those needs with high-quality consumer electronics products. Sales in 1984 exceeded $5 billion.
Description of S:	Sony's elegant solutions began with a transistor radio that produced a higher quality sound than the cheaper, competitive models. This was followed by the Trinitron TV, the Betamax, the Walkman, and various other products. Even when knocked off by competitors (Akai's "Walkman look-alike" was 40 percent cheaper), Sony's name has become synonymous with high-quality innovation.
Members of E:	Norio Ohga, president; Makoto Kikuchi, Ph.D., director of Sony's Research Center
Size of V:	The approximately 231 million shares of common stock outstanding traded in a range of $13¾ to $17⅜ in 1984 for a valuation of $3.5 billion.
Social Utility:	The company has taught many American consumer electronics companies how to build and market high-quality products with consumer satisfaction as a prerequisite.

Principal Sources   The sale of a truck in 1948 for $500
of Venture
Capital:

MASARU IBUKA and AKIO MORITA founded Sony Corporation
and built it into a giant among consumer electronics firms with an un-
believable stream of ingenious inventions, because of a series of fiascos
and failures in conventional areas. Ibuka failed the entry exam for lifetime employment at Toshiba. Then he met Morita on an electronics research project for the Japanese Navy, and the two conspired to produce
automatic rice cookers. They made 100 rice cookers, most of which
burnt the rice. From the sale of Morita's dilapidated Datsun truck, the
two failures formed Sony Corporation (then TTK Ltd.) with $500 and
wrote the following introduction to their prospectus:

> At this time of inception of the New Japan, we will try to create
> conditions where persons could come together in a spirit of team-
> work, and exercise to their hearts' desire their technological ca-
> pacity . . . such an organization could bring untold benefits . . .
> [We will] eliminate any untoward profit-seeking [and] expansion
> of size for the sake of size . . . . Rather, we shall emphasize activi-
> ties . . . that large enterprises, because of their size, cannot enter
> . . . Utilizing to the utmost the unique features of our firm, wel-
> coming technological difficulties . . . focusing on highly sophisti-
> cated technical products of great usefulness in society . . . we shall
> open up through mutual cooperation channels of production and
> sales . . . equal to those of large business organizations."[63]

These words, more than any others written about entrepreneurs, can
stand for the entrepreneur's *credo*.

Ibuka and Morita kept their lights on and the paychecks coming by
producing voltmeters at night and on weekends, while Ibuka worked
weekdays on his dream: a consumer tape recorder. He had seen a military tape recorder one day in Occupation Headquarters, and the idea

---

[63]Nick Lyons, *The Sony Vision* (New York: Crown, 1976).

began to take shape in 1948. But Ibuka had no patents, no recorder, and no tape. Japan had no plastic and an import license was not permitted. Thus, Ibuka and Morita had to create the technology of magnetizing tape, and capturing sound on it. They did just that, and when they had created this unique innovation, nobody wanted it; because, as Ibuka and Morita were to have etched in their brains via their thin billfolds, nobody needs an innovation until they are sold on the idea of their need.

Out of sheer desperation, Morita stepped into a proverbial phone booth, changed clothes, and blasted out of the phone booth as one of the greatest salespeople the electronics industry has ever seen. He called on schools, government agencies, individuals in their homes, and shopkeepers, always listening to the customer while accepting the turndown. Finally, he found a secret: a new product must be a solution to a problem in order to generate sales. The need that Morita found was education, and Sony Corporation's tape recorder began to penetrate Japanese schools in the early 1950s. The company quickly penetrated other markets; then Ibuka became concerned that the technological brains he had assembled would grow bored without new challenges. He flew to America to explore transistor technology in 1953, and for $25,000, Ibuka purchased a license from Bell Laboratories to use transistors. On the ride home, Ibuka became fixated with another idea: "Radios small enough so each individual will be able to carry them around for his own use, with power that will enable civilization to reach even those areas with no electric power."[64] MITI (The Ministry of International Trade and Industry) prevented Ibuka from patenting the idea, saying that if transistorized radios were such a good idea why had Hitachi and Toshiba failed to build them. Ibuka kept his engineers busy developing radios, while he put his documentation together to persuade MITI to change its mind. The arguments prevailed a year later, and Ibuka and his chief engineer then left for the United States to learn all they could about photographic etching and advanced crystallography. After three months, Ibuka returned, but his chief engineer remained. Each day he telephoned Ibuka about the things he had learned at conferences and in laboratories.

In 1954 Texas Instruments, Inc. (TI) announced the first transistor-

[64]Ibid, p. 41.

ized radio. Although it initially jarred Ibuka, he used the defeat as fuel to galvanize his team and himself into a mind-set that created heroic achievements. Thereafter, all major breakthroughs in consumer electronics for nearly 30 years were to come from Sony, as it rocketed past Hitachi, Toshiba, Matsushita (Panasonic), TI, RCA Corporation, Westinghouse Electric Corporation, and General Electric Company. Notwithstanding Sony Corporation's higher priced transistor radio—$40 per unit versus TI's $12.95—Sony Corporation was delivering *consumer satisfaction*. It advertised "the radio that works." To stay ahead, Ibuka badgered his engineers and production chiefs to make the radio smaller and smaller. He wanted a pocket radio. His experts said it was impossible, but Ibuka was relentless in his desire.

From its successes in transistor radios, Sony Corporation was able to fund the development and manufacture of the Trinitron one-lens color TV (1968) and the Betamax VCR in 1975. Thereafter have come the Tummy TV, the Walkman, a musical calculator, a personal computer, the Mavica digital disc still camera, the Digital Audio Disc system, the BVP 330 professional video camera, and a fully equipped van to permit film editing in under 10 days.

Ibuka and Morita created Sony Corporation's achievements by fulfilling human needs, frequently before humans realized they needed the things Sony Coporation made for them. Always the innovator, eventually Sony Corporation built a reputation of customer satisfaction that heightened the consumers' awareness of their needs with Sony Corporation's announcement of its solution. Few entrepreneurs have achieved a corporate identity synonymous with innovation as well as Ibuka and Morita.

DAVID JACKSON

Name of Company:	Altos Computer Systems
Date Founded:	1977
Location:	San Jose, California
Description of Business:	The company designs, develops, manufactures, and markets 16-bit, multiterminal, multiuser computer systems.
Description of P:	Jackson perceived the opportunity to sell multi-user microcomputers in the minicomputer marketplace. He positioned his products as business machines and avoided the personal computer image and direct competition with IBM Corporation.
Description of S:	Altos Computer Systems' (ACS) engineers designéd microcomputers to handle the most important tasks normally assigned to minicomputers: business applications and communications. A typical Altos computer can handle up to 800 terminals at a fraction of the price of a minicomputer. Because minicomputer manufacturers Digital Equipment Corporation, Data General Corporation, and Wang Laboratories had a vested interest in the mini, they left the supermicro market to ACS and others. Of these, ACS has achieved the greatest success.
Members of E:	David Zaccarias, vice-president—finance.
Size of V:	The approximately 15 million shares of common stock outstanding traded in a range of $8½ to $12¾ in 1984 for an average valuation of $150 million.
Social Utility:	ACS has created 525 jobs in San Jose. At the time the company had its initial public offering in 1982, Jackson received $5.9 million in cash and

transferred $3 million of it to the Altos Foundation to aid indigents.

Principal Sources   Jackson invested $100,000 earned from a previous
of Venture   venture.
Capital:

DAVID JACKSON directed ACS into a relatively small niche in 1977: the multiuser segment of the microcomputer market, which is the lower end of the minicomputer, office-automation market. Any business that was using DEC, Data General, or Wang computer, and any distributor handling the more expensive minicomputers, was a target for Jackson. In 1984 when ACS's sales exceeded $90 million and its net income $9 million, Digital Equipment Corporation, Data General Corporation, Wang Laboratories, International Business Machines Corporation, Apple Computer, American Telephone & Telegraph Company, NCR Corporation, and five Japanese manufacturers tried to squeeze into Jackson's niche. They were unsuccessful.

I got a call from Jeffrey Boetticher, Pathfinder Computer Center's president and chief operating officer, in mid-December 1984. "We're having our best month in history," he said. "Should do $500,000 and most of it Altos." That conversation was probably going on between many computer dealer managers in late December, because the Altos microcomputer became a very "hot piece." IBM had pulled its multiuser PC AT from the marketplace, AT&T had not released its multiuser 3B2 to a large enough group of dealers, NCR Corporation and the Japanese were not cracking the marketing code, Apple Computer's LISA was not in the hands of business-oriented retailers, Digital Equipment Corporation, Data General Corporation, and Wang Laboratories each of whom produces excellent personal computers, had a problem called "channel confusion": should their direct salespeople sell their supermicros or should the manufacturer build a dealer network? Confusion in the marketplace does not generate sales.

ACS gets its computers to the marketplace mainly through independent distributors who sell to approximately 1,400 systems houses, office equipment dealers, and computer dealers. A direct sales force sells primarily to manufacturers for resale, large end-users, and service bureaus. Exports account for approximately one-half of the company's sales.

British-born Jackson learned the computer business as a salesperson for Digital Equipment Corporation. Following that, the entrepreneurial bug bit, and Jackson started to manufacture computer output microfilm at Peripheral Technology Company which he sold in 1971 for $100,000. That became his nest egg for Altos, named for the Altos Brand apricots crated near his Los Altos Hills home. Jackson learned several things from his first entrepreneurial experience. He told an *Inc.* reporter: "I learned then that if you want to meet the payroll you'd better have some money in the bank." For this reason, Jackson runs ACS "lean and mean." Pretax margins have averaged 12 percent since 1982, and return on equity has averaged 39 percent over the same period. ACS achieves an unusually high $170,000 sales per employee ratio from its 350 "happy, but serious" employees. Jackson says, "That's the key to this business. If Japan can do it, good luck to them. No competitor can underprice us and survive."[65] Jackson wisely extends dealer credit and provides national advertising in business magazines to create brand awareness. An almost equal amount of dollars is reinvested in research and development to keep the ACS line state-of-the-art.

In 1984 AT&T spent $43 million on advertising to enter ACS's niche and NCR Corporation spent a like amount. Neither one shipped as many multiuser systems as did ACS, even though ACS spent less than $10 million on advertising. Venture capitalists in Silicon Valley pretty much let this niche company slip by them. Don Valentine, the venture capitalist who discovered Apple Computer Inc., provided bridge financing to Jackson. Thus, when ACS went public in late 1982 by selling a 20 percent interest for $62 million, Jackson and his wife, Susan, still owned close to half of its stock. Find a niche and dominate it, is the ACS lesson. Then run lean, mean, and hard because there will be tanks chasing your peashooter.

---

[65]R.A.M., "The Inc. 500 Private Lives," *Inc.*, Dec. 1982, p.43.

CLAUDE AND DONNA JEANLOZ

Name of Company: Renovator's Supply, Inc.

Date Founded: 1978

Location: Millers Falls, Massachusetts

Description of Business: The company began as a publisher of a mail-order catalog of electrical and plumbing fixtures, hardware, and ornaments used to restore old houses.

Description of *P*:   Eight million families received Renovator's Supply's catalog of hard-to-find specialty plumbing, hardware, and electrical items in 1984, up from 6.5 million in 1983. The Jeanlozes were correct in their estimate six years ago that a lot of people were frustrated by their inability to renovate their old houses for lack of the right hardware items. With catalog advertising, a $2 price for the catalog, and revenues from 13 retail stores and other businesses either started or acquired, the "nostalgia P" identified by this company will exceed $40 million in 1985.

Description of *S*:   In a classic use of customer financing, revenues from the catalog, estimated at $13 million in 1983, have financed the expansion into 13 co-owned Renovator's Supply stores, *Victorian Home* magazine, another catalog called *Country Notebook*, a catalog of products for left-handed people, a Play for Growth line of children's toys, and other businesses.

Members of *E*:   Karen Morgan, computer operations manager; Richard Aldrich, product development chief; Cindy Harris, president of mail order division; and William Chagnam, director of manufacturing.

Size of *V*:   Although privately held, a fair estimate of the valuation a potential acquirer would place on Renovator's Supply might be 150 percent of revenues or around $60 million.

Social Utility: The Jeanlozes have created 140 jobs in Millers Falls, plus around 75 in their stores. To renovators of old houses, the social utility of the company is obvious.

Principal Sources of Venture Capital: The Jeanlozes borrowed $50,000 on their renovated home to start the business.

CLAUDE AND DONNA JEANLOZ were tossed out of an African country in 1974 by a dictator who hated the United States and its Peace Corps. They returned to their home in Massachusetts, and for lack of something better to do began restoring their colonial house in Northfield, Massachusetts. Like any homeowners who care about aesthetics and quality, the Jeanlozes ran up against a wall. Many of the authentic fixtures they were looking for were just not made any longer. And when items were available, getting them took infinite patience and dogged pursuit. Sheer desperation finally drove them to manufacturers' directories where they hunted down sources for the things no one else could supply.

Four years later the couple had completely restored their house in Massachusetts and another in Canada. In the process, they had answered dozens of inquiries from people who wondered where they had found their supplies. This prompted the Jeanlozes to start a mail order business, a clearinghouse for exactly the kinds of electrical and plumbing fixtures, hardware, and ornaments that had so many house restorers over a barrel. Their basic catalog offers necessities for fixing up old houses of any period or region. Supplementary catalogs offer specialty products to add finishing touches, nostalgia, and whimsy.

As the business grew, the Jeanlozes moved it into an old garage, which, of course, they restored. Then in December 1983 they moved down the street into a large factory which went through a renovation. Sales grew from $34,000 in 1978 to $12 million in 1983. The introduction of a computer early on to collect subscriber names and inquiries and to store product information has been critical to the company's rapid growth. To generate additional revenues, the Jeanlozes permitted manufacturers to advertise in their catalog.

A stunning cash flow has permitted the couple to rapidly diversify into a chain of retail stores called Renovator's Supply. The first was opened in Flemington, New Jersey, a historic town with a restored old town section; the other 13 stores are primarily situated in New England.

In March 1984 the company purchased the publisher of *Aristera*, a catalog of products for left-handed people, and *Country Notebook*, a catalog of country-inspired home decoration items. Other diversifications included an on-premises blacksmith shop that produces wrought iron items for the home and Play for Growth, a toy line for children.

What better example than Renovator's Supply of the catalysts of entrepreneurship—dissatisfaction, insight, and energy—welded to the Jeanlozes' identification of a mail-order, customer-financed solution to the problem.

STEVEN P. JOBS
STEVEN WOZNIAK

Name of Company:	Apple Computer, Inc.
Date Founded:	1975
Location:	Cupertino, California
Description of Business:	The company is a leading manufacturer of personal computers.
Description of *P*:	The development of microprocessors, their proper arrangement on printed circuit boards, and the connection of the boards to a keyboard and a television terminal in 1975 produced excitement in the engineering departments of most mainframe computer and electronics companies. But only the potential entrepreneurs in these companies saw that these exciting little products were actually computers that people could afford. In 1984 sales of personal computers reached $9 billion, of which Apple had a 15 percent market share.
Description of *S*:	Wozniak and Jobs had very little money and were forced to use the least expensive products, the fewest chips and the most creative arrangement of components. Although Wozniak offered Hewlett–Packard the Apple I they refused it and have been trying to catch up ever since.
Members of *E*:	A.C. Markulla, the first chief operating officer, and John Sculley, chief executive officer
Size of *V*:	The approximately 60 million shares of common stock outstanding traded in a range between $34 and $22 per share in 1984 for a valuation of $1.5 billion.
Social Utility:	Apple Computer has created approximately 4,700 jobs and provided a goal for every engineer who has ever dreamed.

Principal Sources
of Venture
Capital:

A.C. Markulla provided the seed capital, and start-up venture capital came from Don Valentine's Capital Management, Venrock (the Rockefellers' venture capital fund), Arthur Rock, and Henry E. Singleton, the founder of Teledyne Corporation.

STEVEN P. JOBS and STEVEN WOZNIAK, two self-taught engineers and dropouts, introduced the typewriter-sized, $1,350 Apple II in 1977, the state-of-the-art in home and small business computers for the next five years. Notwithstanding the onslaught of practically every mainframe and minicomputer behemoth in the United States and Japan, Apple Computer has held its ground. It is one of the greatest entrepreneurial success stories in the history of the American economy.

An adopted orphan, Steven Jobs wandered through the wilderness of Oregon apple orchards after leaving Reed College in his freshman year. Then he cavorted with gurus and primal scream therapists while searching in sandals for his genetic forebears and his identity until he became reacquainted with a high school friend, Steve Wozniak. Jobs found in Wozniak's engineering brilliance an opportunity to channel the energies of his search into a frenzied five years of scrambling for components, raising money, and selecting business partners that created the mystique and the reality that was and is Apple Computer, Inc.

Jobs and Wozniak met in 1975 when Jobs was a video game designer at Atari, where founder Nolan Bushnell wanted to reduce the number of chips in his Pong game from 150–170 to less than 40. Wozniak, then an engineer at Hewlett–Packard Company, had designed a version of Pong that used about 30 chips. Bushnell told Jobs and Wozniak that he would give them $700 if they could design "Breakout," a Pong upgrade, with less than 50 chips, and $1,000 if it was under 40 chips. Wozniak and Jobs delivered a breadboard model in four days with 44 chips.

After that chance encounter, Wozniak began designing a personal computer at his bench at Hewlett–Packard Company, because he wanted one for his personal use. Wozniak tells the following story:

One day I mentioned to Steve that I had noticed something interesting in the video addressing. I could make a little change by adding two chips, and then I could just shift each byte out onto the screen and we'd have hi-res graphics. I wasn't sure it was worth the two chips . . . . But Steve was pushing for all the features we could get, so eventually we put it in. At the time we had no idea that people were going to be able to write games with animation and little characters bouncing all around the screen . . . . I would take it into Hewlett–Packard to show the engineers. Sometimes they would sit down and say, "This is the most incredible product I've ever seen in my life!"[66]

His first computer was slow and its timing was off, because Wozniak was using the oldest, cheapest surplus parts he could find, plus a home television set. Wozniak says,

Steve got intrigued with all these ideas and one day he asked me, "Why don't you use these new 16-pin dynamic RAM's?" I had looked at them in my work at Hewlett–Packard, but they were new and I couldn't afford any parts that didn't come my way almost free. I'm a little bit shy, and I didn't know any of the reps, but Steve just called them up and talked them into giving us samples.[67]

The two Steves had become members of the Homebrew Computer Club, a meeting place for high school students and Silicon Valley engineers to discuss microcomputers, and to show one another their designs. Jobs came up with the idea of building a few of Wozniak's computers and selling them to club members. As Wozniak tells it:

We had about 500 members in the club, and I thought that maybe 50 people would buy it. It would cost us about $1,000 to have the board laid out, and each board would cost us about $20. So if we sold them for $40 and 50 people bought them, we'd get our $1000 back. It seemed pretty doubtful. But Steve said, "Well, yes, but at least for once in our lives we'll have a company." So Steve sold

[66]Gregg Williams & Rob Moore, "The Apple Story." Byte, December 1984, p. A67–A71.
[67]Ibid, p. A68.

his van and I sold my HP calculator to raise money to make the PC boards.[68]

Soon thereafter, Wozniak and Jobs received an order from a local computer dealer to supply completely built computers. He ordered 100 units at $500 each, a $50,000 order. To obtain parts, the supplier approved the credit of the dealer, and provided Apple Computer with $20,000 of parts on 30 days' credit. A friend, Alan Baum, loaned $5,000, and Wozniak was able to build the computers and deliver them in 10 days.

To build the Apple II, Wozniak and Jobs needed to raise $250,000. Nolan Bushnell, Jobs' boss at Atari, put Jobs in touch with Don Valentine, a venture capitalist, who had been involved in Atari. Valentine introduced Apple Computer to Mike Markulla, a former marketing manager with Intel Corporation. Markulla wrote a business plan and invested $91,000. He brought in Michael Scott as president and he attracted $600,000 in venture capital plus a line of credit from the Bank of America. Within three years from the time Markulla joined the company, Apple's sales exceeded $100 million and four years after that, the company's sales reached approximately $1.5 billion. As competitors have come and gone, as managers have quit to go elsewhere, and after the venture capitalists have cashed in their chips, Jobs continues to play a leading role in product design and development at Apple. Wozniak left Apple in early 1985 to design computers in a smaller pond.

[68]Ibid, p. A69.

EWING MARION KAUFFMAN

Name of Company:	Marion Laboratories
Date Founded:	1950
Location:	Kansas City, Missouri
Description of Business:	The company derives the bulk of its revenues from aggressively marketing the discoveries of other pharmaceutical companies, mostly foreign firms.
Description of P:	Kauffman began his career as a drug salesperson in 1948. Within a year, his commissions exceeded the president's salary. He left to start his own pharmaceutical marketing company and obtained the rights to market the drugs of foreign firms in the United States.
Description of S:	In his spare time, Kauffman developed the first calcium pill made from crushed oyster shells, which he packaged in the evenings in his basement. The company's other achievements include selecting useful drugs to bring to market. Sales in 1984 were $226 million on which the company earned over $20 million.
Members of E:	F. W. Lyons, Jr., president; Michael E. Herman, chief financial officer
Size of V:	The approximately 19 million shares of common stock outstanding traded in a range of $27¼ to $42½ in 1984 for an average valuation of $655 million.
Social Utility:	Kauffman has funded and promoted a massive public education and training program to train children and adults in life-saving techniques and cardiopulmonary resuscitation techniques. He recently began finding a program which he created to teach sixth and seventh graders how to manage their temptation to try alcohol or drugs.

Principal Sources   Personal savings
of Venture
Capital:

EWING MARION KAUFFMAN, 69, is genuinely giving, and universally regarded as being "too friendly and too eager to accept challenges." Some local businesspeople have been heard to say, "I would have pegged Ewing as a great showman—Barnum, Bailey and Kauffman—if I didn't know about Marion Labs." His success has been earned every inch of the way, notwithstanding a robust cheerfulness that masks his tenacity. Kauffman likes the following old world idiom: "Those who apply themselves unswervingly to a task are amply rewarded."[69]

At age 11, Ewing was involved in all the sports and horseplay of childhood when a severe illness left him with a faulty heart valve. The doctor prescribed a year in bed, flat on his back. Ewing fought it at first, but soon became hooked on reading. He began reading over three books a day, with the supply of 100 books a month met under special arrangement with the local library. In addition to being well read at the end of that year, Ewing developed the ability to speed read at rates up to 3,000 words a minute.

Ewing's parents were divorced the next year. His father had lost the family farm and couldn't find work in Depression-hit Kansas City. His father had four grades of education and impaired vision, but Ewing remembers him as an earthy man with a kind heart. His mother was a college graduate who had seven years of Greek and eight years of Latin studies. She gave Ewing a sense of spirituality and courage. For instance, he always wore a suit to high school, the only one he had. His mother explained to him, "You may not have as much money in your pocket as the others, but there is no one better than you."[70] Kauffman says, "I had this inner feeling of being able to do things. It is like being willing to get up and talk in front of an assembly in the auditorium or volunteer for a task. I got that from my mother. The values of life were important to her."[71]

Kauffman spent two years in junior college, working afternoons and

---

[69]Phil A. Koury, "It Takes More Than a Hit to Get to First Base, A Character Study of Ewing M. Kaufman," p. 4 (pamphlet).
[70]Ibid, p. 7.
[71]Ibid, pp. 7–8.

evenings at a laundry. One day he saw the laundry owner sitting at his desk cutting out little slips of paper. He was designing a form to hold together shirt collars. Later on, Kauffman noticed, the owner received a check in the mail for several thousand dollars for the invention. "I didn't make that much in a year," Kauffman said, "and he got paid for something that came out of his mind."[72]

When World War II started, Kauffman enlisted in the U.S. Navy and was assigned to a flagship convoy that shuttled between the United States and the West Indies. While on board, he read voraciously on the subjects of astronomy and navigation. His expertness led to saving the convoy from running aground, for which feat Kauffman received a deck commission with the rank of Ensign bestowed by the Secretary of the Navy.

After the service, Kauffman went to work for a Decatur, Illinois, pharmaceutical company, calling on doctors' offices. Once again, he dug into every medical book he could find. Within a year's time his income exceeded the company president's, "so they cut my commissions and kept trimming my territory as the sales volume grew. Finally I quit."[73] It was then that he went into his basement where Marion Laboratories was launched.

The initial capital was $4,000. During the day, Kauffman called on doctors to sell his one and only product, a calcium pill made from crushed oysters. At night, he typed up the orders and packaged the merchandise. The next day he took them to the post office. Kauffman operated alone, but accurately, enthusiastically, and thoroughly. He learned the value of thinking smart, and to this day loves the idiom: "You can't stop a man who thinks."

Kauffman is a giver, not a taker. "This community has been good to me," he says. Early employees and early stockholders have been handsomely rewarded. The community has a major league baseball team courtesy of Kauffman. When he bought the Oakland A's franchise from Charley Finley for $8 million in 1970, he stunned the town and upset some of the grey eminences of Kansas City who did not know about him. The Kansas City Royals have become a winning and valuable franchise in a little over a decade.

[72]Ibid, p. 7.
[73]Ibid, p. 9.

His sharing goes further. With his wife, the former Muriel Dennie, the Kauffmans funded and promoted a massive public education and training program aimed at teaching life-saving techniques to 100,000 area residents. The program, which is on-going, teaches cardiopulmonary resuscitation (CPR) technique, which combines chest compression and mouth-to-mouth resuscitation, in the initial phase of heart attack. Not only does Kauffman share his fortune with the community, but he shares credit for the success of Marion with all of his employees. He got people to work for Marion on the promise that "someday they would have a car, someday they would have insurance, someday they would have a profit-sharing plan." Kauffman says, "It takes more than a hit to get to first base." Perhaps it is his humility that has made Ewing Kauffman so successful.

THOMAS L. KELLY, JR.

Name of Company:	TIE/Communications, Inc.
Date Founded:	1971
Location:	Shelton, Connecticut
Description of Business:	The company designs telephone key systems manufactured in Japan, which are imported and marketed primarily to business customers in the United States.
Description of *P*:	Kelly perceived an opportunity to sell to companies telephones with features substantially better than American Telephone and Telegraph Company's (AT&T) for prices significantly less than AT&T's cumulative rental charges. He correctly perceived AT&T as a leasing company, charging monopolistic monthly rates for fully depreciated, ubiquitous equipment. He could sell a better product on a cost efficient basis, after the Supreme Court Carterphone decision in 1965, which permitted telephone equipment manufacturers to hook their equipment onto AT&T's lines.
Description of *S*:	AT&T was a formidable opponent of the interconnect companies. Notwithstanding TIE/Communications' (TIE) superior equipment and price advantages, AT&T resisted interconnecting its equipment, and Kelly frequently had to argue his case to regulators. Institutional barriers to entry were as much his problem as was Ma Bell. Eventually TIE won and American businesses and consumers rushed out to purchase cheaper and better telephones. With MCI Communications Corporation pulling AT&T at one end, and TIE at the other, AT&T threw in the towel and asked to be broken up in order to compete without regulations.

Members of *E*:	Leonard J. Fassler, vice-president, and early investor; William A. Merritt, Jr., executive vice-president
Size of *V*:	The approximately 33 million shares outstanding averaged $9⅜ to $28⅜ in 1984 for a valuation of $610 million.
Social Utility:	TIE has created approximately 1,300 jobs in Connecticut and, in part, caused the deregulation of the telephone industry.
Principal Sources of Venture Capital:	Personal savings of $10,000 from Kelly and $39,000 from Fassler and four others, a grant from the state of Connecticut, and venture capital of $300,000 from Allen & Company

THOMAS L. KELLY, JR., 45, is a five-foot-six-inch tightly wound coil of tense steel, who challenged the mighty AT&T to a fight in the early 1970s. To the surprise of nearly everyone—except those of us who know Kelly—he beat Ma Bell into submission. Kelly's father took away his safety net early, and let him know that if he wanted anything he would have to fight for it. Once Kelly got a job as a truck driver during a college vacation. For amusement the other drivers backed the bespectacled mini-mite into a corner for a little game of torture, so Kelly broke a Coke bottle like John Wayne in a bar fight and took on the whole outfit. They backed down and Kelly won their respect.

While raising venture capital in the capital-thin mid-1970s, Tom Perkins, senior partner of Kleiner & Perkins, poked fun facetiously at Kelly's telephone. Perkins went so far as to say the semiconductor would downsize the telephone to the size of a pocket calculator. Once again Kelly came out of his seat, picked up Perkins' telephone, thrust it in the venture capitalist's lap and said: "Look, Mr. Perkins, your ear is there and your mouth is over here, so you'll always need something to link the two." Perkins still seemed unconvinced. "Okay," continued Kelly, "look at the size of your fingers. See the fat tips. You're going to need 10 buttons at least the size of your fingertips." Perkins began to take notice of Kelly's reddening face and dancing eyes. "Finally, Mr. Perkins, if I may lift the handle of your phone," Kelly said as he raised the handle off the cradle, "some people have a temper like mine and occasionally slam down the phone like this." Which he did. "So they're going to need a pretty strong cradle to catch it." With that, Kelly and this author, his investment banker, left Silicon Valley empty-handed.

Kelly was turned down by dozens of venture capitalists, usually for the same reason: nobody can beat AT&T. He cleverly generated $350,000 from a grant program established by the State of Connecticut to provide funds to scientific organizations in the state. Kelly created subsidiaries that sold interconnect equipment (non-AT&T telephone systems) to businesses in New York City and he borrowed on their receivables.

Through it all, Kelly urged his engineers to design better telephones. He added music on hold, lockout features to ensure privacy, soft paging, and automatic conferencing. Kelly knew that AT&T was not going to react with newer and better telephones because as he said to a *Forbes* reporter in 1981: "Now, what business do you think Bell is in?" Telecommunications, maybe? "No," Kelly replied. "They're a bank. The biggest rental company in the world. They happen to be casually in communications." His point: AT&T's $115 billion plant and equipment is depreciated slowly. It has to think like a leasing company. Kelly added: "What happens if you are a smart guy at Bell Labs? They say, 'Great idea, George. You take your idea and keep thinking about it for three or five years.'" AT&T was employing 3,464 Ph.D.'s at the time, to TIE's 2.[74]

In 1982, due to TIE's increased penetration of AT&T's installed base and its arguments before the Federal Communications Commission, AT&T was ordered to offer a purchase as well as a lease option on its equipment. Once AT&T lost its profitable lease renewals there was no valid reason for it to avoid direct competition with TIE, Rolm Corporation (switchboards), and MCI Communications Corporation (discount long-distance service). Ma Bell asked to be deregulated in order to fight it out in these three enormous markets, and others entered the markets as well.

But Kelly has never had the comfort of mountains of venture capital or dozens of supporters in his camp. In fact, his first and most enduring entrepreneurial achievements have been in Kelly versus Goliath situations. His courage and spirit are indefatigable.

---

[74]William Baldwin, "For whom the bells toll," *Forbes*, Sept. 14, 1981, pp. 188, 191.

AMIN J. KHOURY

Name of Company:	Delmed, Inc.
Date Founded:	1974
Location:	Canton, Massachusetts

Description of Business:
: The company designs, develops, manufactures, and markets specialized parenteral products, including plastic blood banking disposables, intravenous devices, dialysis products primarily for home-care patients, and specialty solutions.

Description of P:
: Khoury observed that one large company had 90 percent of the $200 million intravenous blood bag market and was marketing a fairly old product at a high price. Khoury believed he could design a superior product and sell it at a lower price. Delmed accomplished its goal, although it took longer and cost more money than Khoury believed it would.

Description of S:
: Khoury accepted several major risks: institutional barrier to entry (FDA), one major competitor (Fenwall), and very few customers (the Red Cross accounts for 50 percent of the market). He relied on his ability to produce a technically superior product and deliver it at a lower price.

Members of E:
: Dr. James F. Marten, co-founder

Size of V:
: The approximately 15 million shares of common stock outstanding traded in a range of $4⅝ to $11⅝ in 1984 for an average market value of $113 million.

Social Utility:
: The company has created 700 jobs and it demonstrated entrepreneurial success in an area in which many of the large pharmaceutical companies failed.

Principal Sources of Venture Capital:
: Khoury and Marten invested $500,000 and Fred Nazem was the principal venture capital investor.

AMIN J. KHOURY, a 45-year-old chemist of Lebanese descent, has not led a "risk averse" business life, to use his favorite expression. In the late 1960s, Khoury and his coworker Dr. James F. Marten were working at Damon Corporation on now infamous Route 128 west of Boston. Unable to raise venture capital on their own, they had convinced Damon Corporation to back them on a joint venture basis to make automatic blood analyzers. In six years, sales of their device had risen to $90 million. They suggested a new start-up to Damon Corporation—blood products—but management said no. The two entrepreneurs left Damon Corporation with a six-figure bonus and retreated to Khoury's basement to write a business plan. (Whereas Silicon Valley start-ups—frequently computer- or electronics-based—usually occur in garages, East Coast start-ups—which list more medical companies among their number—occur mostly in basements.)

The business plan called for Delmed to design, develop, and produce a technologically superior polyvinylchloride blood bag, filled with all the blood and chemicals used in intravenous blood delivery. These included anticoagulant solutions, a plasticizer to keep the bag flexible, tubing, and the needle. The product had to pass the Food and Drug Administration's (FDA) inspection and it had to be superior to and less expensive than the competitive product, which had a 90 percent market share. Citicorp Venture Capital, following Nazem's lead, invested $1 million having seen Khoury's and Marten's performance at Damon Corporation.

Murphy's Law applied: the plasticizer was proven to be carcinogenic, the FDA did not approve Delmed's anticoagulant, and the needle hurt the patients when tested by the St. Louis Red Cross. Like great entrepreneurs do, Khoury went about solving his problems. He went to Union Carbide Corporation to make a better plasticizer, he purchased McGaw's line of anticoagulants, which had FDA approval, and he solved the manufacturing problem that made Delmed's needle hurt patients. Of course, the original $1.5 million in venture capital had to be supplemented; Khoury convinced Nazem to stick with him and bring in more investors. There were other problems, primarily caused by Delmed's taking manufacturing to El Salvador where labor costs are one-fifth of U.S. costs, but it took years to get the plant up to speed. The Delmed launch took seven years and $14 million, but its blood bags became the product of choice for the Red Cross and other large customers.

When Delmed proved it could take market share from an industry giant, other giants such as Cutter Laboratories and Bayer, A.G. entered the market. Khoury said, "Now our risks [changed] from production risks to marketing risks. We . . . kill our customers with kindness."[75]

Khoury was one of the first entrepreneurs to start a medical products company with all of the risks facing him: development, manufacturing, marketing, management, and growth, plus institutional barriers to entry. Although it took twice as long and cost 10 times as much, Delmed has been a lamplighter for medical industry entrepreneurs.

[75]Jane Carmichael, "Perseverance or Pigheadedness," *Forbes*, Dec. 7, 1981, pp. 62–65.

RAPHAEL KLEIN

Name of Company:	Xicor, Inc.
Date Founded:	1978
Location:	Milpitas, California

Description of Business: The company designs, develops, and manufactures nonvolatile reprogrammable semiconductor memory products.

Description of P: The personal computer created an insatiable demand for memory. Klein anticipated the need for customized memory devices, at mass production prices, delivered in days with a high reliability factor.

Description of S: The company manufactures electrically erasable programmable read only memory (EEPROM) semiconductors. EEPROMs are unique memory devices that can be programmed, randomly erased, and reprogrammed either through the keyboard or remotely through a modem without removal from the system and will retain stored information if system power is lost or turned off.

Members of E: Richard T. Simko, vice-president—research and development; William H. Owen III, vice-president—engineering; Wallace E. Tchon, vice-president—strategic planning; and S. Allan Kline.

Size of V: The approximately 11 million shares of common stock outstanding traded in a range of $8½ to $19¾ in 1984 for an average valuation of $155 million.

Social Utility: Raphael Klein has built one of the fastest growing semiconductor companies in the world, in defiance of proclaimed Japanese superiority and the turn-downs of Silicon Valley venture capitalists.

Principal Sources
of Venture
Capital:

The seed capital was provided by Raphael Klein and the members of the entrepreneurial team; venture capital was raised from the public via D. H. Blair & Company.

RAPHAEL KLEIN, 41, is the entrepreneur of whom the Silicon Valley venture capitalists like least to be reminded. He built the kind of company that venture capitalists like most to finance—productivity-improving, electronics-based, capital goods—without a dime of their money. He was trained at National Semiconductor Corporation and Fairchild Semiconductor Corporation from whence came the brilliant triumvirate who founded Intel Corporation, as well as Jerry Sanders, who launched Advanced Micro Devices Corporation. Klein's entrepreneurial team includes experienced semiconductor engineers and executives from Intel, Fairchild, Texas Instruments, National Semiconductor, Data General, and Honeywell. Klein is a physics graduate from Technion, Israel's equivalent of M.I.T., and his team graduated from California Institute of Technology, University of Chicago, University of California, and so forth. Klein and his co-founders, to top it off, invested over $160,000 of their personal savings in Xicor. Notwithstanding, Klein could not generate any interest from the professional venture capital community. The alternative, a public offering, was the route taken, and D. H. Blair & Company, one of the best at judging which new issues to back, did its usual admirable job.

Klein and his wife came to the United States in 1974 with one suitcase and a ticket to fly to San Jose, California to begin working for Monolithic Memories, Inc. The Kleins had no money. But he had a job offer.

Soon after joining Monolithic, Klein left for National Semiconductor, continuing to learn about semiconductors. The reputation of Fairchild Semiconductor as the "University" that graduated Noyce, Grove, and Moore (the founders of Intel) was too great a magnet. Thus, he joined Fairchild where, from 1975 to 1976, Klein was manager of technology and manufacturing engineering for charge-coupled-memory devices. He moved on to Intel in August 1976, and remained there until August 1978 as program manager for research and development of an advanced memory device. For his unique contribution to Intel's product line, Klein received a cash award of $70,000. He was launched.

Xicor's initial offices were in Klein's home and subsequently the home of a co-founder, where the NOVRAM memory device was developed. The need for a facility to test design concepts became apparent in late 1978, and Klein convinced Ebauches in Marin, Switzerland, to undertake a cooperative development effort in exchange for a minority equity interest. Ebauches received one board seat as well. The founders kept Xicor alive with personal investments and loans and with two private placements: $476,300 in June, 1979 at $1.18 per share and $2,487,100 in April, 1980 at $3.80 per share (most of it purchased by Ebauches).

In October 1980, D. H. Blair took Xicor public. It sold 1.98 million shares of common stock at $6.50 per share. In December 1980, CIN Industrial Investments, Ltd., a subsidiary of the British coal miners' pension fund, invested $2 million and committed another $4 million. Another D. H. Blair offering at $7.15 per share in May 1982 brought in $10 million.

The financial history bears pointing out because it shows that major amounts of money can be raised for a high technology company even when the traditional and most likely investors turn thumbs down. Xicor is today considered a leader in the EEPROM niche. How big is this niche and how fast is it growing? Dataquest projects EEPROM sales of $1.1 billion in 1989. *Electronic Design News* projects that over half of all design engineers will be using EEPROM within six months to two years. Each microcomputer includes $6 of nonvolatile memory, most of that soon to be EEPROM's.

I asked Raphael Klein if he would launch his company any other way if he had it to do over again. His reply: "I owe everything to the American public. They believed in me when no one else did. I am glad that they are benefiting now."

PHILIP H. KNIGHT

Name of Company:	NIKE Inc.
Date Founded:	1972
Location:	Beaverton, Oregon

Description of
Business:
The company designs, manufactures, and markets a broad line of high-quality athletic footwear for competitive and recreational purposes.

Description of *P*:
Knight formulated the problem in 1963 in a student term paper: with the demographic shift toward health care and physical fitness, more people would be running or, at least, recreating. They would become conscious of what the professional athletes were wearing, and seek to emulate them. Thus, if Knight could produce a high-quality, low-cost shoe for professional athletes, he would open up a mass market.

Description of *S*:
Knight found Japanese manufacturers who could produce higher quality athletic shoes at considerably less cost than the European manufacturers. To assure proper design, he formed NIKE with his college running coach, William J. Bowerman. After several years of market research and product testing, the NIKE line was launched for the 1972 Olympics.

Members of *E*:
Philip H. Knight, president; James L. Manus, vice-president—finance

Size of *V*:
The approximately 19 million shares of common stock outstanding traded in a range of $7⅞ to $16⅜ in 1984 for an average valuation of $437 million.

Social Utility:
The company has created employment for 3,600 people and a rate of return on stockholders' equity of more than 30 percent per annum since 1980.

Principal Sources   Personal savings of the co-founders Knight and
of Venture   Bowerman
Capital:

PHILIP H. KNIGHT joined the CPA firm of Coopers & Lybrand (C&L)
in 1963 after graduation from Stanford University's MBA program, but
his mind was not on debits and credits. A better than average miler at
the University of Oregon, Knight was struck with the idea of capturing
a large share of the athletic shoe market by offering higher quality—so
high that professional athletes would wear and endorse the shoes—at a
lower price. An MBA term paper formulated the market. If the Japanese
could underprice the Germans in electronics, they could probably do it
in running shoes as well.

He contacted his former running coach Bill Bowerman and, with
$1,000, they formed Blue Ribbon Sports which imported Tiger shoes
from Japan. While working at C&L during the day, Knight peddled
Japanese-made track shoes in the evenings and on weekends, mostly to
school athletic teams. Meantime, Bowerman was tinkering with new
designs. It was a good thing that he was doing things like pouring rub-
ber into his wife's waffle iron, because in 1972 Tiger demanded 51 percent ownership of Blue Ribbon Sports, or the company would lose its
franchise.

Knight refused. He took the waffle sole design to a manufacturer and
began producing his own shoes at a desperation-induced pace, because
the 1972 Olympic trials were only months away. The night before the
product's name had to be imprinted on the boxes, employee Jeff Johnson came up with the name NIKE, the Greek goddess of victory. The
company was nearly put out of business in 1972 by a dock workers'
strike and a sharp rise in value of the yen. It had to pull out of its deficit
working capital position in 1973 or go out of business.

Fortunately, the quality of the shoes carried the company through.
Serious athletes began requesting NIKE shoes and from that point on
Knight knew an emphasis on research and development would be
required to maintain the company's dominant position in the United
States. To that end, Knight tests new models on 15-mile jogs to work.
He laughingly says, "If a model is not a success, it's embarrassing when
I walk around crippled all day."[76]

---

[76]"The Richest People in America, The Forbes 400," *Forbes*, Fall 1983.

NIKE's sales for 1984 exceeded $1 billion and the company has become the dominant name in running and recreational shoes in this country and second to Adidas worldwide. Knight is diversifying NIKE into apparel, other footwear, and into foreign markets. NIKE is living proof that a carefully formulated problem can lead to a huge success even though the solution is nonproprietary.

DAVID I. KOSOWSKY

Name of Company:	Damon Corporation
Date Founded:	1961
Location:	Needham Heights, Massachusetts

Description of Business:

The company is a leader in the clinical diagnostics industry, operating a nationwide network of clinical laboratories and manufacturing instrumentation and diagnostic products.

Description of P:

Kosowsky perceived a need for a highly reliable chain of clinical laboratories to test blood and urine chemistry, electrocardiography, kidney dialysis, and pulmonary function. The business grew to $140 million in revenues and began to level off, at which point Kosowsky began looking for meaningful diversification opportunities. Damon Corporation went into clinical diagnostic instruments, veterinary biologicals, and educational toys. The research activities of two of these divisions—physics and biology—led to a new breakthrough, ENCAPCEL, the ability to encapsulate living cells, a breakthrough in genetic engineering.

Description of S:

Kosowsky saw the need twenty years ago to gain credibility with pathologists who would send work to his labs. Thus, Damon Corporation bought a well-known manufacturer of centrifuges to impress his customers. In 1981 physicists at this company spotted the breakthrough: a membrane barrier that would hold uniform amounts of chemicals, and the knowledge for producing the capsules. Scientists in the veterinary products division contributed their knowledge of biological mechanisms. The result is a capsule that can contain new genetic information to fight disease inexpensively and efficiently.

Members of *E*:   Robert P. Schneider, president; and Vernon Sherman, Jr., vice-president treasurer.

Size of *V*:   The approximately 7 million shares of common stock outstanding ranged from $11½ to $19⅞ in 1984 for an average valuation of $100 million.

Social Utility: The company created 4,000 jobs and it has been a leader in reducing the cost and improving the efficiency of U.S. health care delivery systems.

Principal Sources of Venture Capital: The new issue market of 1967 provided much of Damon Corporation's capital along with venture capitalists Peter A. Brooke and Charles L. Lea, Jr.

DAVID I. KOSOWSKY, 54, is part of a special breed of man. A brilliant scientist, he wrote his doctoral thesis at Massachusetts Institute of Technology (MIT) in 1955 on "The Synthesis and Realization of Crystal Filters," under Jerome Weisner, subsequently MIT's president. It was business that appealed to him, however, not academia. In 1961, Kosowsky started a clinical laboratory. His timing for launching an expensive start-up such as this was excellent, because the new issues market was boiling and bubbling in 1967 when Damon Corporation's funds had been exhausted on newer and better equipment and better and better lab technicians.

The law of the big-*P* was very much present. This law says that if you convince the market that the problem you intend to solve is sufficiently large and if your entrepreneurial team has on it the likes of Kosowsky, the market will value your company at the size of the problem and patiently wait years for the solution. After all, brilliance works slowly through big problems. Indeed, Damon Corporation's stock roared to a high of $63 in the early 1970s and stayed there until 1974 when the lab business was clearly not going to be the solution that everyone expected. Kosowsky had directed his business at hospitals leaving over $15 billion worth of lab business generated by local physicians for other companies.

Undaunted by this miscalculation, Kosowsky borrowed $30 million to buy his way into other businesses. These included veterinary medicine, where Damon developed vaccines to protect poultry from immunological disease. The acquisition of a rocket toy manufacturer has produced stable earnings growth while the health-care businesses stumbled.

In 1984 the federal government began forcing hospitals to seek the lowest cost health care services, through regulations called diagnostic related groups (DRG), and they have been forced to utilize Damon Corporation's labs. At the same time, its scientists have found the company's future in the field of encapsulating monoclonal antibodies. Damon Corporation's ENCAPCEL product, the result of combined research in all its divisions, can enclose living cells. Kosowsky points out, "When you grow cells in a flask, they just kind of float around, and they don't grow very well. But, when you push them up against one another inside a sphere, they grow very well . . . the genetic messages seem to get passed from cell to cell more efficiently."[77] By concentrating on scientific innovation, Kosowsky is doing what he knows best—research and development—and returning Damon Corporation to prominence in the market of big-Ps. It may become the first double big-P company in recent memory.

[77]Stephen Kindel, "Management, Know Thyself," *Forbes*, Aug. 16, 1982, pp. 69–70.

RAYMOND A. KROC

Name of Company: McDonald's Corporation

Date Founded: 1961

Location: Northbrook, Illinois

Description of Business: The world's largest food service company with 7,400 restaurants located throughout the world.

Description of P: Americans were beginning to eat out with great frequency in the 1950s and 1960s. The trend was led by teenagers for whom eating hamburgers in their cars at noisy, filthy drive-ins was adequate. Kroc, a milkshake machine salesperson, visited the original McDonald's in 1954 and stayed on as a franchiser until 1961, at which time he bought the business for $2.7 million.

Description of S: Kroc's solution to the problem of providing a clean, sit-down, fast-food hamburger restaurant was a departure from the drive-in craze of the 1950s with carhops and loud noises. He redesigned the restaurants to attract families. The food was consistent, warm, and pleasantly serviced. Working women—an increasing percentage of all women—could then recommend a dinner at McDonald's.

Members of E: Richard J. and Maurice (Mac) McDonald founded the original McDonald's in San Bernadino, California, in 1948 with $5,000.

Size of V: The 87.2 million shares of common stock outstanding traded in a range of $40⅞ to $55⅞ in 1984 for an average valuation of $4.2 billion.

Social Utility: McDonald's created employment for 125,000 people and Kroc's charitable contributions to alcoholism rehabilitation, abused children, and cancer research, among others, are of legendary proportions.

Principal Sources   Customer financing
of Venture
Capital:

RAYMOND A. KROC, who died in 1984 at the age of 82, was raised by his mother after his father "worried himself to death." He attended public school with Ernest Hemingway and dropped out of high school to become a musician. Later he served in World War I with Walt Disney, who enlisted at the age of 16. While in his early twenties, Kroc got a job as a musical director of a Chicago radio station and discovered the singing comedy team of Sam and Henry, later to be known as Amos 'n' Andy.

In the 1920s he drove to Florida to try to make a fortune in real estate. He drove back "stone broke." He was a failure by his thirtieth birthday. He bounced around, finally becoming a milkshake machine salesperson. Orders frequently came from a drive-in restaurant in San Bernadino, California, owned by the McDonald brothers. Like so many crazes, the drive-in began in California. The McDonald brothers had so many hungry adolescents clamoring for their 15-cent burgers stuffed into paper bags, that the day Kroc visited the restaurant, security guards were needed to quell the mob. Kroc saw an opportunity to sell franchises, so he asked for the job. Kroc gave the brothers 0.5 percent of the gross receipts of franchise fees and royalties. After six years of paying the brothers, and 300 franchises later, Kroc found the brothers "were beginning to get on my nerves." He bought them out for $2.7 million in cash.

Kroc was a self-taught businessperson with numerous one-line prescriptions for success. For example, to select sites, he recommended flying over neighborhoods to count church steeples and schools. Service personnel who deal with customers cannot have long hair, sideburns, moustaches, bad teeth, severe skin blemishes, or tatoos. A vicious competitor, Kroc is remembered as having said: "It's dog-eat-dog and if anyone tries to get me I'll get them first. It's the American way of survival of the fittest."[78]

[78]Tom Robbins, "Ray Kroc Did It All For You," *Esquire*, December 1983, p. 344.

For all his toughness in business, Kroc and his third wife Joan are renowned for their charitable contributions. Ronald McDonald House is an extremely important "giving" institution. Kroc never gave money to colleges, only to trade schools. He valued hard work rather than "phony intellectuals." As one economist once wrote about Kroc: "His enterprise expresses the prosaic idea on which American prosperity rests: things add up."[79] Kroc's entrepreneurial genius was acting boldly on the obvious and never stopping to rest.

[79]Ibid.

SANDRA L. KURTZIG

Name of Company:	ASK Computer Systems, Inc.
Date Founded:	1974
Location:	Los Altos, California

Description of Business:

The company designs, develops, and produces MRP turnkey systems: software that is marketed along with minicomputers to industrial corporations to assist them in improving manufacturing productivity through optimizing inventories, reducing operating expenses, and improving customer service.

Description of P

Industrial computer users began purchasing computers for the plant and warehouse, but they lacked the in-house software capability to generate the desired efficiencies and cost savings. Computer manufacturers focused on financial and information systems applications. Thus, a niche was created for independent software companies. ASK Computer Systems' (ASK) sales in 1984 reached $65 million.

Description of S:

Kurtzig designed software modules for the factory and warehouse, integrated them into a well-known minicomputer, the Hewlett–Packard 3000 series, and began selling and installing software, with the customer's needs in mind. With customer input, the modules became a complete manufacturing information system called MANMAN, and further refinements have included a network and microcomputer system for smaller users.

Members of E:

Ronald W. Braniff, president; and Robert J. Riopel, executive vice-president—finance

Size of V:

The approximately 12 million shares of common stock outstanding traded in a range of $13 to

$20¼ per share in 1984 for an average valuation of $200 million.

Social Utility: Kurtzig has demonstrated the ability of a female to succeed in a male-dominated business. ASK has created 250 jobs and its investors have earned an average of more than 25 percent return on equity since 1981.

**Principal Sources
of Venture
Capital:**   Kurtzig's personal savings of $2,000

SANDRA L. KURTZIG, 38, was trained in math, engineering, and computer systems marketing but in 1972 wanted to start a family so she quit her job at General Electric Company. Feeling the need to work part-time, she took $2,000 of her savings and started a contract programming business in a spare bedroom of her California apartment. "My part-time job was taking up to 20 hours a day. I had the other 4 to start my family."[80] Her first program was one that let weekly newspapers keep track of their newspaper carriers.

She recruited several bright computer and engineering graduates and directed them to write applications to solve problems of local manufacturers. Manufacturers' needs were well known to Kurtzig. She says,

When you spend a fortune buying expensive equipment and end up following some manufacturer's programming book one-two-three-four, it gets frustrating. You want someone to come up with easy answers, and the big companies are not aggressive or creative enough to supply them. The big companies put in the computers and open the doors for the new, aggressive companies to nibble away at the business. In general, the small companies are better at this business because the employees feel they can make a difference.[81]

[80]"A Most Successful Part-Time Job," Forbes, Fall 1983, p. 198.
[81]Joel Kotkin, "New Money," TWA Ambassador, April 1982, p. 48.

Kurtzig has always been cash conscious. Initially she stashed all her business funds in a shoe box in her closet. If there was more money in the shoe box at the end of the month than the beginning, her company made a profit. The Silicon Valley venture capitalists would not contribute to her shoe box so Kurtzig had to launch ASK on retained earnings alone.

Friendly executives at a nearby Hewlett–Packard Company plant permitted Kurtzig and her programmers to use one of the company's 3000 series minicomputers at night to try to develop a manufacturing inventory control program. The group slept in sleeping bags at the company, and by 1978 it had a salable product. The breakthrough was the result of putting useful, easy-to-use software on a well-known, highly reliable computer. ASK's sales soared. From $1.9 million in 1980, the company achieved revenues of approximately $65 million in 1984, with profits of $6.1 million.

Unable to interest many investors in her stock when ASK was privately owned, Kurtzig is one of the wealthiest self-made women in America. The Small Business Administration reports that businesses founded by women are increasing at the current rate of 35 percent per annum versus 17 percent per annum for men. Success stories like this one surely help the shoe box producers.

FRANCIS LABRECQUE

Name of Company:	American Discount Auto Parts
Date Founded:	1975
Location:	Avon, Massachusetts
Description of Business:	The company owns and operates a retail chain of 45 discount auto parts stores.
Description of *P*:	The runaway inflation of the 1970s and long gasoline lines forced many Americans to keep their cars longer. In 1975 Americans held onto their cars for six years on average; by 1983 the average had increased to 7.4 years. This meant a greater demand for auto parts.
Description of *S*:	Labrecque introduced the concept of discount auto parts at a time when Americans in the industrial northeast were looking for the least expensive way to hold their cars together. With computerized control of inventory introduced from the beginning, American Discount Auto Parts (ADAP) could expand geographically without a major capital investment.
Members of *E*:	Donald Brabants, executive vice-president; Michael Shaw, real estate director; and Robert Romanow, financial backer
Size of *V*:	The company was acquired by Rite Aid Corporation in 1984 for $28 million.
Social Utility:	The company created 600 new jobs under a management team of young car buffs, many of whom never attended college.
Principal Sources of Venture Capital:	Robert Romanow's initial $10,000 investment

FRAN LABRECQUE has had a love affair with cars for as long as he can remember. While growing up in Boston, Massachusetts, this hard-nosed kid valued friendship and loyalty above all else. "You are what you drive," might have been his motto. Naturally, the friends he associated with in the 1960s shared his love of cars as well. Visions of *American Graffiti*?

When Labrecque turned 16, he owned 13 cars, all of which he had tuned and rebuilt in one way or another. All of his spare change and all of his time were invested in cars. "I knew about three people who went to college," Labrecque told *Esquire*.[82] He worked in a car dealership and did very well, until the civil rights conflagrations in Roxbury in the late 1960s led to rampant car thefts, repossessions, and fear. After the dealership closed, Labrecque took a job helping Bob Romanow run his small foreign auto parts importing business. He left Romanow after a few years to work for a competitor, and once while "peeking out from under the hood," Labrecque conceived the notion of selling a discount-card that would permit auto parts customers to go into any auto parts store and get a discount. He described his idea to Romanow and American Discount Auto Parts (ADAP) was born.

For management, Labrecque turned to his friends of the 1960s, fellow car afficionados. His assistant, Jack Vinchesi, had taken a Fortran course and run a McDonald's to put himself through college. He knew ADAP needed on-line inventory controls if it were to grow beyond a handful of stores. Vinchesi found Jim Barry, a computer whiz working behind the counter of the Somerville store, and the two of them wrote the software system to control the point of sale, back office, and warehouse. Labrecque told *Esquire*, "I knew it would work when Jack got the computer to open the cash drawer."[83] The computer system cost less than $1 million and every employee learns how it operates. Without it, ADAP could not have grown to 45 locations in five years.

All of Labrecque's fellow managers and employees had a strong drive to succeed, to show the "collegiates" that they could do it. But Labrecque did not ignore the printed word. After a 14-to-18-hour day at ADAP, he would go home and read Peter F. Drucker, Abraham H. Maslow, and B. F. Skinner; he also studied Japanese management strat-

[82]Joseph Dalton, "Do-It-Yourself Dynasty," *Esquire*, Dec. 1984, p. 341.
[83]Ibid, p. 342.

egies and analyzed which strategies worked best for him. Labrecque calls the ideas from Drucker and others, "tools in my tool box." He even hired Louis Brandeis's law firm to help find an investment banker to take ADAP public. When he could not get the price he wanted, Labrecque went looking for a buyer. He played the public offering off against the buy-out until he got the price he wanted: $28 million. Such a return in nine years on a $10,000 investment is about as good as any 36-year-old ever got.

CHARLES LAZARUS

Name of Company:	Toys 'R' Us, Inc.
Date Founded:	1978
Location:	Rochelle Park, New Jersey
Description of Business:	The company owns and operates a large chain of toy stores. It is diversifying into a chain of children's apparel stores called Kids 'R' Us.
Description of *P*:	Lazarus was the first entrepreneur to grab the opportunity to build a national chain of high-quality toy stores.
Description of *S*	Lazarus built Toys 'R' Us (TOYS) to four stores in 1966 and sold it to Interstate Stores, Inc., which filed for bankruptcy in 1974. Lazarus became the dominant manager of Interstate, whose parts he sold off while building TOYS. When it emerged from bankruptcy in 1978, TOYS had 63 stores. Over the last seven years, its stock has increased 20-fold.
Members of *E*:	Milton S. Petrie, a director and "grey eminence"; former managers W. John Devine and Sy Ziv; and present senior managers, Norman Ricken, Howard Moore (former owner of Toy Town), Michael Goldstein, and Joseph Baczko
Size of *V*:	The approximately 54 million shares of common stock outstanding traded in a range of $31¾ to $52⅞ in 1984 for an average valuation of $2.2 billion.
Social Utility:	Toys has created 1,400 jobs and granted stock options to several thousand employees. The company has maintained high-quality standards, an important flag to wave in an industry notorious for ripping off children.

Principal Sources of Venture Capital:	Bankruptcy work-out: the sale of assets to satisfy debts

CHARLES LAZARUS, 61, relentlessly drives himself and the management of TOYS as if it were 1974. That was the year the retail chain that purchased his chain of four toy stores went bankrupt; Lazarus would have lost everything unless he took charge. The TOYS story begins in the early 1960s when Lazarus took over his father's bicycle shop and converted it to a juvenile furniture store and then to a toy store. He grew it to four stores and sold them to Interstate Stores, Inc. in 1966 for $7.5 million. The chain grew to 47 stores under the Interstate umbrella, but Interstate was poorly managed and too financially strapped for the expansion of its other chains, Topps and White Front, along with TOYS. It filed for protection under Chapter 11 in 1974.

TOYS was the healthiest chain and the creditors wanted its assets. Lazarus fought to control TOYS. To do so, he emerged as the head of Interstate and sold off other chains and assets while keeping TOYS intact. By 1978 TOYS had grown to 63 stores, and Interstate emerged from bankruptcy with a new name, Toys 'R' Us. Creditors were paid in full.

The chain is around 200 strong and opening over thirty stores per annum. It is expanding into Canada, England, the Middle East, and the Far East. Lazarus has launched a new children's apparel chain, Kids 'R' Us, which presently has 15 outlets. Securities analysts believe in Lazarus, and give the TOYs stock a p/e ratio of 30x. Lazarus is a hands-on manager who walks the toy show aisles checking the quality of goods himself. He is a dynamic speaker and an evangelist for the art of the possible.

While Interstate was in trouble in 1974–1978, its stock was trading at between $.125 and $.50 per share (adjusted). Roughly 10 million shares were acquired by Milton S. Petrie, founder and chief executive officer of Petrie Stores and a very capable businessperson with an unblemished history of greater profitability than all of his competitors. Initially Lazarus and Petrie did not get along, both of them having strong personalities and entrepreneurial egos. However, Petrie has proven to be a wise counselor and good friend to Lazarus, and today they are inseparably good friends.

TOYS is somewhat of a tollgate into the home computer and home software markets. Approximately 18 percent of its sales of $1.5 billion are in computers and software. Entrepreneurs in these fields must learn to deal with TOYS to see their products realize their true potential in the marketplace. TOYS's terms are stiff. Vendors must have high-quality items, they must be selling well before TOYS takes them on, and the vendors must be willing to take back slow-moving items.

To facilitate its rapid growth, TOYS has developed a cookie cutter store opening formula: 18,000 square feet, located near high-traffic malls, 18,000 stockkeeping units, low retail prices, and a liberal return policy. Lazarus sees no reason why the company's sales cannot exceed $2 billion in a couple of years and maintain a 6.5 to 7 percent return on sales. The market believes him and has made TOYS a blue-chip stock.

LAWRENCE F. LEVY

Name of Company:	The Levy Organization
Date Founded:	1976
Location:	Chicago, Illinois
Description of Business:	The company owns and operates restaurants, cafeterias, a gourmet food store chain, apparel stores, and rental property.
Description of *P*:	In Larry Levy's own words, he has an ability to "understand the upper-income consumer better than others."[84]
Description of *S*:	Levy opened an old-fashioned delicatessen in Chicago's most fashionable shopping mall and the cash flow therefrom permitted him to open other retail establishments including an even fancier shopping mall across the street, One Magnificent Mile.
Members of *E*:	Mark Levy, brother; Eadie Levy, mother; Aunt Rosie; and Martin and Jack Weiner who built the apparel operation.
Size of *V*:	*Forbes* estimated the value of the Levy Organization in 1981 at $25 million. It has probably doubled since then.
Social Utility:	The Levy Organization employs 2,500 people. A family business that has become an empire in less than eight years, it is an inspiration to other entrepreneurs who seek to keep their activities private and within the family.
Principal Sources of Venture Capital:	Personal savings

[84]Larry Marion, "Pile on the Corned Beef, Add to the Price," *Forbes*, Oct. 12, 1981, pp. 145–147.

LARRY LEVY, 40, walks and talks quickly and throws himself into his businesses with a contagious, youthful zest. But when he happens to overhear his customers talking, he stops to eavesdrop. For example, he heard negative reviews on some of the items he was serving at D.B. Kaplan's, a delicatessen that he opened in 1976 in Water Tower Place, the heart of Chicago's fashionable near north side. As a result, his mother Eadie's chicken soup was substituted and other menu items were changed. Eadie Levy gave up her telephone advice business in St. Louis to come help her sons at D.B. Kaplan's, and soon more than a dozen relatives were sprinkled through the organization. In-laws and close family friends help operate the Atlanta and Los Angeles delicatessens as well. D.B. Kaplan's serves a corned beef sandwich with 5.5 ounces of meat for $3.95. A nearby delicatessen charges $2.85 for 4 ounces. The original deli has revenues of $3.5 million per annum.

To hold down the cost of food, Levy integrated forward and backward. First he bought $70 million (revenues) Hillman's in a leveraged buy-out for $5 million. Hillman's owns and operates 10 supermarkets, a catering business, and other food interests. The purveyor of food to Hillman's is also the same as to Levy's restaurants, hence the cost savings. A hidden value in the Hillman's purchase was the land under the stores in Chicago's expensive Loop area.

Forward integration has included a chain of stylish saloons named Hillary's after Levy's daughter, that serve the best of D.B. Kaplan's offerings; The Chestnut Street Grill seafood restaurant; Dos Hermanos Mexican restaurant; and the Eaternity Cafeteria spread from coast to coast. Max Pine, a 20-year veteran of the restaurant business is Levy's joint venture partner in the restaurant field. Levy invested in and subsequently purchased the $35 million (sales) Robert Vance Ltd. apparel chain built by Martin and Jack Weiner, clustered principally in Chicago's downtown and suburban fashion malls.

It was not always this easy. Levy's father did well as a record distributor in St. Louis, but became ill in the mid-1960s and lost the family's money. Both Levy and his mother went to work. In 1969 Levy was selling lamps from a derailed freight train and low-cost flights to Europe to pay tuition at Northwestern University where he earned an MBA in marketing. He went into real estate development and in the recession of 1974–1976 was handed his hat. So Levy turned his thoughts to retail.

As he told a *Forbes* reporter, "With retail, you know if you have a winner in one day. It is instant gratification or instant death."[85]

The formula for success at the $150 million (revenues) Levy Organization is minimize risk by integration to reduce cost, select skilled management, and stick to the business you know best. It also helps to have your mother at the cash register.

[85]Ibid, p. 146.

SYDNEY LEWIS

Name of Company:	Best Products Company, Inc.
Date Founded:	1957
Location:	Richmond, Virginia

Description of Business:

The company operates one of the largest discount catalog merchandise firms in the country with over 150 showrooms and sales in excess of $1 billion.

Description of *P*:

Lewis challenged the fair trade laws in the late 1950s and sold quality consumer products via mail order at prices below the minimum retail prices set by manufacturers. Lewis proved that the giant manufacturers indeed needed "protection" from entrepreneurs such as himself because Best's growth has been dramatic compared with conventional retailers.

Description of *S*:

Best Products Company sells quality merchandise through catalogs and showrooms. The showrooms have unique facades, which reflect Lewis's interest in modern art. Best Products Company's labor and inventory costs are low and its turnover is high.

Members of *E*:

Frances A. Lewis, executive vice-president (Mrs. Sydney); Dora Lewis, Sydney's mother and self-styled "watchdog"; Andrew M. Lewis, president and chief operating officer; and Alan Werner, executive vice-president

Size of *V*:

The approximately 27 million shares of common stock outstanding traded in a range of $10\frac{5}{8}$ to $19\frac{1}{4}$ in 1984 for an average valuation of $405 million.

Social Utility:

The company employs 19,491 people and the Lewises have used their wealth to endow the Virginia Museum of Fine Art and the Eastern Virginia Medical College, and to make generous donations to Washington & Lee University and to other causes.

Principal Sources of Venture Capital: Customer financing

SYDNEY LEWIS and his wife, Frances, have a giant Claus Oldenburg "clothespin" in their front yard in conservative Richmond, Virginia. Lewis began collecting art after he had a heart attack 24 years ago and his doctor suggested that he acquire a hobby. Since then he and Frances have been among the most avid collectors of contemporary American art in the country. The Lewises recently donated 3,500 pieces of art to the Virginia Museum of Fine Art along with $6 million to double its size. Lewis has also been very generous to Washington & Lee University with an estimated $11 million in gifts.

The elder son of a Russian emigre who sold encyclopedias by mail order, Lewis was accepted by Washington & Lee University on a scholarship. He played basketball, worked in the school cafeteria, and met his future wife. They married in 1942 and Lewis went on to get a law degree at George Washington University, which launched him into a tax law practice in Washington, D.C.

In 1955, upon learning that his father was too ill to work, Lewis returned to Richmond ostensibly to take over the encyclopedia business. Instead, he and his wife launched Best Products Company in 1957 in an 8-by-19 foot space in his father's Richmond warehouse. He started a business that relied on his legal training as well as his upbringing in a merchandising household. Lewis understood that the fair trade laws of the late 1950s were anticompetitive. Thus, he flouted the laws and began selling quality consumer products at prices below the manufacturers' minimum retail prices. Sometime later in describing how fair trade laws were fostered by big business under the guise of protecting the little man—the consumer—Lewis quoted Milton Friedman: "Every businessman and every business enterprise is in favor of freedom to compete for everybody else, but when it comes to himself, that's different—he needs protection."[86]

[86]Best Products Co., Inc. 25th Anniversary Report, Jan. 30, 1982.

Dora Lewis, the entrepreneur's mother, was one of Best Products Company's first employees. Lewis called her one day during the company's first year and said: "There's a guy over here with a gadget called a hooded electric hair dryer—do you have any ideas about it?" She said: "Well, if it works, it's a fantastic object." He said it was a Sunbeam—a good brand. She said: "Yes, I think you ought to experiment with it in one of your circulars."

So, we sent out 3,000 circulars that month, with the hooded electric dryer insert. And we only sold two. It was one of the most depressing things that ever happened to me in retailing.

Of course, the hooded electric hair dryer eventually became a fantastic seller, when people like Sunbeam and General Electric started to put a lot of money into promotions.[87]

The company doubled its warehouse space to 1,600 square feet after one year. A manufacturer's representative, Charles E. Argenzio, tells what it was like to make a sales call on Sydney Lewis: "On my first sales job—with Eversharp pens—I got a sales lead, and I followed it up. I went to the address given me, and met Sydney Lewis. What struck me was that there I was, just a young kid, and Mr. Lewis was explaining his idea to me. He treated me like I knew what was going on. At the time, I think he had this idea of assembling catalog pages that manufacturers had supplied."[88]

There are many stories of Lewis' Best savvy, as well as that of his wife and mother, and even more stories about his generosity. It is not unique for an entrepreneur to be charitable; but, it is unusual for him to be recognized for it. Sydney Lewis lowered prices on billions of dollars of consumer products, a charitable act in and of itself. Then, so many consumers flocked to his catalog showrooms that at 65 he has been able to give over $50 million of his wealth to enrich the lives of others.

[87]Ibid.
[88]Ibid.

ROYAL LITTLE

Name of Company:	Textron, Inc.
Date Founded:	1954
Location:	Providence, Rhode Island
Description of Business:	The first multi-industry company or conglomerate with seven operating divisions managing dozens of companies in unrelated fields.
Description of *P*:	Little was the first entrepreneur to fully understand the leveraged buy-out. He located undervalued manufacturing companies, those with fully depreciated plants and equipment, and acquired them by borrowing on their reappraised assets. Little merged them into Textron, then bought more companies with Textron's publicly traded stock. He retired in 1962 and formed Narragansett Capital Corporation, a small-business investment corporation (SBIC) that created a leveraged buy-out fund, and enjoyed considerable success as a venture capitalist. Textron's acquirees include American Woolen Company, Bell Helicopter, AVCO Corporation, Homelite, Jacobsen Turf, E-Z-Go, Sheaffer-Eaton (pens), Bostitch, and many more.
Description of *S*:	Little identified companies whose managements did not know their true worth. He convinced them that by becoming part of a multi-industry company, their cycles would be smoother and their return on equity increased. Little understood financial leverage and implemented it with outstanding success.
Members of *E*:	Little's original partner was Jerome Ottmar, who also left Textron to launch an SBIC.
Size of *V*:	The approximately 35 million shares of common stock outstanding traded in a range of $25⅞ to

$35¼ in 1984 for an average valuation of $1 billion.

Social Utility:	Narragansett Capital Corporation has launched more than 100 companies in its 23-year history. Little is one of the most extraordinary human beings in American history. His goal is "to die broke," and to do so, Little is actively passing his wealth through the Little Family Foundation to a variety of charities including Junior Achievement.
Principal Sources of Venture Capital:	Financing provided by companies that Textron acquired

ROYAL LITTLE is an active financier at age 88. In 1980 he helped Raytheon Company arrange the $800 million purchase of Beech Aircraft Corporation, for which he and his associates earned a $1 million fee. He recently arranged the leveraged buy-out of six Sara Lee Corporation hardware subsidiaries, and he has been working on several large acquisitions this year. His consulting firm shares office space with Narragansett Capital Corporation, an SBIC he started at age 65. Narrangansett Capital Corporation is run by his son Arthur D. Little.

Little graduated from Harvard College in 1919 and apprenticed himself for free to a silk mill in order to gain practical experience. He remained in the textile industry for 33 years. In 1954 the idea of the multi-industry company occurred to him as a solution to the problem of intense cyclicity in textile companies. He tendered for cash-rich American Woolen Company, in a stormy, hostile takeover fight, the only unfriendly takeover in Textron's history. Years later Little would say that one of the keys to success in hostile takeovers of much larger companies is to "be sure to pick a company whose board of directors isn't smart enough" to fight back with a reverse takeover offer.[89]

Little is under doctor's orders: "He says I've got to get my heart beating hard at least once a day, so I walk all the way up the hill to the

---

[89]William M. Bulkeley, "Royal Little, Who Built Up Textron Inc., is Still Active in Business Ventures at 88," *Wall Street Journal*, Oct.2, 184, p. 4.

Hope [Club]."[90] He goes to work every day, taking a bus 32 miles from a rented house on the shore. Little plays golf frequently, using a caddy rather than a cart, and he takes exciting, stimulating vacations with his grandchildren.

He is optimistic about the future of the American economy. Little told a *Forbes* reporter: "Fortunately, there's an enormous amount of venture capital out there now to back businesses, which eventually will be some of our bigger businesses. A good example is Wang, and of course Digital Equipment was started with $70,000 . . . . there will be a lot of interesting opportunities."[91] Little does interesting, value-added things with his life. He consults, recommends, and suggests without being dogmatic. He leaves companies at the top rather than holding on and becoming a bother. In 1962 he retired from Textron and gave up his seat on the board as well, telling a *Wall Street Journal* reporter: "If I'd stayed on, I'd have been a pain to my successors."[92]

The first entrepreneur in a new industry operates in a very sure, simplistic method. Little profited from capital gains in Textron, but he probably created less personal wealth in a lifetime than Saul Steinberg or Irwin Jacobs makes from one or two greenmail plays. Who will have created the life that generations of people will honor and revere: Royal Little or the modern-day raider-liquidators? There is no contest.

[90]Richard Greene, "Up the Hill With Royal Little," *Forbes*, April 26, 1982, p. 42.
[91]Ibid, p. 43.
[92]Bulkeley, *Wall Street Journal*, p. 4.

GEORGE LUCAS

Name of Company:	Lucasfilms, Inc.
Date Founded:	1975
Location:	Lucas Valley, California
Description of Business:	The company is the leading producer of science fiction "chase" movies, including the *Star Wars* saga.
Description of *P*:	Lucas discovered a subject matter that appealed to the greatest number of moviegoers: chase films (bright young boy and girl armed with a magical Force attempting to rid the world of evil) that blended high tech—computer-controlled space ships—with high touch—warm, fuzzy animal creatures and humorous robots.
Description of *S*:	Lucasfilms has attracted some of the most technologically competent cinematographers and optical technicians in the world and it exploits the most advanced computer-aided design (CAD) and computer-aided engineering (CAE) technology to make movies.
Members of *E*:	Early partners included Francis Ford Coppola and Gary Kurtz.
Size of *V*:	Although a privately held company, the value of the film properties, toys, books, and publishing rights is probably in excess of $500 million.
Social Utility:	*Star Wars* lifted the movie business out of a down cycle and introduced the concept of blockbusters: movies that gross more than $100 million.
Principal Sources of Venture Capital:	Movie entrepreneurs leverage everything to get their first move released, but they keep a portion of the bottom line for themselves.

GEORGE LUCAS, 40, has brought many innovations to the movie industry: blockbusters; high-tech chase scenes with high-touch characters battling machinelike, Nazi-type enemies; the summer spectacular (all *Star Wars* movies were released as schools let out); the use of CAD and CAE to lower the cost of producing movies; and the multiplier effect: generating 10 to 20 revenue sources from a single idea.

Lucas began like movie producers always begin, with a screenplay and lots of desire. This one was *American Graffiti*, a story about teenagers growing up in a small town in the 1960s: cars, music, a gang fight, love affairs ended by college and the draft. To get a studio to finance the low-budget movie, Lucas brought in Francis Ford Coppola, of *The Godfather* fame. *American Graffiti* was a hit and gave Lucas the credibility to launch *Star Wars*.

Like all the successful entrepreneurs who fill these pages, Lucas watched every detail. He sent his partner Gary Kurtz with a microphone and announcer and actor James Earl Jones into a sewer to obtain the unique voice of Darth Vader. He shot most of the scenes in England to avoid higher unionized costs of labor. Snow scenes were shot on location. Bullets slashing through the air were digital signals generated by CAD/CAE.

Lucas bought an old egg factory near United Artists and pulled together a movie production company that licensed everything "except the squeal." The CAD/CAE engineers remained in San Raphael, California, in an inconspicuous building near a strip center called Industrial Light and Magic. Lucas's desire for anonymity is towering: many employees wear beards and glasses like his (and Coppola's) so the visitor who does not know Lucas cannot identify him.

Twentieth Century Fox reluctantly agreed to put up some of the capital for *Star Wars*, after a prolonged negotiation on dividing the net profit (after the exhibitors' 50 percent). They did not share Lucas's belief in the *Star Wars* saga. On the next film, *The Empire Strikes Back*, Lucas did not have to find financial partners; Lucasfilm's income was in the range of $10 to $12 million per month for the year that *Star Wars* was being shown. Thus, Lucas had the distributors begging for *Jedi*. He also kept all of the rights—no need to sell VCR, cable, network, and so forth to raise capital. And he kept the rights to toys, books, clothing, calendars, masks, and the other paraphernalia, selling off licenses whenever he felt the price was right. Utilizing vertical integration at its best,

Lucas could have helped Xerox Corporation integrate from copiers to computers, so awesome was his control of the property.

Lucas can make us laugh or grab the edge of our chairs; we return again and again to see his films. He is the dominant entertainment entrepreneur of the last decade.

ALEX MANOOGIAN

Name of Company:	Masco Corporation
Date Founded:	1929
Location:	Taylor, Michigan

Description of
Business:

The company is the nation's largest manufacturer of plumbing supplies; it also makes other unattractive products that solve mundane, unattractive, unnoticed problems. A careful diversification plan over the last 25 years has created an impressive record of sales and earnings growth.

Description of *P*:

Manoogian introduced a less-expensive, single-handled faucet during the late 1950s building boom. With a strong earnings base, the company diversified into other mundane, but highly profitable industries.

Description of *S*:

"Nothing we develop is the stuff dreams are made of," says Masco Corporation's president, 48-year-old Richard Manoogian. "They just make lots of money."[93] Masco Corporation also sells water filters, thermal vent dampers, pumps and piping, gear blanks, and wheel spindles for the automotive industry, scanning radios and cordless telephones, in addition to its broad line of plumbing supplies.

Members of *E*:

Richard Manoogian, president and son

Size of *V*:

Approximately 56.5 million shares of common stock outstanding traded in a range of $33⅞ to $22½ in 1984 for an average valuation of $1.59 billion.

Social Utility:

The company employs over 12,000 people and its script for profitable growth should become part of more business school textbooks.

[93]Steven Flax, "Faucets that Drip Money," *Forbes*, March 16, 1981, p. 132.

Principal Sources   Personal savings
 of Venture
Capital:

ALEX MANOOGIAN, 84, is an Armenian who emigrated from Turkey in 1920 to escape persecution. He landed a job in Detroit by claiming to be an experienced machinist. He was not so he got fired. Once Manoogian learned the trade, he was rehired but he quit in 1929 to form Masco Screw Products Company. The company supplied nuts and bolts to the automotive industry. In the mid-1950s, Manoogian became concerned that he could count his customers on the fingers of one hand. He developed a single-handled faucet, which the major plumbing supply companies eschewed. So Manoogian decided to market it on his own. The Masco "Delta" faucet has been advertised on the "Tonight Show," where Johnny Carson and Ed McMahon made numerous jokes about it. This attracted attention for the faucet, and helped it to gain a 32 percent market share and 23 percent of Masco Corporation's $107 million of 1983 earnings.

Manoogian's son, Richard, joined the company in 1968 and began one of the cleverest diversification strategies in recent memory. Masco Corporation acquired dozens of little companies making humdrum products like luggage racks, gear shift levers, and wheel spindles. In the late 1970s, Masco Corporation began acquiring oil tool companies, in areas like drilling heads, rock bits, and pumping engines. Its six acquisitions in the oil industry now generate about 11 percent of Masco Corporation's earnings. The company penetrates an industry deeply enough to capture market share, but not to the extent of relying on it. Richard made that mistake once when he plunged into the CB radio field. He learned to avoid industries where the government can change the rules. He told a *Forbes* reporter: "When the government allowed CBs to have 40 channels, we were doing $10 million a month in sales of 23-channel sets. They became obsolete immediately."[94]

In the automobile industry, Masco Corporation acquired a German company that owned a hot forging technology. This allows Masco Corporation to make the most economical and strongest gear blanks, wheel spindles, and other parts for today's popular front-wheel-drive cars.

[94]Ibid, p. 132.

Masco Corporation puts about $8 worth of parts on all front-wheel-drive cars being made. That begins to sound like a growth market.

The last thing on the Manoogians' minds is a glamorous acquisition. Richard Manoogian says:

> I think that our business, as lousy as it looks, is really much more solid than Xerox or IBM. We've built a diversity and balance that would be hard to imagine being disrupted. But I can think of lots of things that could put Xerox or IBM within five years where Burroughs is right now."[95]

The Manoogians have multiplied the success of a mundane plumbing product by acquiring miserable little companies in forgotten areas into a balanced work of financial art that happens to be one of the country's most profitable companies.

[95]Ibid, p. 135.

PATRICK J. McGOVERN

Name of Company:	International Data Group, Inc.
Date Founded:	1964
Location:	Framingham, Massachusetts

Description of Business: The company has two divisions: International Data Corporation gathers and sells market research on the computer industry; International Data Group publishes 62 different computer magazines, and weekly newspapers on the computer industry in 19 countries. *Computerworld* with 120,000 subscribers is the largest specialty publication in the country.

Description of *P*: McGovern was the first person to see the need for information in the fledgling computer industry. In 1964 when IBM had a 73 percent market share, the other vendors had no way of knowing what computer users were interested in. He sent a letter to 25 vendors offering to gather market research for a $15,000 fee. Eighteen of the companies responded positively with payment in advance.

Description of *S*: International Data Group, Inc. (IDG) is in the business of gathering data on various phases of a single subject, the computer industry. Various marketing research clients pay IDG $25,000 annual retainers. That covers a lot of overhead. Magazine subscriptions to 62 different publications pay a lot of bills as well. Advertising in the publications is yet another source of revenue. Thus, McGovern has found a way to sell essentially the same product in several channels.

Members of *E*: Walter Boyd, president of the publishing division; C. Oakley Mertz (now with rival Gartner Group); E. Drake Lundell, former editor of *Computerworld*.

Size of *V*:   IDG is privately held. Its revenues are estimated at
                      $250 million on which it earns approximately 10
                      percent. At a p/e ratio of 15x, IDG's valuation is an
                      estimated $375 million.

Social Utility: IDG employs approximately 1,400 people and
                      provides useful information to 9 million readers.
                      McGovern is a benevolent and generous person
                      who is genuinely interested in encouraging prob-
                      lem-solving entrepreneurship.

Principal Sources   Customer financing
  of Venture
  Capital:

PATRICK J. McGOVERN, 48, is the most successful marketer of information since Paul Revere. I wrote a book in 1982 called *UpFront
Financing*, whose premise is that there are roughly 20 ways to finance a
start-up company, but the least expensive is customer financing. Moreover, if entrepreneurs select areas where there is a lack of information
about the nature of the problem and the quality of the solutions, and
where buyers and sellers have a great deal of uncertainty about each
other, they can sell information to both of them. In fact, in most new
markets, the first multimillionaire is the journalist, the person who
sells information about the market. Subscribers will pay in advance for
the information as well as market research clients, so the journalist
need not dilute his equity ownership by selling some of his stock.

If this sounds too hypothetical, note that one of IDG's publications,
Computerworld, has 120,000 subscribers and annual advertising revenues of $42 million. The research division had estimated revenues of
$25 million in 1984, while IDG had aggregate revenues of approxi-
mately $250 million. McGovern owns about 85 percent of the company,
having given away 15 percent to key employees. IDG began with approximately $170,000 of customer financing.

When McGovern was 15 years old he became so interested in computers that he decided to build a version of his own. "I spent about $20
of my newspaper route money and wired up a computer system with
carpet tacks and bell wire, plywood boards, and flashlight bulbs . . . and
made a machine that played tic-tac-toe in a way that was unbeatable."

McGovern told a reporter for *Business New Hampshire*. "Except, I found people didn't like to be unsuccessful continuously, so I made it make a mistake every 40th move, so in somewhat unpredictable style, they could win occasionally."[96] The tic-tac-toe machine earned McGovern a scholarship to Massachusetts Institute of Technology (MIT).

At MIT McGovern noticed he was not alone in his fascination with the computer. "People would wait six or seven hours in the early morning, 4 or 5 a.m., to get access to one of those large vacuum tube machines or transistor machines that were around then."[97] His own interest grew and after graduation he accepted a position as associate editor of *Computers and Automation*, one of the early computer magazines.

While honing his reporting skills for six years, McGovern became convinced that most computer companies knew little about who was buying computers and what they did with them. He approached the head of Univac with a proposal to "organize a market research program and create a census that [would indicate] where all the computers are and how they're being used." McGovern says the executive liked the idea and agreed that most computer manufacturers had only limited information about the marketplace. McGovern asked for $7,000 or $8,000 to do the study.

The Univac executive replied, "That's completely unrealistic."

McGovern lowered the price of the project to $5,000. But he had misread the Univac officer's concern. McGovern says the executive told him, "You don't understand. I couldn't get anyone to use information that was too cheap. Charge at least $12,000 and sell it to a lot of other companies, too."

McGovern immediately wrote a proposal and mailed it to Univac and the other major computer manufacturers. Within a week, "I got probably $70,000 of prepayments." Nearly every company had forwarded a $6,000 advance toward the project.[97]

With money in hand, McGovern founded IDG. Within three years, the business was grossing an annual $600,000 and McGovern was searching for new ideas that would expand the company's base of business.

One idea was *Computerworld*, a trade publication for the computer

[96]John Milne, "The Entrepreneur," *Business New Hampshire*, August 1984.
[97]Ibid.

industry. "We found that managers of computer systems were very un-aware of what people were achieving with computers. So we thought that it would be useful for them to get rapid-access information about the new products and services."[98]

The decision to launch *Computerworld* was made shortly before a Boston trade show in 1967. Faced with a two-week deadline, Mc-Govern and his staff scrambled to produce a 16-page tabloid and sub-scription materials. Originally, he intended to call the magazine *Computer World News*, but this was shortened when, at the last moment, the typographer could not fit the entire name across the page. At the trade show, McGovern was able to attract enough subscribers to pub-lish. As with his first research project, he got his money up front.

Other journalistic entrepreneurs have entered the computer indus-try, but none has achieved IDG's level of success. What is McGovern doing differently? His senior officials call him "one of the nicest men on the face of the earth." His entrepreneurial energy is unabated. Mc-Govern still travels 60 percent of the time: high for a manager, normal for an entrepreneur. McGovern says that he enjoys spotting needs that IDG can fill, while leaving the publishing and market research opera-tions in the hands of capable managers. Thirteen of *Computerworld's* original 18 staffers are still with IDG. Other insights about McGovern are that he sleeps very little, works relentlessly, remembers small de-tails about people and does not let people know what he is thinking. McGovern is a pure play in entrepreneurship.

[98]Ibid.

WILLIAM G. McGOWAN

Name of Company:	MCI Communications Corporation
Date Founded:	1968
Location:	Washington, D.C.

Description of Business:
The company provides long-distance telephone and telecommunications services over the network of a company-owned microwave system, and to a lesser extent, facilities leased from other commercial carriers.

Description of P:
American Telephone and Telegraph Company (AT&T) monopolized the long-distance telephone business, until MCI Communications Corporation (MCI) came along and offered a 50 percent cheaper alternative microwave service. AT&T sued, but after three years, MCI won; once again David beat Goliath. MCI won $1.8 billion in damages—AT&T appealed and the award was reduced—and today MCI has more than 1 million customers and dozens of competitors.

Description of S:
McGowan detected that "AT&T had never expressly been given a monopoly in the [long-distance telephone] market. Everyone just thought they had." He challenged the monopoly by applying for a microwave voice communications link from Chicago to St. Louis. When he won, long-distance telephone calls became cheaper by half and AT&T had to be broken up and deregulated to permit it to compete.

Members of E:
John D. Goeken, who hired McGowan in 1968 to solve his problems at Microwave Communications, MCI's predecessor.

Size of V:
The approximately 233 million shares of common stock outstanding traded in a range of $7⅛ to $16¼ in 1984 for an average valuation of $2.8 billion.

Social Utility:	MCI has created jobs for $10,000 people and lowered the cost of long-distance communication.
Principal Sources of Venture Capital:	McGowan invested $50,000 of his personal savings, and received unswerving financial support from Chicago merchant bankers, Baker, Fentress & Co.

WILLIAM G. McGOWAN is a 55-year-old confirmed bachelor who works a 70-hour week to broaden MCI's penetration into all aspects of telecommunications. In 1983 he announced a billion-dollar expansion of MCI's long-distance voice and digital network; acquired 24 satellite transponders, the largest such purchase ever; and announced plans to lay more than 4,000 miles of fiber optics telephone lines which will increase the company's capacity by half. In 1984 McGowan entered the electronic mail and cellular mobile radio telephone business. McGowan drives himself relentlessly with shibboleths such as: "The worst thing that could happen to MCI is to think we have succeeded. We have not yet succeeded. We succeeded at previous incarnations, and those gave us the opportunities to be where we are today." He continues with this final charge: "We will have succeeded only when MCI is considered the single most significant factor in telecommunications-oriented services, domestically and internationally."[99]

McGowan was born and raised in a large Irish family in Wilkes-Barre, Pennsylvania. While in high school and college, he worked nights on the New Jersey Central Railroad. While at Harvard Business School, the dean recommended McGowan to movie entrepreneur Mike Todd, who was then launching a wide-screen innovation called Todd A-O. He left Todd after a few years, joined Shell Oil Company, but was turned off by the corporate environment and hung out a shingle as a financial consultant to troubled businesses. McGowan had numerous business experiences over a ten-year career as a workout and turn-around consultant, including once getting paid "with one hundred and twenty sets of men's two-suiter luggage." Another time, he ended up with 20 percent of a building on Fourth Avenue in New York City that was mortgaged to the limit. Mayor Robert Wagner changed the name of the street to Park Avenue South and the building shot up in value.

[99]Joel Mahower, "The Maverick Mogul of MCI," *Mainliner*-United Airlines, June 1983, p. 78.

Soon after, McGowan was contacted by John D. Goeken, who was attempting to build a microwave system between Chicago and St. Louis, as an expansion for his mobile-radio business. Regulatory approval had been held up for five years at the Federal Communications Commission (FCC) because of AT&T's strong opposition, and Goeken was practically insolvent. McGowan bought the company for $50,000 and took on AT&T. As he told *Money*: "The fact that it had never been done before made the idea all the more irresistible." In 1969, one year after his bold acquisition, the FCC approved the Chicago-to-St. Louis link of the MCI network. Meantime, McGowan hit the road in search of capital. Says he: "I went up to bankers and venture capitalists. I even hit my brother up for $15,000."[100] He was a fund-raiser extraordinaire. Within four years of acquiring MCI, he had pulled in more than $100 million. McGowan had also opened the maiden link of a nationwide network and, most important, got the FCC to endorse the concept of nationwide long-distance phone competition. McGowan expanded MCI as fast as he could. It turned its first profit—$345,000—in 1977.

All this came in the face of tough competition from AT&T. It fought MCI in the marketplace, before the FCC, in Congress, and the courts. "Why do you think I moved the company to Washington, D.C., half a block from the Federal Communications Commission?" he asks.[101]

AT&T's brawl with MCI has proved expensive for both sides but may be more costly for Ma Bell. In June 1980 a federal jury in Chicago found AT&T guilty of antitrust violations and ordered it to pay MCI $1.8 billion in damages—the largest antitrust judgment awarded to a company in U.S. history. The case was appealed by AT&T and the award was lowered in 1985 by a considerable amount.

McGowan credits MCI's achievements to his hardworking employees. He drives them as hard as he drives himself and demands absolute loyalty. In return, McGowan has created a stock purchase incentive system that helps the employees build substantial net worths.

IBM knows a good thing when it sees one. In June 1985, it announced that it would purchase an equity interest in MCI equal to 16 percent for nearly $500 million. Many analysts feel IBM will eventually acquire all of MCI in order to compete more effectively in the telecommunications industry.

[100]"Six Who Succeeded," *Money*, December, 1982 p. 65.
[101]Ibid.

MALCOM P. McLEAN

Name of Company:	Sea-Land Services, Inc.
Date Founded:	1961
Location:	Port Elizabeth, New Jersey
Description of Business:	The largest container-shipping company in the world, Sea-Land Services (SLS) was acquired by R.J. Reynolds Industries in 1969 for $160 million.
Description of *P*:	A considerable amount of scotch and other liquor shipped from Europe in barrels stacked in the hulls of ships was not making it to the American bottlers.
Description of *S*:	McLean conceived the idea of shipping products in sealed containers, the same ones that fit onto the backs of trucks. To do this he bought moth-balled ships used during World War II and put "honeycombs" into their hulls to hold truck containers. As trucks pulled up to the dock, a crane lifted the containers onto the ship and stacked them in the honeycombs. The opposite process happened at the receiving end. Turnaround time improved dramatically and shrinkage dried up.
Members of *E*:	Disque Deane, a brilliant investment banker at Lazard Frères, was McLean's partner and the other half of his brains.
Size of *V*:	SLS became a $525-million entrepreneur's dream (McLean's share, $160 million). Since then McLean has had other "ideas" as he calls them, probably worth a billion dollars all told.
Social Utility:	McLean's idea reduced the cost that all of us pay for imported products.
Principal Sources of Venture Capital:	Beginning with one used truck in the Depression, McLean built McLean Trucking to the industry's fourth largest firm, selling out in 1955 for $6 million.

MALCOM P. McLEAN is described by his friend and partner Disque Deane as "a poor old North Carolina farm boy who made a ton of money off some good ideas." At 71, McLean is a member of a vanishing breed of entrepreneur: the old-style tycoon. Compared to some of the one-shot entrepreneurs who grow dimes into dollars in 15 years, McLean starts with dollars and grows them into manhole covers in five years. Not once, but many times. He once told Business Week in a rare interview: "I am a builder, and I guess I engage in fantasies about as much as any other builder."[102]

Indeed, McLean's fascination is with dreaming up new enterprises, not with operating existing ones, and few can claim such rich corporate offspring. Starting with one used truck during the Great Depression, he built McLean Trucking Company into what was then the industry's fourth largest company before selling out for $6 million in 1955. Reinvesting those funds, he revolutionized the transportation of freight by putting cargo in standardized containers that can be moved across land on trucks and railroad cars and across water in ships; now 75 percent of U.S. dry-cargo shipping is containerized. With that breakthrough, McLean built SLS into the largest U.S. shipping company before selling it in 1969 to R.J. Reynolds Industries in a deal that brought McLean $160 million in Reynolds preferred stock and a seat on that company's board.

Financing for the ships that SLS purchased was very imaginative. Ocean-going vessels had been assigned a 40-year life by the Internal Revenue Service (IRS). McLean was buying fully depreciated ships; in the eyes of the IRS, reconstituted ships could have any life that McLean selected. He chose seven years, and wealthy investors bought them for the rapid depreciation and tax shelter value. SLS was my account at Chase Manhattan Bank in 1964–1965 and we provided most of the financing to the container partnerships. The financing scheme was ingenious and extraordinarily profitable to McLean, Deane, and the investors.

McLean has since used that wealth to invest heavily in real estate (Diamondhead Corporation), life insurance (Loyal American Life Insurance Company), and even corporate farming. His First Colony Farms broke new ground in mechanized hog raising and is attempting to build

[102]"Malcom McLean's $750 Million Gamble," Business Week, April 16, 1979, p. 80.

this country's first commercial peat operation to harvest what might be $1 billion worth of peat. "Malcom has the capacity to come up with ingenious plans almost daily," says Deane.[103]

The pattern of his start-ups is to buy assets cheaply, borrow liberally to expand them, and sell out early. "I don't have much nostalgia for anything that loses money," McLean told *Business Week*.[104]

After selling SLS, McLean bought 126,000 acres of land near major cities and built and sold condominiums; he bought the Pinehurst golf resort in North Carolina as well. The value of his real estate holdings is estimated at $275 million. In 1970 he bought Loyal American Life Insurance Company for $5.2 million. Its stock is worth more than five times that amount today. In 1973 he bought 400,000 acres of North Carolina land for $51 million and began raising hogs on it. In 1978 he sold 100,000 acres and the hog-raising operation for $30 million. The remaining 300,000 acres are believed to be worth between $200 million and $1 billion, if peat deposits become commercial. In 1978 he purchased U.S. Lines from Walter Kidde & Company for $160 million and plunged back into container shipping with a $750 million expansion program. McLean cherry picks his former businesses, and puts their managers into key management slots in his new ones. "It's very hard to build with strangers," he says.

McLean's finest hour was putting together SLS. He bought Pan-Atlantic Steamship Corporation in 1955 with the $6 million he got from selling McLean Trucking Company. The Waterman family wanted to dispose of their fleet of ships, and a Citibank loan officer named Walter B. Wriston provided $42 million. McLean put up $10,000. Waterman then declared a $20 million cash dividend and McLean began unloading real estate. Within a few years he had recouped $39 million. He then gave away 25 percent of the stock in McLean Industries, the holding company for his shipping interests, to stockholders of McLean Trucking Co. When asked why he decided to be this generous, McLean told the shareholders that he got the idea for containerization when he was running their company.

Waterman's 30 ships became the nucleus of SLS's fleet. The rest were purchased from the U.S. Navy by investors and leased to SLS.

[103]Ibid, p. 80.
[104]Ibid, p. 81.

McLean took on the dockworkers and the teamsters' unions. When they struck, they nearly broke the young company. Bailout financing came from Freuhauf Corporation, a trailer manufacturer that could benefit from containerization, and two other investors, Daniel K. Ludwig and Litton Industries. McLean's equity dropped to 35 percent, but he held on until containerization caught on. The company was a massive capital eater and McLean had too much of his capital tied up in it. So, when Reynolds came along, he bailed out. As one of SLS's first officers said some years later, "Malcom does everything he wants to when he wants to, and everybody had better understand that."[105]

[105]Ibid, p. 84.

SY SYMS MERNS

Name of Company:	Syms Corporation
Date Founded:	1959
Location:	Lyndhurst, New Jersey
Description of Business:	The company owns and operates 12 "off-price" apparel retail stores on the East Coast. Expansion is planned into Chicago.
Description of P:	Merns identified two problems: Luxury apparel manufacturers occasionally have oversupplies which they need to unload for cash. Intelligent consumers will seek out retailers who offer famous brand apparel at a significant discount.
Description of S:	Merns opened the first Syms store in the Wall Street area to be near the greatest number of brand name and money conscious people.
Members of E:	Marcy Merns (daughter), president and chief operating officer; Richard Diamond, vice-president —finance; Irwin Shirek, vice-president—operations.
Size of V:	The approximately 17.7 million shares of common stock outstanding traded in a range of $15⅞ to $10 in 1984 for an average valuation of $228 million.
Social Utility:	Syms Corporation employs approximately 1,100 people and saves consumers millions of dollars per annum on their clothing bills. Merns gave $1 million from his initial public offering to Yeshiva University.
Principal Source of Venture Capital:	Personal savings

SY MERNS was working behind the counter of his haberdashery when I went to work on Wall Street in 1964. My bosses at Chase Manhattan Bank expected me to dress very nicely, but at a salary of $7,700 per year, I could not wear the Brooks Brothers label. A few inquiries led me to Syms, located behind Trinity Church, where Sy Merns was selling the Brooks Brothers look at half the price. The suits and shirts were "overstocks" and "imperfects." His customers ranged from partners and senior officials of commercial and investment banks to budget-conscious trainees like me. The selection was—and still remains—broad, interesting, and very well priced. The crowds of customers are thick.

When the script was ready to be rolled out, Merns opened stores uptown and in Westchester County, Long Island and New Jersey. He followed his customers to their homes; he made it easier for them to buy his goods. When you have a simple idea, Merns learned, to stay ahead of the competition you have to stay close to your customer. As it is carved in stone in the law of supply and demand: if it is worth doing, it is worth duplicating. Syms Corporation has many replicators, so steady, purposeful expansion was a must, and Merns knew it.

How many merchants have you known who worked hard all their lives and finally packed it in with varicose veins, a liquidation sale, and Social Security payments to sustain them during retirement? What did Merns do right to generate a valuation of $228 million of which he owns more than 80 percent? He multiplied, or cookie-cuttered, a simple solution—"off-price, famous brand men's apparel"—to a large problem—looking well-dressed for less money.

Merns was the eighth child born to Russian immigrant parents 58 years ago in Brooklyn, New York. After graduating from college he tried to become a sports announcer, but did not succeed. He joined his family's haberdashery in the Wall Street area in 1952 and worked there until he opened the first Syms store in 1959. His elegant solution, plus the desire to be his own boss, created one of the simplest, nonproprietary entrepreneurial success stories of the postwar economic period.

WILLIAM H. MILLARD

Name of Company:	ComputerLand Corporation
Date Founded:	1976
Location:	Oakland, California
Description of Business:	Franchisor of nearly 800 computer and software retailers
Description of *P*:	Millard saw the opportunity to satisfy the desire of many people to own their own personal computer store without knowing much about business, the traditional opportunity addressed by franchisors.
Description of *S*:	Franchising is a means of raising capital via customer financing. ComputerLand has sold more than 791 franchises, and it will generate revenues of more than $1.4 billion in 1984 from franchise fees and royalties (8 percent on sales).
Members of *E*:	Edward Faber, president; Patricia (Mrs. William) Millard, director
Size of *V*:	*Forbes* recently estimated ComputerLand's earnings at $35 million after taxes. At a p/e ratio of 20x, the company would be worth about $700 million.[106]
Social Utility:	ComputerLand has 1,200 corporate employees and about 11,000 chain-wide.
Principal Sources of Venture Capital:	Customer financing. In 1981, Millard borrowed $250,000 for IMSAI, a predecessor company, but provided the lender the right to convert the promissory note into 20 percent of Millard's holdings. The note was purchased by John Martin-Musumeci, a former Millard associate, who sold inter-

[106]Kathleen K. Wiegner, "Bill Millard's Private War," *Forbes*, July 2, 1984, p. 43.

ests in the note to 60 individuals. Martin-Musumeci sued Millard for the 20 percent interest, a
process that lasted over three years. In March
1985, Martin-Musumeci won the lawsuit, plus
$125 million in punitive damages. His victory
will probably cause a public offering for ComputerLand stock.

WILLIAM H. MILLARD, 52, oversees a rather troubled empire, of
which both the trouble and the empire are of his making. He built one
of the largest franchisee organizations ever, but he has not elected to
make his franchisees wealthy. The trouble also comes from human nature. As Milton Friedman has told us so frequently, "It is the nature of
cartels to disagree and break up." The same applies to franchisees.
Therefore, the franchisor who does not create a mechanism for rolling
up his franchisees into company-owned stores by (1) acquiring the best
of them (see Frank Carney, Pizza Hut) or (2) arranging a public offering
of a part of the ownership of many of them, will find his "cartel" breaking up. Millard at this moment is in a pivotal stage of his maturity. His
larger franchisees need only to read the prospectuses of the publicly
held computer retailers—Math Box, Pathfinder, Businessland, to name
the most recent new issues—to see that some computer retailers are becoming wealthy.

Millard has been working on a solution for some time; he indeed, has
even suggested various methods of pooling store interests with those of
the parent, and doing a public offering for the pooled company. A top-
drawer investment banker has been retained to develop alternative
plans. Moreover, Millard is a survivor of numerous business crises,
several of them more desperate than the present one. To bet against him
would not be wise.

Millard grew up in Oakland, California, in the Depression. His father
worked for the railroad and his mother for Montgomery Ward. Although he had great respect for his parents, he resented the fact that his
father was locked into an optionless career, where he chose security
over upward mobility and was never acknowledged for his performance. Millard's parents were strict and demanding. There was no al-
lowance waiting for him at the first of each week. Millard had to contribute to the family's earnings, and this meant a paper route in the

afternoon, 365 days a year for seven years. It was demanding and it pre-
cluded sports or afternoon activities of any kind.

After high school, Millard continued to work. He went to Nevada
and worked in a copper mine. He dug ditches. He worked on a train. He
tried college for three semesters while holding down two jobs, but left
because he didn't have a goal.

At 21, Millard became a bill collector for Pacific Finance. In his first
job requiring customer relations, Millard developed a successful persuasive style, and Pacific Finance promoted him rapidly to branch
manager. Pacific Finance bought one of the first Sperry Univac Computers in 1958 and Millard was offered a chance to join the data processing division, which he gladly took. He moved quickly through the
data processing department, but was told that the next highest job, that
of controller, would not be his because he lacked a college degree. Millard left to become director of data processing for Alameda County, California. He told the editors of The Computer Entrepreneurs:

> It was an incredible time in my life. I loved it. It was a perfect job
> . . . the thing I loved about it . . . here's this kid—and I had a free
> license to go anywhere in the county. I was a department head . . .
> I got to play, "How could computers help the hospitals? How can
> computers help the police, the tax assessors, the county control-
> ler?" I mean, hey, I was in my glory.[107]

This experience was perfect for International Business Machines
who recruited Millard as their industry specialist for state and local
government. He traveled around the world for IBM from 1961 to 1965.
He then joined San Francisco County as director of data processing,
and in three years brought them up to the level of Alameda County.
Feeling he had built a base of contacts and experience, Millard left in
1969 to start his own company, Systems Dynamics. His goal was to
write better software than IBM. As other entrepreneurs who take on
IBM directly have found, life is not easy in that arena. Systems Dynamics was closed down in 1972. Millard realized that being a division
manager is no training for a businessperson. A second realization was
that he was a 40-year-old business failure, unacceptable to his former
employers. He had to generate income to feed his family.

[107]Robert Levering, Michael Katz, Milton Moskowitz, The Computer Entrepreneurs
(New York: New American Library, 1984), p. 347.

Millard heard that Los Angeles County was going to seek bids for the design of an on-line information retrieval system. Millard bid and won jointly with TRW. He called his new consulting company IMS Associates.

Millard was learning the consulting business, and how to smooth the cycles, an excellent training ground for entrepreneurship because it develops most of the necessary skills. In 1973, he underbid a contract for a General Motors dealer, and had to find the cheapest possible components for a computer system in order to avoid losing his shirt on the job. He got wind of Intel's 8080 microprocessor and learned that MITS in Albuquerque had built a small computer using the 8080. He bought two Altair microcomputers from MITS, tore them apart and then built his own version called the IMSAI 8080. He placed a one-inch ad announcing its availability in *Popular Electronics* and received 3,500 responses. Most of the orders came with a check for $699. Millard was ecstatic. For the first time in 45 years, he had a chance to perform and be well compensated for it.

Millard left the consulting business immediately and became a manufacturer of industrial-quality personal computers. From 1975 to 1978, he sold 13,000 IMSAI 8080's. But Millard would not take in outside partners, venture capitalists, public stockholders, or strong managers. Customer service suffered. Capital became scarce. And the IMSAI factory was shut down in mid-1979.

However, in 1976, Millard had begun a pilot ComputerLand store in Hayward, California, installing Ed Faber, IMSAI's sales manager, as president. Sales of franchises began in 1977 and Millard had his back door in good shape and on high ground when the creditors gathered up the remains of IMSAI. Except for one claim against IMSAI that is collateralized by 20 percent of ComputerLand stock, Millard protected ComputerLand when IMSAI crashed.

Trial and error; failure turned into a learning experience, and a desire never, ever to return to the hard, spiritless days of the paper route; and a strict, insecure father who removed his options appear to be Millard's drivers. He began on one of the lowest rungs of the ladders that our society has to offer, and the hill was steeper, harder, and more arduous than it was for many of the people Millard competes with. As a result, he keeps the thumbscrews on them fairly tight.

PHILLIP MOFFITT
CHRISTOPHER WHITTLE

Name of Company:	13-30 Corporation
Date Founded:	1969
Location:	Knoxville, Tennessee

Description of Business: The company publishes *Esquire* magazine, which it acquired at *Esquire's* nadir in 1979. It also publishes "target" magazines, generally by suggesting a subject and a target audience to a large advertiser who underwrites the costs.

Description of *P*: Moffitt and Whittle identified the need for magazine advertisers to reach target audiences and the need for these audiences to get certain valuable pieces of information in a regular, reliable format. They began publishing information magazines for college students and broadened to larger and more varied audiences.

Description of *S*: Facilities management is the solution to the problem of serving target markets. If Kimberly-Clark Corporation wants to reach high school senior women, 13-30 Corporation (13-30) will design a publication for it. If Johnson & Johnson wants to reach new parents, 13-30 will design a publication for it called "New Parent" and get it in the hands of 1.9 million new parents. 13-30 publishes 19 magazines, of which 15 are for specific advertisers. Revenues in 1984 are estimated by management at $100 million.

Members of *E*: David White, former president, and Nicholas Glover, president

Size of *V*: The company is privately held. Assuming $5 million in earnings and a p/e ratio of 20x, 13-30 is probably worth $100 million.

| Social Utility: | The company has created 400 jobs and its success with *Esquire* will make it easier for other entrepreneurs to take over struggling but useful magazines. |
| Principal Sources of Venture Capital: | Tony Spiva, Moffitt's economics teacher, guaranteed a bank loan for the two entrepreneurs. |

PHILLIP MOFFITT, 39, and CHRISTOPHER WHITTLE, 38, are the H. Ross Perots of magazine publishing. They are in the facilities management segment of publishing, a niche that Perot nailed down for himself in data processing. Moffitt and Whittle approach a large advertiser, such as Nissan Motor Corporation, R.J. Reynolds Industries, or Ralston Purina Company and they say, "We'll publish a magazine targeted at college students, or moviegoers or veterinarians and you'll be the principal advertisers." Nissan Motor Corporation then hires 13-30 to publish *America*, R.J. Reynolds Industries contracts for *Moviegoer*, and Ralston Purina Company signs up for *Veterinary Practice Management*. They have repeated this scenario more than a dozen times and then used the ample cash flow therefrom to purchase *Esquire*, whose revenues they have increased to $35 million in 1984 from just a couple of million when they bought it in 1979. Moffitt and Whittle are a very private publishing team that has come up with a new medium one would expect of a Rupert Murdoch or some other Madison Avenue publishing guru. But Moffitt and Whittle did their problem formulating in a very unlikely spot, Knoxville, Tennessee. How unlikely is it? The town has not had an entrepreneurial success since the Dempster Dumpster some 30 years ago.

Approach 13-30 Corporation, as it was first called, got into business with *Knoxville in a Nutshell*, a primer for freshmen entering the University of Tennessee. Even then Moffitt and Whittle were thinking target audiences. The expansion phase came early, as *Nutshell* was produced for other campuses. Writing for students was easy and cheap; the team hired student writers.

A commercial banker played venture capitalist to 13-30. Moffitt's economics teacher, Tony Spiva, put his personal guarantee on the line, but Valley Bank officer Lawrence Frierson, who died in 1973, made loans in excess of Spiva's net worth. Total borrowings reached $1 million by 1973, the first time 13-30 began to show profits. In 1974 the company made $300,000 and began paying off the loans.

Moffitt explained his feelings, when 13-30 owed $1 million and was unprofitable, to Jane Gibbs DuBose of the Knoxville *News-Sentinel*:

> I never saw on any logical level any reason that it would not work, and that has turned out to be a tremendous asset for the company. We are strategic people and the reason it is so instinctive to us is because of those early days. The only thing we could go on was the soundness of the strategy.[108]

The founders of the single-sponsor magazines keep rolling. They signed Seagram Company, Ltd. to a multimillion-dollar contract to publish a magazine for waiters called *Tables*. The U.S. Army signed up for a magazine for high school seniors called *On Your Own*. There seems to be no end to target publishing on a single-sponsor basis. Even *Esquire* is a target publication, with each issue dedicated to a central major theme such as style, soul, or careers. Specific advertisers are approached for each issue and the targets are reviewed with them in advance. When Whittle predicted sales of $250 million by 1984, the Madison Avenue gurus who chortled when the hillbillies bought *Esquire* did not scoff anymore. They took notes.

[108]Jane Gibbs DuBose, "2 ol' East Tennessee Boys Teach Publishing World a Thing or Two," *Knoxville News-Sentinel*, Oct. 21, 1984, p. C1.

PARKER G. MONTGOMERY

Name of Company:	Cooper Laboratories, Inc.
Date Founded:	1958
Location:	Palo Alto, California

Description of
Business:
The company manufactures drugs, lasers, devices, and diagnostic instruments used in specialty medical practices.

Description of *P*:
Cooper Laboratories has been a leader in developing innovative medical solutions for medical specialists. It listens to what the market needs and finds the scientists and engineers who can deliver the solution. Sales reached $363 million in 1982, the year before Montgomery began splitting off Cooper Laboratories' key divisions and selling them to other pharmaceutical companies, much like Charlie Finley split up and sold the Oakland A's.

Description of *S*:
The areas Montgomery selected were eye-surgery equipment (Coopervision), medical lasers and ultrasound equipment (Cooper LaserSonics), the Oral-B toothbrush (Cooper Care) and internal medicine (CooperBiomedical). Believing that the sum of the parts would be worth more than the whole, Montgomery began selling and spinning them off for huge prices in 1983.

Members of *E*:
A. Kenneth Nilsson, John H. Williford, John Edwards, and Martin Koffel

Size of *V*:
The approximately 16.5 million shares of common stock outstanding traded in a range of $10⅜ to $27 in 1984 for an average valuation of $205 million.

Social Utility:
Montgomery has made some important business statements while achieving Cooper Laboratories'

spin-offs, not the least of which is that investors have a difficult time judging the worth of multidivision companies. If they are spun off, the investors can then choose which ones to put into their portfolios.

Principal Sources of Venture Capital:	American Research & Development provided $600,000 in 1958, along with $400,000 from Montgomery, his family, and friends.

PARKER G. MONTGOMERY, now 56, left the security of a distinguished Wall Street law firm in 1958 and purchased a money-losing obstetrics and gynecology pharmaceutical company, the Martin H. Smith Company, with revenues at the time of $165,000. He immediately changed its name to Cooper–Tinsley Laboratories and changed marketing and manufacturing procedures as well. Within a year, revenues had tripled and the company was profitable. In 1962, with $1 million of venture capital, Cooper–Tinsley acquired Aveeno Pharmaceuticals, a manufacturer of dermatology products. Cooper Laboratories continued to make acquisitions and by 1968 Montgomery had formulated his strategy: "surround the professional" with products designed to meet the full needs of each medical profession.

Cooper Laboratories had grown at the rate of 95 percent per annum and Montgomery believed his strategy was invulnerable. Thus, Cooper Laboratories made over 20 acquisitions between 1968 and 1973. But in 1973, the company's income dropped from $5 million the previous year to a loss of $800,000. Several start-up operations failed, including an ultrasonic denture cleaner, and management's attention was diffused due to rapid expansion. A number of unrelated businesses had to be sold off.

The worst blow was that Montgomery's reputation as a manager and his credibility, especially on Wall Street, suffered. Cooper's stock fell from a high of $30 to less than $4 a share. Wall Street labeled Montgomery a financial risk taker, and he was determined to prove them wrong.

He streamlined the company's goals in four areas: dentistry, vision care, internal medicine, and surgical instruments. Cooper Laboratories made over 30 acquisitions from 1978 to 1982 in these areas. He split off component parts that did not fit and was fairly single-minded in his pursuit of a narrow business objective.

To strengthen management, Montgomery hired John Williford in 1978 as vice-chairman. Williford had engineered Revlon's growing health-care division from $18 million to $500 million. In 1979 Williford sold Cooper Laboratories' internal medicine division, with sales of $36 million and net assets of $23 million, to Schering-Plough Corporation for $90 million. Practically all of Cooper Laboratories' debts were extinguished thereby. The sale focused Cooper Laboratories on the fast-growing, high-technology aspects of its business.

But Cooper's stock price did not recover. Montgomery came up with a new strategy called "Operation SuperNova." He perceived that the company was being inadequately analyzed by the stock market. He told *In Vivo*:

> There are three tiers to the market and Wall Street is interested in properly analyzing only the top and bottom tiers—the billion-dollar-plus companies which they have to analyze, and the small, single-product companies with first-class R&D. The middle-level companies, with revenues between $100 million and $1 billion, are by and large ignored.[109]

In accordance with this hypothesis, Montgomery began spinning off Cooper Laboratories' parts toward the goal of realizing $100 per share for Cooper Laboratories' investors, by retaining 80 percent ownership in each spun-off company. Young managers could bubble to the top and receive equity rewards as well, along with autonomy. From the time the "SuperNova" plan was announced in mid-1982 through mid-1984, Cooper Laboratories' stockholders have received $121.20 per share in the form of dividends and share value. Montgomery's entrepreneurial career demonstrates unusual flexibility and resiliency along with high goal setting. His drive has not been purely financial. Cooper LaserSonics is at the forefront of a new laser-based cancer therapy called photodynamic therapy that may prove to be the treatment of choice for many forms of cancer.

[109]Clare Starrs, Editor, Tucker Swan, Roger Longman, Wendy Cooper, "Growth Company Cooper Laboratories," *In Vivo*, 1984, p. 33.

THOMAS S. MURPHY

Name of Company:	Capital Cities Communications, Inc.
Date Founded:	1954
Location:	New York, New York
Description of Business:	The company is a diversified radio, television, and cable broadcaster and a newspaper and special interest publisher with $939.7 million in 1984 revenues. Capital Cities in March 1985 announced that it will purchase 100 percent of American Broadcasting Companies, Inc., which had 1984 revenues of $3.7 billion, subject to Federal Communications Commission approval.
Description of *P*:	Murphy has the ability to view individual broadcasting and publishing properties as solutions to specific regional and industrial problems or market niches that have certain monopolistic features that make them unusually profitable when managed well.
Description of *S*:	Upon assuming the top job at Capital Cities in 1964, Murphy began acquiring broadcasting and publishing properties, and reducing overhead through economies of scale. In this manner, Capital Cities' earnings are nearly as large as ABC's even though ABC has four times more revenues.
Members of *E*:	Daniel B. Burke, president; Joseph P. Dougherty, executive vice-president; and Warren Buffett, personal advisor and largest individual investor in Capital Cities
Size of *V*:	The approximately 13 million shares of common stock outstanding of Capital Cities traded in a range in 1984 of $123½ to $174½, for an average valuation of $1.9 billion.
Social Utility:	The company has created 15-fold appreciation for its investors over the last 10 years and built a rec-

ord of consistent profitability that is the envy of most broadcasting company managers.

Principal Sources
of Venture   Leveraged buy-outs of radio stations in the 1960s
Capital: provided positive cash flow for future growth.

THOMAS SAWYER MURPHY, 59, is a tall, athletic, shy and intensely private individual. He was born in Brooklyn, New York, and raised in a devoutly Catholic home by a strong-willed mother from whom, it is said, Murphy gained much of his optimism and faith in individual achievement. Murphy's father, Charles, an attorney, was appointed a justice of the New York Supreme Court in 1947. He served in that capacity until his death in 1959.

Murphy enrolled in Cornell University and earned a BSME degree in 1945. After serving in the U.S. Armed Forces and then selling oil for Texaco for a year, he entered Harvard University and earned an MBA degree in 1949.

After Harvard, Murphy joined the Kenyon & Eckhardt advertising agency as an account executive for several years and then moved on to Lever Brothers as a product manager. When a group of investors formed Capital Cities Communications in 1954 to purchase Hudson Valley Broadcasting Company in Albany, New York, Murphy joined the company as general manager of the Albany television station. Capital Cities also bought WTVD, a Raleigh-Durham, North Carolina station, hence its corporate name. Within three years, Murphy became a director and within 10 years, president of Capital Cities.

Under his leadership, the company has grown by acquisition to include 19 television and radio stations in major markets throughout the United States; 54 cable television systems in 16 states; 10 daily newspapers in 8 markets; 36 business and specialized newspapers and magazines; 36 weekly community publications; and it is an electronic distributor of information and databases. Three of the company's electronic databases include financial information sold to the investment community, medical supplies information sold to hospitals and other health care providers, and a database of electronic components, complete with technical specifications, prices, and delivery schedules sold to electronic designers and partially supported by advertising.

Murphy's diversification into electronic databases makes him a high technology entrepreneur as much as his acquisition of more than 100 broadcasting and publishing companies makes him one of the pre-eminent leveraged buy-out entrepreneurs. When Fairchild Publications, publisher of *Women's Wear Daily*, *Daily News Record*, *Electronic News*, and many other trade newspapers, was seeking to be acquired 15 years ago, John Fairbanks contacted Murphy. Fairchild instantly liked him as do most people who meet Murphy. He liked his optimism and his openness and willingness to consider new ideas. Fairchild told *The New York Times*, "He has big blue eyes . . . and when he gets excited about an idea, they roll."[110]

Thus, when Leonard S. Goldenson, 79, founder of ABC, began to face the issue of management succession, he looked outside his company to Capital Cities. ABC television provides programming for more than 200 affiliates and owns five television stations. ABC radio has 1,596 affiliates and owns five FM and seven AM radio stations. Until the FCC decides which of the television and radio stations must be sold in order to meet its guidelines, Capital Cities-ABC's combined stations will serve one-fourth of the nation's population. Goldenson saw in Murphy perhaps the same management abilities that attracted Warren E. Buffett, Capital Cities' largest individual investor. Capital Cities has consistently earned more than 15 percent on revenues over the last 10 years, and more than 20 percent on stockholders' equity. Indeed, to finance the purchase of ABC, Buffett invested over $517 million in Capital Cities. (Buffett's investment philosophy, which will assist in an understanding of what attracted Murphy to him, is explained in detail under Warren E. Buffett.)

[110]Pamela G. Hollie, "An Empire Builder Without Usual Ego," *The New York Times*, March 20, 1985, p. 38.

LANE NEMETH

Name of Company:	Discovery Toys
Date Founded:	1977
Location:	Pleasant Hill, California
Description of Business:	The company sells a private label line of educational toys, games, and books on a party plan basis.
Description of P:	Nemeth grabbed an opportunity to sell high-quality educational toys direct to the consumer on a party plan basis.
Description of S:	Party plan selling is a marketing channel directly into the home; the inventory is financed by the sales consultant who purchases exclusive rights to a territory. The consultant is financed by her customers when she makes sales. Although it takes longer to get a party plan marketing company up to positive cash flow, it can become a cash cow in four to five years.
Members of E:	Nemeth developed Discovery Toys on her own.
Size of V:	Although privately held, based on sales of similar companies to Colgate-Palmolive Company and Dart & Kraft, Inc., it is probable that Discovery Toys' valuation is about one times sales or $40 million.
Social Utility:	The company has created 250 jobs at headquarters and 10,000 jobs in the field.
Principal Sources of Venture Capital:	$25,000 borrowed from family members and friends

LANE NEMETH, now 37, worked for three years as the director of a state-funded day-care center in Concord, California. When her husband's employer moved them to Concord, Nemeth was basically a housewife who thought she might go to work. But she worked very hard and, she told *Esquire*, "I burned out on my work."[111]

One day eight years ago, she went shopping for an educational toy for a friend's one-year-old son. She could not find one anywhere. So Nemeth went home, sat on the living room floor, and sketched out a business plan. The problem was the absence of educational toys in the toy stores and qualified sales personnel to describe the educational qualities of entertainment toys. Her solution: select a line of educational toys, make the sales presentation in the home, explaining to the parent the skill that the toy is developing. Operating out of her garage in the first year, sales were $280,000. In 1985 they are projected to be $40 million.

Along the way, there were some fits and starts, but the purpose of trouble is to instruct. In one instance, when Discovery Toys needed money very badly, it had to borrow at an interest rate of 27.5 percent per annum. At another time, the company underordered and was out of stock on 35 items.

The company has 10,000 people (mostly women) in a pyramidlike sales force. The sales consultant who arranges the party receives a 26 percent commission on sales and a smaller cut on sales made by her recruits. Achieving sales goals is rewarded with cars, fur coats, vacations, and jewelry. The marketing format is not unique: Mary Kay Cosmetics, Amway Corporation, Transart Industries and others have been doing it for years. What is unique is that the product is educational—toys for the mind—and upscale. In fact Nemeth may have found a second product line, perhaps for the husbands of her consultants: software for home computers.

[111]*Esquire*, Dec. 1984, p. 29.

WILLIAM C. NORRIS

Name of Company: Control Data Corporation

Date Founded: 1957

Location: Minneapolis, Minnesota

Description of Business: The company designs, develops, and manufactures large-scale scientific and engineering computers.

Description of P: At a time when "experts" in computer technology decided that six big computers could handle the whole world's computing needs for all time, Norris launched Control Data to build and market super-computers. Revenues have grown to over $4 billion per annum.

Description of S: Most of the initial computer manufacturers (IBM Corporation, Honeywell Corporation, NCR Corporation, Burroughs Corporation, RCA Corporation, and Sperry Corporation) were interested in business applications. Norris and his entrepreneurial team designed their computer for the scientific and engineering markets.

Members of E: Co-founders included Willis K. Drake, Arnold Ryden, Robert Perkins, Seymour Cray, Frank Mullaney, James Miles, William Keye, James Thornton, and Henry Forrest.

Size of V: The approximately 38 million shares of common stock outstanding traded in a range of $24⅜ to $48½ in 1984 for an average valuation of $1.4 billion.

Social Utility: The company has maintained a spirit of entrepreneurship since inception by encouraging its employees to be innovative, by assisting them in obtaining venture capital when they become entrepreneurs, and by applying the computer to some of society's major problems such as illiteracy. It has created employment for 60,000 people.

Principal Sources of Venture Capital: The company was one of the first start-ups to do a self-underwritten public offering.

WILLIAM C. NORRIS, now 72, was one month away from graduation from the University of Nebraska in 1932 when his father collapsed with a heart attack. He earned his engineering degree by accelerating the remaining requirements into a few days and returned to his desperate mother's farm in southern Nebraska. To save the farm, Norris preserved its sole remaining asset, cattle, in an unconventional manner: he cut all of the thistle and fed it to the cattle over the winter. They thrived on the thistle and bore calves in the spring. The cattle was marketed in the summer and the proceeds were used to put the fields back to work. The lessons of his Nebraska farm days were to see Norris through some tough times in his entrepreneurial days.

Norris left the farm in 1934 to take a job with Westinghouse selling x-ray equipment. He left to join the Navy in Washington, D.C. as an electrical engineer. When World War II began, he was assigned to Communications Supplementary Activity (CSAW) or "seesaw" for short, a select team of cryptologists, chess masters, bridge masters, physicists, and engineers. Their goal was to break enemy codes. These code-breaking exercises represented the seeds of the computer era. At the end of the war, one of Norris's CSAW colleagues, Howard Engstrom, suggested that he and Norris start a company to continue the work that CSAW began. Venture capital was nonexistent in 1945. However, an investment banker named John E. Parker had some experience in small, technological companies, and he agreed to put up $200,000 for 50 percent ownership. The company, known as ERA, attempted to design and develop computers—then called electronic data-processing and storage devices. The design team included subsequent computer industry giants such as Seymour Cray, Bill Keye, and Frank Mullaney. In a short period of time, ERA computers became known for their sophisticated engineering features, careful design, and reliability.

As *Self-Made* authors Carol Pine and Susan Mundale report:

The little company in St. Paul was making a name for itself, but journalist Jack Anderson's "Washington Merry-Go-Round" column published in 1950 provided too much attention. Anderson and his colleague Tom McNamara complained that the Navy had entrusted a vital project "involving complex engineering and construction to an inexperienced company." Not only that, the newshounds pointed out, former Navy officers including William Norris and Howard Engstrom just happened to be "highly salaried" ERA vice presidents. A "juicy" multimillion-dollar contract had been awarded to ERA even though 12 established companies were available to do the work.

The enterprising little computer company that landed that "juicy" contract also attracted the attention of Remington Rand Corporation. James Rand had already purchased Eckert-Mauchly Computer Corporation, the developer of the UNIVAC Computer and ERA's arch-competitor. Like ERA, Eckert-Mauchly had suffered chronic cash shortages and finally succumbed to acquisition just before the start of the Korean War.

John Parker had begun thinking about selling out, too. ERA had been a good investment, he reasoned, but strictly a business deal. While ERA was growing, month-to-month financing was tough. Parker guessed that ERA needed at least $5 million, maybe $10 million, if it seriously hoped to enter the computer business in a major way.

Parker decided he would find a buyer for this promising but expensive enterprise. IBM Corporation, Honeywell Corporation, and NCR Corporation were among the companies quietly examining ERA, but it was James Rand who finally bought ERA for 73,000 shares of Remington Rand Corporation common stock worth about $1.7 million on the New York Stock Exchange. Parker and Rand arrived at that sum by multiplying $5,000 times 340, the total number of engineers employed by ERA. "That may have been one of the few times since the Civil War," computer historians and engineers Arnold Cohen and Erwin Tomash observed later, "that individuals have been sold by the head outside the professional sports world."

When Parker announced the sale to ERA's shareholder-engineers in December, 1951, they were shocked. Especially William Norris. The sale meant that Norris and his cadre of bright, young engineers would lose their creative freedom. They would be absorbed into massive Remington Rand Corporation, an entity about as fast on its feet as an aging government bureaucrat, an entity fiercely committed to the prosaic—electric shavers and typewriters. Equally important, the sale of ERA extinguished—at least for a while—an entrepreneurial flame.[112]

Remington Rand Corporation was acquired by Sperry Corporation in 1955, and Norris was put in charge of all computer activities—research, engineering, manufacturing, marketing, and finance. Sperry's senior management did not appreciate the magnitude of what it had gotten into. It did not understand the level of risk or reward. Hence, it cut off capital in each one of Norris's areas of responsibility one by one. As Bob Perkins, one of Control Data's early employees says of these days, "Entrepreneurs [like Norris] have trouble if they have to climb up through a heavy organizational structure. They don't all quit. Some adapt, and that's the end of their entrepreneurial spirit. Bill Norris chose not to adapt."[113]

Norris was ripe for a change when Arnold Ryden, a financial consultant, Byron Smith, a UNIVAC executive, and Willis K. Drake, Norris's assistant (later the founder and Chief Executive Officer of Data Card Corporation), approached him in early 1957. They planted the seed in his mind to launch a new company—another ERA—free to grow without a corporate bureaucracy. Ryden wrote a business plan. Norris reached the end of his rope at Sperry and resigned. Drake became Control Data's first employee and it was his task to raise the initial capital. As it is described in Self-Made:

Sell stock, his collaborators said. It was an extraordinary idea. Never in history, the Minnesota securities commissioner told

[112]Carol Pine and Susan Mundale, Self-Made (Minneapolis, Minnesota: Dorn Books, 1982), p. 106.
[113]Ibid, p. 110.

Drake, have the founders of a new company personally tried to sell their own stock.

Drake showed the commissioner the Control Data prospectus. Control Data's mission statement was thin. The company would engage in research and development of electronic equipment. Nothing was said about building computers. Furthermore, the company said it did not intend to compete directly with giants like IBM, Sperry Rand and General Electric.

The securities commissioner searched his rule books looking for some regulation that outlawed personal sale of new company stock by its founders. There was none. He handed Drake all the forms he needed and expected never to see him again.

"The idea that we could sell stock in a company with no product, no employees and no facility seemed totally preposterous to him," Drake recalls. Drake set about trying to sell the stock anyway. He drank countless cups of coffee at Mrs. Strandy's Coffee Shop in St. Paul with potential investors. He met others at the Parker House Restaurant in Mendota ("when people didn't want to be seen with me"). But the process was too slow. Drake invited a dozen people to his home instead.

"One engineer said he wanted 10,000 shares," Drake recalls. "Up to that time I had sold 500. The second night we had another meeting; this time 25 people showed up. The third night, there were cars parked for blocks up and down the street in every direction. People called from New York and California. The whole thing cascaded. Investors were buying the principals led by William Norris as much as they were buying the idea for a company."

One objective was to distribute Control Data stock as widely as possible. The future of this new venture, the co-founder decided, would not be vested in a single large shareholder like John Parker.

The stock sold easily—615,000 shares at $1 a share in less than two weeks. About 300 people, chiefly UNIVAC employees and personal friends of Control Data officers, invested. Norris himself bought 75,000 shares—having "mortgaged nearly everything to do that," according to a colleague. Then Norris and Ryden arranged a two-year note with First Bank of Minneapolis for the principal investors. The bank was willing to lend each man four times his investment, with his Control Data stock pledged as collateral. ("That," Bill Drake says, "was an enlightened bank.") Even Jane Norris, Bill Norris's wife, put in some of her own money for Control Data stock. "If we lose all of it," she said at the time, "we'll just move ourselves and our six children back to the farm in Nebraska."[114]

In attempting to build a strong, local board of directors, Norris visited the elder statesman of 3M Corporation and painted a vivid picture of Control Data's future. "Hell," the 70-year-old 3M chairman said, "if I were 20 years younger, I'd invest. And I'll tell you this, too, sonny: If I were UNIVAC, I'd sue your ass." In fact, Sperry Rand sued Control Data, forcing Norris to sign a consent order. In the meantime, Control Data's stock rose from 33 cents to $11.25 per share. Norris began growing Control Data's revenues rapidly. He also saved money wherever he could.

Control Data staffers always told a manufacturer's representative selling electronic parts to arrive at 11:30 A.M., hoping he would buy them lunch. "I don't mind feeding the company," the representative said one day when he was asked to leave yet another armload of parts behind, "but I'll be damned if you're going to build your computer with my samples."

That computer was Seymour Cray's 1604—an instrument that would set Control Data's course for years to come and pull it out of its early poverty. Cray's 1604 meant that Control Data would not be the company described in the original mission statement. CDC would instead build a large-scale computer, and it would compete with the majors. The 1604 was compact, extremely versatile and, most important, priced at about half the cost of a competitive IBM computer. The 1604 was predicated on transistors, not vacuum tubes, and designed with complex printed circuit cards. "Printed building blocks," Cray called the cards. With

[114]Ibid, p. 112.

those as a starting point, he theorized, a computer of almost any size could be built.

"No one else at Control Data would have thought of it," says Robert Kisch, a CDC engineer during that period. "No one else had the capability. The initial success of Control Data was due to Seymour Cray."

The 1604 had its debut eight months after Control Data was incorporated. Two months later the company had its first order from the U.S. Navy Bureau of Ships. The $1.5-million sale to a "prestige customer" was crucial to the young company's credibility. About the same time, Norris, the man responsible for fund-raising, had also convinced Allstate Insurance to buy 350,000 shares of preferred stock at $25 per share. "We were rolling again on a full stomach," Norris recalls.

After the Navy order, new buyers of the 1604 fell into line, and Cray continued his imaginative tinkering. In 1959, Cray's Model 160 desk-sized computer selling for $90,000 enhanced the company's growing reputation for innovation. A year after that, Cray started work on the CDC 6600—bigger than IBM's "Stretch," until that time the largest computer ever built. The 6600 would cost $7 million per unit, and Norris offered a reporter the following understatement: "We won't have to make very many to make money. . ."

When Norris said in 1961, with similar understatement, "There are certain advantages to size," perhaps even he did not envision the momentum of that decade. After its first, unprofitable year, when total sales hovered around $780,000, CDC's figures were stunning: 1959, $4.5 million; 1960, $28 million; 1963, $100 million; 1965, $160 million; 1968, $841 million; 1969, $1 billion.

In 1961, only IBM, with a hammerlock on 82 percent of the computer market, and Control Data, with 1.6 percent of the market, were operating in the black. The computer divisions of Philco, Bendix, RCA, Packard-Bell and Honeywell all saw red ink. Norris's nemesis, Sperry Rand, was only just approaching profitability with its computers.[115]

[115]Ibid, p. 117.

The rest of the story is as fascinating in many ways as the beginning. Norris diversified Control Data into financial services and peripheral equipment. When he felt that the company was safe from uncertainty and sudden shocks, Norris began directing the company's efforts into solving society's problems in education, health care, agriculture, technology transfer, and job creation. Norris believes in cooperative efforts between corporations and the government.

Norris believes as well in the importance of entrepreneurship. He helped to fund a venture capital fund, a seed capital fund, and an innovation center in Minnesota. He also helped to found two consortium organizations to aid the rebuilding of decaying inner cities and poverty-stricken rural areas. America's signature Renaissance Man of the present entrepreneurial revolution is Norris.

KENNETH H. OLSEN

Name of Company:	Digital Equipment Corporation
Date Founded:	1956
Location:	Lincoln, Massachusetts
Description of Business:	The company is a leading manufacturer of mini-computers and the second largest computer manufacturer in the world.
Description of *P*:	Olsen believed that he could design a computer to perform 80 percent of the functions of a main-frame computer and market it for 20 percent of the price of International Business Machines Corporation's (IBM) mainframes.
Description of *S*:	Digital Equipment Corporation (DEC) has an untarnished 25-year reputation of manufacturing spectacular computers in the under $600,000 price category. The PDP 11 was the standard low-priced minicomputer (under $100,000) for over 10 years and the VAX has been the standard super minicomputer for over five years.
Members of *E*:	Edward A. Schwartz, vice-president—general counsel, secretary; G. William Helm, Jr., vice-president—finance, and treasurer.
Size of *V*:	The approximately 58 million shares of common stock outstanding traded in a range of $70⅜ to $125 in 1984 for an average valuation of $5.7 billion.
Social Utility:	DEC is the prototypical high technology start-up company; it has created 88,600 jobs and at one stretch increased employment at the rate of 40 percent per annum and made numerous investors wealthy.

Principal Sources of Venture Capital:	General Georges Doriot, the founder of America's venture capital industry, invested $70,000 of American Research & Development's capital in 1957. The investment was returned over 100 times.

KENNETH H. OLSEN was a 31-year-old circuit designer with no prior business experience working at Massachusetts Institute of Technology's Lincoln Labs, when the idea for the minicomputer came to him. He approached General Doriot, then the head of the country's oldest and premier Small Business Investment Company, American Research & Development (ARD) in Boston. Notwithstanding Olsen's lack of business experience or a businessperson partner, Doriot invested $70,000 to enable Olsen to develop a prototype minicomputer. When the product worked, the officers at ARD could see that it performed many of the functions of IBM's million-dollar mainframe computers at 20 percent—or less—of IBM's price. ARD invested another $1 million to begin production, build a marketing team, and launch sales. DEC's success has become legendary. It has surpassed all computer manufacturers, save IBM; spawned numerous entrepreneurial spin-offs such as Prime and Apollo; and trained many of the industry's best managers.

DEC continues to operate out of the abandoned textile mill in Lincoln, Massachusetts, where it began 27 years ago. Money is not spent on lavish furnishings or offices. The management structure is organized to encourage ideas to flow up. Olsen is accessible, easy to reach. DEC's technology and experienced sales and service team carry the company. Olsen says, "You make the best products you can, and you grow as fast as you deserve to."[116]

For all its successes in minicomputers, DEC has had a terrible experience in personal computers. Its Rainbow personal computer is technically second to none in the industry, but it has not sold very well. DEC opened over 50 retail stores, featuring its makes and models and none other. The stores competed with the direct-sales force, and both channels had unhappy soldiers. Further, customers left the DEC stores empty-handed because they wanted a wider variety of computers to

---

[116]"The Richest People in America, The Forbes 400," *Forbes*, Fall, 1983.

choose from. Thus, DEC's profits skidded in 1984 and its stock price fell.

At 59, Olsen is being tested as a manager for yet another time. Will he make the right moves to position DEC properly in the personal computer industry? Or, will DEC suffer the defeats of other tired giants, unable to make the transition to the "managed" stage of their development, only to be picked apart and finally mortally injured by the quicker entrepreneurs?

ELISABETH CLAIBORNE ORTENBERG

Name of Company:	Liz Claiborne, Inc.
Date Founded:	1976
Location:	New York, New York

Description of Business: This designer of women's clothing made by independent suppliers in the United States and the Far East sells its "better sportwear" merchandise through 3,000 department and specialty stores.

Description of P: Working women want well-made, fashionable sportswear to wear to the office. They are busy, so they will shop mainly in the major department stores. To be certain they are getting quality, women want a fashion image they can trust. Sales at Liz Claiborne in 1984 topped $400 million.

Description of S: Ortenberg has focused her line on the needs of business and professional women. To save costs, 65 percent of the manufacturing is done overseas. Distribution is direct to big department stores. And to maintain a fashionable high-quality image—and the prices of a "designer" label—Ortenberg appears frequently on the covers of *Ms.* and *Savvy*.

Members of E: Arthur Ortenberg, Leonard Boxer, Jerome A. Chazen

Size of V: The approximately 10.5 million shares of common stock outstanding traded in a range between $16 to $49 in 1984 for an average market value of $347 million.

Social Utility: Fashion entrepreneurs are viewed, perhaps unfairly, as opportunistic. Ortenberg, however, has generated 1,700 jobs in the United States and an average return on equity since 1980 of 50 percent.

Principal Sources   The four co-founders invested an aggregate of
of Venture $250,000 to start the business.
Capital:

ELISABETH CLAIBORNE ORTENBERG, 51, has distinguished herself as one of the best entrepreneurs in America in an industry that has
taken the toll of more businesses and had more grown men crying in
their pillows than any other. In New York it's called the "rag business,"
and its function is to design, produce, and deliver to merchants
throughout the country the clothing that we will select to wear.

Most apparel companies have been fly-by-night, here today, gone tomorrow, primarily because they have addressed a trend or a look, and
not solved a problem. Liz Claiborne, Inc. is different. It solved a problem. Simply stated, women in fast-paced industrial and financial companies do not have time to shop for apparel, stay up-to-date with styles,
yet they cannot afford to look out of step at any time. The solution to
this need was a line of apparel between "classic" and "avant-garde"
that was designed for smart-looking, young female executives. But the
line was marketed like a service rather than a product. Rather than go to
the expense of opening and operating its own stores, where sales personnel would be trained to service the customer, the company provided "Claiboards" to the retailers who stocked the line. As Irene Daria
wrote in Women's Wear Daily: "Claiboards [are] a trademarked concept
using sketches, photos and printed explanations showing how merchandise should be displayed in groups."[117] Claiboards explained to
the retailer how to mix and match the apparel to maximize the appearance for the customer. The sales and service tool said in effect, "Here's
how to service the customer so she'll keep coming back." There are at
least 30 computer manufacturers who possibly could have gotten shelf
space in computer dealer stores had they discovered "Claiboards," or
their equivalent. Products in a competitive marketplace keep selling
and selling if the customer feels he or she is receiving service, not because the product is substantially unique, which in the case of apparel
is not the case.

Jerome A. Chazen, one of the company's four founders says, "We

---

[117]Irene Daria, "Claiborne Priority: Managing its Growth," Women's Wear Daily, June
26, 1984, p. 4.

sometimes fantasize about how wonderful it would be to have our own stores. . . . Then the blouse that goes with group A [wouldn't] be on the other side of the floor."[118] But this is unlikely to happen. Thus, the emphasis on sales training.

Liz Claiborne Inc. may not have happened except for the fact that Jonathan Logan closed Youth Guild in February 1976, a dress division where Ortenberg had worked as a designer for 16 years. Concomitantly, her husband Arthur Ortenberg phased out his consulting business and they went into business together. They advertised for a production partner. This led to Leonard Boxer joining the fledgling firm. Jerry Chazen, Ortenberg's college roommate and a retailer, invested his share of the initial $250,000, but didn't join the company until it could afford him.

After 18 months of operations, Liz Claiborne Inc. was on its way to a $7 million year. The four partners felt they may be on to something big. They went on a three-day retreat to the Poconos to talk about "what success would mean, how it would change each of our lives and whether we wanted those changes to happen," Chazen said. Two of the partners did not want rapid growth but Ortenberg's argument was compelling, for Liz Claiborne, Inc. as well as other rapidly emerging companies: "Once you shape a company to service the marketplace and your services are necessary, the company develops a compulsion of its own to grow."[119] That statement says a great deal about entrepreneurial drive and motivation.

[118]Ibid, p. 4.
[119]Ibid, p. 5.

M. KENNETH OSHMAN
ROBERT R. MAXFIELD

Name of Company:	Rolm Corporation
Date Founded:	1969
Location:	Santa Clara, California
Description of Business:	The company is a leading producer of computer-controlled business telephone switching systems.
Description of *P*:	Rolm Corporation is an elegant example of the vertical integration of the microprocessor. The company attempted to develop more technologically superior switchboards than American Telephone and Telegraph Company (AT&T) and it succeeded. Sales in 1984 exceeded $650 million.
Description of *S*:	Rolm Corporation did what Silicon Valley high-technology companies are good at: invoked the law of 30-30-30. It made a private branch exchange (PBX) system that was 30 percent better, 30 percent faster, and 30 percent cheaper than AT&T's. And Rolm Corporation improved on it every year.
Members of *E*:	Eugene Richeson and Walter Lowenstern, co-founders; Richard Moley, vice-president—marketing
Size of *V*:	International Business Machines Corporation (IBM) paid $1.5 billion for Rolm Corporation in 1984.
Social Utility:	The company employs 10,000 people and it made over 9,000 stockholders a significant capital gain on the IBM merger.
Principal Sources of Venture Capital:	Reid Dennis of Institutional Venture Associates and Robert Perring of Wells Fargo SBIC invested $1.2 million in a second stage financing. A tiny publicly held SBIC called Continental Capital

Corporation invested $200,000 in 1970 for 13.5 percent ownership.

EUGENE RICHESON, M. KENNETH OSHMAN, WALTER LOWEN-STERN, and ROBERT R. MAXFIELD conceived their billion-dollar baby at a monthly poker game in 1968. The first letters of their last names spell Rolm. The game included engineers from IBM and GTE-Sylvania and they talked about what they would do when they grew up. The four founders were graduates of Rice University who met again as graduate students at Stanford University.

Lowenstern talked the others into setting up their own shop in a prune-drying shed in Santa Clara in 1969. Oshman was named president because he had dreamed of having his own company. Lowenstern and Maxfield preferred engineering. Richeson became the marketer because he was comfortable selling Rolm Corporation's initial product, fail-safe computers for the military.

Five years later when sales hit $3 million, Oshman convinced the team to spend $1 million to diversify into the microprocessor-based PBX business because the Intel 8080 chip had arrived on the scene. This decision put the company squarely into the office automation business.

Rolm Corporation's bread and butter product, the ROLM CBX, is a PBX designed for business with 16 to 10,000 telephone extensions. Its microprocessor-based telephone sets interface with the PBX unit. The system integrates voice and data signals. Messages can be sent, received, and answered electronically through a video terminal connected to one of Rolm Corporation's telephones.

Each year, Rolm Corporation seems to come out with new features that are 30 percent better, 30 percent faster and 30 percent cheaper than competitive systems. In 1983, for instance, the company introduced Phone Mail, a PBX enhancement that combines telephone answering, message notification, and voice store-and-forward features with a new digital feature. IBM has found its own Western Electric Company.

Oshman built Rolm Corporation to be a "great place to work." Rolm's campus headquarters has sports and wellness facilities. One Halloween, three of the founders—who are all in their mid-forties—came to work dressed as three of the Seven Dwarfs. Their fortunes are anything but dwarflike.

DAVID PACKARD
WILLIAM R. HEWLETT

Name of Company: Hewlett–Packard Company

Date Founded: 1939

Location: Palo Alto, California

Description of
Business:
    The company is the largest manufacturer of electronic test and measurement instruments and the second largest manufacturer of minicomputers in the world.

Description of P: Packard and his partner, William Hewlett, have built a highly regarded, professionally managed company with a focus on electronic devices that test and measure signals. In the 1960s, Hewlett–Packard Company (H–P) entered the minicomputer field; revenues therefrom now account for 51 percent of the total, and profits 46 percent. To gain entry into personal computers, H–P introduced a lap portable in 1984 which has been the best-selling of that species.

Description of S: H–P is a happy place to work. It encourages entrepreneurship among its managers. If an engineer develops a new electronics device, he estimates market size, prepares a business plan and then recommends to his manager that H–P create a new division to manufacture and sell that product. If H–P management agrees, the engineer gets to entrepreneur the project through development, test, manufacture, and marketing. If H–P rejects it the engineer is free to leave and start a company to make and sell the product, so long as he gives H–P a nonexclusive license. With the entrepreneurial spirit alive and well at H–P, it continues to grow at a fast pace ($884 million revenues in 1974 to over $5 billion in 1984) with return on sales of more than 9 percent.

Members of *E*:	The 257 million shares of common stock outstanding traded in a range of $31⅛ to $45½ in 1984 for an average valuation of $9.9 billion.
Social Utility:	H–P has created 83,000 jobs and trained some of America's most outstanding electronics industry entrepreneurs.
Principal Sources of Venture Capital:	Packard and Hewlett chipped in $538 and their wives worked in the early days to support them.

DAVID PACKARD and his partner WILLIAM R. HEWLETT have created a company that would have been included in a book of the 100 best entrepreneurial companies founded prior to 1960. Reiteration in this book is justifiable because the company has remained intensely entrepreneurial in the last 25 years. Not only that, H–P's senior managers are beginning to tell us some things about the next 25 years that bear listening to.

The late Frederick E. Terman, whose teaching career began at Stanford University in 1925, is responsible for beginning H–P. Professor Terman encouraged his students to start their own businesses when they had an idea, and the most notable of the students that he encouraged was William Hewlett. He encouraged Hewlett to lure David Packard away from General Electric Company to start work on a resistance-tuned audio oscillator. They began work in Packard's Palo Alto garage in 1939. Hewlett, a brilliant engineer, made sure that the products were of the highest standards, while Packard made sure they were sold. As a leading manufacturer of electronic test and measurement instruments, company sales grew to $500 million by the end of the 1960s.

A second entrepreneurial life struck H–P in 1972. At this time, most engineers were still using slide rules to calculate. Hewlett thought it would be easier and more accurate if they would use a scientific calculator. H–P's management and market research department concluded that there would be no demand for a $400 calculator so long as slide rules cost $20. Hewlett told me he barked: "I don't know if anyone else wants one, but I do. Build it." The HP–35 calculator, with performance features equal to that of the ENIAC computer of the late 1940s, was introduced and became the hottest product in the electronics industry for several years. The slide rule was history, H–P's sales tripled to $1.8 billion by 1978.

Although H–P is admired for its test instruments, calculators, and computers, its medical instruments are exceptional products as well. They account for a mere 8 percent of revenues and profits. One of them, an ear oximeter, can measure blood oxygen levels without obtaining a blood sample. The oximeter shines light from optical fibers through the translucent part of a person's ear. The light that is emitted is electronically measured to determine blood oxygen levels.

H–P's third entrepreneurial life is with minicomputers and personal computers. Its minicomputers, topped off by the powerful, popular H–P 3000, have captured the number two position behind Digital Equipment Corporation (DEC). H–P management has its eye on the number three position in the personal computer industry, behind International Business Machines Corporation and Apple Computer. Others seeking that spot include AT&T, Compaq Corporation, DEC, NCR Corporation, Data General Corporation, TI, ITT, and at least five Japanese electronics and computer companies. H–P has entered the market with a lap portable, rather than confronting IBM's strength with a desk top model. Most of the components of its lap portable are Japanese made; it has two popular software packages imbedded in the hardware: a word processor and a spreadsheet package. H–P does not try to be all things to all people. It bought chips from Hitachi in 1981, which sent the American semiconductor industry into convulsions and accelerated its search for capital (hence IBM's investment in Intel Corporation). It bought 3.5 inch disc drives from Sony Corporation in 1982 which sounded the death knell for U.S. disc drive manufacturers Shugart Corporation and a division of Control Data Corporation, among others. And the screen in the H–P lap portable is made by Toshiba.

While H–P remains competitive in its markets, 79-year-old Hewlett and 73-year-old Packard place their time and fortunes in charitable, cultural, and governmental endeavors. As is their company, they are the finest mature entrepreneurs our country can point to with honor and pride.

ROY HAMPTON PARK

Name of Company:	Park Communications, Inc.
Date Founded:	1962
Location:	Ithaca, New York
Description of Business:	The company is a media holding company that owns and operates 70 publications, including 23 dailies, 18 nondailies, 27 controlled circulation weeklies, and broadcasting properties including 14 radio stations and 7 television stations.
Description of P:	The need for people living in small towns to have first-rate broadcasting and newspapers is the opportunity that Park perceived. In 22 years, Park Communications has assembled 91 small town media and grown to revenues of just under $100 million. It is the 96th largest broadcasting company in the country.
Description of S:	Park learned that he could borrow on the assets of a broadcasting property in order to acquire it. Once he got control, he altered the format to provide lots of important local news.
Members of E:	Kenneth B. Skinner, Wright M. Thomas, and Dorothy D. Park (Mrs. Roy H.)
Size of V:	Forbes estimates Park's wealth at $230 million.[120]
Social Utility:	Broadcasting does not create a great deal of employment. In fact, the company employs 1,700 people in the aggregate. However, Roy Park's entrepreneurial achievements are legendary in his birthplace, near Raleigh, North Carolina, and in his adopted hometown, Ithaca, New York.

[120]"The Richest People in America, The Forbes 400," Forbes, 1983 edition, Fall, 1983.

| Principal Source of Venture Capital: | The proceeds of the sale of Hines-Park Foods to Procter & Gamble Company for more than $2.5 million. |

ROY H. PARK, 73, was born on a farm in Dobson, North Carolina, but his father could afford to send the four children to college. His first job came in 1931, while Park was still a student at North Carolina State University in Raleigh.

I saw a want ad in *The News and Observer*. . . . Someone was looking for a young man to do some writing. Those days many ads like that were come-ons, and I wanted to be sure this one was legitimate. The ad said to write Box 731, Raleigh, so I did. But I put the letter in a pink envelope. Then I went to the post office the next morning and waited till I saw someone take that pink envelope out of the box. Then I eased over and found out who was offering the job." It was the North Carolina Cotton Growers Association. Anticipating that he would be interviewed for the job, "I had bought myself a white cotton suit and showed up for the interview wearing it."

The Cotton Growers Association was reluctant to hire him. So Park told his prospective employer, "I had my own typewriter and didn't need an office. If they'd just find me a table in a corner somewhere, I'd work three months for nothing."[121]

Park was hired and he stayed with the Association for 11 years, editing a magazine and taking care of public relations and sales promotion.

One day out of the blue, Park received an invitation from Dr. H. E. Babcock, head of a farmers' cooperative called GLF, now known as Agway, to come to Ithaca to discuss an opportunity. Park replied that he would move only to have his own business. "Young man," Dr. Babcock said, "you just bought it."

"What business did I buy?" Park asked.

"Your own ad agency," he replied. "If you need money, we'll lend it

[121]Guy Munger, "Farm Boy to Boss of a Communications Empire," *The (Raleigh, NC) News and Observer*, July 29, 1984, p. 3D.

to you."[122] Dr. Babcock was also Chairman of the Board of Trustees at Cornell University.

Park grew the business steadily and wisely, sticking to advertising for farm businesses. He opened branches in five other cities and expanded to 125 employees in six years. Then, "I fell on my face."

"My mistake was getting into political advertising, where we did several campaigns for Tom Dewey, including appeals for the farm and small town vote in 1948."[123] When Truman beat Dewey, many clients identified Park's firm as a "loser" and switched to other agencies. Park had to come up with a new idea.

The farm cooperatives had shown the need to Park for a consumer brand name of their own. Extensive market research indicated to Park the enormous consumer appeal of the name Duncan Hines. At that time, Hines was America's most famous restaurant reviewer, and the author of guidebooks that rated restaurants. Park felt that a line of Duncan Hines food products would be potent. There were two obstacles, however: (1) Hines had never permitted his name to be used and (2) Park didn't know how to get to Hines. To prepare for his eventual meeting with Hines, Park read everything he could find on the man. He knew that Hines did not want to license his name for the wealth it might bring him. Park was introduced to Hines by a mutual friend, and Hines asked the young man: "So, you're going to make me a millionaire?" Park said, "No . . . [but] you can help upgrade American eating habits." Knowing also that Hines never endorsed anything, Park came prepared to the meeting with completely finished Duncan Hines labels, in full color, on dummy cans, cartons and jars so that Hines could see what the concept looked like. They shook hands on a deal.

Park and Hines began product planning and testing immediately. All products underwent blind tests before market introduction to assure consistency from one product to the next. Rigid quality control standards were set by Hines and he saw that the company's manufacturers met those standards.

In the meantime, Park's farm cooperative clients backed out of their commitment to pay some of the up-front costs for an interest in the

[122]Roy H. Park, "Building a Business with no Outside Stockholders," a speech delivered Nov. 2, 1976, at Cornell University Graduate School of Business and Public Administration.
[123]Ibid.

profits. Park had to raise money quickly, which he did from family and friends and by pulling cash out of his advertising agency and letting it slide away. To save production and shipping costs, Park mailed the labels to the packages rather than the other way around. Soon after its introduction, Duncan Hines cake mix captured a 48 percent market share. Pillsbury, Swansdown, Aunt Jemima, and Betty Crocker brands took the hit. As Park says, "We could never outspend those giants—so we out-thought them."[124]

Duncan Hines was the first cake mix to be advertised on television. In the late 1940s, Mr. Hines acted in the commercials, which was also a first in consumer products advertising. Hines-Parks Foods was also the first company to use 4-color ads in newspapers. Park also used outdoor ads to remind the housewife of the commercial she saw the previous evening on television. Park took Hines on the road, talking mayors and governors into declaring "Duncan Hines Days," and presenting him with keys to the city. The Duncan Hines Days generally ended with a big dinner, to which the governor, the mayor, city big-wigs, and the key chain store buyers were invited, along with their wives. The latter were presented with a corsage and an autographed Duncan Hines Cookbook on arrival. Park instructed his people to sell nothing at the party. "Next day was another story," says Park.

With distribution in 23 states and 120 different cake mixes, the Duncan Hines brand was second in sales among all brands by the mid-1950s.

A buy-out offer from Procter & Gamble Company was accepted, for a price never made public. Park stayed at Procter & Gamble Company for seven years under the terms of a noncompete agreement, and in 1962 he left in order to begin his third career—and in a sense a return to his first love—journalism.

Park is a frequent speaker to business school and journalism students. His basic rules include the following:

1. Pay attention to details.

2. Get things done on time.

3. Delegate to others all that they can handle as well or better.

4. Use showmanship, imagination. Dramatize what you are doing.

[124]Ibid.

5. Take action. If you have the facts and a little common sense, and you move, you've got better than a 50 percent chance of being right.

6. Do your business homework.

7. Reinvest the cash flow as it is generated—but always keep a liquid position.[125]

[125]Ibid.

JOSEPH C. PARKINSON
WARD PARKINSON

Name of Company: Micron Technology, Inc.

Date Founded: 1978

Location: Boise, Idaho

Description of   The company designs, develops, and manufac-
Business: tures high performance microprocessors, includ-
                       ing 64K and 256K chips, used to manufacture per-
                       sonal computers.

Description of *P*:   In 1978–1981 U.S. semiconductor manufacturers
                       were losing market share to the Japanese, who had
                       gotten the jump on the 64K dynamic random
                       access memory (DRAM) chip, a principal com-
                       ponent of computers and telecommunications
                       systems. Most U.S. companies retreated to high-
                       performance, specialty chips: the markets are
                       smaller but the margins are higher and competi-
                       tion is less intense. The Parkinsons seized the op-
                       portunity to be the only American company to
                       make 64K DRAM chips and they are beating the
                       Japanese in this market.

Description of *S*:   Despite proclamations of doom befalling them
                       from semiconductor industry gurus such as L.J.
                       Sevin (founder of Mostek Corporation) and others,
                       Micron Technology has succeeded on less capital
                       than these experts said it would need ($9 million
                       versus $100 million) and against a competitive
                       force that many of these experts call formidable.
                       But, the experts did not count on the advantages
                       of Boise, Idaho. As Joe Parkinson told a *Forbes* re-
                       porter: "You just don't grow up in our neck of the
                       woods believing that someone can outwork
                       you."[126]

[126]Subrata N. Chakravarty, *Forbes*, Dec. 31, 1984, p. 36.

Members of _E_:	Juan Benitez, a plant manager at Mostek, who responded to a three-line ad in the _Wall Street Journal_: "Small start-up semiconductor company in the Pacific Northwest looking for individual to be responsible for overall construction of a metal oxide semiconductor facility."
Size of _V_:	The approximately 19 million shares of common stock outstanding traded in a range of $14 to $40¼ in 1984 for an average valuation of $513 million.
Social Utility:	The company has created 800 jobs in Boise, has beaten back the threat of Japanese dominance of the semiconductor industry, and has pointed up some sclerosis in older U.S. semiconductor companies.
Principal Sources of Venture Capital:	Idaho businesspeople Ronald Yanke, Allen Noble, Thomas Nicholson, and successful entrepreneur, J.R. Simplot

WARD PARKINSON, 39, and JOSEPH C. PARKINSON, 41, attribute the success of Micron Technology in the semiconductor industry to the fact that their competition threw in the towel to the Japanese. In 1979, Hitachi, Fujitsu, and NEC Electronics got the jump on Intel Corporation, Mostek Corporation, and American Micro Devices in developing 64K DRAM chips and the United States companies retreated to the specialized chip markets. Micron began in the basement of a dentist's office in Boise, Idaho, with a contract to design a 64K chip for Mostek Corporation. When United Technologies Corporation bought Mostek Corporation later that year, the contract was cancelled but Ward Parkinson, the principal design engineer, and his colleagues, Douglas Pitman and Jim O'Toole, redoubled their efforts and completed the design.

Parkinson began turning over every rock for money. L.J. Sevin, Mostek Corporation founder-turned-venture capitalist, turned him down. Venture capitalists Hambrecht & Quist and Sutter Hill followed suit. Silicon Valley hubris has let many good deals escape.

The experts all said it could not be done. So Micron was launched with funding from three Boise residents: Ron Yanke, a machine shop owner; Allen Noble, a potato farmer; and Tom Nicholson, a wealthy sheep rancher. For "real gambling money," as he puts it, J.R. Simplot, Idaho's potato billionaire, had to be brought in.

The company was helped by the fact that construction costs are lower in Boise than in Silicon Valley and that the 64K's development costs were largely paid for by the Mostek Corporation contract. But the key saving was in equipment costs. Micron Technology bought one machine and kept it well oiled, because everything relied on its not breaking down. Today, Micron Technology has $84 million worth of equipment, and it produces 6 million chips a month.

In September 1984 Micron Technology made another bold move. Seeing a coming softening of demand, it dropped the list price of 64K DRAM chips from $3.40 a chip to $1.95. The competition became outraged. The president of NEC Electronics said, "I don't see marketing expertise in what they are doing."[127] Orders flooded in following the price cut, and Micron Technology claims it is booked solid through 1985, while other American chip makers are 61 percent backlogged. Meanwhile, the company has come up with a 256K chip, which it has begun shipping directly in competition with NEC Electronics and Hitachi. The Micron Technology chip is said to be technologically superior; it has 50 percent more cells (the slots that hold information) than its competitors, and contains certain error correction capabilities.

By running a lean operation and doing all its manufacturing in Boise, Micron Technology saves on inventory and transportation costs. Thus, Micron Technology has achieved significant cost advantages over the Japanese. Still the experts put down Micron Technology. The Japanese say Micron Technology cannot maintain the advantage, and Silicon Valley venture capitalist Pierre Lammond told *Forbes*, "I think their luck is going to run out."[128] And the stock market has not run up the price. In fact, 70 percent of Micron Technology's stock is owned by Idaho investors. All of this proves the stubbornness of Boise entrepreneurs and the stubbornness of the entrepreneurs and investors who preceded them.

[127]Ibid, p. 35.
[128]Ibid, p. 36.

ALLEN E. PAULSON

Name of Company:	Gulfstream Aerospace Corporation
Date Founded:	1970
Location:	Savannah, Georgia
Description of Business:	The company designs, develops, and manufactures luxury corporate jets.
Description of P:	The private corporate jet business was treated as an appendage by most major aircraft manufacturers in the 1970s. Paulson saw the opportunity to capture the high end of the market and develop it into a sizable business by marketing the plane to high-income, fast-moving executives.
Description of S:	Paulson was in the right place at the right time when Grumman Corporation offered to sell its corporate jet division in 1978 for $52 million. Within four years, Paulson had grown the business to approximately $580 million in revenues, and he offered shares to the public at a valuation of $700 million. The luxury private jet business is an excellent example of an overlooked, but profitable, niche market seeking an entrepreneur to exploit it.
Members of E:	A.H. Glenn, executive vice-president, and James Brandbury, vice-president—finance
Size of V:	The approximately 33 million shares of common stock outstanding traded in a range of $13 to $20¼ in 1984 for an average valuation of $1.1 billion.
Social Utility:	Gulfstream Aerospace Corporation employs roughly 3,000 people.
Principal Sources of Venture Capital:	Paulson's sweat equity

ALLEN E. PAULSON, 63, grew up on a farm in Iowa during the Depression. At age 13 he was supporting himself and at 15 he went to California to work on a dairy farm. There he fell in love with the airplanes at a nearby airport. An advertisement he saw in 1941 changed his life; Trans World Airlines (TWA) wanted mechanics. Paulson took the job at $.30 per hour.

He served in the U.S. Army Air Corps from 1943 to 1945, finishing ground school and flight training before the end of the war. Following his discharge, Paulson finished pilot training and rejoined TWA in his prewar job. When the Federal Aviation Administration (FAA) first required flight engineers on all passenger flights, TWA did not have enough engineers so they promoted some of their mechanics. Paulson was one.

As a flight engineer, Paulson became aware of problems with Lockheed Corporation's engines and the growing need for engine parts by airline companies. He purchased and dismantled a surplus B-29 engine and modified the parts to improve their performance and dependability. Though Paulson offered his ideas to his employers, TWA did not accept them, so he sold them to other airlines. Later TWA also placed orders for enough of his parts to modify over a hundred engines. He soon became one of the major suppliers for new and reconditioned aircraft engine parts in the United States.

In 1951 Paulson founded California Airmotive Corporation to convert surplus airliners to carry cargo. By 1953 the company was doing so well that Paulson left TWA. While running his own company, he started a Learjet distributorship and became its number one sales outlet. In 1970 Paulson formed American Jet Industries, to convert general aviation piston powered aircraft to propjet configurations and to develop special purpose aircraft.

Paulson became proficient at aeronautical design for in-line, combination power aircraft and, as a result, he was awarded five patents. In 1978 Grumman Aerospace offered to sell its Savannah, Georgia, subsidiary for $52 million. American Jet had sales of $35 million by then, and enough credibility with lenders to obtain financing to buy the division.

Paulson renamed his new acquisition Gulfstream American Corporation and turned it around by increasing sales, cutting costs, increasing productivity, and discontinuing unprofitable lines. He focused on the Gulfstream II, the ultimate corporate jet, and the Gulfsteam III, then in development. Paulson made more improvements to the Gulfstream III and started a completion center to provide interior outfitting services and reduce his dependence on other suppliers.

In February 1981 Gulfstream acquired the Commander Jetprop manufacturing facilities in Oklahoma City from Rockwell International. This division currently produces four models of twin engine, prop jet powered aircraft. New Commander jet prop models are in various stages of development for future additions to the Gulfstream line, such as the development of a new medium-size business jet, the Peregrine. It is the first single-engine jet ever designed specifically for business use. In May 1985 Chrysler Corporation obtained an option to invest in or purchase Golfstream for a significant valuation.

When an entrepreneur starts out at 13 to make his or her way in the world and if he or she learns a set of skills that are timely and relevant, the American system rewards the entrepreneur with wealth, esteem, and honorariums: our gratitude for showing us once again how fortunate all of us are to have these opportunities.

LUIGINO FRANCO PAULUCCI

Name of Company:	Chun King Corporation, Jeno's, Inc.
Date Founded:	1946, 1967
Location:	Duluth, Minnesota
Description of Business:	Chun King Corporation processed and distributed canned Chinese foods. Jeno's, Inc. processes and distributes frozen pizzas and snack foods.
Description of *P*:	Paulucci recognized the opportunity in ethnic foods sold through supermarkets rather than restaurants. He has achieved two consecutive entrepreneurial successes: first in Chinese foods (1946 to 1966) and second in Italian foods (1967 to the present).
Description of *S*:	Paulucci learned how to package and sell various foods based on ethnic appeal as a child; his business successes with Chun King and Jeno's are extensions of childhood achievements. Working at Hibbings Downtown Daylight Market at age 14, from 6 A.M. to midnight during the Depression, Paulucci learned merchandising out of desperation; he had to work to feed his family. The refrigerator broke down one day and 18 crates of bananas turned an oily, speckled brown on the outside; otherwise they were unharmed. The store manager ordered Paulucci to take them into the street and get rid of them at bargain prices. Paulucci hauled them out front, hand lettered a sign saying "Argentine Bananas," and began shouting out news about this exotic fruit. A crowd gathered and he sold all 18 crates in three hours at four cents a pound higher than the price of ordinary bananas. These and similar marketing strategies, refined and repackaged, have provided the keys to Paulucci's many successes.

Members of *E*:	David Persha, first employer and later a partner, and Paulucci's wife, Lois. Paulucci's advice to entrepreneurs: "Get a mate who will allow you to work day and night seven days a week, if need be. Otherwise stay single."[129]
Size of *V*:	*Forbes* estimates the value of Paulucci's holdings at $200 million.[130]
Social Utility:	Paulucci has been responsible for the creation of an estimated 2,000 jobs in Minnesota, Ohio, and Florida.
Principal Source of Venture Capital:	Paulucci's sweat equity

JENO F. PAULUCCI, now 67, has driven himself and others to succeed since he was a child. There does not appear to be any way to slow him down, notwithstanding that Paulucci is a centimillionaire many times over. He is an incurable, successful entrepreneur. According to his autobiography, the Paulucci family was poor even by Depression standards. Paulucci's father, Ettore, had migrated to Aurora, Minnesota, to work in the iron mines. The work, however, was irregular and food for the family of four was available only when everyone scrounged. Young Jeno walked along the railroad tracks looking for fallen lumps of coal, pulling a little red wagon held together by discarded parts. He gathered cardboard boxes to sell for a penny each to the Pauluccis' landlord who burned them for fuel.

By age 12, Paulucci figured that there was more to work than muscles. He peddled iron-ore samples in glass vials to tourists who came to visit the iron ore mines, and he conducted guided tours of the mines. Paulucci's father abandoned the family shortly thereafter, but returned when Paulucci was successful. In 1933 his hardworking mother opened a grocery store in the family's living room and Paulucci took a job at a downtown grocery. He developed an awe-inspiring reputation for hard work, 16-hour days and salesmanship that the small chain's

---

[129]"The Richest People in America, The Forbes 400," *Forbes*, Fall, 1983.
[130]Ibid.

owner, David Persha, admired. Always combative, Paulucci led two strikes at high school: one against long homework assignments for students who held jobs and the other against learning poetry. At 16 he became the Minnesota sales representative for a food wholesaler after negotiating a 50 percent profit split.

During the Second World War, fresh vegetables were in short supply, and Paulucci observed that Oriental families in Minnesota were growing their own bean sprouts in hydroponic gardens. Paulucci experimented with growing soybeans, and he and David Persha became partners in the new venture. Persha was an experienced businessperson, reasonable and cautious. Paulucci was young, energetic, abrasive, combative, and full of ideas. Paulucci at five feet five was known to take on an entire barroom; and later when Chun King had management meetings, to jump onto the conference table, stare down at his vice presidents and terrorize them.

Chun King toughed it out through the late 1940s, and Paulucci's marriage tempered his pugnacity somewhat but not entirely. It was for pure spite that Paulucci started Northland Foods, predecessor to Jeno's, Inc. In the book *Self-Made* by Carol Pine and Susan Mundale, the beginning of Northland Foods is described:

It was 1947, and Jeno owed everybody money—his packers, his suppliers, even some of his customers who had credit memos. A federal investigator, moreover, determined that Paulucci owed his employees $15,000 in back pay for time-and-a-half over 40 hours instead of 48 as stated in their union contract. Jeno bid on a government contract to pack boned turkey on the basis of a verbal loan agreement from a Duluth bank. When the bank backed out, he had to tell the government to take the next lowest bid. Finally, a small Duluth bank granted him a loan.

In an effort to settle one debt, Jeno made an agreement with the packer who had won the lawsuit. Jeno would act as a field broker, selling the packer's canned pie fillings at a low brokerage rate. But the packer, who had been so prompt about collecting payments on the settlement, proved slow to pay the brokerage fee. Again Jeno took matters into his own hands. He telephoned the packer's company with a fictitious order for $9,000 worth of pie filling. When the cans were in the truck and on their way to Duluth, he phoned the packer again. "If I don't get $5,000 by tomorrow, I'm going to dump this stuff in the Twin Cities for bargain prices," he said. "Furthermore, I'm going into the pie-filling business myself, and it's a vendetta." Northland Foods, later Jeno's, Inc., was thus born.[131]

Chun King began to attract acquisition interest in the 1960s. Paulucci rejected a Chef Boy-Ar-Dee offer for $4 million. But in 1966 R.J. Reynolds Industries bought the company for $63 million, freeing Paulucci to work on the expansion of Jeno's. He certainly was not going to stay at Chun King, with the new corporate regime in place. Paulucci says: "When I showed up for work at my usual time the first morning, the guard wouldn't let me into the building. I suddenly realized that I was in a different world! These people came to work at nine in the morning. I thought I was late walking in at six!"[132]

[131]Carol Pine and Susan Mundale, Self-Made (Minneapolis, Minnesota: Dorn Books, 1982), p. 28.
[132]Ibid, p. 29.

H. ROSS PEROT

Name of Company:	Electronic Data Systems Corporation
Date Founded:	1962
Location:	Dallas, Texas
Description of Business:	The company manages data processing departments of large industrial companies and government agencies under facilities management contracts. The company was recently acquired by General Motors Corporation (GM) for $2.5 billion, but some analysts believe that Electronic Data Systems Corporation (EDS) management will soon be running GM.
Description of P:	Perot identified one of the largest and easily soluble industrial problems of the 1960s: purchasers of million dollar computers were unable to process their data—receivables, payables, inventory, and so forth—and data processing managers were under enormous pressure to find a solution.
Description of S:	A former International Business Machines Corporation (IBM) salesperson, Perot left to form EDS. He called on his former customers and offered to manage their data processing facilities under contract. EDS bought their computers and equipment, assumed the salaries of their employees, and contracted to deliver the solutions for the amount of the customers' budgets. EDS sold off excess equipment, laid off excess people, and earned as much as 40 percent profit on sales.
Members of E:	Morton H. Meyerson, president; Claude K. Chappelear, vice-president—secretary; R. Michael Farmer, treasurer.
Size of V:	The company was acquired in mid-1984 for $2.5 billion.
Social Utility:	EDS created 27,326 jobs and invented a unique method of doing business: facilities management.

Perot has been emulated by numerous entrepreneurs who are running government agencies and corporate divisions under contract.

Principal Source of Venture Capital: Perot and family members launched EDS with $25,000.

HENRY ROSS PEROT at 55 has achieved greater wealth in a shorter period of time than any other entrepreneur in the history of the American economy. In a span of six years, 1962 to 1968, the value of Perot's holdings in EDS grew from $25,000 to $1 billion. By 1970 Perot had wasted an estimated $600 million in an attempt to purchase and turn around a major Wall Street brokerage firm, Francis I. duPont, Glore Forgan & Company. Many of duPont's brokers resigned upon receiving a memorandum from Perot which recommended push-ups and knee-bends before beginning work. The crash on Wall Street killed off the remains of duPont and lowered the value of EDS's stock. Perot lost over three-fourths of his wealth. The press attempted to further diminish Perot's credibility by chastising him for a POW Christmas dinner airlift that he funded during the Vietnam War. The mission was unsuccessful.

Entrepreneurs of Perot's class must never be counted out. He made back his fortune at least twice over, and with a seat on GM's board and lots of its voting stock, Perot is in a position to influence one of America's largest companies and bring it into the age of technology. Perot's most frequently quoted remark is: "Eagles don't flock, you have to catch them one at a time."

Perot's most significant contribution to our economy has not been in the field of data processing. It was his invention of a unique method of solving large problems for large corporations, hospitals, insurance companies, and government agencies. EDS hired the customers' data processing personnel and purchased the customers' data processing equipment. It ran the customers' work for the customers' budget (EDS's revenues). If it brought in the job for less than the budget, the difference was EDS's profit. Additional customers meant fewer personnel and less equipment per job, hence more profit. The eight factors of success for EDS, which I call DEJ factors for "demonstrable economic justification," are described in Chapter 4.

MILTON S. PETRIE

Name of Company:	Petrie Stores Corporation
Date Founded:	1932
Location:	Secaucus, New Jersey
Description of Business:	The company operates a large number of women's specialty apparel stores under various names throughout the United States, plus a 25 percent interest in Toys 'R' Us Corporation.
Description of *P*:	Many entrepreneurs have discovered the women's apparel opportunity. Petrie markets more clothing to more women at a greater profit than anyone else in the country.
Description of *S*:	By acquiring nine chains since 1979, Petrie has built an empire of 1,365 stores and $1 billion in revenues. Petrie stores earn over 10 percent on revenues and 24 percent on assets, margins usually associated with high tech companies.
Description of *E*:	Petrie is searching for an heir apparent.
Size of *V*:	Petrie Stores has approximately 21.1 million shares of common stock outstanding which traded in a range of $26½ to $37½ in 1984 for an average valuation of $672 million. The founder owns more than 60% of the stock.
Social Utility:	Petrie has become the example of successful retail entrepreneurship to which others aspire. He is a quiet, but significant, philanthropist as well.
Principal Sources of Venture Capital:	Supplier financing

MILTON S. PETRIE, 82, invited me to lunch at his club in New York City in early 1985 for an interview. I was excited to have lunch with a legend.

We met at 12:30 P.M., but there were two other people at lunch: The president of a small, midwestern apparel chain and a merger broker. "David is a venture capitalist," Petrie said to the other people. And to me he said, "These gentlemen have a business that I'm thinking of buying." Then he leaned over to the midwestern people and negotiated for a few minutes. Then back to me and said, "My sister got me my first job: advertising manager for an Indianapolis newspaper. I was fired in a short period of time and heard there was more going on in Detroit. So I moved there, and talked my way into a job in an advertising agency. After a few years, and many ads for socks and hats, I opened a hosiery store in Cleveland. My suppliers provided the capital because they could not crack another account in town and figured they could do no worse than bet on me."

Then he leaned back over to the midwestern side of the table and continued his negotiations. I was enraptured by the energy and intelligence of this 82-year-old dynamo. In a single investment last year—the Irvine land deal—Petrie turned $10 million into $100 million; possibly more than the entire U.S. venture capital industry made in 1984. His purchase of 25 percent of Toys 'R' Us at a total cost of $40 million in the 1960s produced a $400 million capital gain.

He operates the largest, most successful chain of budget-priced women's apparel stores in the country. The names are Petrie's, Marianne, G & G Shops and Miller-Wohl. The profits are the largest in the industry and it is due to Petrie's attention to detail. He is a shrewd strategist and has been known to acquire suppliers in order to obtain important lines. He failed once in 1937, "but I paid my creditors 100 percent on the dollar."[133]

Rallying from the setback, Petrie opened a number of women's shops in downtown areas. As the shopping center boom began in the late 1940s and 1950s, he became one of the most active tenants in strip centers, then moved heavily into the big suburban centers.

Even though Petrie has been married three times, and has three children, none of them takes an active part in the business.

---

[133]Isadore Barmash, "The Acquisition Kings of Women's Wear," The New York Times, March 31, 1985, p. 6F.

JOHN WILLIAM PODUSKA

Name of Company:	Apollo Computer Inc.
Date Founded:	1980
Location:	Chelmsford, Massachusetts

Description of Business: The company is a leading manufacturer of computers used mainly for computer-aided design (CAD) and engineering (CAE).

Description of *P*: CAD and CAE are rapidly becoming among the most important technologies because they permit more rapid, more accurate, and less expensive design of integrated circuits, tools, and numerous industrial items. CAD and CAE are critical to further innovation and cost reduction in the electronics industry. Poduska foresaw the need for a computer specifically designed for the use of CAD and CAE programmers.

Description of *S*: Minicomputers such as Digital Equipment Corporation's VAX, selling for $600,000, were initially adopted by CAD/CAE programmers until Apollo introduced its DOMAIN system at 20 percent less than the cost of a VAX, while offering most of the computing capability of the VAX.

Members of *E*: Charles P. Spector, executive vice-president; Robert M. Antonuccio, vice-president—manufacturing; Barry J. Fidelman, vice-president—marketing; J. Michael Greata, vice-president—research and development; and David G. Lubrano, vice-president—finance

Size of *V*: The approximately 30 million shares of common stock outstanding traded at an average price of $15⅝ to $25⅛ in 1984 for an average valuation of $600 million.

Social Utility: The company has created roughly 500 jobs and accelerated the development of CAD/CAE software applications.

Principal Sources of Venture Capital: A syndicate of venture capital firms including Hellman Ferri, Genstar, and Venrock invested approximately $15 million.

JOHN WILLIAM PODUSKA, 47, launched what Wall Street loves to call a pure play in a breakthrough industry. A pure play is a company that has built a solution to a large problem and has managed to sell the solution time and again at a profit that grows quarter by quarter. His "pure play," Apollo Computer, was accorded a p/e ratio as high as 90x in 1984, and there is nothing to suggest it might fall off the scaffold in the next few years.

The problem that Apollo Computer and others are solving is productivity stagnation in American industry; that is, helping American industry remain competitive. The solution is CAD, CAE, and their offshoot, computer-aided manufacturing (CAM).

CAD of CAD/CAM is basically designing, drafting, and analyzing with computer graphics displayed on a screen. Anything that a draftsman conventionally does using triangles, pencils, and compasses is done mathematically within this system. CAD not only speeds up slow, laborious drafting, but also enables the designer to study various aspects of an object or assemblage by rotating it on the computer screen, separating it into segments, or enlarging or shrinking details.

Gene Bylinsky wrote:

What makes CAD so effective a way to design and analyze products and components is that the computer communicates with the designer in pictures. The mind absorbs the information content of a displayed diagram or drawing much faster than it can take in an array of numbers or words and mentally translate them into images. "Computer graphics," a scientist says, "seems to tape the way the brain is designed to work."

What's more, if the necessary programming has been done, the designer can analyze and test the things he designs right in front of his eyes, subjecting them to electronically simulated temperature changes, mechanical stresses, and other conditions that might impinge a real life. This on-screen testing can save the huge amount of time and expense involved in fabricating prototypes, then testing, modifying and retesting.[134]

The payoff from CAD—or from CAE, which is similar software used to solve engineering and architectural problems—comes when it is linked to CAM. The on-screen designs and tests of new products generate a bank of instructions for their manufacture. The tool paths can be specified on the computer as well. The time between design and production shrinks dramatically. Pratt & Whitney Group, an aircraft components manufacturer deeply involved in CAD/CAM, reports a reduction in labor costs and lead time of 50 to 1 in some instances.

For integrated circuit design CAD/CAE has been imperative for American industry to regain its lead. For example, a microchip at the level of complexity of large scale integration (LSI) can control all of the traffic lights in a city of half a million people. Theoretically putting 10 times the number of transistors on a chip would advance the science to very large scale integration (VLSI) and control all of the traffic lights in the United States. Regrettably, there are not enough hours in the day or available engineers to be very effective in designing VLSI chips. The solution is CAD/CAE. We are just beginning to see the results of CAD/CAE on commercial products. The full effect of this revolution will be American dominance in electronics, vast cost reductions in all electromechanical products, and life-saving or life-enhancing, inexpensive medical products.

Several computer manufacturers modified their hardware for the CAD/CAM industry, and DEC skimmed the cream off the top. Apollo was created to serve engineers striving to achieve breakthroughs in VLSI. A massive undertaking, and Poduska had the credentials to attract $15 million in venture capital from three of the most highly regarded funds: Venrock, Hellman Ferri, and Genstar (Sutter Hill). Poduska had been a co-founder of Prime Computer Corporation, a successful, middle-of-the-pack minicomputer company, and he served as

---

[134]Gene Bylinsky, "A New Industrial Revolution Is on the Way," *Fortune*, October 1981.

its head of research and development from 1972 to 1980, when he left to found Apollo. He learned high-level programming while working on interactive systems for future manned space flight missions, including the earth-orbiting laboratory, while at NASA's Electronic Research Center in Cambridge, Massachusetts, from 1966 to 1970.

SOL PRICE

Name of Company:	The Price Company
Founded:	1976
Location:	San Diego, California
Description of Business:	The company operates Price Club cash-and-carry membership-only wholesale outlets in California and Arizona. The outlets sell a variety of goods and services to member businesses that buy for their own use or for resale, and to a selected group of retail customers.
Description of P:	Consumers and businesses need a convenient means of shopping and low prices for bulk purchases.
Description of S:	Price conceived a novel idea for consumer goods marketing, featuring low prices and convenience, seven days and 61 hours per week, achieved in part via selling prepaid memberships to customers.
Members of E:	Robert E. Price, son, co-founder, and president
Size of V:	The approximately 23 million shares of common stock outstanding traded in a range of $23¾ to $48¾ in 1984 for an average valuation of $828 million.
Social Utility:	The company has created 1,054 full-time jobs and 1,404 part-time jobs.
Principal Sources of Venture Capital:	Accumulated gains from previous venture, Fed-Mart Corporation

SOL PRICE practiced law for 17 years and then quit to launch Fed-Mart Corporation, a mass merchandiser and supermarket chain. Price pioneered private label brands and the one-stop shopping concept. In 1975 he sold Fed–Mart to a West German buyer who fired him. Fed–Mart subsequently failed without him.

In 1975 with his son Robert, Price formed The Price Company and introduced the concept of selling to members only in large warehouses. Businesses or individuals with retail sales licenses may become wholesale members by paying an annual $25 membership fee; for an additional $10 per person, a wholesale member may designate two additional buyers. Group memberships are available to bank and savings and loan employees, state and local government employees, certain utility and transportation workers, certain savings and loan customers, certain hospital workers, civilian federal employees, and members of certain credit unions. Just as prepaid health maintenance is becoming the toll gate in the health care market, prepaid consumer buying plans are beginning to play a role in the consumer products market.

There are presently over 170,000 active wholesale members and some 800,000 group members. The 20 Price warehouses are each 100,000 square feet and open seven days per week. The company does not advertise. Marketing is word-of-mouth. The company sales are derived from appliances (20 percent), food (22 percent) and hardgoods, liquor, softgoods, and sundries (28 percent).

At 69, Price is an astute marketer trained in the law in a field where many of the best practitioners are subtle but excellent salespersons. Price is clearly among the best. "Merchandising is not a science," he says, "it is an art."[135]

[135]"The Richest People in America, The Forbes 400," *Forbes*, Fall, 1983.

BARBARA GARDNER PROCTOR

Name of Company:	Proctor & Gardner Advertising, Inc.
Date Founded:	1970
Location:	Chicago, Illinois
Description of Business:	The company is one of the fastest-growing advertising agencies in the country. It specializes in the black consumer market.
Description of P:	Proctor realized that large advertisers wished to appeal directly to the black consumer and needed guidance to do so. She also wanted to protect the black community from ethically dubious advertising pitches.
Description of S:	The company designs, develops, and implements advertising campaigns for large consumer products companies to reach the black community. Billings exceed $15 million annually.
Members of E:	George Miller, executive vice-president; and Eular Jones, creative art director
Size of V:	The company is privately held but its dominant position in its niche would fetch a higher than expected valuation, perhaps greater than the size of its billings.
Social Utility:	Proctor is a beacon for women entrepreneurs the world over to follow.
Principal Sources of Venture Capital:	An $80,000 SBA loan.

BARBARA GARDNER PROCTOR has achieved financial and professional success at 51 without sacrificing her ethical standards. "In the public-trust category," she told the *Wall Street Journal*, "our advertising business is in a dead heat with the used car salesman. And justifiably so. Advertising's only goal seems to be to move goods and services at a profit."[136]

She decries the effect of advertising on women, claiming that they have fallen prey to dubious pitches for psychoactive drugs and sleep inducers that have very little medicinal value. Women smokers, she says, can thank advertisers as well. Sounds like a soap-box orator or some flake who calls up radio talk shows?

Not at all. Proctor is the owner of one of the fastest-growing advertising agencies in the country, Proctor & Gardner Advertising, Inc. It reaches the black community for Dark & Kraft, Inc., Jewel Food Stores, Sears, Roebuck & Company, Alberto-Culver Company, and CBS, Inc. Further, Proctor is vice chairman and a director of Illinois Bell Telephone; a director of Bingham Companies, Mid-City National Bank of Chicago, the Better Business Bureau, and The Executives' Club of Chicago; a trustee of Mundelein College and Talladega College; and a committee member of 16 different charitable and cultural organizations.

After a short career with Vee-Jay Records from 1961 to 1964 and a divorce, Proctor worked for three Chicago advertising agencies in the 1960s, rising to the level of copy supervisor by 1970. Then she was fired. She says that the agency wanted her to write a shaving cream TV commercial to parody the civil rights sit-ins of the time by calling it a "foam-in." She refused, because it demeaned the civil rights advocates.

With no alternative but to put her own ideas to work, Proctor formed her own advertising agency. The proof of the pudding for this single parent, who was put out on the street in 1970 for standing up for her beliefs, is a successful enterprise, financial comforts, and recognition from her industry. President Ronald Reagan cited Barbara Proctor in his 1984 State of the Union Address as an example of one of "the heroes of the eighties."

[136]Earl C. Gottschalk, Jr., "More Women Start up Their Own Businesses, With Major Successes," *The Wall Street Journal*, May 17, 1983, p. 1.

JAMES W. ROUSE

Name of Company:	Rouse Company, The Enterprise Development Company
Date Founded:	Rouse (1939); Enterprise (1984)
Location:	Columbia, Maryland
Description of Business:	The Enterprise Development Company is a not-for-profit company that renovates dilapidated downtown buildings, creating housing for the very poor—with annual incomes of less than $9,000. The Enterprise Development Company also involves minorities in owning and operating shops and housing in the rebuilt communities. Rouse & Company is known for its festival marketplaces, such as Faneuil Hall and South Street Seaport, that have made urban centers exciting and profitable shopping and living areas.
Description of P:	Rouse identified urban blight and decay as a problem capable of entrepreneurial solution.
Description of S:	Rouse developed the know-how to pull together capital, local government support, and the sweat equity of the urban poor to rebuild blighted urban areas into festivals of small shops and clean, inexpensive housing.
Members of E:	Charles Tuchfarber (Rouse) and Charles Evans (Rouse)
Size of V:	The approximately 15 million shares of common stock outstanding traded in a range of $28\frac{3}{4}$ to $37\frac{3}{8}$ in 1984 for an average valuation of $495 million.
Social Utility:	Rouse is deeply concerned for the urban poor; by using all of his skills as an entrepreneur, he is making a positive impact on their lives.

Principal Source   Rouse borrowed $20,000 from family and friends.
of Venture
Capital:

JAMES W. ROUSE retired in 1984 at 70 from Rouse Company, a redeveloper of downtown American cities whose common stock sells at 50 times earnings because the company solves *big problems*. (See the law of the big-P in Chapter 4.) Rouse's purpose in retiring was to start a new company, one that would aid the poor in a meaningful positive way.

His new company, The Enterprise Development Company, pulls together capital, local government support, and the sweat equity of poor minorities into a powerful force, one that is rebuilding downtown slums and putting poor people in charge of businesses and apartment houses in the rebuilt downtowns. Enterprise Development Company's first project, Waterside, was completed in June 1983 in Norfolk, Virginia. Its second was the $14.5 million renovation of Toledo's Portside. Projects are in process in Flint, Michigan, and Richmond, Virginia. The most difficult chore Rouse faces is assembling capital. Federal funding for urban projects is scarce so Rouse asks for charitable contributions from individuals and corporations, solicits government grants, persuades major lenders to make below-market-rate loans, and packages tax shelters, using the 25 percent historic renovation investment tax credit for leverage. Equitable Life Assurance Society and United Virginia Bank, among others, have provided loans at single-digit interest rates.

Orphaned as a teenager at 16, Rouse saw his family's home foreclosed on because of his father's business debts. With his sister's financial help Rouse studied at the University of Hawaii for a year. A scholarship enabled him to enroll in the University of Virginia, but he left in March 1933 because the Depression obliged him to go to work. In Baltimore he found a job parking cars at the St. Paul Garage. From 1934 to 1936, while studying law at the University of Maryland at night, Rouse worked as a legal clerk in the Baltimore office of the newly created Federal Housing Administration (FHA). Giving up his position with that New Deal home financing agency in 1936, he persuaded the Title Guarantee and Trust Company of Baltimore to inaugurate a mortgage department, which he was then hired to run until 1939. Meanwhile, in 1937, he was awarded an LL.B. degree and admitted to the Maryland bar.

Instead of setting up a law firm, Rouse borrowed $20,000 from his family and friends. In 1939 with real estate appraiser Hunter Moss, he opened the Moss-Rouse Company, a mortgage banking business. The pair represented Continental American Life Insurance Company and Connecticut General in a practice that concentrated on FHA loans for one family houses. Before Rouse entered the Naval Reserve as a lieutenant (j.g.) in 1942, the company was servicing payments on a mortgage loan portfolio of about $6 million. For the remaining years of World War II he was on the staff of the Commander, Air Force Pacific Fleet. On his return to Baltimore, Rouse enlarged his business by underwriting apartment houses and shopping centers. By 1954 he had bought out his partner and formed James W. Rouse and Company, Inc., whose loan portfolio in 1970 reached $885 million worth of mortgages for about 70 life insurance companies, bank pension funds, and other lenders. The Rouse Company's revenues for just that section of its operations came to $1.4 million annually.

Concurrently, Rouse was becoming known nationally as a housing expert dedicated to improving urban environments. As chairman of the Mayor's Advisory Committee on Housing in Baltimore from 1949 to 1952, he helped to shape one of the nation's first efforts at upgrading slums, although the accomplishments were impermanent. Active in a local group called Volunteers for Ike, in 1953 Rouse was named chairman of the subcommittee on rehabilitation, redevelopment, and conservation of President Dwight D. Eisenhower's Advisory Committee on Government Housing, Policies, and Programs. The committee's proposals to expand federal programs against slums became a part of the 1954 Housing Act. With Nathaniel Keith, Rouse wrote No Slums in Ten Years (1955), an audacious but unheeded plan for the redevelopment of Washington, D.C. that would have utilized the new government jurisdiction and other provisions granted by the act. A founder and vice-chairman (in 1956, 1957, and 1962) of the Greater Baltimore Committee, a corps of some 100 businesspersons, Rouse was a dominant presence in downtown Baltimore's Charles Center redevelopment project.

Another way in which Rouse exerted influence on urban renewal was through a national antislum organization, which he founded with other businesspersons and housing-industry leaders. He served as president in 1958–1959 and in 1967–1968 of the Ameri-Council to Improve Our Neighborhood, as it was first called, later to become ACTION Inc. Still later, in 1970, as Urban America Inc., it was incorporated into the Urban Coalition, headed by John W. Gardner. Rouse was a member, moreover, of the Rockefeller Foundation's advisory committee on urban design.

Piecemeal, through dummy buyers, over a ten-month period in the early 1960s Rouse quietly bought up some 14,000 acres of open land in the rolling countryside of Howard County, between Baltimore and Washington, D.C. After assembling a planning staff of architects and engineers, Rouse for the first time in the history of city planning, convened a panel of 14 academic experts on human behavior to hold a running seminar discussion and to serve as consultants to the physical planners. Rouse, whose suggestions were generally more radical than the panel's, forged the character of his city, Columbia, sometimes imperceptibly.

For years a foe of segregated housing, Rouse insisted on racial as well as economic integration. In an effort to recapture the old sense of village community, the planners clustered seven villages around an urban downtown and oriented neighborhoods to schools. While preserving the natural terrain, they added three lakes. Construction began in June 1966, and the first homes went on sale in July 1967. Originally planned as a balanced, self-sufficient city of 110,000 to be completed in 15 years, Columbia housed about 56,000 residents by 1981, approximately 20 percent of them black.

In an interview in *Time*, Rouse exulted over "the marvelous advance in race relations in Columbia."[137] He believes that his town "raises a banner for a new America," as he was quoted in the *Saturday Review*. "It isn't a perfect city, but it is a better city," he maintained. "It is a city that works for its people."[138]

The Faneuil Hall Marketplace resulted from a restoration in three phases of 150-year-old, block-long, abandoned Greek Revival buildings near Boston's Faneuil Hall. It includes the Quincy Market, which opened in August 1976, with tempting restaurants and an informal, in-

[137]M. Demarest & others, "He Digs Downtown," *Time*, Aug. 24, 1981, pp. 42–44.
[138]G. Breckenfeld, "The New Entrepreneur: Romantic Hero of American Business," *Saturday Review*, July 22, 1978, pp. 12–15.

novative Bull Market of colorful kiosks and pushcarts; the South Market building completed in August 1977; and the North Market completed in 1978. Rouse had been brought into the enterprise, which later stimulated a major development boom in the city, by architect Benjamin Thompson in 1973. Together they repeated the Boston feat on three acres of open space along Baltimore's resurrected Inner Harbor. Opening in July 1980 and drawing 18 million visitors—more than Disney World in its first year—Harborplace was heralded as "the most brilliant showcase of Rouse's craftmanship." Its two translucent pavilions—with 134 restaurants and cafes, fresh-food booths, specialty shops, kiosks, and pushcarts—fulfills Rouse's ideal of the center city as a warm and human place with diversity of choice, full of festival and delight.

When New York City Mayor Edward Koch first saw Faneuil Hall Marketplace, he announced: "I want one of those for New York." South Street Seaport brought Rouse's brand of festival shopping to Manhattan. Also on the Rouse Company's drawing boards are St. Louis Station, to be built on the site of an old railroad terminal and surrounding rail yards; Yerba Buena Gardens in San Francisco, which will convert a former skid row into a marketplace complex with an amusement park inspired by Copenhagen's Tivoli Gardens; a three-level mall in the heart of downtown Milwaukee, the Grand Avenue, which will connect two existing department stores; and Gallery II in Philadelphia, which will also link department stores. "A city is hollow without a lively, effective retail core," Rouse maintains.[139]

"The Most Happy Fella among all the strollers and browsers" at Harborplace, as he has been described in *Time*, Rouse often dresses in casual attire that is likely to include loafers and a madras jacket or shirt. He said in the interview for *People*, "I have a conviction that optimism is a value, not a sentimental state of mind. It helps to bring about what ought to be."[140]

[139]G. Breckenfeld, "Rouse Show Goes National," *Fortune*, July 27, 1981, pp. 48–55.
[140]Demarest, *Time*, p. 43.

W. JEREMIAH SANDERS, III

Name of Company:	Advanced Micro Devices, Inc.
Date Founded:	1969
Location:	Sunnyvale, California
Description of Business:	The company is one of the leading manufacturers of integrated circuits, focusing on specialty markets and high-value products.
Description of *P:*	Sanders broke away from Fairchild Semiconductor Corporation where he had been in marketing. Rather than pioneer the new market in microchips, Advanced Micro Devices, Inc. (AMD) made them under license from those who had the technology. Once the company had built itself up, it acquired the technology and has been an industry leader ever since.
Description of *S*:	AMD has focused on fast chips: bipolar MOS and its energy-saving complement, C-MOS. It is a back-up supplier of Intel Corporation's 8088 chip, the brains of the IBM Personal Computer. The company has avoided diversions that have been expensive lessons to other chip makers, such as digital watches and calculators.
Members of *E*:	Anthony B. Holbrook, chief operating officer; James B. Downey; Richard Previte; and Stephen Zelencik.
Size of *V*:	The approximately 50 million shares of common stock outstanding traded in a range of $25⅛ to $41⅛ in 1984 for an average valuation of $1.6 billion.
Principal Sources of Venture Capital:	Severance pay from Fairchild Semiconductor Corporation plus $1.5 million in venture capital.

JERRY SANDERS, 49, always wanted to make a lot of money. He experienced a higher degree of deprivation as a child than most entrepreneurs, but has channeled the pain in two directions: AMD's magnificent bottom line and his personal luxurious style of living. For 1984 AMD's sales were approximately $700 million and net profits were $100 million, a 32 percent return on stockholders' equity. His homes in Bel Air, Malibu, and San Francisco, California, house Rolls-Royces, Bentleys, and other beautiful cars.

His drive comes from a brutally poor and lonely childhood on Chicago's South Side. Sanders's divorced parents left him to be brought up by grandparents who did not want him. Sanders's first memory was that of a 4-year-old arriving at his grandfather's house to find workmen refurbishing the first floor. When he asked where his grandparents were, a workman joked that they no longer lived there. Shaken but unbelieving, Sanders finally located his grandparents in the basement, where they had moved temporarily.

Sanders was required to work. At 12 he began a variety of menial jobs to help pay for his keep. Soon Sanders realized that education was to be his rope ladder out of the hole fate had dug for him. Sanders became valedictorian of his graduating high school class and studied electrical engineering at the University of Illinois. He joined Douglas Aircraft Company at 21 and while redesigning the air-conditioning system on the DC-8 jetliner, a components salesperson took him out in his company car for a fancy lunch. Sanders could see that the salesperson was living a lot better than he was. He became a salesperson at Motorola, where his abilities were noticed by Fairchild Semiconductor Corporation. He joined Fairchild when it was a nursery for two dozen integrated circuit start-ups. Two Fairchild engineers approached Sanders to break off and start a new company with them and he did.

Because AMD has always had less capital and less of a proprietary position, Sanders has stressed other things in order to keep near the head of the pack: company loyalty, low employee turnover, high-quality products, and maximum profitability. AMD is split up into 13 "managing directorates." At other corporations they might be known as profit centers, but these are profit centers with a difference. For all practical purposes, a managing director at AMD runs an independent entrepreneurial company, with full command of the resources needed to conduct business.

The directorates' strength lies in their self-contained nature. They work directly with customers and design their own products. How they go about that seems unique in the industry. At other semiconductor companies, a designer will typically come up with an idea for enhancing a chip. The new circuit works its way through the company product-development operation and finally reaches the outside world—a better mousetrap designed without consulting the market.

At AMD, by comparison, company personnel constantly look for new or unmet needs. AMD engineers then conceive a new design for a chip, or system of chips, aimed at solving a specific problem. The company takes the idea to potential customers, asking them how they would like the chip or chip system to work. The responses are collected and documented. Then the directorate decides what technology is best for the new chip or chips. The chip is then produced and becomes part of AMD's line of proprietary products. The best indication of the success of AMD's marketing approach is the fact that 40 percent of the company's sales now come from proprietary chips, and the percentage continues to rise.

As a result of this approach, when AMD makes a proprietary product, that product is usually a winner. Among the company's recent offerings are a single-chip modem used in sending computerized data over telephone lines and a chip for tying office telephones into switchboards. AMD prices these chips according to their value to the customer rather than marking them up a set amount over costs or predicted costs. AMD also surrounds its proprietary chips with a whole family of auxiliary, or peripheral, circuits making it more difficult for competitors to imitate the entire set, since many of these peripherals are highly complex.

Sanders worked seven days a week for 10 years to get AMD off the launch pad. Now its stock is listed on the New York Stock Exchange and he is on one of the Exchange's advisory committees and a director of numerous corporations and organizations. When your life has a purpose as Jerry Sanders's has, you keep your head down, your feet moving fast, and your eye on the ball for a long time, because you never ever want to go back to the beginning again.

CHARLES SCHWAB

Name of Company:	Charles Schwab & Company
Date Founded:	1971
Location:	San Francisco, California
Description of Business:	The company is the largest discount stock broker-age firm in the country.
Description of *P*:	When the securities industry was deregulated in 1974, most established firms believed that invest-ors would continue to pay high commissions to brokers in order to receive other services such as research. Schwab believed there was a need for a discount brokerage service.
Description of *S*:	Charles Schwab & Company offers a 24-hour stock trading service with commissions 30 to 40 percent below the industry average.
Members of *E*:	Larry Lawrence Stupshi, president; Robert Fivis, executive vice-president, chief financial offi-cer/treasurer; Barbara Wolfe, vice-president—ad-ministration.
Size of *V*:	In 1982 BankAmerica Corporation acquired Charles Schwab & Company for $53 million.
Social Utility:	The company has created 1,500 new jobs and re-duced the price of a standard service for thou-sands of people.
Principal Sources of Venture Capital:	Personal savings, family and friends

CHARLES SCHWAB raised chickens in his parents' yard in Wood-land, California, when he was 10 years old; he also sold chickens and eggs door-to-door. He went to Stanford University, earned an MBA de-gree, and headed for the securities industry. Wanting to be his own boss, the chicken-and-egg man opened his own brokerage firm in 1971 at the age of 34. Within a year, Charles Schwab & Company had a dozen employees and about 2,000 clients. Then the Securities & Exchange Commission discarded the fixed rate system for buying and selling securities in favor of negotiated rates in which investors are free to haggle with brokers over commissions. This drastically altered the ways of doing business in a venerable old industry; the brokerage firms least able to compete went out of business or were acquired.

Schwab embraced negotiated rates and immediately changed his operating method to no-frills, discount pricing for fast, accurate trades. No research, no tips, no hand-holding, all of which he figured his clientele would choose to do for themselves.

By 1981 Schwab's company had earnings of $5 million, and he plowed the cash back into new products for his customers: cash management and insurance. By 1982 BankAmerica Corporation thought Charles Schwab & Company fit nicely into its expansion plans and paid $53 million to own it.

A few years earlier, the banks and brokerage firms conspired to make life difficult for Schwab. He spent hours combating rumors spread to stock exchanges that he was going out of business. Banks refused to lend to him. Office space was hard to come by, because large brokers were telling landlords that they would pull out of buildings if they rented to Schwab. Many of these brokerage firms have gone out of business due to a paucity of fresh ideas. Today at 48, Schwab has offices in 50 American cities and is expanding overseas.

DAVID B. SHAKARIAN

Name of Company:	General Nutrition, Inc.
Date Founded:	1955
Location:	Pittsburgh, Pennsylvania
Description of Business:	The company is engaged in the production, distribution, and sale—mostly under its own brand name—of vitamins, minerals, nutritional foods, and personal care products sold largely through company-owned retail stores.
Description of *P*:	Nutrition has been one of the most neglected areas of health care. Until recently medical schools did not teach the subject at all; information on the subject was provided by "vitamin evangelists," who came and went like any other fad. Shakarian took hold of the crusade and made it an important *P*; then he sold solutions into the market that he created.
Description of *S*:	In 1984 General Nutrition (GNC) had sales of more than $400 million on which it earned over 20 percent after taxes. Nutritional foods and vitamins are healthy for the bottom line as well.
Members of *E*:	Gary A. Daum, president and chief operating officer
Size of *V*:	The approximately 33 million shares of common stock outstanding traded in a range of $5⅛ to $13½ in 1984 for an average valuation of $300 million.
Social Utility:	Shakarian created 7,500 new jobs and increased the country's awareness of nutrition. Today, 88 percent of American medical schools teach nutrition.
Principal Sources of Venture Capital:	Shakarian's sweat equity

DAVID B. SHAKARIAN died in 1984, and many people in Pittsburgh, his hometown for 70 years, learned about their city's wealthiest citizen for the first time. He was the son of Armenian immigrants who had fled Turkish persecution. His father operated a yogurt importing business, which folded during the Great Depression. Young Shakarian was a quiet, introverted young man, who was seized on a cold day in 1932 by a public lecture given by Gaylord Hauser on the value of eating "natural foods."

The next day Shakarian convinced a bank to lease him a vacant storeroom for $100 per month rent, payment of which he had to defer. He stocked the store with 40 items including wheat germ and yogurt. The going was tough, but Shakarian's purpose was messianic. "I never worked a day in my life," Shakarian was heard to say. "It's not work when you love what you're doing."[141]

Shakarian's first big break was the popularizing of synthetic vitamins shortly after World War II. As vitamins became a drugstore staple, he went to the manufacturers of brand name vitamins, such as Squibb's Theragram and Miles's One-A-Day, and arranged to buy the same tablets, package them with his own label, and sell them for a fraction of the cost. "We sold Geritol tablets for 79 cents when Geritol was selling it . . . for five or six dollars a bottle," he said.[142] Next, Shakarian began selling vitamins by mail order. Customer financing gave GNC sufficient cash flow to open four new stores by 1960. There are now 250 stores and 12,000 mail orders per month.

"Having a battle with that sluggish lower digestive tract? . . . our Acidiphisus tablets act as friends to your system, cleaning and absorbing unfriendly waste and gas," suggests GNC's mail-order catalog. In addition to offering an immense variety of vitamin and mineral supplements, the catalog also lists products which range from unusual food supplements—Potent Yeast Food with Aspertame, for example, and English bee pollen—to patent remedies, such as "Stop Snore," billed as "a new invention that instantly stops snoring!" There are even a few products intended for nonhuman consumption, such as Organic Formula 52 Dog and Cat Shampoo and Vi-Pet tablets—"The best friend your pet may ever have." Although retail is now a bigger portion of GNC's business, on a good day the clerks at GNC's Penn Avenue head-

---

[141]"GNC Founder Dies", September 11, 1984, p. 1 (Press Release).
[142]Pat Tierney and Patrick Kiger, "The Emperor of Vitamins," *Pittsburgh*, November 1983, p. 87.

quarters may process as many as 8,000 to 10,000 orders with the help of computers; some orders come from as far away as Mexico or Europe.

In terms of both mail-order and the retail stores, it's really no longer accurate in the strictest sense to refer to GNC as a "health food" company. Vitamins, minerals, and supplements, which amounted to 68 percent of sales in 1982, are the biggest part of GNC's business. Actual foods—yogurt, juices, and whole grain cereals—totaled 23 percent, and cosmetics and other products accounted for the remaining 9 percent.

Who is buying all these products? GNC's customers number in the millions. Market studies show that the average customer is a fairly typical middle American: over 35, female, white-collar, earning $22,000 a year. Why are they buying several hundred million dollars' worth of vitamins, bee pollen, and other GNC wares? Shakarian's answer was simple:

> The Social Security system is broke. Medicare and Medicaid can't cover the enormous doctor bills we have in this country. We are shifting from an institutional health care society to a self-help society, where more are going to be concerned about their own personal health and their diet and they'll be taking it into their own hands. Instead of depending on government and the Food and Drug Administration and the Federal Trade Commission . . . there's going to be a trend to do this yourself.[143]

Shakarian took longer than most successful entrepreneurs to get into the megamillion revenue category, but to his way of thinking, he was an evangelist for better health, not Pittsburgh's best entrepreneur since the Industrial Revolution.

[143]Ibid, p. 88.

LEONARD SAMUEL SHOEN

Name of Company:	The U-Haul System
Date Founded:	1945
Location:	Scottsdale, Arizona
Description of Business:	The company operates the largest one-way truck and trailer rental business in the country.
Description of *P*:	Shoen perceived the need for Americans to be able to move their belongings from place to place, simply, inexpensively, and without hiring professional movers.
Description of *S*:	The solution to this problem is elegant and logistical. Shoen, who had been in business since his teens and used to thinking big—seven sons and five daughters—figured it out. Gasoline stations throughout the country became outlets to handle the rental and paperwork needs of the system. Once that kind of network is set in place, it is difficult for a competitor to enter.
Members of *E*:	Anna Mary Shoen, wife of the founder, and other family members have been active in the business.
Size of *V*:	*Forbes* estimates U-Haul's valuation to be $300 million.[144]
Social Utility:	The U-Haul System has created approximately 20,000 jobs and there are 6,000 independent business people who earn a substantial portion of their income through U-Haul commissions. It also solved the relocation problem for millions of Americans.
Principal Sources of Venture Capital:	$5,000 in personal savings plus unique financial leverage.

[144]"Richest People in America, Forbes 400," *Forbes*, Fall 1983.

LEONARD S. "SAM" SHOEN, 69, has built one of America's best-known businesses using sale-leaseback techniques and customer financing. When an entrepreneur doesn't use equity financing, he holds onto most of his company's common stock. Shoen owns 92 percent of The U-Haul System, whose revenues are in excess of $750 million. I called on Shoen in the late 1960s to sell him the investment banking services of my employer, Kuhn, Loeb & Co. After reviewing his exquisite use of financial leverage, I realized that Shoen knew more about investment banking than did most of us on Wall Street.

He would purchase trailers and trucks and sell them to employees, family members, friends, and investors who would then lease them back to AMERCO, the parent company of U-Haul. The equipment had tax advantages and generated income for the trailer owners from their continual rental. The equipment was eventually packaged, and the offerings became larger and more popular and were registered with the Securities and Exchange Commission. But, they were never equity-linked.

While leveraging the capital equipment needs at one end, Shoen leveraged the customer at the other. He made gasoline stations into U-Haul dealers, thus eliminating his need for retail outlets and the cost of carrying labor. The advertising was largely paid for by the person who drove a U-Haul trailer down the highway. It was a moving billboard seen by thousands. The general and administrative costs were also largely born by the dealers, who handled the paperwork at the rental and receiving ends. You would have to look long and hard to find a more elegant service business than the U-Haul System.

Shoen was born on a farm near McGrath, Minnesota, in 1916, the second of seven children. "I owe much of my understanding of a business operation to my father who can best be characterized as a 'jack of all trades' . . . He is not awed by the new and the different," Shoen said in his book. "My father moved his family from Minnesota to Oregon in . . . 1923. Because I was the oldest boy, he secured my help in all his business ventures and was quite free with his advice and with the details of the business operations."[145] Many of his father's ventures were unsuccessful and Shoen worked on nearby farms and in local stores throughout his teens. Finding business to be unrewarding, Sam regis-

[145]L.S. Shoen, *You and Me* (Las Vegas, Nevada: AMERCO, 1980), p. 2.

tered in the premedical program at Oregon State University in 1937. To pay for medical school, he learned how to be a barber.

In his sophomore year in college, Shoen leased the barber shop in a hotel in Corvallis and within six months he had four barbers operating for him. With cash flow from this barber shop, Shoen opened a three-chair barber shop in Albany, Oregon. He expanded with two shops later in the year. When World War II began, Shoen lost his barbers to the draft. He closed his shops and put the equipment into storage.

Notwithstanding his business distractions, Shoen's grades were good. Yet, in his senior year of medical school Shoen was suspended for answering in class for his lab partner. Shoen enlisted in the Navy, but in 1944 contracted scarlet fever and was hospitalized for five months. It was the first time in his life that he had not been active. But his mind was; Shoen conceived the business plan for the U-Haul System while on his back in the hospital.

Shoen had seen trailers in Los Angeles made out of parts of old automobiles. Rental lots were renting 20 to 40 of these "junkers" per day for $2.00. The trailers would usually fall apart and the tires would go flat within 100 miles of use. Plus, the trailers had to be returned to the rental lot after use. Servicemen were the primary customers. Shoen saw an enormous need for one-way rentals and more substantial trailers.

Upon his release from the hospital, Shoen did some extensive market research. He examined the reasons why the trailer rental industry had not developed: poor materials, tire shortage, weak bumpers, and a lack of convenience. Trailers were so inexpensive to make that people who needed their convenience usually bought rather than rented them.

It was necessary that Shoen think big: produce his own trailers, conceive the entire system, and put it into place quickly and efficiently. With $5,000 in personal savings, and newly married, Shoen decided to chase his dream rather than buy a house. He writes:

> Since my fortune was just about enough to make the down payment on a home and furnish it, and knowing that if I did this we would be sunk, we started the life of nomads by putting our belongings in a trailer and living between in-laws and parents for the next six months. I barbered part-time and bought trailers of the kind I thought we needed to rent from anybody who happened to

have one at the price I thought was right. By the fall of 1945 I was in so deep into the trailer rental deal economically that it was either make it or lose the whole thing.'[146]

U-Haul has been the dominant factor in the one-way trailer rental business for more than 30 years with very little effective competition. As Shoen says, "I believe in luck. The harder I work the luckier I get." Along the way, Shoen thought an understanding of the law might be useful. Thus, while building the U-Haul System, he earned a legal degree in 1955 by going to night school at Lewis and Clark College in Portland. He graduated at the head of the class.

[146]Ibid, p. 12.

MORRIS J. SIEGEL

Name of Company: Celestial Seasonings, Inc.

Date Founded: 1970

Location: Boulder, Colorado

Description of
  Business: The company is the largest producer of herbal teas in the country.

Description of *P*:   The tea market had been largely ignored by large consumer food processors, and one product was pretty much like any other. Siegel saw the herbal tea segment as a viable expandable niche, and it coincided with his health food philosophies. The herbal tea market is now $100 million per annum and Celestial has about half of it.

Description of *S*:   "We see a nice botanical niche for us," Siegel told the *New York Times*. "We're not operating on the super weapon theory; we can't launch a Pert like Procter & Gamble did for $50 million and blow the market out. But we can be successful building on our own strengths of herbs, beauty and service. It's not a bet-the-company strategy at all."[147]

Members of *E*:   John Hay, co-founder

Size of *V*:   Dart & Kraft, Inc. (Kraft cheese, Tupperware) acquired Celestial Seasonings in 1984 for an estimated $25 million.

Social Utility: Siegel created 200 jobs in Boulder and installed an unflagging sense of mission in all of his employees.

Principal Sources
  of Venture
  Capital: Personal savings, family and friends

[147]Thomas C. Hayes, "Celestial Seasonings Pins Its Hopes on More Than Herbal Tea," The *New York Times*, April 3, 1983, p. 6F.

MORRIS J. SIEGEL, 35, pedals his bicycle five miles from his home to the Celestial Seasonings plant most weekdays listening to tapes by Peter F. Drucker and others on his Sony Walkman. The tapes have helped this entrepreneur make tough decisions, now that he has created a market large enough for Thomas J. Lipton, Inc. and Procter & Gamble Company to jump into. Lipton actually aided the growth of Celestial Seasonings with its heavy advertising campaign showing that "real men" like tea. Siegel had been advised by management consultants trained at PepsiCo, Quaker Oats Company, and Coca-Cola Company to raise some big bucks and go after Lipton toe-to-toe. But one day, he took the bicycle ride without the Sony Walkman and arrived at the decision on his own. "Comparative advertising is not our style," Siegel told the *New York Times*. "Basically . . . if it doesn't follow the Golden Rule, I don't want to participate in it. We've never made any money bad-mouthing anyone else."[148]

Celestial Seasonings was founded when Siegel was 20. He had picked berries as a child and given them to ladies to make jelly, and he had an awareness of plants. "I started mixing herbs and making blended tea. I figured that if you could make the stuff taste good, you'd have an idea," Siegel said.[149]

His first concoction made up of 36 herbs was a hit and came to be known as "Mo's 36." He and his wife Peggy packaged the tea, put it in the back of their dilapidated Datsun and traveled coast to coast to sell it to grocery and health food stores. Then came "Red Zinger," still one of Celestial's best-selling teas. Now there are 70 teas which health food advocates claim taste good, are healthier due to an absence of caffeine, and have miscellaneous soothing qualities. Sales are growing at the rate of approximately 30 percent per annum, and Siegel is developing new product lines including "Mountain Herbery" shampoos.

"Mo" Siegel grew up in Palmer Lake, Colorado, the son of a furniture retailer who was at work practically all the time. Siegel's mother died when he was 2 and he was raised by one of his three sisters. Siegel mowed lawns, pulled weeds, and became self-supporting at the age of 15. When his friends went off to college, Siegel stayed back and managed a health food store in Aspen. A combination of his childhood de-

[148]Ibid, p. 6F.
[149]Ibid.

privation and his desire to succeed beyond the level of his peers created in Siegel a burning desire "to do a big idea." He has achieved his goal in a highly competitive industry and like many elegant S companies, acquisition is the appropriate exit route.

ROBERT F. SIKORA

Name of Company:	Bobby McGee's U.S.A., Inc.
Date Founded:	1971
Location:	Phoenix, Arizona
Description of Business:	The company owns and operates 16 dinnerhouse discotheques in four western states plus Hawaii.
Description of P:	When Americans began eating out in large numbers in the 1970s, Sikora created a different kind of night out: a theme restaurant with dancing.
Description of S:	People go to a Bobby McGee's restaurant for the experience, not just the meal. The waiters and waitresses are dressed in costumes of comic book or Hollywood characters and they perform skits at the customers' tables. Later in the evening, patrons move to the dance floor for some of the best dance music they will ever dance to. Sales for 1984 are estimated at $48 million, that is, $3 million per restaurant, which puts Bobby McGee's restaurants among the largest in the country.
Members of E:	John L. Schwimmer, chief operating officer
Size of V:	The company is privately held, so valuation is unknown. Sikora has rejected acquisition offers in excess of $30 million.
Social Utility:	Bobby McGee's has created 1,700 jobs, trained 10 times that number in waiting tables and food service, and created the concept of "theme restaurants."
Principal Sources of Venture Capital:	Personal savings and loans from individuals and banks

ROBERT F. SIKORA, 47, smiles when he describes the lines 200 and 300 deep waiting to get into one of his Bobby McGee's Conglomerations dinner house discotheques. He came upon the idea for a theme restaurant in 1971, after having opened Mr. Lucky's King of Clubs, a 19,000-square-foot country and western nightclub, which still pulsates every night in Phoenix, Arizona. "Why can't regular people have as much fun at night as cowboys?" Sikora asked me rhetorically a few years ago when I was helping him restructure his balance sheet. "So, I came up with an idea that would make eating out fun for all ages and all kinds of people." Music is the key that makes Bobby McGee's so successful.

As the early dinner patrons come in, the music is 1940s style and the waiters and waitresses perform skits at their tables. The Groucho Marx impersonator at the Scottsdale, Arizona, restaurant is so funny that Sikora flew him to Los Angeles to wait on the original Groucho's table. Children and grandparents alike roar with laughter at the antics of Superman, Jose Jimenez, Harpo Marx, and others who serve and entertain them.

As the evening wears on and the nine-year-olds go home with their grandparents, the beat picks up: Simon & Garfunkel, Carly Simon, and Neil Diamond. The laughter continues and the bar becomes more active as well.

By 11:00 P.M. food service is over and the disc jockey is playing hard rock. The discotheque has been carefully constructed. "I found some electronic engineers," Sikora says. "I told them to create a sound system that hit the dancers at their navel and made the center of the dance floor too loud to hear anything but the music, while two feet off the dance floor, a table of four could have a normal conversation." Sikora's dance floor idea worked, and for the last 10 years, his discos have had standing room only on weekends.

On weekdays Bobby McGee's does a large lunch business because it offers fresh foods, well prepared and served ingeniously. The salad bars are nine-foot-long antique bath tubs. Thirty percent of Bobby McGee's revenues are from customers celebrating birthdays, anniversaries, and other happy occasions.

Sikora was born in West Virginia and moved with his family to Arizona when still very young. The family was hard-working but poor, and Sikora went to work as a teenager in the kitchen of a McDonald's.

He worked at every job in a variety of different restaurants, and while in his mid-twenties, Sikora began building, opening, and selling restaurants to others. When the theme restaurant with discotheque idea took root in his imagination, Sikora had the experience, a few dollars, and the credibility with banks to pull it off.

JACK R. SIMPLOT

Name of Company:	J.R. Simplot Corporation
Date Founded:	1927
Location:	Boise, Idaho
Description of Business:	Largest potato processor in the country with a patent on frozen French fries.
Description of *P*:	Simplot has consistently jumped into opportunities, justifying it with the message on a small metal plaque that has been on his desk for the last 25 years: Nothing will ever be attempted if all possible objections must first be overcome. This spirit got him into producing dried onion powder and flakes, freezing French fried potatoes, and investing venture capital in Micron Technology.
Description of *S*:	Simplot learned the principles of investment while still a teenager. When the farmers feared a pork surplus and slaughtered their hogs, 16-year-old Simplot collected and fed hogs and waited out the period until hogs were in short supply. He made a profit that financed his first potato processing plant. Timing, hard work, and doing what was necessary for the business at all times, have been Simplot's trademark solutions to problems.
Members of *E*:	Scott Simplot, a son; Ray Dunlap, chemist; Richard Tobin and Ray Kueneman, engineers
Size of *V*:	*Forbes* estimates the value of Simplot's holdings at $500 million. Simplot stated, "I wouldn't sell for that, that's for sure."[150]
Social Utility:	J. R. Simplot Corporation employs 10,061 people and Simplot's investment in Micron Technology was critical to its launch.

[150]"The Richest People in America, The Forbes 400," *Forbes*, Fall, 1983.

Principal Sources	Teenaged Simplot's $7,800 profit from feeding,
of Venture	caring for, and selling 700 hogs in 1927.
Capital:	

JACK R. SIMPLOT, now 76, was born in a one-room cabin in Declo, Idaho, where he was raised by a stern father and loving mother. Except for hunting to put food on his family's table, young Simplot's life was one of work on his family's 120-acre farm, where he pulled out rocks and sagebrush by hand. In town, Simplot was variously a paper boy, scrap collector, and caddy. Driven by an intense desire to succeed, he dropped out of school in the eighth grade and left the father he feared and the mother he loved.

He learned to live on his entrepreneurial instincts at 14, when he made $7,800 in a year on his pork "corner." For the next three years, he went into farming, trading animals, and learning how to survive on sparse land and in hard times. He heard of an electric potato sorter in 1928, bought it for $345 and began sorting and storing potatoes for other farmers. The Great Depression increased the demand for potatoes and Simplot's business expanded. By 1940 he employed about 1,000 workers at 30 potato and onion warehouses, each of which had three electric sorters.

He got into the onion powder and flake business in a classically entrepreneurial manner, cleverly described by George Gilder in *The Spirit of Enterprise*:

Then in the spring of 1940, Jack Simplot decided to drive to Berkeley, California, to find out why an onion exporter there had run up a bill of $8,400 for cull (or reject) onions without paying. . . . The girl in the office said the boss wasn't in. Fine, said J.R., he would wait until the man arrived. Two hours later, at ten o'clock, a bearded old man walked in. Assuming this was his debtor, Simplot accosted him. But he turned out to be a man named Sokol, inquiring why he was not getting his due deliveries of onion flakes and powder. They sat together until noon, but still the exporter failed to arrive.

As the noon hour passed, Simplot was suddenly struck with an idea. He asked the bewhiskered old trader to a fateful lunch at the

Berkeley Hotel. "You want onion powder and flakes," said J.R. "I've got onions. I'll dry 'em and make powder and flakes in Idaho."

The two men shook hands on the deal and returned to the exporter's office. Mr. J.R. Simplot had entered the food processing business, without any clear notion of how to produce dried onion powder or flakes. Once again he followed his lifelong precept of entrepreneurship: "When the time is right, you got to do it." The objections to signing a contract for delivery of 500,000 pounds of dried, powdered, or flaked onions—without drier, pulverizer, or flaker or any clue of how to build them—seemed altogether prohibitive. But J.R. Simplot struck when the time was right.

Finally, the owner returned to his office and surprised Simplot by agreeing to pay off the debt, albeit on a slow schedule. Simplot then casually asked him where he performed the processing. The man avoided the question, thus heightening the Idahoan's curiosity. Leaving the office, Simplot noticed one of the exporter's trucks pulling out of the driveway. He followed it out to the plant, where he identified the equipment as Nipchild Prune driers from St. Helena, California. Simplot then rushed to his car and drove out through the Napa Valley to St. Helena, arriving just before dark. Before he left Nipchild Prune, he had made a down payment on six tunnel driers, and he had learned from Nipchild how to manufacture a vertical hammer mill and shaker to produce the powder and flakes. It had been a good day's work, Simplot thought as he returned to his car.[151]

Simplot quickly learned that other foods could be dried as well, and that the process reduced the storage requirement to one-seventh the warehouse space required prior to drying. When America entered World War II, Simplot's dried potatoes were in enormous demand as field rations. To get more potatoes, he bought and cleared more land for farming. To dispose of the endless skins, he bought a feedlot for 3,500 hogs. To get more fertilizer, he bought mineral rights to 2,500 acres of phosphate-rich Indian land. Each production obstacle was met with

[151]George Gilder, *The Spirit of Enterprise* (New York: Simon & Schuster, 1984), p. 30.

vertical integration. Although he worked day and night to increase productive capacity to feed the Army, the IRS sued him for tax evasion and war profiteering in the late 1940s. In addition, labor unions closed a plant and Simplot was hit with unfair labor practice suits. Fearing the worst was to come, Simplot's partners including his father demanded to be bought out in cash on the spot.[152]

Once again, Simplot saw an opportunity of Rothschildian proportions. While his partners saw another depression hitting Idaho, Simplot gladly went into debt to buy out his partners. He told one of them, "I ain't no economist, but I got eyes to see. This here state is going to boom for a long time to come." A Rothschild had said the same thing two hundred years earlier in the following words: "Buy when blood is running in the streets and sell when the fatted calf is lowing in the fields."

In 1946 a Simplot chemist came up with a process to freeze dry French fries. Frozen french fries did not catch the attention of consumers or restaurants until 1960, making the intervening 14 years very tough at J.R. Simplot Corporation. But the entrepreneur's patience and belief in this innovation paid off fully in the mid-1960s when Ray Kroc, head of McDonald's, ordered the frozen French fries to be tested in a few stores. The customers kept coming back for more. McDonald's soon accounted for 40 percent of Simplot's revenues. The J.R. Simplot Corporation had ridden through another period of holding onto an investment until it had become valuable, then selling it when, "the fatted calf is lowing in the fields."

---

[152]Ibid, p. 36.

HENRY E. SINGLETON

Name of Company:	Teledyne, Inc.
Date Founded:	1960
Location:	Los Angeles, California
Description of Business:	A diversified manufacturer of electronics equipment, avionics, consumer appliances, and insurance.
Description of *P*:	Warren S. Buffett considers Singleton the best manager in America and points out that Teledyne's four divisions earn a return of more than 50 percent on assets every year, notwithstanding each is in a very competitive industry. Buffett would like to see business schools teach Singleton, instead of producing executives cut from a McKinsey & Company cookie cutter.
Description of *S*:	Singleton has built a company that makes high-quality products and a great deal of profits. His management abilities are legendary.
Members of *E*:	George Kozmetsky, co-founder; and George Roberts, president
Size of *V*:	The approximately 12 million shares of common stock outstanding traded in a range of $147¼ to $302⅜ in 1984 for an average valuation of $2.7 billion.
Social Utility:	Teledyne is an example of superb management benefiting stockholders
Principal Sources of Venture Capital:	Venture capitalists Tommy J. Davis and Arthur Rock provided $1 million.

HENRY E. SINGLETON, 68, learned discipline at Annapolis, engineering at Massachusetts Institute of Technology (MIT) where he earned three degrees, research at a General Electric Company laboratory, and management first at Hughes Aircraft Company and then under Charles (Tex) Thronton at Litton Industries. In 1960 he left Litton to pursue a childhood dream, to build a giant company. His management style is to watch the thundering herd, then frequently to trot off in his own direction. When other companies are looking for acquisitions, Singleton abstains. When nobody wanted to buy stocks in 1978, Singleton went on a buying spree.

When I first met Henry Singleton in 1967, he operated in a tiny office in the low rent district in Hawthorne, California. His desk and chair were reclaimed Navy furniture. The office next to his was occupied by Themos Miklos, an acquisition lawyer. Miklos was up to his armpits in acquisitions because between 1960 and 1972, Singleton made 130 acquisitions. He used "Chinese paper," that is, higher and higher priced Teledyne common stock, using the previous acquisition to drive the price of the stock higher. When the market and the price of his stock dropped, Singleton reversed his field and did not make another acquisition for eight years, while buying his own stock back.

In 1976 the stock market caught on to what Singleton was doing: Teledyne's shares jumped from $20 to $80 in the space of a few months. He could have reduced debt with his cash in 1978, for instance, but that would have only fractionally increased earnings. Instead, Singleton bought back Teledyne stock and increased earnings from $10 to $16 per share. While earnings tripled during the mid-1970s from operations, they grew seven-fold from asset management.

Singleton thinks in terms of 130 different businesses or profit centers. Each one reports to Roberts or to an executive who reports to Roberts. Singleton told *Forbes*, "Teledyne is like a living plant, with our companies the different branches and each putting out new branches and growing so no one business is too significant."[153] He means what he says. Without a single acquisition since 1972, Teledyne's sales have soared from $1.3 billion to over $3 billion.

In 1983 Singleton bought back 43 percent of Teledyne's stock and drove the price over $300 per share. An investment in Teledyne at $3 per share in 1972 would have grown 100-fold in 11 years. That is better than most entrepreneurial returns of the last 25 years.

[153]Robert J. Flaherty, "The Sphinx Speaks," *Forbes*, Feb. 20, 1978, p. 35.

FREDERICK W. SMITH

Name of Company:	Federal Express Corporation
Date Founded:	1973
Location:	Memphis, Tennessee
Description of Business:	Through an elegantly integrated air-ground transportation system, the company provides overnight delivery of small packages throughout the United States and Canada. It recently introduced ZapMail, a same-day electronic mail service.
Description of P:	The airfreight companies shipped packages on commercial airplanes. If weather or equipment problems prevented takeoffs or landings, the packages did not get shipped. The reliability was low and the price was high.
Description of S:	In a paper for an economics course at Yale University, Smith proposed the idea of an airline that would carry small packages overnight from city to city. The airline would have its own aircraft and truck fleet, operate independently of the commercial schedules and routes, and deliver its cargo anywhere in the United States between dusk and dawn. He received a grade of C on the paper, but the nation got Federal Express Corporation, whose revenues exceeded $1.4 billion in 1984.
Members of E:	Peter S. Wilmott, Roger Frock, Michael Fitzgerald, Arthur Bass, and Vincent Fagan
Size of V:	The approximately 46 million shares of common stock outstanding traded in a range of $27¾ to $47 in 1984 for an average valuation of $1.7 billion.
Social Utility:	The company employs approximately 25,000 people, but its primary validity is in getting life-saving blood and medical supplies to people overnight.

Principal Sources   Charles L. Lea of New Court Securities (now Roth-
of Venture   schilds, Inc.) was the lead investor among 26 ven-
Capital: ture capital funds; Smith invested his $3.8 million
                        inheritance and personally guaranteed more in
                        debt.

FREDERICK W. SMITH, 41, was given a sizable inheritance on his
21st birthday and a letter from his father who died when Smith was
four years old. The letter urged Smith to put the inheritance to work to
build something great, and not to become part of the idle rich whom his
father despised. Smith was raised by his mother in Memphis, Tennessee. Although he was born with a birth defect—a bone socket hip disorder called Calve-Perthes disease—she encouraged him to enter into
all sorts of physical activities. Throughout grammar school he wore
braces and used crutches, but nothing really slowed him down. He
grew out of his disease and in prep school Smith played both basketball
and football.

At the age of 15, Smith learned to fly. That same year with a class-
mate he organized Ardent Record Company, a business that still exists
today. The company recorded "Rock-House" and "Big Satin Mama" in
its first year and broke even. Smith withdrew from the business when
he left for Yale University in 1962. Four years later, upon graduating,
Smith joined the Marines and was shipped off to Vietnam where he
flew 200 missions in forward-control planes. Smith developed an ad-
miration for the grit and determination of Ho Chi Minh and for the an-
cient landscape and protected culture of Vietnam before it was brutal-
ized by military confrontation. Most entrepreneurs are economically
deprived, but Smith was not. It has been suggested that his experiences
in Vietnam enabled Smith to intuit deprivation and perhaps desperation.

In 1969 Smith purchased a Little Rock company called Arkansas
Aviation Sales, a fixed base operator which provided maintenance services for corporate aircraft. Smith began brokering corporate jets; the
company became profitable and well regarded by the Little Rock financial community.

From 1969 to 1972 Smith investigated the needs of the U.S. Postal

Service and the Federal Reserve System for an overnight mail service. His most likely customer, Smith felt, was the Federal Reserve System, which could save $3 million per day in float. The word "Federal" is in the company name because Smith anticipated that his company would soon be hauling their checks from bank to bank. He put in his own funds and guaranteed a $3.6 million bank loan to buy two Dassanet Falcon 20 Fan Jets from Pan American World Airways. Weeks later the Federal Reserve backed out, and Smith had two jets and a partially formulated business plan.

In 1972 and 1973 Smith dived back into market research to attempt to develop a business plan. He hired two consulting firms, one large and the other small, to study the domestic air freight industry. The research pointed up the need for an air cargo service to provide a network among 100 large cities. This network would offer priority air service and would also have ground legs to offer service between the shipper and consignee. The small consulting firm provided Smith with future managers who knew the airline industry thoroughly.

What happened next in Smith's life was a marathon, nonstop journey into the canyons of Wall Street where he raised $96 million from venture capital funds, banks, and corporations; in one instance, Smith convinced his employees to pawn their watches to raise a short-term bridge loan. Smith's business plan had to be modified continually particularly when the price of gasoline quadrupled in the mid-1970s. Many of Smith's venture capital backers deserted him as the stakes were raised and breakeven seemed to be missed month after month. New Court, First Chicago, and Citicorp Ventures stuck by him and, most important, his management team stuck by him when the venture capitalists thought that another chief executive officer could do a better job than Smith. Arthur Bass told the board that if they replaced Smith, there would be a mass resignation of Federal Express Corporation's key officers. Crisis was a way of life at Federal Express Corporation because the company could not get its revenues up high enough to cover its constantly increasing expenses. An aggressive advertising campaign, and the development of the slogan "absolutely positively overnight" finally led to the company's profitability and its ability to go to the public market for much needed capital in 1977.

Federal Express Corporation is a miracle. As Robert A. Sigafoos writes in *Absolutely Positively Overnight*: "It is a good bet that the restless entrepreneur within Fred Smith and his compulsion to build will motivate him to try for greater success . . . he sees himself as a leader in the forefront of exploiting the hot, new high technologies."[154]

[154]Robert A. Sigafoos, *Absolutely Positively Overnight* (New York: New American Library, 1983), p. 250.

RAYMOND STATA

Name of Company:	Analog Devices, Inc.
Date Founded:	1965
Location:	Norwood, Massachusetts
Description of Business:	The company is the leading producer of precision data acquisition components and subsystems used in measurement and control instruments and computerized control systems. The company has made venture capital investments aggregating $10 million in 10 high technology companies.
Description of *P*:	Stata spotted a very large problem in 1965—operational amplifiers ("opamps") used in electronic test and measurement instruments were of poor quality and marketed without a service component.
Description of *S*:	Analog Devices was launched to manufacture, sell, and service opamps. It subsequently broadened into devices that monitor and control medical instruments, aircraft, automobiles, temperature of electrical equipment, and similar industrial products.
Members of *E*:	Matthew Lorber, co-founder; and Richard Burwin, first employee.
Size of *V*:	The approximately 25 million shares of common stock outstanding traded in a range of $19⅜ to $30 in 1984 for an average valuation of $500 million.
Social Utility:	The company has created 4,500 new jobs and has earned approximately 18 percent on equity for its investors over the last 10 years.
Principal Sources of Venture Capital:	Stata and Lorber made $100,000 on the sale of their first company to Kollmorgen Corporation. The Kollmorgen stock was used as collateral for a bank loan to start Analog Devices.

RAYMOND STATA, now 50, and his Massachusetts Institute of Technology (MIT) roommate, MATTHEW LORBER, founded Analog Devices in 1965 to make analog components. Stata and Lorber were college acquaintances who bumped into each other on the street one day six years after graduation. Stata had been selling electronic instruments for Hewlett-Packard Corporation. Lorber was working at the Instrumentation Lab at MIT. Both were looking for an apartment-mate to help save money. Over the course of rooming together, they talked one another into starting a company. On weekends and evenings they built power supplies and began selling them. Stata left Hewlett-Packard in 1962 to operate their company—Solid State Instruments—full time. Stata said in an interview with Goodloe Suttler of the Amos Tuck School of Business Administration in 1980:

> In many ways it turned out to be an ill-conceived business and it really didn't do all that well; we didn't have any capital, we didn't have any experience and the business was badly strategized—it was a really bad deal.

> But the thing that really sustained it was this urge to try something on our own. And after a while we did, in fact, get a little something going with those power supplies, although we never really foresaw that they would be the sustaining opportunity for the company—it was just something to take off on. Having done that we pooled our relative skills and experiences and looked around for more meaningful products. Sort of after the fact we came across an opportunity in gyro instrumentation, which is an area in which Matt and I had worked at M.I.T.

> So we shared a knowledge about gyro instrumentation and we developed this product which turned out to be pretty good: it was a rate table and the vendor of the motor and the tachometer (which was the heart of the technology) recognized it as a significant development. So they became interested in us more than the product because they wanted to get the know-how that we had of that technology.

> We finally worked out a deal and sold Solid State Instruments to them. We each got fifty thousand dollars in Kollmorgen stock. We

had an agreement to stay with them and build that business and we did; we worked for them for a couple of years after that and, in fact, built a very successful small business in exploiting that technology.

This is like '63. So we only had Solid State Instruments going for maybe a little over a year before we sold it. We developed in that two year experience in terms of how to do it and how not to do it and learned a lot more about running a small business.

As the two year contract period came to an end, Matt and I began to sit around and drink coffee again and talk about the future and essentially establish the fact that we would find something else and get the hell out of there. An idea emerged from our experience of shifting from making to buying certain components we used in our gyro test instrument—namely operational amplifiers. Prior to buying those products, we made our own, i.e. we designed our own operational amplifiers for use as servo amplifiers in our gyro test instrument.

All of a sudden we see these little black boxes showing up for very cheap prices and we began to evaluate the "make/buy" decision. We concluded that their deal was a hell of a lot better: we shouldn't be wasting our engineering resources because we were pretty thinly staffed.

So we had made the make-to-buy transition ourselves and started doing business with these companies only to find that the service and support that they were providing us with was poor: getting information, help or support was like pulling teeth. The salesmen never showed up, and the companies just weren't sales oriented. Well, countless other companies had made the same decision to buy rather than make and we presumed a whole bunch of people are going to start doing that. We could see some ways of developing, selling, and marketing the products better than what was being done. So we came on the idea: well, that's it, we will strike out and set up a business to make operational amplifiers in competition with our vendors.

We were pretty busy, though: we were both V.P.'s at the time and had a lot of responsibility. So we went out and found a very competent circuit designer by the name of Dick Burwin. He was a consultant around the area at the time. I met him when I was a salesman and we sort of knew about him. We went to Dick and said, "Look, Dick, here's the competition; we would like to come up with some products that are distinctly superior, what do you think" and so forth. For a year we worked with Dick at nights and on weekends. Then when the magic day came, and we thought we were far enough along to exit, about the end of our two year contracts, we went in and told management that the ball game was up. Matt left and went to set up an operation to start doing this thing. I stayed on and worked for another three or four months making the transition and then we struck out into Analog Devices.[155]

Stata and Lorber flipped coins to see who would do which tasks. The jobs were divided according to talents and interests. Lorber took engineering and manufacturing. Stata opted for marketing and finance.

Analog Devices' first office was in an old building near MIT. Rent was cheap and the only other expenses were Dick Burwin's salary of $35 per hour, some of which he took in stock and $50 per week to each of the founders. Kollmorgen liked the young men and gave Analog Devices a small contract to generate some cash flow while Burwin designed the company's opamps. The company broke even in its first year of operations and in 1966, sales tripled to $1.4 million. By 1968, sales were $5.7 million and the company went public in the buoyant new issue market in order to generate capital.

Stata credits Analog Devices' rapid sales rise to thoroughly understanding the competition's opamp business and improving the product, the price and the after-sale support. To reach the broadest number of potential customers for opamps without a sales force, Stata relied on "the paper salesmen." He said, "My concept was to come up with a literature approach where we could access ourselves to the whole world . . . I started writing a series of application notes—opamps part one, two, three and four. The concept was to use these as drawing cards to get attention because that's what people wanted at the time. What they

[155]Goodloe Suttler, "Analog Devices, Inc.," a paper prepared for class called Entrepreneurship at The Amos Tuck School of Business Administration, pp. 2–3.

wanted was not so much the products, they wanted the knowledge . . . we used to get tens of thousands of inquiries. We put these things in magazines: send in your bingo cards and we'll send you an opamp application note on such and such."[156]

The inquiries for applications notes were converted to a mailing list which produced qualified leads. Stata hired and trained technically qualified salespeople to follow up the leads. The high-quality image of the company generated by the applications notes had to be matched by technically confident and qualified salesmen. Thus, Analog Devices was launched by mailing information about the kinds of problems opamps could solve to thousands of interested engineers. In the years prior to easy access to venture capital, entrepreneurs frequently generated their capital via the customer financing route.

After its initial public offering in 1968, Analog Devices continued to grow by launching new products that it could manufacture and send down the marketing channel that it had created. It had its second major hit with analog-to-digital converters. Over the last 15 years, sales have grown to more than $250 million per annum, divided into data conversion devices (55 percent), signal conditioners (31 percent) and instruments and systems (4 percent).

In order to maintain its technical leadership, the company became a venture capitalist. Standard Oil of Indiana invested $10 million in the company for the purpose of permitting it to make venture capital investments in emerging high technology companies. Although these have not flowered into companies as dynamic as Analog Devices, they have provided the corporate banker with windows into new technologies.

In *Managing Corporate Culture*, Stanley M. Davis says of Ray Stata:

Analog has a founder and leader. He is . . . universally respected, and either liked or loved. "The company was, and still is, the extension of Ray Stata," says one executive. "The atmosphere is considerate, thoughtful, very humane, and averse to open conflict."[157]

[156]Ibid, p. 6.
[157]Stanley M. Davis, *Managing Corporate Culture* (Cambridge, Massachusetts: Ballinger Publishing), p. 96.

Another employee told Davis: "Ray evokes warmth and sincerity. He practices what he preaches. I can speak to him for five minutes and he inspires me and gives me enough to think about for a month, six months. I just enjoy being around that person."[158]

The leader of Analog Devices has begun to use his innovative and managerial skills in public service, particularly in Massachusetts governmental affairs and at MIT. He has written two books, the most recent of which is *The Innovators*, published in 1984 by Harper & Row.

[158]Ibid, p. 97.

ROBERT A. SWANSON
HERBERT W. BOYER

Name of Company:	Genentech, Inc.
Date Founded:	1976
Location:	San Francisco, California

Description of Business: The company is a leader in the development, manufacture, and marketing of pharmaceuticals produced by recombinant DNA technology. Principal products include human growth hormone, gamma interferon, tissue-type plasminogen activator, and bovine interferon.

Description of P: Genentech is the classic big-P company. Swanson began chasing big problems, such as cancer, with brilliant scientists and a magical "force" called interferon. American stock buyers like chase scenes. They bid the value (V) of Genentech's stock to $800 million on the day it went public, years before it began providing the solution.

Description of S: Swanson, a venture capitalist, wanted to run a science-based company that solved some of society's major problems. He met Herbert W. Boyer, one of the first scientists to synthesize life: he and Stanley N. Cohen had taken DNA strands from two different living organisms and glued them together, creating a bit of life that had never existed before. Boyer convinced Swanson that this scientific achievement could be commercialized, and the two became partners to create solutions to various medical problems utilizing recombinant DNA methods.

Members of E: Thomas J. Perkins, chairman; Donald L. Murfin, an active investor-director from Lubrizol Corporation; and David Goedel, chief scientist

Size of *V*:	The approximately 14 million shares of Genentech common stock outstanding traded in a range of $28¾ to $42¼ in 1984 for an average valuation of $490 million.
Social Utility:	Genentech is beginning to deliver solutions to serious medical problems including diabetes, short stature, certain forms of cancer and other diseases.
Principal Sources of Venture Capital:	Swanson and Boyer each invested $500 to begin Genentech. Kleiner & Perkins has been the principal backer.

ROBERT A. SWANSON, 37, and HERBERT W. BOYER, 48, have formed the most potent entrepreneurial team in biotechnology acceptable to investors, the scientific community, and the large pharmaceutical companies. When the chase is to conquer life-threatening diseases, the ingredients are capital, great scientists, and outstanding marketing companies, such as Eli Lilly & Company. Genentech has won the hearts, minds, and pocketbooks of all three. It has raised over $125 million—much more aggregate capital than its aggregate revenues since 1976 of $98 million—and licensed Eli Lilly & Company, Hewlett–Packard Company, Boehringer Mannheim Corporation, Miles Laboratories (subsidiary of Bayer A.G.) and others to market its products or codevelop new ones. How did Swanson, who left Kleiner & Perkins at 28, and Boyer, a scientist, pull off this miracle, where so many others have failed?

Boyer had agreed to leave academia, a difficult step for a distinguished scientist to take. Swanson had telephoned him out of the blue; but Swanson had a record of impetuousness. When he completed his undergraduate work at Massachusetts Institute of Technology (MIT) in chemical engineering in three years rather than four, Swanson had convinced the Sloan School of Management to let him begin graduate school early. Later Citicorp Venture Capital hired him, and although he was just 25, sent him to San Francisco to open an office for them. A year later, Kleiner & Perkins hired him. Swanson was an entrepreneur, however, not a venture capitalist; so, his next step was to find a problem that he could be happy solving.

After learning about Cetus Corporation, a 1971 biotechnology start-up, Swanson focused his investigations at the local library on the infant science of bioengineering. He compiled lists of authors and started telephoning the scientists one by one for their opinions on commercializing gene splicing. Each call would give Swanson more and more data, but none of the scientists believed that recombinant DNA could be bottled and sold as a remedy. Then he called Boyer to find out if this technology could be commercialized. Boyer replied that it could.

The two repaired to a local saloon and several beers later agreed to invest $1,000 to exploit recombinant DNA technology through a new company called "Genentech": genetic engineering technology. Their strategy violated several implicit rules of high-tech entrepreneurship, as promulgated in Silicon Valley during the 1970s. Instead of raising millions of dollars through an offering to plow into huge expenditures for plant and equipment, and instead of going on a hiring binge, Swanson and Boyer acted on Tom Perkins's advice and contracted out their early research to university labs. Rather than attempting to bring a product to market immediately (which was, after all, the goal), they opted simply to demonstrate that the technology would actually work—that through genetic engineering a microorganism could be made to produce a substance that it ordinarily does not make. In the original experiments by Boyer and Cohen, an artificially created gene had simply been replicated or cloned. Now they were trying not only to create and clone a gene in a laboratory, but also to place it inside bacteria and cause the bacteria in turn to manufacture a useful protein. This had never before been accomplished. This certification of the technology, the principals believed, would generate the excitement and money necessary to finance a continuing operation.

For their experiments, Boyer selected somatostatin, a hormone found in the brain. It has no market to speak of, but Boyer felt certain it could be synthesized. Its structure is simple, consisting of four amino acids. They would synthesize the DNA fragments at City of Hope National Medical Center, recombine the DNA, insert it in a bacterium (in this case E. coli, a fast-reproducing bacterium found in the human intestine), and then assay the "molecular soup" back at City of Hope to detect somatostatin.

The first test, which took seven months, was unsuccessful. Swanson was worried. Then one of the scientists thought of protecting somatostatin from some proteins in E. *coli* that might be attacking it. Says Robert Crea, a chemist at City of Hope, "We found that by playing this genetic trick of protection, there was really that thing in the soup."[159] Swanson and Boyer had the beginnings of a new pharmaceutical company: recombinant DNA was a replicable technology.

Swanson and Boyer then decided on a first product: synthetic human insulin. For this they needed to raise capital and recruit scientists. Swanson went after the best molecular biologists, protein chemists, and fermentation experts he could find. The accomplishment was similar to compressing at least 10 years of new product development at a major pharmaceutical company, because Genentech was only two people.

Manufacturing synthetic insulin was integral to Swanson's business strategy. Immediately after the somatostatin synthesis, Swanson informed Eli Lilly & Company, the $3-billion pharmaceutical giant, of their insulin plan. Eli Lilly & Company had begun marketing insulin in 1923; by 1979 it held 85 percent of the American insulin market. Swanson had no intention of competing with Eli Lilly & Company; it would have been futile, perhaps suicidal, to challenge its advanced sales and marketing staff.

But Swanson knew that the mere existence of synthetic human insulin would seem a threat to the giant. Swanson wanted to license Lilly to market insulin to raise capital.

In early summer of 1978, the final breakthrough occurred—the recombination and the expression of the insulin gene. Genentech was at last a company. It had the credibility to attract major financing, and to find scientists to join it. Like Luke Skywalker hiring Han Solo to join in attacking the EMPIRE, Swanson and Boyer have found their own FORCE—interferon—to attack the big-Ps of cancer, diabetes, and other serious diseases. The future of entrepreneurship as a mechanism for solving major social problems owes a large debt to the initiative of Swanson and Boyer.

[159]Randall Rothenberg, "Robert A. Swanson, Chief Genetic Officer," *Esquire*, December 1984, p. 372.

SIRJANG LAL TANDON

Name of Company:	Tandon Corporation
Date Founded:	1975
Location:	Chatsworth, California
Description of Business:	The company is a leading manufacturer of random access disc drives for data storage in personal computer systems.
Description of *P*:	Like Borg-Warner Corporation and the many other parts makers for the automobile and steel industries, Tandon saw the need for a parts maker for the computer industry. His company got in early and became the high-quality, low-cost supplier of disc drives.
Description of *S*:	In an industry which had as many as 110 competitors, Tandon captured a 60 percent market share. Tandon saw the price elasticity in the personal computer industry. He developed the manufacturing skills to lower the price of disc drives, and in so doing, expanded their market.
Members of *E*:	Ranjit Sitlani, vice-president—planning; and Clarice Gerkey, vice-president—finance
Size of *V*:	The approximately 51 million shares of common stock outstanding traded in a range of $3 to $20⅜ in 1984 for an average valuation of $600 million.
Social Utility:	Tandon has created 1,600 jobs in the United States and has proven that low costs can indeed be achieved by American manufacturers.
Principal Sources of Venture Capital:	Tandon's $65,000 bonus earned at Pertec Corporation.

SIRJANG LAL "JUGI" TANDON, 44, is an American-educated mechanical engineer from northern India's Punjab region. Like every other successful manufacturer before him, Tandon has built his company by paying constant attention to details and cutting costs to the bone.

Tandon Corporation makes disc drives for personal computers. Housed in boxes that resemble cassette tape players, the drives sit alongside or inside computers, providing memory storage. In each drive a recording head reads or writes magnetic information on the floppy disc that is inserted into it. One or two disc drives are sold for each personal computer. Tandon shipped over 3 million in 1984 for a 60 percent market share. With 110 competitors Tandon's achievement is quite remarkable.

Tandon comes from a frugal culture although he was not raised in a deprived environment. He simply believes that every penny counts. One of eight children of a Punjabi lawyer, Tandon came to the United States in 1960 to finish his last two years of college. He earned a B.S. in mechanical engineering at Howard University, then went to Kansas State University for a master's degree before joining International Business Machines Corporation as a junior engineer. He picked up an MBA degree later on in the evenings. After a brief visit to India in 1967 and marriage, Tandon returned and joined Memorex Corporation where he was asked to develop a floppy disc drive. The project was ignored until IBM introduced a small disc drive. Alan Shugart left Memorex Corporation to start his own disc drive company. Tandon wanted to leave as well, but could not attract any capital.

He jumped to Pertec Corporation where he was offered a $65,000 stock bonus (later renegotiated to cash) to develop a disc drive for them. In 1975 he left Pertec Corporation with $65,000, put all but $7,000 in real estate, and with his wife and brother to assist him, began making recording heads for disc drives.

Why recording heads? Because Tandon put his ear to the market and heard it calling for efficiently manufactured heads. He figured that he could sell heads for $18 each. The going rate then was $40. As Tandon told *Forbes*: "One man's fat margins are another man's opportunity."[160] By 1978 Tandon was the largest independent supplier of recording heads with sales of $3 million.

The head is the most costly part of the disc drive, and Tandon by

[160]Kathleen K. Wiegner, "The Hard Driver Atop the Disk-Drive Heap," *Forbes*, Nov. 7, 1983, pp. 216–217.

then was the established low-cost head producer. By 1979 Tandon had decided to produce the entire drive. Here again the competition's high margins came to his aid. Tandy Corporation, whose Radio Shack stores were heavily committed to the personal computer business, was having problems with their principal disc drive source. John Roach, Tandy's chairman, set out looking for alternative drive sources. But wherever Roach went, potential suppliers informed him that they could only supply Tandy with more drives if Tandy could supply them with more Tandon recording heads. Roach tracked down Tandon. Says Tandon:

> We were in this tiny building that John Roach said looked like a high school cafeteria. We had a prototype of a disc drive. That's all. I said to Roach, "When do you want production?" This was in May [1979]. Roach said, "July." I said to our engineers, "We have a chance to really grow this company or we're totally going to screw it up." We spent ten minutes, and everybody said, "We're going to go at it."[161]

Tandy got its drives on schedule; the order eventually totaled 50,000 units. A flood of orders soon came from other microcomputer makers and finally from mighty IBM itself for the PC. IBM currently ships the majority of its PCs with Tandon drives.

Tandon is a manufacturing whiz. Where does one go with an elegant S company? Usually it is growth via acquisition and diversification. Will Tandon become the shark or the minnow?

[161]Ibid.

CHARLES TANDY

Name of Company:	Tandy Corporation
Date Founded:	1963 (Radio Shack acquisition)
Location:	Fort Worth, Texas
Description of Business:	The company is the largest retailer of consumer electronics products, operating through approximately 6,000 owned and 3,000 franchised Radio Shack and other outlets. Personal computers and related products represent one-third of revenues.
Description of *P*:	Tandy saw an opportunity to become the largest retailer of personal computers in the mid-1970s, eight years ahead of most major computer manufacturers. "It helps not to know what you're doing," Tandy told me one evening in his Ft. Worth office in 1976. "That way you don't know what to be scared of."
Description of *S*:	Although his father handed him the opportunity to build a leather goods retail chain, Tandy sold it and plunged into a market that he felt had more opportunity. He bought the nine-store Radio Shack chain in 1963 and has since opened nearly ten thousand outlets. When he learned about personal computers in the mid-1970s, Tandy took his second plunge into a new area. Sales have quintupled from $579 million in 1974 to over $2.5 billion in 1984.
Members of *E*:	James V. Roach, chairman and president; and Phil R. North, interim president, following Tandy's death in 1978.
Size of *V*:	The approximately 82 million shares of Tandy Corporation common stock traded in a range of $23¼ to $43⅜ in 1984 for an average valuation of $2.7 billion.

Social Utility:	Tandy has created approximately 31,000 jobs and trained three to five times that number in retail store management.
Principal Sources of Venture Capital:	Consumer financing

CHARLES TANDY, who died suddenly in 1978, left Harvard Business School in 1948 to join the Navy. Upon his return home later that year he asked his father, David Tandy, to let him operate Tandy Leather Company's small leathercraft division. The principal business of Tandy Leather Company was filling mail orders for shoe findings and selling shoe repair supplies through retail outlets. The son's division specialized in handicraft supplies and soon overtook the father's; they bought out a disgruntled partner and began an expansion campaign that took the chain to 150 units by 1968. Do-it-yourself was a powerful trend sweeping the country and Tandy Leather Company was in the middle of a fast current.

In the late 1950s, Tandy went on an aggressive acquisition binge that resulted in serious indigestion, conflicts among the divisions, and by 1960, a drop in sales and the company's first loss. The entrepreneur had gotten his taste of diversification and it did not sit well with him. He spun-off Pier I Imports to its managers, and although he didn't realize it then, his feelings for the long-term prospects of the leather handicrafts business were not bullish.

In 1962 Tandy became intrigued with the operations of one of his acquisitions, Electronic Crafts of Fort Worth. He began looking for a larger company to graft it onto and he found Radio Shack Corporation, a nine-store Boston-area consumer electronics chain with sales of $9 million per annum mostly to ham radio buffs. Although in deep financial trouble, Tandy turned Radio Shack around by concentrating selling efforts on fast turnover items with broad consumer appeal. He insisted that buyers work constantly to develop new ideas for exclusive products and then buy properly so that products were competitive. When manufacturers in the United States were inadequate for this purpose, he developed resources abroad. *Realistic* and *Archer* became the company's trademarks. Retail stores were expanded rapidly so that today there are nearly ten thousand Radio Shack stores in the United States and abroad. In 1979 the leather business and the remainder of the acquisitions were spun-off to finance Tandy's expansion into personal computers.

Tandy did not live to see his personal computer bet pay off. The TRS-80, the company's initial product, became the most widely used personal computer until the Apple II and IBM PC bumped it into third place. Further research and development brought the company back to prominence with the TR1000 in 1984, an IBM PC compatible computer that Radio Shack store managers cannot keep on the shelves. Once while leaving his Fort Worth office at 8:00 P.M. for a dinner meeting, I asked Tandy, then in his late 60s, why he was taking home a briefcase full of work. He replied, "I'm not ready for computers, so I've got some catching up to do."

HENRY TAUB
FRANK LAUTENBERG
JOSEPH TAUB

Name of Company:	Automatic Data Processing, Inc.
Date Founded:	1949
Location:	Clifton, New Jersey
Description of Business:	The company is the leading independent supplier of data processing services, including payroll, accounting, and tax services for commercial business; back office processing, recordkeeping, and services for financial institutions; and network services.
Description of P:	Henry Taub decided that there would be a market for a trustworthy service company that prepared payrolls for small businesses, delivering to employers either their workers' checks correctly made out or pay packets ready to be filled, with all of the associated documents for the files and government agencies.
Description of S:	By separating out the payroll processing service from other accounting functions, Automatic Data Processing, Inc. (ADP) was able to offer a standardized product at a much lower price. The company's revenues exceeded $888 million for the fiscal year ended June 30, 1984, on which it earned 16 percent before taxes.
Members of E:	Joshua S. Weston, president and chief executive officer
Size of V:	The approximately 35 million shares of common stock outstanding traded in a range of $29½ to $39½ in 1984 for an average valuation of $1.2 billion.
Social Utility:	ADP has created 16,000 jobs, has produced a U.S. Senator (Lautenberg), a sports entrepreneur

(J. Taub), and two leaders in charity for Israel (H. Taub, Lautenberg).

Principal Sources   The founders' sweat equity
of Venture
Capital:

HENRY TAUB, 57, worked his way through high school as a bookkeeper for a small company. He paid for college by working part-time for a one-person CPA firm. He did client write-ups for five years—billings, receivables, and payrolls. As he told *Forbes*,

> In those days, payroll was regarded with a high degree of confidentiality. The employer did it himself, or if he had a bookkeeper and she went on vacation, he took the payroll home to work on it at night. Then payroll became more complicated . . . all the state programs began, taxes, unemployment, workers' compensation. Payroll became a burden for a small business.[162]

Upon his graduation at the age of 21, Taub formed Automatic Payrolls, Inc. He put a cot in the office and he and his brother Joe took naps on it, while working around the clock to get the payrolls out on Friday mornings. JOSEPH TAUB brought the work in, Henry processed it, and Joe delivered it.

FRANK LAUTENBERG, 57, a Columbia University Business School graduate was working as a sales trainee for Prudential Insurance Company of America in the same building as Automatic Payrolls. He began moonlighting with the company in 1952 and signed on full-time in 1954, becoming the chief salesman. The business was labor-intensive with low capital requirements; the demand for outside payroll processing services required incubation of the idea with the customers. Small businessmen do not make sudden changes in their accounting systems. Thus, ADP grew slowly and purposefully.

Wall Street was made up of hundreds of small brokerage businesses whose back offices were in serious need of management. ADP had gone

---

[162]Martin Mayer, "How to Manage a Revolution," *Forbes*, April 23, 1984, p. 97.

public in 1961 with one of its Wall Street payroll clients, Oppenheimer & Company, whose senior partner, Jack Nash, suggested that ADP explore handling Wall Street's back office services—clearing, account maintenance, and general ledger. Henry Taub opened an office in the area and began to learn the business, amidst the confusion of International Business Machines Corporation, RCA Corporation, Honeywell, and Sperry Rand Corporation each claiming they could handle Wall Street's needs. Like the tortoise and the hare, ADP became the best back office management company. When brokerage firms failed in the late 1960s, ADP's clients did not.

The company became very skilled in the management of accounting functions for thousands of small businesses in New Jersey and New York City. With a publicly traded stock, Lautenberg took to the road to cookie cutter the ADP script in other cities. He formed ADAPSO, an association of service bureaus, and convened numerous meetings at which he accumulated numerous financial statements, frequently on the backs of menus or on napkins, of service bureaus seeking to be acquired. Lautenberg's aides de camp were Bruce K. Anderson, now a venture capitalist in New York; Gilbert J. Mintz, now a leading merger and acquisition broker in the computer software industry; and the author, at that time an employee of ADP's investment banker, Kuhn, Loeb & Co. We traveled around the country making dozens of service bureau acquisitions, using ADP's stock. With each acquisition, the payroll and accounting processing systems would replace the services that the acquiree had been providing. ADP grew handsomely in this fashion: a "computing" company rather than a "computer" company, never quite trusting technology, but always listening to what the customer needed and wanted. Eventually large clients began to seek out ADP to have their payrolls processed and conversely by acquisition ADP found new services that it could offer its large clients. ADP even acquired some on-line services and technology-based services, such as Comtrend, a commodities futures market report service; but ADP has never relied on them to replace its basic problem-solving services. As the information revolution expands, ADP is beginning to become more network oriented in order to deliver its services more quickly and at lower costs.

WILLIAM Y. TAUSCHER

Name of Company:	FoxMeyer Corporation
Date Founded:	1978
Location:	Denver, Colorado
Description of Business:	The company is the fourth largest drug wholesaler in the country with revenues of more than $700 million; in addition, it provides support services to drug retailers including a franchise program and computer systems.
Description of *P*:	Many independent pharmacies and small chains are poorly managed and require assistance in inventory control, advertising, store layout, and marketing. Without these tools and central purchasing to contain costs, the independent pharmacies would be unable to survive.
Description of *S*:	FoxMeyer delivers several elegant solutions to pharmacists: facilities management, private-label brands, computer software, and franchising services.
Members of *E*:	Richard H. Bard, executive vice-president
Size of *V*:	The approximately 6.6 million shares of common stock outstanding traded in a range of $20 to $26¾ per share in 1984 for an average valuation of $154 million.
Social Utility:	The company employs 1,100 people.
Principal Sources of Venture Capital:	The author with the assistance of Stephen W. Fillo, formerly with Quidnet Capital Corporation, along with Sprout Capital Groups and First Century Partnership.

WILLIAM Y. TAUSCHER, 35, bought a lemon and then made lemonade. When I met Tauscher in 1978, he told me a little about himself. "I was admitted to Yale University and given financial aid, but I spent the money before I got to school," he said. "And I had to get a job in a restaurant to pay for tuition. Finally, I opened a restaurant, and ran it for the whole time I was at Yale." Upon graduating, Tauscher joined International Business Machines Corporation as a computer salesman, but he did things a little differently there as well. "I wouldn't sing the company song," said Tauscher. "So I was pretty much branded as stubborn and independent."

IBM assigned Tauscher to sell computers on Chicago's South Side, which is the equivalent of trying to sell tennis rackets in the Amazon. Undaunted, Tauscher found that the South Side was rich in wholesalers. As he made various computer installations, Tauscher learned the distribution business. One customer, Lag Drug Company, hired him to convert their massive inventory, accounts receivable, and accounts payable from a manual system to the IBM mainframe Tauscher had sold them. When Lag's president died, the owners asked Tauscher to run the company. He was 29 years old.

Once the computer was in operation, Tauscher had audited financial statements prepared and realized Lag was broke. To avoid succumbing to the laws of gravity, Tauscher decided to buy a healthy company in the same business. He found Fox-Vliet, a Wichita-based drug wholesaler whose owner wanted to sell. Both companies were in the $85 to $100 million per annum sales range, and Tauscher arranged a leveraged buyout of Fox-Vliet that required $4.6 million in equity. Three venture capital funds invested $4.6 million to effect the purchase.

Life with the venture capital funds was uncomfortable at first. They squeezed Tauscher and he left LFV Corporation, as he named the new company, to let the investors try to run things. When losses became frighteningly high, they asked Tauscher to return. He did, but on new terms, and he began buying more drug wholesalers, particularly in the midwest and Rocky Mountain region. The company name was changed to FoxMeyer when LFV bought Meyer Drug Company in Denver.

When there was sufficient scale, Tauscher began a unique strategy of changing FoxMeyer into a computer systems house and drugstore franchising company. The idea for a computer system to help pharmacists manage their business and place orders with FoxMeyer on an on-line, realtime basis, came from Tauscher's IBM experience. But where did he learn franchising and private labeling of health and beauty aids? "I looked at this half-a-billion-dollar business and decided that I would try to take as many cost centers as I could find and convert them to profit centers," said Tauscher. "That's just being practical."

Practical maybe, but smart for sure. Franchising brings in a lot of cash at the front end, and private labeling of health and beauty aids is profitable. Computer systems have higher margins than drugs. Tauscher even went into the trucking business because some of Fox-Meyer's 25 trucks were coming back empty. The trucking operation is a new profit center, controlled by a software system that assures optimal utilization. It seems that Tauscher has gotten himself into a low margin, antiquated industry and leveraged every possible asset and liability to bring the bottom line up. In about two or three years, FoxMeyer will probably be considered a high technology company with a variety of side businesses. Pass the lemonade!

JAMES G. TREYBIG

Name of Company:	Tandem Computers Inc.
Date Founded:	1974
Location:	Cupertino, California
Description of Business:	The company makes fault-tolerant, multiple processor computer systems for on-line transaction processing.
Description of *P*:	Treybig became aware of the serious needs of certain kinds of computer users to avoid downtime or breakdowns. These users include banks, hospitals, travel agencies, racetracks, and others.
Description of *S*:	Tandem developed a way of linking two or more central processing units, so that if there was a failure anywhere in the system, work would automatically shift to another part of the system, while the faulty parts were fixed.
Members of *E*:	Thomas J. Perkins, chairman and principal investor, and R.C. Marshall, chief operating officer.
Size of *V*:	The approximately 40 million shares of Tandem common stock outstanding traded in a range of $16 ¼ to $40 ¼ in 1984 for an average valuation of $1.1 billion.
Social Utility:	The company has created 5,365 new jobs and it has introduced some innovative management concepts, such as easy access to the president, many recreational facilities for employees, and stock options for all employees.
Principal Sources of Venture Capital:	Thomas J. Perkins' venture capital fund, Kleiner & Perkins, invested $1.5 million and pulled together a total of $3.1 million of launch capital in 1975.

JAMES G. TREYBIG, 44, was a professionally incubated entrepreneur. Like the merchant bankers of the late 19th century who would take promising young men under their wings, Thomas J. Perkins, one of the most experienced venture capitalists in the United States, incubated Treybig for a year at Kleiner & Perkins. Perkins had been personal assistant to William Hewlett and David Packard; in 1971 he joined forces with Eugene Kleiner, one of the founders of Fairchild Semiconductor Corporation, to form Kleiner & Perkins. The venture capital fund achieved an average rate of return of approximately 50 percent per annum through 1983.

In the mid-1970s, rather than wait for top-drawer entrepreneurs to knock on his door with elegant business plans under their arms, Perkins believed that great business plans could be created at Kleiner & Perkins and married to outstanding entrepreneurs. He also believed that outstanding entrepreneurs could be found to learn the entrepreneurial process at Kleiner & Perkins and create elegant business plans, which Perkins would bankroll. Tandem Computers Inc. was the first product of Perkins' fertile plan, and there have been several others as well.

Treybig earned a bachelor's degree in electrical engineering and an MBA from Stanford University before going to Hewlett–Packard Company as a marketing manager for five years. Perkins got wind of this bright, energetic young man and asked him to come to Kleiner & Perkins and read business plans and listen to the proposals of other entrepreneurs for a year, then write down his own business plan. Treybig was not like other venture capitalists who did not quite grasp the technology. Treybig dug into the proposals and asked penetrating questions about the need for the product and how the product answered that need. He was animated, constructive, and helpful.

When his incubation period was over he forsook the gasoline pump of the venture capitalist for the automobile of the entrepreneur. Treybig had formulated one of the largest problem areas of the day: the need for a double fail-safe computer. One that had a very long mean time to failure. The industry has competitors, eight years later, and a name: fault-tolerant computers. But Treybig built Tandem from sales of $8 million in 1977 to more than $440 million in 1984 and a market value of more than $1 billion.

At Tandem all employees get stock options. Every Friday afternoon Tandem holds beer bashes on the company's patio, where suppliers, managers, and assembly workers swap information and complaints. In the Silicon Valley, where skilled people are hard to find and often harder to hold on to, Tandem's tennis courts and flexible work hours are not merely examples of laid-back California, but practical industrial relations tactics.

Life at Tandem is anything but relaxed. Worker productivity is twice the average for the computer industry, which is as a whole devoutly entrepreneurial and fiercely competitive. Treybig's paradox is that Tandem must grow big or be swallowed up by a larger competitor; yet, to grow, it must keep the kind of people who often function best in small, freewheeling organizations.

Credit for Tandem's continued growth and valuation belongs as well to the company's outside directors, three of whom are among the most astute venture capitalists in the country: Thomas J. Perkins, Tommy J. Davis, and Franklin P. "Pitch" Johnson, Jr.

ROBERT EDWARD TURNER III

Name of Company:	Turner Broadcasting System Inc.
Date Founded:	1969
Location:	Atlanta, Georgia
Description of Business:	The company operates the first cable television Superstation—WTBS—and has introduced a 24-hour, all-news service, Cable News Network (CNN), seen in 85 percent of homes that have cable television hookups.
Description of *P*:	Turner saw an opportunity to build a major cable television network. He observed correctly that NBC, CBS, and ABC would not enter the cable market to compete against themselves and that Westinghouse Electric Corporation and other large cable television station owners could not move as rapidly as an entrepreneur.
Description of *S*:	Turner began with a bankrupt Atlanta television station, WTBS-Atlanta, whose programs he sold to cable TV stations across the country. This not only increased the number of viewers, but also attracted national advertisers to WTBS and increased Turner Broadcasting's cash flow. With the cash he launched Cable News Network.
Members of *E*:	Robert W. Wussler, executive vice-president, and William C. Bevins, Jr., chief financial officer
Size of *V*:	*Forbes* estimates Turner's worth at more than $400 million.[163]
Social Utility:	Turner Broadcasting System Inc. (TBS) has created roughly 1,800 new jobs and brought better programming to millions of television viewers.

---

[163]"The Richest People in America, The Forbes 400," *Forbes*, Fall 1983.

Principal Sources of Venture Capital:	Loans collateralized by television stations

ROBERT EDWARD "TED" TURNER, 45, has been complaining about the poor quality of programming on the three major television networks for 10 years. His style is more than brash. It is antagonistic. The rude barbs draw the bears out of their caves and make them say silly things as did ABC program advisor Mike Dann: "The days of Mr. Turner's clear sailing are over."[164] What Turner knows, of course, is that entrepreneurs *always* beat corporate managers at the same game, and Turner is merely having his laughs as he goes along, rather than after he has scaled the mountain.

Turner is used to living on the thin edge. Intense, arrogant, full of braggadocio, combative for the sheer hell of it—all the adjectives have been pulled out to describe this phenomenon and they all miss the mark. They are form. The substance is this: Turner has made a career of taking on apparently impossible challenges and making spectacular successes of them against all odds.

He is also a canny opportunist. Enthusiastic about CNN, he hardly sounds like the man who said in 1974: "As far as our news is concerned, we run the FCC minimum of 40 minutes a day."[165]

While Turner has decried for years the "crappy programs" the networks have produced, he did not hesitate to run junky sitcom series he could buy for a song. Professional wrestling is junky, too, and Turner embraces it as well.

This ability to rationalize has enabled Turner never to paint himself into a corner. When trapped, he just knocks down the wall. Consider the fortunes of CNN, which created a $24 million working capital deficit at TBS before Turner was able to convince Manufacturers Hanover Trust Company and Citicorp to loan TBS $50 million for three years. No matter that the loan cost him—three points over prime, a $3 million fee, and tying up TBS's advertising accounts receivable for three years —Turner did not have to give up any equity. Cleverly, TBS borrowed $50 million when its retained earnings deficit was $9 million. How

---

[164]Howard Rudnitsky, "Don't Count Ted Turner Out," *Forbes*, Aug. 31, 1981, p. 31.
[165]Ibid, p. 32.

many entrepreneurs have pulled off that pretty a piece of leverage? Not too many would even dare to ask.

Turner began with a bankrupt billboard advertising company in 1969, which he forsook to purchase WTBS, a UHF station in Atlanta, whose future looked bleak. It was losing half a million dollars a year, was last in a market dominated by three network stations, and its signal was often weak and distorted. Through purchases of other stations for stock and debt, WTBS improved its stature in the Atlanta marketplace.

Turner bought up old movies on the cheap, including the *Star Trek* series, and ran them against the network stations' newscasts. Then, when the local NBC affiliate refused to take some network programs, Turner picked them up. He also paid to get the Atlanta Braves telecasts on WTBS. By 1974 Turner Broadcasting was operating in the black and Turner bought out his three largest stockholders for a debenture, Rice Broadcasting, and the billboard business. With 87 percent ownership, Turner became more aggressive. He paid $1.3 million for a Charlotte UHF station that was later sold to Westinghouse Electric Company for $20 million to help Turner finance CNN. He bought the Atlanta Braves and the Atlanta Hawks that same year with financing provided by the sellers.

Meanwhile, Turner had long been interested in cable television as a way to break out of his limited Atlanta market. But building a string across the South to reach cable operators was out of the question. When RCA Corporation launched a commercial communications satellite in late 1975, Turner jumped at this chance to build a $750,000 earth station. That way he could send his signal not just across the South but *everywhere* in North America, and at a fraction of the cost of a ground system. In 10 years' time Turner has built the fourth major network. In May 1985 he began a campaign to acquire CBS, and many analysts believe he will succeed.

Frequently an entrepreneur is driven to succeed to overcome the business failures of a father. Turner's father sold his failing billboard business to his son, and then killed himself. This may or may not be Turner's principal driver. But he has accomplished things in an intensely competitive market that men with 100 times the money and corporate juggernaut have not been able to do. He has moved mountains using verbal skills, financial leverage, and initiative.

ALBERT L. UELTSCHI

Name of Company: FlightSafety International, Inc.

Date Founded: 1951

Location: Flushing, New York

Description of Business: The company provides high-technology training programs to private and commercial aircraft pilots and technicians and to crews of ocean vessels. It also manufactures sophisticated training equipment including flight simulators.

Description of *P*: Ueltschi was the first to seize the opportunity to train pilots and technicians in the increasingly complex aircraft brought about by the introduction of commercial jets. The Federal Aviation Administration's requirements for certification provide increased pressure on pilots and technicians to have their training continually upgraded.

Description of *S*: FlightSafety's professional pilot training, which accounted for approximately 90 percent of 1984's revenues of $90 million, includes advanced education in the operation of aircraft, air traffic control skills, and flying proficiency as well as instruction in new aviation developments and training to help pilots maintain their status as certified operators of various types of aircraft.

Members of *E*: Bruce N. Whitman, executive vice-president; and John P. McIntosh, vice-president.

Size of *V*: The approximately 15 million shares of FlightSafety common stock outstanding traded in a range of $19½ to $30¼ in 1984 for an average valuation of $375 million.

Social Utility: The company has created approximately 1,300 jobs and its return on equity over the last 10 years has averaged over 25 percent per annum.

Principal Sources   Ueltschi second-mortgaged his house to buy a
of Venture $10,000 flight simulator.
Capital:

ALBERT L. UELTSCHI, now 69, was born on a dairy farm in Frankfort, Kentucky, in 1915, one of seven children. Life on the farm was difficult, and young Ueltschi had to milk the cows before school, bottle
the milk, and sell it in town for a nickel a quart. He attended a one room
school and graduated high school in the mid-1930s with a burning desire to fly. He told reporter Jerry Wakefield of the *Frankfort State Journal*, "I always had a feeling I'd like to fly. I remember Lindbergh cross-
ing the Atlantic and when I was in grammar school I always read all the
aviation books I could." He learned to fly when he was 16 on an old
grass airstrip. "A fellow named Charlie Black had a farm out on the
Georgetown Pike where he had built a hangar for me. So I ran some ads
in the paper for the Frankfort Flying School. We'd put on a little air
show and charge everybody about $3.00 or something like that."[166]

Ueltschi ran a restaurant during his college years, then he became a
barnstorming pilot until World War II, briefly serving as Juan Trippe's
(PanAm's founder) pilot. With the growth in commercial aviation after
the war, Ueltschi observed that industrial corporations were having
trouble finding trained pilots, and aircraft manufacturers were getting
out of the pilot training business in order to concentrate on aircraft
manufacture.

In 1951, Ueltschi jumped into the pilot training gap by renting space
at LaGuardia Airport's Marine Air Terminal and renting flight simulators. In 1954, when the business appeared viable, he mortgaged his
house to buy a $10,000 training simulator from Link. A cautious man,
Ueltschi remained a Pan Am pilot until 1968, running FlightSafety on
off-hours. He took the company public in 1968, and began to give it his
full-time attention.

The company owns and operates approximately 75 flight simulators
which duplicate nearly every flight experience and are identical in instrumentation and appearance to the cockpits of actual aircraft. The
simulators cover a broad range of aircraft, with an emphasis on smaller,

---

[166]Jerry Wakefield, "Al Ueltschi," *The Frankfort State Journal*, p. 75.

business aircraft, as opposed to commercial airlines. FlightSafety has an estimated 30 percent market share of the general aviation training market. It is the authorized training organization for 17 aircraft manufacturers. Some might say Ueltschi has a lock-up.

A $2.5 billion giant has said just that. Singer Company has asked a federal court to nullify FlightSafety's agreements with major aircraft manufacturers including McDonnell Douglas, Lockheed, and the Sikorsky division of United Technologies. These manufacturers steer their customers to FlightSafety and Singer says the practice is anticompetitive; they want easier access into the market. Ueltschi is defending his position vigorously. He recently told *Forbes*: "I built this damn thing from nothing and I did it clean. Nobody can take that away from me."[167]

[167]Anne Bagamery, "Dogfight," *Forbes*, July 30, 1984, p. 68.

HOWARD VOLLUM

Name of Company:	Tektronix, Inc.
Date Founded:	1946
Location:	Beaverton, Oregon
Description of Business:	The company is the world's leading producer of cathode ray oscilloscopes. It also manufactures a broad range of electronic test and measurement instruments as well as terminals for the computer graphics industry.
Description of *P*:	Vollum saw the need for mass produced oscilloscopes that measure electrical and mechanical energy and reproduce it in graphic form.
Description of *S*:	The entrepreneur was introduced to radar in World War II. Afterward with his partner, M.J. Murdock (d. 1971), Vollum worked in a radio and appliance shop. He designed the company's first oscilloscope in 1946 and with five employees took on DuMont, then the industry leader, and drove it out of the market.
Members of *E*:	M.J. Murdock, initial partner; Earl Wantland, president and chief executive officer; William D. Walker, vice-president—test and measurement industry division
Size of *V*:	The approximately 19 million shares of common stock outstanding traded in a range of $58⅛ to $78¾ in 1984 for an average valuation of $1.2 billion.
Social Utility:	The company has created 20,693 jobs and fostered numerous entrepreneurial spin-offs in Oregon.
Principal Sources of Venture Capital:	The founder's personal savings

HOWARD VOLLUM, now 72, built a company that has continually served the fastest-growing segments of the electronics industry: computers and communications. As a result, its sales grew faster than any other electronics company in the 1970s, from $337 million in 1974 to $1.3 billion in 1984, and earnings increased from $26 million to $118 million. Following the successful launch of its oscilloscope in the early 1950s, Tektronix built the product to a position of market dominance. Hewlett–Packard Company became its principal competitor.

Then, entrepreneur Vollum successfully led the company into a second product line and it became dominant there as well. This was the field of color graphic computer terminals: high resolution display monitors for industrial designers, plus ancillary equipment including logic analyzers, microcomputer development products, semiconductor test systems, hard copy units, ink jet printers, and plotters. This division now accounts for 40 percent of Tektronix's sales, practically equal to that of the instrument division.

A third diversification took the company into communications; Tektronix sells television waveform and picture monitors used to analyze video signal transmission quality and special effects systems used for television. The company follows an axiom of successful selling: rapidly growing companies buy more, faster, and pay more quickly than do companies in low growth industries.

Vollum's achievements came from selecting excellent managers. Earl Wantland, now the company's president, selected Lawrence Mayhew to head up the company's graphic terminal division in 1964. The first product was overpriced and had only a limited market appeal. Mayhew had it redesigned and cut the cost in half. The product became a hit and took Tektronix though the 1974–1975 recession with ease.

In 1974 Tektronix went outside Beaverton to acquire Grass Valley Group, a California company making television switching systems for special effects. The company formed the basis of Tektronix's communications products division and has been a strong contributor to profits, with a 24 percent pretax margin.

For most of Tektronix's rapid growth period, securities analysts could not believe that an electronics manufacturer outside of Silicon Valley could thrive. Thus, its price/earnings ratio has averaged around 14x over the last 10 years, versus 20x or more for its competitors in better neighborhoods. That's a large discount to pay for success.

SAM MOORE WALTON

Name of Company:	Wal–Mart Stores, Inc.
Date Founded:	1962
Location:	Bentonville, Arkansas
Description of Business:	The company is a rapidly expanding chain of discount stores that operates stores in 750 small towns from South Carolina to Texas.
Description of *P*:	Walton believed that people in small towns—he favors county seats—need large general merchandise stores offering name brand goods at discount prices.
Description of *S*:	Wal–Mart Stores are generally 50,000 square feet in size and have 36 departments. Walton told *Forbes*, "There was a lot more business in those towns than people ever thought."[168] He and top executives visit all of the stores several times a year. Sales are over $5 billion per annum.
Members of *E*:	David D. Glass, president; and James L. Walton, senior vice-president
Size of *V*:	The approximately 140 million shares of common stock outstanding traded in a range of $30¼ to $47 in 1984 for an average valuation of $5.4 billion.
Social Utility:	Wal–Mart Stores employ over 30,000 people; they have filled a major need in 750 small towns.
Principal Sources of Venture Capital	Self-financed until 30 stores were opened; then public market.

SAM MOORE WALTON was a J.C. Penney trainee after graduating from college and admires James Cash Penney a great deal. In 1945 at the age of 27, he opened his first Ben Franklin store, in Newport, Arkansas.

---

[168]Harold Seneker, "A Day in the Life of Sam Walton," *Forbes*, Dec. 1, 1977, p. 47.

In 1950 Walton's store folded. He reopened another Ben Franklin five-and-dime in Bentonville, Arkansas, immediately and by 1962, he had 16 of them. His brother James gave Walton the idea for discount stores, and the Ben Franklins were converted to form the base for what has become one of the greatest family fortunes in America. Walton owns 39 percent of a business valued at $5.4 billion. What did he see 22 years ago that others overlooked?

Walton knows small towns. With a twin engine Piper Aztec, he flies from small town to small town, often visiting four stores per day, and spending a couple of hours with the store managers, the associates who run the various departments, and the customers. He told *Forbes*: "We like to let folks know we're interested in them and that they're vital to us. 'Cause they are. Those department heads are the only ones who *really* know what's going on out there in the field, and we've got to get them to tell us."[169]

Walton carries an idea that works in one town to another town. He will ask the manager if the idea will work, and discusses its pros and cons. Walton knows the names of thousands of employees and he has their loyalty.

There is often a Penney's store in town, but he does not worry about it. Wal–Marts have a wider merchandise mix with more hard goods. His real competitors are K-Mart Corporation, Gibson's (a southern chain) and TG&Y Stores (a division of Household Finance). They find Wal–Mart Stores very tough competitors. Often when they find an attractive town a Wal–Mart is already there. When it is not, Wal–Mart is not above putting a bigger, brighter store in wherever competitors show the slightest vulnerability. Some of them have even been run out of town.

Wal-Mart's boundaries are set by one-day truck routes from six warehouses; 80 percent of its goods pass through these huge company distribution complexes for trans-shipment. That way, volume discounts and its own trucking save 2 to 5 percent on cost, no small matter to a company with a 7 percent pretax margin.

Success for Wal–Mart is the result of caring. The stores are big and attractive and they say to the customers, "You may be small town people, but you have big town taste!" Walton pays his customers a compliment and they have paid him back many times in return.

[169]Ibid, p. 47.

AN WANG

Name of Company:	Wang Laboratories, Inc.
Date Founded:	1955
Location:	Lowell, Massachusetts
Description of Business:	The company is a leading manufacturer of small computers and word processing systems.
Description of *P*:	Wang identified a need in the 1960s for advanced office automation systems, that is, word processing systems that could handle other functions, at a price most businesses could afford.
Description of *S*:	Wang products include electronic mail, file management, time management, digital voice exchange, and other add-ons that automate the office. The company is known for exceptional customer service and after-sale support.
Members of *E*:	John F. Cunningham, president, and Fred Wans, director of research and development
Size of *V*:	The approximately 138 million shares of common stock outstanding traded in a range of $23 to $37⅝ in 1984, for an average valuation of $4.1 billion.
Social Utility:	Wang has created over 30,000 jobs and brought prosperity to an abandoned mill town, Lowell, Massachusetts. Wang's generosity to educational, medical, and cultural institutions is legendary.
Principal Sources of Venture Capital:	Personal savings earned from licensing a magnetic pulse controlling device (known as magnetic core memory) to International Business Machines Corporation.

AN WANG came to the United States from China in 1945. "I was fortunate that as soon as I got to the United States I was admitted to

Harvard."[170] He rapidly earned his master's degree and then a Ph.D. in physics in 1948. He invented magnetic core memory, essential to computers for 20 years, which he licensed to IBM. With the cash flow, he set up his first factory over a garage in South Boston. Wang Laboratories earnings in that year were $15,000. They have grown by an average of 40 percent a year ever since. The company's products range in price from $6,200 to $200,000 and are available as stand-alone or multiple workstation systems. The company is generally regarded as the leader in office automation systems. To maintain its leadership role, Wang recently bought minority interests in VLSI Technology, Inc., a microchip manufacturer, and InteCom Inc., a maker of voice and data communications and switching systems.

An Wang is Boston's leading benefactor, having recently pledged $4 million to save Boston's main performing arts center, $4 million to Harvard University, and $1 million to Wellesley College. In addition Wang Laboratories' $15 million factory provided 300 jobs for inner city residents. Wang also created the $6 million Wang Institute for Graduate Studies for software engineers and Chinese scholars and donated $1 million for the John K. Fairbank Center for East Asian Research, where young Chinese scholars will study. In 1981 he donated $1 million to Harvard University for four science fellowships to be named in honor of his physics professor at Harvard and has made other gifts of $2 million to Harvard.

This level of generosity and achievement is remarkable for a 65-year-old man who emigrated to America in 1945. Wang credits much of his success to being quickly accepted by Harvard University where he was introduced to computers.

There is irony in Wang's generosity to Boston. The fortunes of many of that city's great families were made in the early 19th century, when they sold opium to the Chinese.

---

[170]Fox Butterfield, "Chinese Immigrant Emerges as Boston's Top Benefactor," *New York Times*, May 5, 1983, p. 1.

SANFORD I. WEILL

Name of Company:	Shearson Lehman Brothers
Date Founded:	1960
Location:	New York, New York
Description of Business:	Investment banking firm with numerous branch offices providing stock brokerage services
Description of P:	Weill recognized the need to "rationalize" the securities industry. He was one of the first to do so by acquiring larger firms and taking Shearson public.
Description of S:	Weill used financial leverage, including the public's money and the cash flow of the brokerage firms he acquired for Shearson.
Members of E:	Co-founders Marshall Cogan, Roger Berlind, and Arthur Levitt; plus Peter Cohen, Shearson's president
Size of V:	American Express Company acquired Shearson in 1980 for $930 million.
Social Utility:	Shearson Lehman Brothers has become a survivor in a highly competitive industry that has seen the number of competitors shrink from 600 in 1969 to fewer than 100.
Principal Sources of Venture Capital:	Personal savings

SANFORD I. WEILL, 51, has risen to the heights of the investment banking industry with speed and grace. Born in Brooklyn, New York, the son of middle-class parents, Weill attended Cornell University. His father abandoned the family in Weill's senior year. Simultaneously, all of the brokerage firms he had interviewed with rejected his applications. The double shock delayed his diploma and Weill took a messenger's job on Wall Street in 1955 for pennies. The next year he was hired as a stockbroker by his employer, Bear, Stearns & Company.

Although not particularly adept at first, by 1960 Weill had earned $30,000 in excess capital and he left to form a partnership called Carter, Berlind, Potoma & Weill to develop an investment banking and brokerage business. In 1967 the Weill firm acquired a money management company, Bernstein, MacCauley, and two of Weill's original partners were replaced. Wall Street had its best years in 1968 and 1969, but then the bottom fell out and many firms folded or became insolvent and needed to be acquired when their back offices could not handle the increased volume of business. The final nail in the coffin was the introduction of flexible commission rates in 1971.

Brokerage firms had to learn how to compete. Weill had been in a race for approval since his personal crisis of 1955, and competition was a way of life for him.

In 1973 he became the head of Cogan, Berlind, Weill & Levitt and managed the integration of the much larger Hayden, Stone. (This well-known and highly regarded national firm had at one time employed Arthur Rock, the successful venture capitalist for Teledyne, Scientific Data Systems, Intel Corporation, and Apple Computer, among others.) Weill's firm assumed the name Hayden, Stone and in 1974, he acquired the still larger Shearson, Hammill & Co.

Needing capital, Weill approached the Securities and Exchange Commission (SEC) for permission to go public. Weill and Levitt went to Washington to plead their case before SEC chairman William Casey. When they were stood up, they tailed Casey to the street, jumped into a cab with him, and bent his ear on their urgent need to go public. Weill and Levitt prevailed.

As early as 1975, Weill put out feelers to American Express that Shearson would like to be acquired. But it was not until 1980 when he met Jim Robinson, American Express' president, that Weill made a formal pitch. Shearson's revenues had grown to $936 million and it was profitable. Prudential Insurance Company of America had recently acquired Bache, and Weill with an uncanny sense of timing, struck when the iron was hot.

Weill is an expert acquisitions negotiator. He knows when to bore in and when to back off. He limits direct contact during the hard negotiations to avoid arguments that could burden relationships after the merger is completed. He has helped American Express grow to sales of over $19 billion with further acquisitions, including the mutual fund giant, IDS; the old line investment banker, Lehman Brothers Kuhn Loeb & Company; and the international bank, Trade Development Bank.

American Express elected Weill president in 1982, but he resigned in June 1985 when he became confined in a position subordinate to Jim Robinson. Prior to leaving American Express, Weill attempted to purchase its Fireman's Fund subsidiary via a leveraged buy-out, but Robinson rebuffed him. Entrepreneur watchers anxiously await Weill's next move.

CHARLES KEMMONS WILSON

Name of Company: Holiday Inns of America, Inc.

Date Founded: 1952

Location: Memphis, Tennessee

Description of
Business: A successful formula of standardized rooms, quality control, reasonable prices, and family accommodations conveniently located near major travel arteries is what made Holiday Inns the largest motor-hotel chain in the world.

Description of *P*:   After a 1951 family vacation to Washington, D.C., Wilson realized the need for providing affordable, convenient, comfortable lodging to the hordes of traveling Americans taking to the nation's highways.

Description of *S*:   Holiday Inns provided standardized, clean rooms equipped with air conditioning, television, 24-hour phone service in every room, ice and soft drink machines in the halls, a swimming pool just outside, and doctors, dentists, babysitters, and clergymen on call. "I put into Holiday Inns what I like," Wilson says, "and I think the public will like what I like."[171]

Members of *E*:   Wallace Johnson was Wilson's business partner during the rapid growth period.

Size of *V*:   The approximately 35 million shares of common stock of Holiday Inns outstanding traded in a range of $35¼ to $51¾ per share in 1984, for an average valuation of $3.7 billion.

Social Utility: Wilson and Johnson have epitomized the manner in which gentlemen do business. In one instance, a venture of theirs was taken public with an ac-

[171]*Fortune*, March 22, 1982, p. 105.

counting error and the stockholders began to litigate to recapture their investment. Although not implicated personally Wilson and Johnson repaid all claims made by stockholders, no questions asked, from their personal resources.

Principal Sources of Venture Capital: Personal savings opened the first motel. Johnson's contacts and experience were subsequently called upon to raise expansion capital.

CHARLES KEMMONS WILSON was born in 1913 in Osceola, Arkansas. When he was nine months old his father died and soon afterward, his mother, Ruby "Doll" Wilson moved with her son to Memphis, Tennessee. "My mother instilled in me the thought that I could do anything in the world I wanted to do, because I was her son," Wilson told *Fortune* magazine in March 1982.[172]

When his mother got sick, Kemmons dropped out of high school and took to the streets. He bought a $50 popcorn machine with nothing down and $1 a week. He installed the machine in a Memphis theater and brought home $30 a week. In one of his most daring gambles of those early years, he purchased 250 cigarette machines plus a supply of cigarettes with six postdated checks for $10,000 each. In order to make the checks good, he had to empty the machines three or four times a day.

From 1943 to 1945 he served as flight officer in the Air Transport Command threading the Himalayan passes from Dum Dum to Shabru, the takeoff point for the cargo flights over the Hump to China. He returned to civilian life in 1946 and expanded his home building business while also operating theaters in Memphis, Tennessee, St. Louis, Missouri, and Louisville, Kentucky.

In 1951 Wilson took his family on what he refers to as "the most miserable vacation trip of my life" because of the cramped, costly lodging available. The motels charged $2 per child even though they bunked in the same room as their parents. Little did Mrs. Wilson realize that her husband's ranting about building a chain of motels that would never charge extra for children would turn into a reality. In 1952 the first Hol-

[172]Ibid.

iday Inn was built on Summer Avenue, one of the main arteries into Memphis. Since that time the chain has grown into 1,750 establishments in 50 states and on every continent except Antarctica. The company has now branched into casinos, bus transportation, and steamship services.

Wilson retired from Holiday Inns in 1979 due to a heart attack, but has now branched into other entrepreneurial activities. "Retirement" is a superfluous word in the vocabulary of developer and entrepreneur extraordinare Kemmons Wilson. He is owner and director of a variety of real estate development and financial service companies, plus Orange Lake Country Club of Orlando, Florida, a time sharing condominium project; Nacho's, Inc., which makes dips and chips, and American Devco, Inc. Wilson is also active in civic organizations, such as the American Heart Fund, March of Dimes, and the President's Council of the University of Alabama. For a young man who started with a few cents to buy popcorn, Kemmons Wilson learned how to make money, in order to survive, then he converted this talent into problem-solving entrepreneurship. With the wealth that he created, and the honor he earned, Wilson is now giving back to his country the skills and capital he has learned and earned.

EPILOGUE

What you have just read is the story of how the American economy was transformed over the last 25 years by 100 heroes and their loyal, hard-working associates. We are in an age of entrepreneurship that will last perhaps a century because the process is exhilarating, exciting, fun, and worthwhile. Being an entrepreneur is like being the builder of civilization: like the pioneers who opened the Far West, after America inherited the land from Mexico in 1821. The frontier was unsettled then; 100 years later, it is a bustling, vibrant center of trade and culture. The entrepreneurs who began around 1960 have transformed the American economy in much the same way as the frontiersmen built the Far West. And as the poet of the men of the mid-nineteenth century, we might say of the men and women in the age of entrepreneurship:

> Bring me men to match my mountains,
> Bring me men to match my plains,
> Men with empires in their purpose
> And new eras in their brains.[173]

Sam Foss

When the next list of great entrepreneuers is compiled, perhaps in another decade, it will look back at the excitement and electricity of the 1980's as the beginning of an age when the fundamentals of entrepreneurship became well known to many people who began applying them to social and medical problems and opening the frontiers of disease, drug abuse, and social disorder to entrepreneurial solutions.

[173]As quoted by Irving Stone in *Men to Match My Mountains* (Garden City, New York: Doubleday, 1956).

≡ INDEX ≡

Numbers in *italics* refer to pages where main entry on each entrepreneur is listed.